The Trophies of Time

The Trophies of Time

English Antiquarians of
the Seventeenth Century

GRAHAM PARRY

Oxford New York
OXFORD UNIVERSITY PRESS
1995

Oxford University Press, Walton Street, Oxford OX2 6DP
Oxford New York
Athens Auckland Bangkok Bombay
Calcutta Cape Town Dar es Salaam Delhi
Florence Hong Kong Istanbul Karachi
Kuala Lumpur Madras Madrid Melbourne
Mexico City Nairobi Paris Singapore
Taipei Tokyo Toronto
and associated companies in
Berlin Ibadan

Oxford is a trade mark of Oxford University Press

Published in the United States
by Oxford University Press Inc., New York

British Library Cataloguing in Publication Data
Data available

Library of Congress Cataloging in Publication Data
Parry, Graham.
The trophies of time: English antiquarians of the seventeenth
century/Graham Parry.
Includes bibliographical references and index.
1. Great Britain—History—To 1066—Historiography.
2. Historiography—Great Britain—History—17th century. 3. Man,
Prehistoric—England—Historiography. 4. England—History, Local—
Historiography. 5. Antiquarians—England. I. Title.
DA135.P27 1995   941.06—dc20   95–8870
ISBN 0–19–812962–9

1 3 5 7 9 10 8 6 4 2

Typeset by Cambrian Typesetters, Frimley, Surrey
Printed in Great Britain on acid-free paper by
Bookcraft Ltd,
Midsomer Norton, Bath.

for
BILL CLEGHORN

Acknowledgements

Antiquarianism is so broad and diverse a subject that in compiling this book I have benefited from the conversation and opinion of people in many disciplines.

A *sine qua non* for writing a book of this kind is an intellectual base close to a great library, and Clare Hall, Cambridge, where I have spent several sabbatical terms, has met that requirement to perfection. I am most grateful to the President and Fellows of Clare Hall for providing such a stimulating research environment. The flow of visiting scholars there has often produced helpful contacts at just the right moment. Among those scholars I would like in particular to name Glyn Parry, Tim Murray, Ian Gentles, Lynn Hulse, and Karl and Sue Bottigheimer. I should also like to thank the staff of the Rare Book Room at the Cambridge University Library for their friendly and efficient service. The confraternity of the tea-room in the University Library should not go unappreciated here: although its membership is ever-changing, it has proved over the years a reliable source of information and illumination.

One of the pleasures of writing this book has been the opportunity for a number of conversations with Professor Stuart Piggott, who must surely be Britain's leading antiquary in our own time. His books have done much to arouse my own interest in antiquarianism, for they convey most intensely the stimulus and pleasure to be derived from this aspect of the history of ideas. In the course of our encounters he has done much to clarify my own thoughts and has helped me to understand the interconnectedness of the antiquarians in the seventeenth century. I have had some enjoyable meetings with Michael Hunter, whose own work on Aubrey has given him a wide experience of seventeenth-century antiquarianism, and has supplied me with a number of valuable leads. The Dugdale Symposium that was held at the University of Virginia in October 1993 provided a rare occasion for intensive discussion of antiquarian matters, and the participants in that gathering helped to give a sharper focus to my sense of Dugdale and his circle; my particular thanks go to Marion Roberts and Everett

Crosby of Virginia, and to David Howarth and Alastair Fowler of Edinburgh University. For all manner of miscellaneous help and advice over the last few years, I should like to thank the following: John Morrill of Selwyn College, Cambridge; Peter Thomas of the University of Wales at Cardiff; Tim Raylor, formerly of Sheffield University and now at Carleton College, Minnesota; Iain Brown of the National Library of Scotland; Tom Corns of the University of Wales at Bangor; and A. Kent Hieatt of the University of Western Ontario. I have read through a good number of Latin works in the course of my research, often with difficulty. I am most grateful to Sally Guthrie for help with Latin and Greek, and to Mark Vessey of the University of British Columbia for looking over and improving my Latin translations in the latter stages of editing.

Marlene Godfrey, the Librarian of Trinity and All Saints College, Horsforth, has often managed to produce a critical book for me at the appropriate moment, and has maintained a continuing interest in this book. Among booksellers, Peter Miller of York and Colin Stillwell of Edinburgh have drawn my attention to relevant antiquarian items in their stock, which have been very useful to me. For various kinds of assistance, I would also like to thank John Axon, Mrs Elsie Duncan-Jones, David and Margarita Stocker, Ken Spelman, Andrew McRae, Stephen Briggs, Nina Collins, Jacques Berthoud, Chris Ridgway, Stephen Longstaffe, and Frank Wilson. In the final process of editing, I have enjoyed the use of Paul Stanwood's library and desk-top facilities in Vancouver, whilst on an academic exchange with him.

My wife Barbara has listened to a good deal of talk about the seventeenth-century antiquaries, whose names have become familiar as household words. She knows how grateful I am for her tolerance, support, and encouragement, which have been as valuable as her practical attention to the minutiae of the text and the mechanics of the manuscript.

G. P.

University of York
15 March 1994

Contents

List of Illustrations   xi

Introduction   1

 1. William Camden   22

 2. Richard Verstegan   49

 3. Sir Robert Cotton   70

 4. John Selden   95

 5. James Ussher   130

 6. Sir Henry Spelman and William Somner   157

 7. John Weever   190

 8. Sir William Dugdale   217

 9. A Mid-century Miscellany: Thomas Browne,
    William Burton, and Thomas Fuller   249

10. John Aubrey   275

11. Phoenicia Britannica   308

12. *Britannia* Revised   331

Conclusion   358

Select Bibliography   367

Index   375

List of Illustrations

1. William Camden, Portrait Frontispiece from
   Britannia, 1695.   24
2. *The Tower of Babel*, by Richard Verstegan.   54
3. *The Idol of the Sun*, by Richard Verstegan.   61
4. *The Idol Seater*, by Richard Verstegan.   61
5. *Fossils*, by Richard Verstegan.   63
6. *The Arch of State*, by Sir Henry Spelman, adapted
   by Thomas Fuller.   158
7. *The First Church at Glastonbury*, by Sir Henry
   Spelman.   171
8. John Weever, Portrait Frontispiece to *Ancient
   Funerall Monuments*.   191
9. Title-page to *Ancient Funerall Monuments*,
   by John Weever.   201
10. Portrait of Sir William Dugdale, by Wenceslaus Hollar.   218
11. Title-page to *Monasticon Anglicanum*, by
    Sir William Dugdale.   233
12. *An Ancient Briton*, by Aylett Sammes.   318
13. *The Wicker Man*, by Aylett Sammes.   322
14. *A Druid*, by Aylett Sammes.   322
15. *Stonehenge*, from *Britannia*, 1695.   338
16. *Miscellaneous Antiquities*, from *Britannia*, 1695.   350

Introduction

Haile bold Researcher! With thy rich returnes
From the darke coasts of Monuments and Urnes.

So sang an obscure Kentish physician, enraptured at the publication
of William Somner's *Dictionarium Saxonico-Latino-Anglicum* in
1659.[1] There is a note of high enthusiasm here, a sense of
antiquarian enquiry as an exciting venture that was opening up the
remote past in a way comparable to the discovery of geographical
space in the previous century. The lines might serve to remind us
that antiquarianism in the seventeenth century had a heroic quality
to it, and its achievements aroused powerful emotions. When
Dugdale's *Antiquities of Warwickshire* appeared, the Oxford
scholar Anthony Wood wrote, 'My pen cannot enough describe
how [my] tender affections and insatiable desire of knowledge were
ravished and melted down by reading of that book.'[2] As a result of
reading the same work, a Norfolk gentleman, Thomas Pecke, wrote
to Dugdale promising, 'I will erect a Statue of gilded Brasse in the
Market-place at Norwich to your memorie, and for the encouragement of ingenious posteritie.'[3] The books of the antiquaries
themselves resound with mutual praise as they salute each other's
accomplishments and urge their colleagues on to new victories. Yet
these volumes, which contributed so much to the intellectual
vitality of the seventeenth century, now lie, for the most part, dusty
and neglected on library shelves. It was a desire to restore these
remarkable works of scholarship to modern awareness that first
caused me to undertake this book. To do so, I have cast my eye over
a whole century of antiquarian writing, from the first publication of
Camden's *Britannia* in 1586 to the elaborately revised and enlarged

---

[1] William Jacob, 'To the much admired Antiquary, William Somner, the great
restorer of the Saxon tongue' in Somner, *Dictionarium Saxonico-Latino-Anglicum*
(Oxford, 1659).
[2] W. Huddesford (ed.), *The Lives of those Eminent Antiquaries John Leland,
Thomas Hearne and Anthony Wood* (Oxford, 1772), 95.
[3] Thomas Pecke to William Dugdale, 22 June 1659, in *The Life, Diary and
Correspondence of Sir William Dugdale*, ed. W. Hamper (1827), 353.

edition of *Britannia* which was published in 1695. Between these dates, antiquarianism developed from being a diversion of a few learned scholars, mainly lawyers and heralds, to the common pursuit of a large number of gentlemen scattered all over the British Isles.

The antiquarian movement in England developed out of the convergence of Renaissance historical scholarship with Reformation concerns about national identity and religious ancestry. The existence of well-edited and annotated texts of the Greek and Roman historical and geographical writers made it possible to form a fairly complex understanding of how Britain, Gaul, and the Northern nations bordering the Roman Empire appeared to the observers of the ancient world, and fuelled a curiosity to know more about the character of Britain, both as a part of the Empire and, before that, as a vigorous primitive society in its own right. The Reformation and the growing sense of national destiny that accompanied the improving fortunes of England in the sixteenth century caused scholars to try to form a clearer understanding of the origins of the nation, and to trace the verifiable course of English history through Saxon times, rather than rest content with old British fables deriving from Geoffrey of Monmouth, which described a colourful but undocumented association with princes from Troy. In ecclesiastical matters, the need to establish the existence of an early Christian Church in Britain that developed independently of Rome was an incentive to seek materials for an authentic Church history. On the secular side, the Italian humanist Polydore Vergil compiled the first objective history of the nation in the reign of Henry VIII, using the critical methods associated with Renaissance historiography. John Leland, under licence from the same King, travelled around the country making an inventory of English antiquities that illustrated the diversity of ancient monuments in the land and drew attention to the complexities of local history. Tudor Church antiquaries such as John Bale and John Foxe made a start on reconstructing the early history of Christianity in Britain, although they were limited by their entanglement with old fables and handicapped by the narrow range of documents available and by their ignorance of Anglo-Saxon. This last problem was alleviated in some measure by the work of Matthew Parker and his circle, who began the long task of recovering the lost language of Saxon England.

The appearance of Camden's *Britannia* in 1586 transformed the state of antiquarian studies and gave all future research a starting point and a base of reference. Here was a comprehensive work of enquiry into national origins and a description of the land unprecedented in its fullness of detail. It was conducted on sound historical principles, using ancient sources whose reliability could be established, it reviewed the evidences of antiquity with an unbiased critical judgement, and it contained much first-hand observation of historical sites. As its title indicated, *Britannia* was primarily concerned with assessing Britain as a province of the Roman Empire, but an important conseqence of Camden's chorography, or description of the land, was that it made evident, from the abundance of material remains, that there was much more history to be investigated than that relating to the Roman occupation. Camps, ditches, stone monuments, ruins of many kinds, urn-fields, mass graves, all suggested that there had been a great deal going on in the past of Britain, much more than was recorded by the ancient historians or the chroniclers. The evidences were there, faint, broken, largely incomprehensible. Could they be reconstructed and interpreted? What shadowy people had left their marks upon the land, and when? Where had they come from, and what had become of them? *Britannia* systematically addressed these questions for the first time. Broadly speaking, during the course of the century the method of enquiry moved from the study of texts to the study of objects, though it must be said that books and documents had a far greater authority over the imagination of English scholars than had artefacts or fieldwork. Camden's career reflected this shift, for in the course of a long life he moved from a position where the past was recovered mainly by means of ancient authors, with the uncertain aid of etymology, to one where material objects became of greater significance and could be used to interact with the written record.

Successive editions of the *Britannia* show greater attention being paid to the Saxons and their religious and political life, and the publication in 1605 of Camden's popular collection of essays, *Remains Concerning Britain*, was further evidence of the growing importance of Saxon studies in his thought. Richard Verstegan's little book, *A Restitution of Decayed Intelligence in Antiquities*, also appeared in 1605, and reinforced the impression that the Saxons were much more significant than the Romans in the formation of the institutions, religious centres and even the character of the English. And, of course, Anglo-Saxon was the immediate ancestor of the English language. To underline his sense of the importance of the Germanic heritage, Verstegan began by proclaiming the Saxon descent of King James, his dedicatee, in a break with the convention that traced James's pedigree back to the British kings of Arthur's line. By 1619, Camden was willing to honour Queen Anne at her death not so much as Queen of Great Britain but for her descent from the Goths and Vandals.[4]

Verstegan's *Restitution* was the first book to be devoted exclusively to Saxon matters, and its success helped to reorient antiquarian studies somewhat. The cultural superiority that Rome enjoyed in the Renaissance made it difficult for educated men to give their serious attention and even respect to the semi-barbaric races that had harassed Rome's northern frontiers, but slowly the balance of interest shifted as the seventeenth century wore on. Tacitus's ancient admiration of the Germans greatly helped in this revaluing of the significance of the Saxons. So much needed to be done to form a proper estimate of their achievements, and it was obvious that no real advance would be made without an understanding of the Anglo-Saxon language, the recovery of which became an important part of antiquarian studies. As the Oxford scholar White Kennett observed, looking back from the end of the century: 'The Saxon Language was extinct, and the monuments of it so few and so latent, that it required infinite courage and patience to attempt and prosecute the knowledge of it. . . . The knowledge of the Saxon Language was so far necessary, as without it, the Antiquities of England be either not discovered, or at least imperfectly known'.[5]

The secular side of antiquarian studies forged ahead thanks to Camden's impetus. The ecclesiastical side was slower to develop. Camden's friend Robert Cotton had ambitious plans for a great ecclesiastical history of Britain that would document as fully as possible the germination and growth of the Church in Britain. This work would confirm the early arrival of Christianity in Britain, emphasize the primitive vigour and independent constitution of the

---

[4] Epitaph on Queen Anne, in William Camden, *Epistolae*, ed. T. Smith (1691).
[5] White Kennett, 'The Life of William Somner' in William Somner, *A Treatise of the Roman Ports and Forts in Kent* (Oxford, 1693), 22.

Church, and demonstrate the continuity of faith from Romano-British to Saxon times. Cotton's celebrated library, which was to become the central resource of Stuart antiquarianism, was assembled to some extent with this plan in mind. Camden hoped to assist Cotton with this work, and King James encouraged it as part of his design to strengthen the intellectual foundations of the Church of England, and to promote ecclesiastical scholarship in his own time. Cotton never made much headway with the project, which passed, with James's approval, into the industrious hands of James Ussher, who found his life's work shaped by it.

The publication of Camden's *Britannia* in 1586 coincided with the foundation of the Society of Antiquaries, and it would seem that the two events were not unrelated. Camden's book provided both a stimulus to and a focus for enquiry into the origin of national institutions, offices, and customs, the subjects that most exercised the members' skills during the twenty years of the Society's existence. I have not discussed in detail the activities of the Society of Antiquaries here, for they have been well described elsewhere;[6] but it is important to remember that the Society's proceedings were the incunabula of antiquarian research, that its meetings provided a forum for co-operative enquiry, and its membership enables us to observe that antiquarians were beginning to multiply as a species. Although Jan Gruter remarked to Camden in a letter of 1618 that he and Cotton formed an oasis of antiquarian learning in a desert,[7] this was far from the truth. John Speed had a creditable record, John Selden and James Ussher were already raising impressive scholarly memorials, and Henry Spelman was showing the promise of his considerable powers. The desert was in fact becoming populated; the oasis was Cotton's library, to which all scholars came for refreshment. Cotton himself acted as a scholarly godfather offering encouragement and timely help. The books of the first age of Stuart antiquarianism abound with expressions of gratitude to Cotton, and his name was invoked as the patron saint of learning who never failed his suppliants, just as Camden was invariably mentioned with reverence and affection as the inaugurator of a new

[6] e.g. in Joan Evans, *A History of the Society of Antiquaries* (Oxford, 1956), May McKisack, *Medieval History in the Tudor Age* (Oxford, 1971), and Kevin Sharpe, *Sir Robert Cotton 1586–1631* (Oxford, 1979).

[7] Gruter to Camden, 10/20 Nov. 1618, in Camden, *Epistolae*, 265.

kind of study of the past. Within a generation of Camden's death in 1623, antiquarian studies were flourishing all over the land. Regional studies, enquiries into the origins of the laws and Parliament and the condition of the primitive Church, burial customs, essays in comparative religion, disquisitions on coins and medals, decipherment of inscriptions—the activity was exhilarating and wonderfully diverse. The 1634 edition of Henry Peacham's *The Compleat Gentleman* included a chapter 'Of Antiquities', a sure sign that the subject was now socially acceptable.

The antiquaries of each generation were mostly known to each other, bound by ties of common interest and friendship in an interwoven pattern that ran right through the century. The most common meeting-places were Cotton's library, the Heralds' Office, the Inns of Court, and the Record Office in the Tower. After the Restoration, the Oxford colleges attracted them in unusual numbers. Antiquarianism was for the most part a co-operative endeavour: the older ones fostered the younger ones, and of the antiquaries described in this book only Aylett Sammes was really working in isolation, and the idiosyncratic nature of his ideas is partly due to his solitariness. Usually friendship and mutual help prevailed. Camden, Cotton, and Selden operated in the midst of a numerous body of shared friends—poets, lawyers, courtiers, politicians—who were serviceable to their studies and companionable in time of leisure. Cotton was very helpful to John Weever, drawing him in to the charmed circle where antiquarian knowledge sparkled in the air. Selden was a close friend and admirer of Ussher, in spite of the wide gap in belief between the secular-minded scholar and the archbishop. Ussher raised up the Irish antiquary James Ware to succeed him in illustrating the antiquities of Ireland. Ussher and Spelman enjoyed a warm friendship cemented by a common concern for the well-being of the Church. Spelman encouraged the career of William Dugdale, opening many doors for him and connecting him to a network of metropolitan and provincial antiquaries who would ensure the productivity of his tireless searches in the records. Dugdale repaid his debt to Spelman by completing his unfinished works, the book on Church Councils and the Glossary of obsolete terms, after the Restoration. Dugdale in turn brought forward William Somner and Abraham Wheelock, the genii of Saxon studies, and amongst the younger men he gave invaluable help to Anthony Wood and to Elias Ashmole, who eventually became his son-in-law. John Aubrey too benefited from Dugdale's assistance, though the two men were temperamentally poles apart, and when we look at Aubrey's circle of friends, it seems to contain the entire antiquarian confraternity of Great Britain. Aubrey himself was a fitful inspirer of a younger generation of Oxford antiquaries, many of whom were recruited by Edmund Gibson to contribute the additions to the 1695 *Britannia*, the project with which this book ends.

Nowhere was the force of friendship more evident than in the co-operation to finance the publication of major works of scholarship, and this feature was particularly noticeable in the political climate of the 1650s, when antiquaries were 'in no better visibility than ye flies in dead winter'.[8] Scores of well-wishers came forward with their £5 to donate an engraved plate to the *Monasticon* or to *The History of St. Paul's*. William Somner's Dictionary, widely recognized to be the essential book for the revival of Anglo-Saxon studies, had its publishing costs defrayed by an odd miscellany of supporters, ranging from a bishop to an astrologer, united in a common cause. Antiquarian works throughout the century tended to be prefaced by congratulatory poems which launched the work with acclamation and applause, and friends willingly mustered to these literary send-offs. Sometimes the verse was of an exalted strain and from a noted pen, as Ben Jonson's poem for Selden's *Titles of Honor*, or Dryden's for Walter Charleton's *Chorea Gigantum*, but as often as not the lines came from gentlemen of towns and shires, friends of the author who were moved by the spectacle of antiquarian scholarship to celebrate 'Those radiant Starrs, those Suns of Fame | Our English Varros'.[9]

Lines of friendship extended across the sea to European antiquaries. Camden's initial impetus to compile the *Britannia* came from the Flemish geographer Ortelius, and Camden engaged in extensive correspondence with scholars in the centres of learning in northern Europe: the best contemporary minds in classical scholarship, epigraphy, law, and political science were in communication with him. He had particularly close relations with the

---

[8] William Higgins to William Dugdale, 9 Feb. 1657, in *Sir William Dugdale*, ed. Hamper, 321.

[9] Poem by Henry Hugford, prefaced to Somner's *Dictionarium*. Varro was a Roman philologist and antiquary of the second century BC.

French polymath Nicholas Fabri de Peiresc, who visited England in 1606 to make Camden's personal acquaintance, at which time he also met Robert Cotton, with whom he developed a warm friendship based on their common fascination with manuscripts.[10] (Peiresc it was who begged the loan of Cotton's priceless fifth-century manuscript of Genesis for purposes of collation, and did not return it for five years.) Spelman, Ussher and Selden all had a large network of European friends with whom they exchanged ideas and information. A name common to all of them was Olaf Worm, the Danish antiquary, from whose work on Danish monuments many inferences about British pre-history could be drawn. Worm went into mourning in 1637 when he heard that Selden had died, until Spelman wrote to reassure him that Selden was still hard at work.[11] Spelman had his runes corrected by Worm when he was trying to decipher the carvings on the Bewcastle Cross. Worm was vastly appreciative of Spelman's *Concilia* and *Glossarium*. He also thought highly of Verstegan's work on the Saxons and their gods, and transmitted his admiration of Verstegan to other European scholars. The benefits of Worm's correspondence were still being felt in the 1660s, when Walter Charleton's book on Stonehenge came out showing an indebtedness to the Dane for opinions exchanged over a decade before. There were other closer links with continental scholars skilled in the business of antiquity. The Huguenot Isaac Casaubon, whose reputation in matters classical and theological was immense, moved to England in 1610, and ended up buried in Westminster Abbey. His son Meric became a prebendary of Canterbury Cathedral and an important Saxonist. Francis Junius, who had been born in Heidelberg, and was the nephew of the eminent Dutch classical scholar Gerard Vossius, became the Earl of Arundel's librarian and developed into a profound antiquarian and linguist. So, until the Restoration, when relations with European masters of antiquity grew more tenuous, English antiquarians had numerous channels of access to the more

---

[10] See Peiresc's Life by Gassendi, translated into English and dedicated to John Evelyn by W. Rand as *The Mirror of True Nobility* (1657). On this 1606 visit, Peiresc also met Sir Henry Savile, John Norden, and John Barclay. See also Linda van Norden, 'Peiresc and the English Scholars', *Huntington Library Quarterly*, 12/4 (1948–9), 369–90.

[11] D. R. Woolf, *The Idea of History in Early Stuart England* (Toronto, 1990), 206.

mature scholarship of northern Europe, and benefited from the high critical standards they encountered there.

How might one define an antiquary? The type is perhaps easier to describe than define, for the spread of scholarship they engaged in was so broad and variegated that it defies definition. A concern with origins was certainly one characteristic preoccupation: the origins of nations, languages, religions, customs, institutions, and offices. Etiological enquiry into such questions will inevitably be directed to times when the historical record is imperfect, or when fable has replaced history as an explanation of beginnings. A great deal of intellectual energy was expended in dispersing the accumulated legends generally known as the British History that filled in the vacant stretches of the remote past with shining princes from Troy and a long line of sturdy British kings that included such familiar names as Locrine, Lud, Lear, and Cymbeline. The existence of these figures could be doubted on the grounds that no ancient historians had ever mentioned this race of heroes, and Caesar had plainly reported his encounters with an almost savage people. The stories were in fact hard to dismiss out of hand, for they had been accepted for so long that they were part of the national consciousness. And what was one to put in their place? That was the task of the antiquary. The problem was clouded by the existence of another spurious history besides that of Geoffrey of Monmouth, and that was one purported to be the work of a Babylonian writer named Berosus. This had been found (or rather invented), edited, and annotated in the late fifteenth century, and provided an invaluable bridge over the chaos of the remote past by enumerating the descendants of Noah and tracing the ways in which these heroes became the founders of the nations of Europe. A fair number of seventeenth-century English antiquaries were prepared to retain some of the more convenient passages of this work, whilst acknowledging the doubtful authenticity of Berosus's manuscript.[12] The shrewder antiquaries, headed by Camden, were those who ignored or indifferently noted these false trails into the past, and tried to reconstruct a primitive British society by analogy

---

[12] The most comprehensive recent account of the fables that filled up the early ages of Britain is Stuart Piggott, *Ancient Britons and the Antiquarian Imagination* (London, 1989). See also T. D. Kendrick, *British Antiquity* (London, 1950; repr. 1970).

with what was known of the Gauls or the Germans from classical reporters.

By means of an insightful reading of the ancient writers on northern peoples, an idea of the system of government prevailing in Britain might be inferred, as also the ways in which laws were made and administered, as Selden most notably endeavoured to show. The ancient religion of the land could be deduced from Roman commentators, as well as the most notable customs of the people. When did the gospel first reach Britain? Here too legend involved the earliest times, but the story of Joseph of Arimathea's journey to Britain shortly after the death of Christ was too precious to dismiss, in spite of the lack of any credible documentation. So this tradition, unlike the tales of Trojan Brutus, persisted until the end of the century, approved by the most serious Church antiquaries, Spelman, Ussher, and Dugdale; Edward Stillingfleet finally rejected it in his *Origines Britannicae* of 1685. Reliable documentation, however, was usually a high priority for antiquarians. Records of the early Church Councils in Europe were scanned for evidence of British participation. For Saxon times, much needed to be done to fill out the details of the historical and ecclesiastical scenes, and the editing of chronicles and lives was an important antiquarian business, attracting Camden, Selden, Twysden, Wheelock, and Wharton, among others. Dugdale and Roger Dodsworth performed an invaluable service by finding and publishing a large body of documents relating to the foundation and growth of monastic establishments in Saxon and Norman times in their *Monasticon Anglicanum*.

Monastic history was certainly a subject that attracted antiquaries, for it had to be pieced together for the first time from documents, and offered that enticing prospect that was an antiquary's delight, a long perspective through time to origins that were obscure. Monastic history did not exist before the seventeenth century, and was an invention of the antiquarians. Camden had to apologize for raising the matter of monasteries in *Britannia*, for too many of his readers, he believed, still regarded them as objects of opprobrium rather than admiration. But recusant historians in the early seventeenth century were understandably anxious to preserve the memory of their achievements and of the flourishing in England of the orders that still continued on the continent. Protestant antiquaries came round to a recognition of their virtues. John

Weever wrote approvingly of them in his book of 1631. Dodsworth and Dugdale probably had to overcome a good deal of conventional prejudice from contemporaries as they laboriously gathered documents towards the history of the one great institution of medieval England that had been completely extinguished. Their work, published over three decades, made possible the objective study of monasteries as an important part of the social fabric of Saxon and medieval England. They were no longer to be viewed as places of indolence, ignorance, and superstition, but as complex social organisms, with highly evolved administrative systems, and as great landowners with considerable economic power under their control. The tenures by which they held their lands were obviously of interest to lawyers, and also to friends of the Church of England who wondered if those lands might ever be restored to the successor Church. Monasteries came to be represented as centres of piety and learning in their best days, the product of a devotional movement that had no parallel in the reformed world. Their destruction could be felt as a loss, which nothing had replaced. William Somner wrote the first history of a monastery, his native Canterbury, in 1640, and monastic studies continued to attract the attention of scholars as the century advanced, with Thomas Tanner's *Notitia Monastica* of 1695 serving as a summary of what had been learnt.

Monastic buildings began to catch the notice of antiquaries in the 1650s as an adjunct to the study of the institution of monasticism. Though Somner had been a pioneer in this field in his book on Canterbury, it was effectively the illustrations to the *Monasticon* that inaugurated a tradition of architectural antiquarianism, and Dugdale was fortunate to have as his chief etcher Wenceslaus Hollar, who had a clear eye for accurate architectural detail.

Structures of a ruder sort had long been considered to lie in the province of the antiquary. Stone monuments and tumuli were obviously survivals from the ancient world. But who had raised them, and to what end? Pre-eminently, Stonehenge challenged explanation as an 'ænigma' of gigantic proportions. Because most enquiries into the past were conducted by the light of classical texts, and these texts were not explicit about such monuments, ingenious analogies or extrapolations had to be made in order to link ancient texts to the monuments. Inigo Jones fell victim to this method when he tried to make out that Stonehenge was a Roman temple built on Vitruvian principles. If one discounted the old fables about stone monuments erected by giants in the dawn of time, then one had to look for the builders among the nations that had occupied Britain in historical times, for hardly anyone imagined that the primitive British had been capable of constructing such piles. Recognition that the ancient British might have been the authors of these stone works, and possessed a competent technology as well as an extensive economy, was slow in coming, but John Aubrey and Edward Lhwyd at the end of the century began to change the current perceptions about the pre-Roman inhabitants of Britain, and they did this by examining material remains and by making comparisons between similar objects found in different places, using techniques that we can describe as archaeological.

The character of Britain under Roman rule was naturally of interest to generations of scholars trained in classical studies. Most particularly, the configuration of Roman Britain engaged their attention. Where were the sites of the ancient towns whose names survived in imperial lists? Where did the Roman roads go? The emphasis was primarily geographical, right from the beginning, with *Britannia*, and an important consequence of this bias was the growth of county studies throughout the seventeenth century as one of the major areas of antiquarian activity. The administrative shire, Saxon in origin, was a convenient unit for an intensive study of the past, allowing commentary on all the layers of historical occupation within a region well known to the author. The Roman settlement plan was usually the basic template of these studies. The plan lay over the loosely defined British tribal areas, and over it Saxon and Norman settlement patterns had formed. This combination of regional study with a classical underpinning, in which antiquities, local history, and economic development could be considered together, became a peculiarly English art form in the seventeenth century.[13]

Another route into the distant past favoured by antiquaries was custom. Custom preserved the shrivelled remains of ancient beliefs, and was a clue to the habits of mind of long-vanished generations. Funerary customs were an enduring interest, for they spoke of attitudes to death and the afterlife in the great civilizations of the past and among our own ancestors. These customs could be related

---

[13] The subject has been extensively reviewed by Stan E. Mendyk in *Speculum Britanniae* (Toronto, 1989).

to the remains of ancient burials that came out of the earth, such as urns and their contents, and inscribed grave-markers. The recording of epitaphs in churches was something of a duty among antiquaries, often allied to an interest in funerary customs. This was an aspect of local antiquarianism, preserving the identity of monuments, and offering an opportunity to remember old families and notable worthies. These collections of epitaphs helped clarify family descents, and were welcomed in particular by the heraldic establishment. Camden, Weever, Henry Holland, Spelman, Dugdale, Browne, and Aubrey were all attracted by the broad subject of funerary antiquities: 'Out of the depth and darkness of the Earth [they] delivered to us the memory and fame of our dead Ancestors.'[14]

Aubrey entertained the ambition to investigate the whole spectrum of folk customs in Britain, hoping to trace thereby the survival of pagan beliefs and rituals into the modern world. His researches, though inconclusive, were suggestive, and he inspired White Kennett to develop the work, laying the grounds for folklore studies in later generations. Selden's *Historie of Tithes* might be considered an enquiry into another aspect of custom, one that pursued the subject from biblical antiquity through into the author's own age. James Ussher and his protégé James Ware enquired into the significance of many Irish customs, and Edward Lhwyd was conscious of Welsh customs as a topic worthy of antiquarian study. At the end of the century, White Kennett was trying to subject the many strands of practices, beliefs, and ceremonies to methodical scrutiny in a 'History of Custom', but it was never completed.

Working then on many fronts, antiquaries tried to piece together the past of Britain, a task that became more daunting as the years went by and scholars realized how deep the past was, and how complex the evolution of the societies that had possessed the land. From documents and by observation and comparison and deduction, the many pasts of Britain were partially reconstructed, often quite erroneously, 'for who is so skilful that struggling with Time in the foggie darknesse of Antiquitie, may not run upon the rocks?'[15]

---

[14] An observation of Sir Walter Raleigh in *The History of the World* (1611), appreciatively quoted by Dugdale in the Preface to *The Antiquities of Warwickshire* (1656).

[15] William Camden, *Britannia*, trans. Philemon Holland (1610), A5v.

Antiquaries, for the most part, retrieved materials that could be used by historians in the compilations of their narratives, but in the seventeenth century antiquaries greatly outnumbered historians, and their work was more imaginative, varied, and exciting.[16] There was an air of urgency about antiquarian enquiry, for so much of the material seemed on the verge of disappearing. Saxon and medieval manuscripts from the monasteries might have been flying around like butterflies, as Aubrey remembered, but their life expectancy was as precarious as a butterfly's too, and a great many had already been lost. Antiquaries hastened to gather them into collections, where they would be safe, and could be examined. State papers and legal papers were kept in deplorable conditions in their several repositories, disordered, often unregistered, prone to decay. As for ancient artefacts, land development and ploughing turned up great quantities of buried remains, coins, utensils, urns, altars, tessellated pavements, foundations of buildings, but so much was soon dispersed or lost that unless a record was made, these objects might never have been. Many churches had been comprehensively neglected in Elizabethan days, and their contents indifferently treated. The Civil Wars accelerated the process of destruction, and allowed iconoclasm a free hand in many areas. Cathedrals were special targets of malice as the seats of bishops, and several important cathedral libraries and archives were ransacked, notably Lichfield, Peterborough, Worcester, and Canterbury. St Paul's Cathedral in London, a treasure-house of historical monuments, was badly mutilated and abused. Even the rude neolithic monuments of the countryside were not impervious to change, for Aubrey reported the destruction of several of the great stones at Avebury in his own time, as the locals broke them up for building material or lime.

Seventeenth-century antiquaries had an elevated sense of their calling. The noble note was struck early on, when Camden wrote of the powerful appeal of the study of 'Antiquitie (which is always accompanied with dignity and hath a certain resemblance with Eternity)'.[17] John Donne, contemplating the antiquarian endeavour,

---

[16] For recent exploration of the borderline between history and antiquarianism in the seventeenth century, see Woolf, *The Idea of History*; also F. Smith Fussner, *The Historical Revolution: English Historical Writing and Thought, 1580–1640* (London, 1962), and Arthur B. Ferguson, *Clio Unbound* (Durham NC, 1979).

[17] Camden, *Britannia* (1610), A4v.

was moved to write: 'For naturally great wits affect the reading of obscure books, wrastle and sweat in the explication of prophecies, digg and thresh out the words of unlegible hands, resuscitate and bring to life again the mangled and lame fragmentary images and characters in Marbles and Medals, because they have a joy and complacency in the victory and atchievement thereof.'[18] One of Dugdale's correspondents declared to him, 'I have often considered the Antiquary the Encyclopaedia of Learning: most of the liberall Sciences (if they do not centre in him, yet) come within his circle.'[19] Not only for breadth of interest but also for height of design were antiquaries impressive. Many of their projects were immensely ambitious, requiring, one might imagine, several lifetimes or numerous assistants for their accomplishment. Dodsworth's and Dugdale's *Monasticon*, Dugdale's *Baronage*, Ussher's Chronologies and Church histories, Weever's design to record all the epitaphs of England, Aubrey's survey of ancient British field monuments, Spelman's Glossary and his work on Church Councils, and Somner's Anglo-Saxon Dictionary were all vast undertakings. Yet in almost all these cases, these grand projects were just a portion of their authors' overall plans for antiquarian research. In the words of White Kennett, who himself knew well the boundless aspirations of antiquarian scholarship, 'There is a sacred ambition in the spirit of Learning, that it will not let a man rest without new conquests, and enlarged dominions. Especially in Antiquities, every acquist heightens the desire, and the wishes are those of the Eastern Monarchs, to have more than one world to bring into subjection.'[20]

Antiquaries did wield power of a kind familiar to scholars. They had a power over older authors, particularly medieval and Tudor writers, whose opinions they could discredit by their own researches, or drive out by calling in the aid of classical historians. Much of the dispersal of the British History was of this order. They had a power over the past, for they were able to determine what parts of it were vital and should be held in respectful attention; they were judges of

[18] John Donne, *Essays in Divinity*, ed. E. Simpson (Oxford, 1952), 56. I am indebted to Alastair Fowler for drawing my attention to this remark.
[19] William Bromley to Dugdale, 20 Nov. 1653, in *Sir William Dugdale*, ed. Hamper, 242.
[20] Kennett, 'Life of Somner' in Somner, *Treatise*, 22.

what was authentic and what was fabulous in the past. Antiquaries also liked to enjoy power over their colleagues, in a time-honoured way, by disparaging the quality of one another's scholarship. Although the prevailing mood of antiquarian studies was one of mutual admiration and co-operation, every now and then there were critical encounters. One can sense a tension between the secular-minded Selden and the supporter of Church rights, Henry Spelman, particularly in the debate over tithes. Selden often betrays feelings of suppressed irritation at the credulousness of his fellow antiquaries, particularly over their reluctance to abandon the fictions of the British History. A notable focus of controversy was Stonehenge. The question of who had built it, and what was its function, turned the monument into a cockpit of contentious antiquaries. For the most part, however, antiquaries retained a high and respected authority throughout the century, a reputation that was sustained by the existence among them of several sublime figures of Alexandrian learning: Camden, Selden, Spelman, Ussher, Dugdale, and Browne. After the Restoration, the rise of the virtuoso, the gentleman eager to possess a polite knowledge of antiquities, allowed a certain dismissive humour to be directed against those who seemed more preoccupied with the remote past than with the business of modern society; but that is another story.[21]

The triumphal way to the printing press was littered with the remains of enterprises that had failed or been abandoned. For every antiquarian work that was published, there were a dozen that remained in manuscript, for the subject required not only industry and skill, but organizational power. The usual working method of the antiquary was to make what were called 'collections': extracts from works bearing on his subject, copies of documents, lists of inscriptions, miscellaneous jottings, records of conversations, observations, etc. Very often a project foundered amongst these compilations. John Leland, the proto-antiquary of Henry VIII's time, had set a precedent in this respect. He was overwhelmed by the volume of his notes, and seems eventually to have been driven out of his wits by the incoherence of his collections. In the seventeenth century, John Aubrey was the best-known example of a

---

[21] See Joseph M. Levine, *Dr. Woodward's Shield* (Berkeley, Calif., 1977).

tireless scholar who could never complete a work or methodize his papers (though modern editors have put into print a great deal of what he wrote). At the end of the century, White Kennett reflected on the large number of unfinished or unpublished antiquarian works he was aware of.[22] Roger Dodsworth headed the list, with sixty volumes of collections left in manuscript. Sir Simonds D'Ewes was another great compiler of notes, on subjects as diverse as the state of the Ancient British, the history of Parliament, and county antiquities, all of which stayed in manuscript. A similar fate attended the collections of Thomas Allen, Brian Twyne, and William Fulman, all of whom had 'the same ambition to collect, the same misfortune never to methodize or publish'. County surveys were the class of writing that experienced the greatest number of casualties, and Kennett could list twelve counties whose descriptions remained incomplete or in note form. The plaintive utterance of the herald Augustine Vincent, as he sifted and extracted the records towards a history of the Baronage of England, must have been echoed by many other scholars: 'Now I find the further I go in that labour the further I am to seeke, yet it shall not discourage me.'[23] But he grew exhausted by his efforts, and baskets full of his notes were deposited with the College of Heralds at his death. It was a matter of considerable concern to the antiquarian fraternity that such collections should be preserved so that whatever there was of valuable information might not be lost. Death-bed scenes like Anthony Wood's, where he allocated his manuscript collections to trusted friends, were probably not uncommon.

Given the conservative character of most antiquarians, it is hardly surprising that the majority of them were strongly supportive of the Church of England. The researches of men such as Ussher, Spelman, Weever, Somner, and Dugdale tended to demonstrate the extreme antiquity of the Christian faith in Britain, and led them to an interest in the constitution of the early Church, its discipline, and its ceremonies. Their care for the material well-being of the Church, as well as its spiritual health, inclined them to be sympathetic to Laud's efforts to heighten the sacredness of the Church as an institution and to dignify and embellish the church as a place of

---

[22] Kennett, 'Life of Somner' in Somner, *Treatise*, 46–7.
[23] Letter to Sir Robert Cotton, quoted in N. H. Nicholas, *A Memoir of Augustine Vincent* (1827), 75.

worship. Ussher could not be said to favour the Laudian programme of reforms in the 1630s, but numerous antiquaries had High Church inclinations which chimed with their sense of tradition and their fondness for ceremonies. Both Laud and Ussher were patrons of antiquarian studies. The Puritan tendency in the Church was commonly regarded as hostile to antiquarian studies, especially as it was known to erupt in iconoclastic activity. Moreover, Puritans prized the living spirit over the dead letter of tradition (as they saw it); antiquaries did not believe that tradition was a deadening force in religion, but there was no dialogue between them and the Puritan camp. In the 1650s, when the men of plain religion prevailed, major antiquarian projects with a religious subject, such as Dugdale's *Monasticon* and *St. Paul's*, or Fuller's *Church History of Britain*, became rallying grounds for Anglicans in the time of their persecution, as is made clear by the names that appear in the dedications or in the subscription lists for their illustrations.

One would also expect antiquaries to have been supporters of the monarchy in the great division of the times, but in fact their loyalties were divided. In 1642, Dugdale, dressed in his herald's coat, with a trumpet sounding before him, rode about the Midlands demanding that garrisons declare for the King. The youthful Aubrey was an enthusiastic royalist. The elderly Ussher fainted away at the sight of the King's execution. William Somner composed 'A Passionate Elegy' on 'The Insecurity of Princes', to mourn the death of Charles I. Selden leaned strongly the other way, for his investigations into the origins of the laws and of parliaments had persuaded him that they were of greater antiquity than kings, and had an authority above royal power. His suspicion of kingcraft and priestcraft as tending to the diminution of personal rights helped keep him firmly in the forefront of Parliament's supporters. Sir Robert Cotton, in spite of kinship links to the Stuarts, found himself moving into opposition to the King's policies as his researches into the development of the law and into medieval and political legal history made him conscious that parliamentary rights had a greater validity than royal prerogative. Had he lived, Cotton would no doubt have sided with Parliament. Antiquarians with a strong interest in the history of the law tended to support Parliament, as was the case with Sir Simonds D'Ewes and Sir Edward Dering. Dugdale, however, was an exception, and although he had a powerful knowledge of the law and civil institutions, he remained loyal to the King. Conversely, Thomas Fairfax, who was a patron of ecclesiastical studies, was a leader of the Parliamentary armies. The Civil War divided the antiquaries as it divided families. As for the first two Stuart kings, one would have thought they would have been favourable to antiquarian studies, as tending to the honour of the nation, the support of the Church, and the maintenance of kingship. But in practice, both feared those antiquaries who were busy enquiring into parliamentary and prerogative rights, usually to the disadvantage of the latter. King James shut down the Society of Antiquaries, and King Charles closed Cotton's library.

The unsettled years of the 1640s, a decade filled with conflict, were profoundly unfavourable to antiquarian research. 'The ignorance and affectation of those times ... hated all Antiquity, Ecclesiastical and Civil.'[24] In contrast, the 1650s were a productive time, when many royalists excluded from public life took refuge in scholarship. Many substantial volumes were published in this decade: Dugdale's first three works, Fuller's *Church History*, Ussher's Chronologies, William Burton's Antonine Itinerary, James Ware's work on Irish Antiquities, Thomas Browne's *Urne-Buriall*, and Somner's Dictionary. In the Restoration, the atmosphere changed again. Charles II was more encouraging than his predecessors, but prudently he showed no interest in political or religious subjects, expressing only a curiosity about the ancient stone monuments in his kingdom. Charles had some contact with antiquaries such as Aubrey and Charleton through the medium of the Royal Society. The Society, founded in 1660, rapidly became a forum for the intellectual life of the Restoration, but antiquarian studies were marginal to its business. The bias against preconceptions, and the Baconian emphasis on experiment, favoured an attention to 'things' rather than books or persons, and directed antiquaries towards scrutiny of material remains. The measured, methodical exploration of Avebury in the 1660s represented a novel movement towards an archaeological attitude to the past. Some of Martin Lister's presentations in the 1680s, recorded in the *Philosophical Transactions*, mark a growing sophistication in the

---

[24] Kennett, 'Life of Somner' in Somner, *Treatise*, 47.

use of evidence, of a quite modern, systematic kind. He described various types of pottery found in Yorkshire, and tried to identify the source of the clay and the site of the kilns. He could declare the Multangular Tower at York to be Roman on stratigraphic grounds, and by its stone and style.[25] The heightened interest in field observations and in found objects showed up in the county descriptions of the later Restoration period, particularly in those by Robert Plot, and the full benefit of them was felt in the contributions to the 1695 *Britannia* by the Oxford group of antiquaries.

Much could be said about the literary exploitation of antiquarian studies in the seventeenth century. There was a tradition of dramatizing British History that ran from Sackville's *Gorboduc* through *King Lear, Cymbeline,* and *Vortigern* to Fletcher's *Bonduca.* Ancient Britons appeared in masques on the Whitehall stage, and considerable antiquarian learning went into Ben Jonson's recreations of Roman society for his masques on classical themes. Michael Drayton's chorographical poem *Poly-Olbion* was based on Camden's *Britannia,* and the songs of its nymphs and shepherds were accompanied by learned annotations by John Selden. William Browne's *Britannia's Pastorals* was also much indebted to Camden, and mingled topographical description with antiquities. Antiquaries themselves were described in character books by John Earle and Thomas Fuller, and became the subject of comedies by Shakerley Marmion and Thomas Shadwell. They were never tragic figures. The literary representation of antiquarian matters lies for the most part beyond the scope of this book, but it is a rich topic that has been little explored.

The antiquarian movement of the seventeenth century appears now as a remarkable phase of the intellectual history of the nation. In this book, I have tried to put before the reader the record of its achievements. I have restricted myself to the discussion of printed material, for the quantity of antiquarian writings in manuscript is overwhelmingly large and diverse. One of my motives in writing this account has been to draw attention to a great body of work, often profound in scholarship and almost always charged with an

---

[25] *Philosophical Transactions,* 13 (1682), 70–4, 237–42. See also Michael Hunter, 'The Royal Society and the Origins of British Archaeology' in *Antiquity,* 65 (1971), 113–21.

unusual energy of mind, that deserves to be more widely known and understood in the general revaluation of the seventeenth century now taking place. I have decided to concentrate on the career of individual antiquaries rather than to pursue thematic lines through the century, and in reviewing the accomplishments of the major figures, I have become aware of the worth of many lesser-known scholars who deserve to be given a renewed recognition. I hope that the appreciative estimates offered here of Richard Verstegan, John Weever, William Burton, James Ware, William Somner, Aylett Sammes, Robert Plot, and Edward Lhwyd will cause some of my readers to seek them out for larger acquaintance. Beyond them stand numerous other figures with antiquarian interests whose names are only alluded to here, but who would undoubtedly reward further study. In reading so many large folios and quartos for this work, I have often felt that the subject is one without boundaries, and that the sequence of interconnections is interminable, but I have been encouraged by the example of my industrious antiquaries to persevere. As Camden wished 'to restore antiquity to Britain', I have desired to restore the antiquaries themselves to modern understanding.

I

William Camden

Antiquarians, like poets, are born not made. There can be no rational explanation why some people are irresistibly fascinated by the remains of the past, impelled to make long journeys to view mounds of rubble, or moved to spend dim hours in libraries over half-legible manuscripts. It is an instinct, a passion. William Camden experienced it as a lifelong emotion. 'Even when he was a schoolboy, he could neither hear nor see anything of an antique appearance, without more than ordinary attention and notice.'[1] At Oxford in the 1560s 'it was not in his power to keep within doors: the bent of his own Genius was always pulling him out, not to impertinent visits and idle diversions, but to entertainments he relished above all these; stately Camps and ruinous Castles, those venerable Monuments of our Fore-fathers'.[2] He was fortunate to find illustrious and sympathetic sponsors, among whom Philip Sidney and Fulke Greville were persuaded that this passion for antiquities might be made to serve a patriotic cause by illustrating English history, so that Englishmen might better understand the nature and merit of their own country. Such patronage was especially welcome in that it was given without the imposition of specific conditions. Camden continued to make antiquarian expeditions after he left Oxford and became a master at Westminster School, building up 'those Collections and Observations . . . for private satisfaction, and to quench a secret thirst which Nature had brought along with him into the world'.[3]

This engaging if self-indulgent situation was transformed by the arrival in London in 1577 of the Flemish geographer Abraham Ortelius, who urged Camden to draw up his notes into a book in order to display Britain to the scholars of continental Europe.

---

[1] Thomas Smith, 'Life of Camden', trans. from the Latin by Edmund Gibson in William Camden, *Britannia*, ed. E. Gibson (1695), fol. B1v. [2] Ibid.
[3] Ibid.

Ortelius was the modern Ptolemy, ambitious to know the topography of all countries and to turn that knowledge into maps. His reputation had been solidly established by his Atlas of the World, *Theatrum Orbis Terrarum*, published in 1570, and by his *Synonymia Geographia* in 1578. He now planned to bring out a series of maps of the ancient world, to be entitled *Parergon*, and pressed Camden to provide a topographical account of Roman Britain that would both identify the Roman settlements and supply a commentary to the map.[4] Camden's response was the renowned *Britannia*, which gained an international reputation for its author and became the fountain-head of antiquarian research for the next century and beyond.

These circumstances help us to perceive what Camden would have called 'The Platforme' of his *Britannia*, the ground-plan that underlay the whole design. The principal intention was to describe Britain as a province of the Roman Empire (hence the simple classical title) and to locate the towns and camps of the Romans as fully and accurately as possible. As he reminds the reader of the greatly enlarged 1607 edition, 'That which I first proposed to myself, was to search out and illustrate those places, which Caesar, Tacitus, Ptolemy, Antoninus Augustus, Provinciarum Notitia, and other ancient writers have recorded; the names whereof Time has either chang'd, lost or corrupted.'[5] The most significant names mentioned here are the last three, for they are all associated with

---

[4] Ortelius's interest in British matters was sharpened by family ties. He was related to the English Marian exile Daniel Rogers, the scholar-poet and diplomat who had a close association with the University of Leiden. Through Rogers, Ortelius came into contact with the humanist circle around Sidney and Leicester. Rogers compiled a treatise entitled 'De Moribus Veterum Britannorum', which was never published, and in 1572 he wrote to Ortelius that he was preparing an account of Roman Britain, but was having difficulty in finding adequate material. He also mentioned that he had a desire to make a geographical survey of Britain. All of this information would have been useful to Ortelius for his planned work on the topography of the ancient world, and Rogers' failure to realize his schemes seems to have caused Ortelius to look to Camden instead for the information he needed. Ortelius was also responsible for the posthumous publication of the papers of the Welsh antiquary Humphrey Lluyd as *Commentarioli Descriptiones Britannicae Fragmentum* in 1572 (trans. in 1573 by Thomas Twyne as *The Breviary of Britayne*). Besides advancing topography by setting Camden to work, Ortelius also promoted cosmography by persuading Richard Hakluyt to collect and publish the voyages of the English nation. See J. A. van Dorsten, *Poets, Patrons and Professors* (Leiden, 1962), 19–25; I. D. McFarlane, *Buchanan* (London, 1981), 419–21.

[5] Preface, trans. by Edmund Gibson in Camden, *Britannia*, (1695).

1. William Camden. Portrait engraved by Richard White, from the 1695 *Britannia*.

lists of place names in Britain preserved from antiquity. One of the standing challenges to Renaissance classical scholars was to determine where the ancient settlements had been, for many had been transformed into new towns, and others had vanished, leaving scarcely a trace. Eboracum was unquestionably York, but where were Brocavum, Condate, or Leucomagus? Briefly (for this subject is discussed at greater length in chapter 9), Antoninus Augustus was associated with a third-century collection of routes across the Roman Empire, called the Antonine Itinerary, which included fifteen itineraries across Britain, detailing the names of settlements and the distances between them. Ptolemy had given many lists of place names and geographical features in Britain in his Geography, written in the mid-second century, and the *Notitia Provinciarum* (or *Dignitatum*) was a late antique administrative document, a register of offices and ranks throughout the Empire, which contained a section on Britain. Together, these documents furnished a very large number of place names for Roman Britain, but they also posed many puzzling questions about sites. As a result of his antiquarian journeys around the country, Camden probably had a more detailed familiarity with historic places than any other Englishman. Fortified in addition by exhaustive reading of all classical texts that had a bearing on Britain, and possessed of a rudimentary knowledge of etymology, he was well qualified 'to restore Britain to its Antiquities, and its Antiquities to Britain, to renew the memory of what was old, illustrate what was obscure, and settle what was doubtful, and to recover some certainty in our affairs'.

The late-Renaissance fascination with antique geography may well have been a consequence of the humanist study of the classical historians. Where precisely were the places mentioned by Livy, Tacitus, or Caesar as the setting of actions so memorable that they had become almost legendary? What was the line of march of Hannibal and his armies when they invaded Italy? Where did Caesar confront Cassivelaunus, or Suetonius rout Boadicea? The histories were often quite specific, but they needed to be matched with the terrain, and the ancient place names had to be restored, by scholarship, to the land. All over Europe, this recovery of the old configuration of the Roman world was taking place.

Britannia was published in 1586, in Latin, aimed at a classically-educated audience. It was reprinted the next year, and in 1590 an impression came out in Frankfurt, to give continental scholars that understanding of Britain that Ortelius had desired. The book should be seen as an important production of the late Northern Renaissance which was centred on the Low Countries, and characterized by formidable textual scholarship in Greek, Latin, and Hebrew, with an accompanying dense knowledge of the ancient cultures. The *Britannia* made Camden a respected member of that loose confederation of northern scholars whose zeal for learning overrode national boundaries and, to a large extent, religious differences. His correspondence should remind us that Camden was a European figure: Ortelius, Lipsius, Hondius, Puteanus, Gruter, Isaac Casaubon, Peiresc, Hotman, and de Thou were all engaged in discussion with him. Camden certainly regarded himself as a champion of British scholarship in the international arena, and it was generally through his contacts that the antiquaries of the Jacobean age, such as Cotton, Selden, Spelman, and Ussher, were linked to their European counterparts.

The book that finally appeared in 1586 had developed a long way from its origins as a description of Roman Britain. As Camden organized his material, he became increasingly curious about the native people whom the Romans had subdued. Who were the British? Where had they come from? What were their beliefs and customs and forms of government? They were, after all, the first known ancestors of that motley race, the English. The question of origins exercised scholars all over Europe in the sixteenth century, for in the nationalistic ethos that prevailed after the Reformation, men had a heightened interest in the distinctive character of their country, and the first settlers were considered to be a significant factor in national identity. Just as great families liked to trace their lines of descent, preferably from a distinguished ancestor, so with nations. The issue in England was bedevilled by the business of the British History that had been put into circulation by Geoffrey of Monmouth, the *Historia Regum Britanniae*, which had become the accepted orthodoxy of the Middle Ages.[6]

Geoffrey had told in considerable detail how Britain had been settled by the Trojan Prince Brutus and his followers. Brutus was deemed to be the great-grandson of Aeneas, who after years of

---

[6] A compendious account of the British History may be found in Kendrick, *British Antiquity*.

wandering was directed by an oracle to seek a new land on the fringes of the world. Geoffrey described the arrival of Brutus and his followers in the land of Albion, at Totnes. They defeated the few giants remaining from the ancient days, including Gogmagog, and founded as their principal city Troynovant, or New Troy, which became London. The name of the land became Britain, or Brutayne, after the Trojan hero. Brutus ruled the entire island, but after he died his three sons Locrinus, Kamber, and Albanactus divided their inheritance, taking England, Wales, and Scotland respectively. This event was declared by Geoffrey to have been synchronous with the rule of Saul in Israel. Geoffrey had developed the story of Brutus and the Trojan foundation out of Nennius, the eighth-century chronicler, but the elaboration of the history and the long record of British kings (including Lear) who ruled before the Romans came was largely his own invention, as was much of the later matter of Arthur and his knights who enacted a British Götterdämmerung in the days of the encroaching Saxons. The British History had an enduring success until the end of the sixteenth century, and held its ground well into the seventeenth. It satisfied the universal desire for known and illustrious origins: it associated Britain with an ancient high culture, and with the epic story of the Fall of Troy, and it gave Britain an antiquity comparable to that of Rome. All the medieval chroniclers approved this history, and the Reformation did not dislodge it. Henry VIII's antiquary John Leland defended Brutus, as did the ultra-Protestant apologist John Bale; and later, Holinshed and Stow both began their chronicles with the colourful arrival of the enterprising Trojans. Basically, the story was too good to dismiss, even though there was no ancient evidence in its favour.

The only serious refutation of Geoffrey's account of British origins was made by the Italian scholar Polydore Vergil, who had settled in England in the reign of Henry VII. With royal encouragement he wrote the *Anglica Historia* (1534), the first work produced in this country to be based on objective consideration of evidence and comparison of source materials, principles that we associate with the methods of Renaissance historiography. Polydore found no credible records to support the Trojan legends, or the Arthurian stories, and as a foreigner he had little sympathy with the nationalistic sentiments that the British History appealed to. In contrast, he imagined a first settlement of Britain by tribes from northern Gaul moving across the Channel, a movement of barbarians that did not invest the beginnings of the British nation with any dignity or glamour. Polydore's sceptical version of events was reviled in England for the rest of the sixteenth century as an expression of Italian or papal enmity to the ancient traditions and honour of Reformation England. In Europe, however, the *Anglica Historia* was frequently re-published and circulated as the major modern account of its subject.[7]

Camden sided with Polydore Vergil in defining the primitive British, although—mindful of national sensitivities on this issue—he does not deny Geoffrey's version of history; instead, he gently professes to suspend judgement on a matter so involved in obscurity. If the Trojan tales were true,

lovers of Antiquity would be excused from a troublesome and tedious enquiry. For my part, I am so far from labouring to discredit that history, that I assure you, I have often strained my Invention to the uttermost to support it. Absolutely to reject it, would be to make war against time, and to fight against a received opinion. For shall one of my mean capacity presume to give sentence in a point of so much consequence? I refer the Controversy intirely to the whole body of learned Antiquaries.[8]

That is a sham profession, and Camden immediately undercuts it by announcing firmly that nowhere in the classical historians can he find any reference to this Brutus, or to a Trojan expedition to the north. He declares his own working principles: to trust most to writings that are contemporary, or nearly so, with the events described, and to value most highly texts that are supported by other near-contemporary statements. In the case of the ancient British, Caesar and Tacitus are the most reliable authorities, and there is no shortage of Roman writers to substantiate and enlarge what they recorded. All the evidence from these sources points to a primitive tribal society, very similar to the Gauls and the Germans, and there is no indication of any classic Mediterranean culture informing their customs or religion. He regards the Trojan hypothesis as completely irrelevant, and proceeds to sketch in some detail the features of a barbarian society that would have been recognizable to Strabo or to Pliny. Instead of the romantic distinction that a Trojan ancestry bestowed on the nation, Camden

---

[7] For Polydore's career and the reception of his work, see Denys Hay, *Polydore Vergil* (Oxford, 1952).   [8] Camden, *Britannia* (1695), col. vi.

was able to offer the admiration that the Romans expressed for the hardy, vigorous martial spirit of the British, and to suggest that these were the true native virtues of the race.

Besides a careful attention to verifiable sources, Camden claimed a modest expertise in a skill that was much esteemed in the sixteenth century, and continued to be an important means of antiquarian investigation throughout the seventeenth: etymology. Clues to obscure questions of origin and function are often furnished by linguistic trace elements in words, and to make sense of these clues requires an acquaintance with non-classical languages. As Camden observes, 'Plato in his *Cratilus* would have us trace the original of Names down to barbarous tongues, as being the most ancient; and accordingly, in all my Etymologies and Conjectures, I have had recourse to the British (or as 'tis now called) the Welsh tongue, which was spoken by the first and most ancient Inhabitants of this Country.'[9] It is not clear how Camden had learnt Welsh, or how much he knew, but as the language most closely derived from the ancient British, Welsh was very useful to him. One can see its value in his attempts to crack the meaning of the name of Britain. He deduces from the numerous variants of 'Britannia' that appear in the Greek and Roman writers, and especially from Procopius's use of 'Britia' as a name for the island, that the ancient inhabitants called themselves Brits or Briths. He then notes that the word 'Brith' in Welsh means 'painted' or 'coloured', and assumes that the natives called themselves by this name because their distinguishing habit was to paint themselves in striking colours, a feature prominent in almost all the early Roman allusions to the British. Camden proceeds to make another discovery along the same lines which also has a credible ring to it: he perceives

that in the names of almost all the antient Britains, there appears some intimation of a Colour, which without doubt arose from this custom of Painting. The red colour is by the Britains called 'coch' or 'goch', which word I fancy lies concealed in these names, Cogidunus, Argentocoxus, Segonax; the black colour they call 'du', of which methinks there is some appearance in Mandubratius, Cartismandua, Togodumnus, Bunduica, Cogidunus.[10]

[9] Preface, ibid. By the sixteenth century etymology had become an extensive field of study. See E. R. Curtius, *European Literature and the Latin Middle Ages*, trans. W. R. Trask (New York, 1953), 495ff.
[10] 'The Name of Britain' in Camden, *Britannia*, cols. xxix–xxx.

And so with white and blue ('glas', as in King Cuniglas), yellow, gold, scarlet, and green. The enigmatic names of the ancient British leaders suddenly break into parti-coloured life as Camden's etymological imagination touches them.

Camden is aware that the etymological approach is at best only a form of conjecture, and he uses it with discretion, but when 'a cloud of darkness, error and ignorance' lies over the earliest phase of a nation, such learned conjecture is admissible. In the early seventeenth century Francis Bacon, in *The Advancement of Learning*, rightly drew a distinction between 'Words' and 'Things' as unprofitable and profitable means of enquiry. Etymology has to be classed as an art of Words. It was a scholastic art which in Camden's day lacked a precise discipline, and was given to ingenious and fanciful exploitation. What the study of antiquity needed was more attention to Things: inscriptions, coins, physical remains from the earth—other forms of evidence than the verbal. Recognizing this need, Camden was moving in the direction of an improved methodology. He made intelligent use of inscriptions to elucidate the extent and character of the Roman presence in Britain. He provided illustrations of a few examples of British coins in the first edition of *Britannia*, and more (from the collection of Robert Cotton) in the 1600 edition, to demonstrate the existence of a British coinage (hitherto a matter of some doubt, and denied by John Leland, among others): he was able to decipher abbreviated British names on coins, to identify their mints, and to deduce a measure of civil organization from the very fact of their circulation. But when it came to things without words, such as stone monuments, earthworks, barrows, and the debris of the past, Camden made little of them.

However, even without the benefits of an archaeological outlook, Camden achieved the considerable feat of presenting for the first time a coherent picture of the ancient British world at the time of the Roman conquest. He stresses the Britons' wholehearted devotion to warfare, and their barbarous appearance. In the matter of government they were ruled by many kings, but in times of emergency they would call a national council and elect a leader for the duration. He says little about the practice of popular religion, dismissing it as 'a dismal and confused heap of superstition', but he lingers with more fascination over the priests who presided over the religious ceremonies, the Druids. He enlarged the section on them in each new edition of *Britannia*, until the 1607 printing, the last one in Latin and the one that contained his final additions and revisions. The material he sets down about the Druids is almost entirely quotation of classical writers, with very little speculation on his own part. Caesar, Tacitus, Dio Cassius, Pliny, and Lucan contribute to an account which depicts Druids as men who combined the offices of priest and magistrate. The Romans' respect for their wisdom is given prominence, as is their reputation for philosophic profundity, but Camden does not attempt to present the Druids as magi or the possessors of secret knowledge that had been transmitted from earliest times. On the contrary, he selects his quotations to emphasize the barbarity of their rites, which included human sacrifice. He notes Caesar's remark that the Druids used Greek characters in their written communications, but does not speculate on the implications of this detail, although he is willing to derive the name 'Druid' from the Greek δρῦς 'an oak', from their veneration of oak trees and their custom of setting their sanctuaries among oaks. As for the Bards, who were often mentioned in ancient writings in conjunction with the Druids, their function was primarily to praise famous men in song; no theories of divine inspiration are floated. Camden frequently notes the closeness of British beliefs, customs, ways of fighting, government, and even language, to those of the Gauls, and makes no great effort to emphasize the singularity of the ancient British, except in the matter of their body-painting. He is wholly committed to the idea that Britain was settled by migration across the Channel by neighbouring tribes.

From the abyss of time, Camden summons up the ancient Britons and restores them to the Elizabethans. To do so, he draws together an anthology of references from ancient historians and geographers to illustrate their appearance and manner of living. We see the men with their long hair and moustaches, covered in blue woad for war, or variously coloured in peace, with painted images and cicatrices on their bodies, tall, valiant, and wild. They wear skins, and ornaments of iron. They have virtually no knowledge of agriculture, but live on flesh and milk. They live in reed or wooden huts, and have many wives. Fighting is their passion, and in warfare their most distinctive feature is the use of chariots, the axles of which are armed with scythes. They are sunk in superstition, and to propitiate their savage gods, human sacrifices are offered. It is a primitive and barbarous scene, authentic in its detail, and far removed from the dim glories of the pre-Roman past that the Elizabethan chroniclers conveyed.

Although Camden had settled the question of the immediate origin of the British tribes, there still remained the larger question of who these people were who inhabited the northern parts of Gaul: where in turn had they come from? The concern with tracing nations back to the earliest phase of world history by means of the biblical record was universal in the Christian countries of sixteenth-century Europe. Chroniclers such as Geoffrey of Monmouth might be proved fallible and discredited, but sacred history was un-challengeable. The Bible offered a continuous account of human affairs from the Creation, and the books of Moses that constituted the first part of the Holy Writ were considered to be a far older history than anything written among the pagan nations. The true origin of all the nations was deemed to lie at Babel, from where the various nations, with their divers tongues, had been dispersed by God as a result of his displeasure at mankind's attempt to scale heaven. Before the building of Babel, 'the whole earth was of one language and of one speech' (Genesis 2: 1). The genealogical lists of the children of Noah and the account of the dispersal of the nations after Babel, given in chapters 10 and 11 of Genesis, provided vital information to antiquarians concerned with the aetiology of race. The sons of Japhet had peopled Europe, while the offspring of Ham occupied Africa and those of Shem settled in Asia. The progenitors of the British were to be sought for amongst the children of Japhet. The race of Gomer (Genesis 10: 2, 3) was the favourite choice, because the Gomerii seemed etymologically cognate with the Cimmerii or Cimbri, tribes historically recorded by writers such as Tacitus as occupying parts of northern Europe. Camden notes that 'the Welsh to this day call themselves Kumero, Cymro and Kumeri. . . . Why should we not allow that our Britains, or Cumeri, are the true posterity of Gomer, and that from him they derive this name?'[11] So etymology resourcefully throws light on the obscurest portion of our history. Conjecture moves towards certainty when Camden applies the same art to the name of Gomer, and he can announce that 'in the Hebrew tongue Gomer signifieth "bounding"

<hr>

[11] 'The Name of Britain' in Camden, *Britannia*, col. xi.

or "the utmost border" '. The British are thus traced across the Channel to Gaul and back to the ancient lands of the Bible. This need to connect the nations of Europe with the biblical record exerted a distorting influence in antiquarian thought for generations to come, with the result that the most successful speculators about British antiquity were those who ignored this topic entirely, such as John Aubrey and Edward Lhwyd.

Camden's initial intention had been to write a description of Britain as a Roman province, but he had been obliged to bring the Romans to a land that already had a deep history and a distinctive character which clearly fascinated him. The ancient Britons engaged his sympathies as the original possessors of the island, Calibans to the Roman Prospero. However, once entered into his main theme—how the Romans occupied the island, civilized it, and incorporated it into the Empire—Camden writes with steady assurance, for there is now more certainty in his sources. Yet even as the Romans subdue the natives, Camden maintains the honour of Britain—also a professed aim of his patriotic work. After an account of the military occupation, he reminds his reader of the many Roman poets who were moved to write of Britain because the country stirred their imagination by its exotic remoteness and by the bravery of its inhabitants. Virgil, Lucan, Horace, Propertius, and Claudian all expressed admiring sentiments about Britain, praising its climate, fertility, and natural wealth, as well as the virility of the people. From the many classical writers who alluded to British affairs, an almost continuous history can be assembled, and this Camden does. In retelling the story of the Roman occupation, he takes care to emphasize details that give the impression that the greatest emperors and generals were preoccupied with the matter of Britain. He also lingers on an exotic feature (mentioned by Dio Cassius) that will have a special place in the imagination of succeeding antiquarians, and that is the importation of elephants by Claudius in his campaign of 43 AD. These elephants will be invoked with tiresome frequency whenever large fossil bones are unearthed (even in Cornwall or Northumbria), for they offer the only available explanation for gigantic skeletal remains.

With full Roman control came the growth of civility. At first there were the military camps, connected by a network of roads. Around the camps, towns began to develop, marking the start of a new way of life for the British, who had until then dwelt in loose settlements or fortified encampments. The Romans introduced their architecture—temples, basilicas, porticoes, baths—and the structures of civilized life arose. The liberal arts came in the train of the soldiers, and the British were encouraged to acquire a measure of civilization. In towns the use of Latin spread and the toga was adopted. Quick-witted natives were sent to Gaul to learn Roman law. The recognizable processes of imperial rule were taking place, the culture of the conquerors was imposed, and the primitive conditions of continual warfare were replaced by a relatively secure peace. For Camden, this incorporation of Britain into the Roman Empire marked her accession to the full honours of antique civilization. From being a remote and barbarous island, she had become part of the Roman world, and ultimately her inhabitants were entitled to citizenship. Some of the greatest emperors traversed the roads of Britain—Claudius, Vespasian, Hadrian, Severus, Constantine; their presence here was infinitely more suggestive than any imaginary Trojan connection. Britain was a portion of the Empire, and a beneficiary of classical culture, matters which would be regarded as highly significant in the seventeenth century, when writers, artists, and politicians would try to exploit an inheritance of Roman values and Roman aspirations. One should remember that Camden was the teacher of Ben Jonson at Westminster School, and later his friend. He was also acquainted with Inigo Jones. The classical revival of Jacobean times led by these two men was validated by Camden's depiction of Britain as a country with a classical past. Jonson's sustained attempt to cast the men and women of the Jacobean court as figures in a revived Augustan society, and Jones's introduction of an authentic classical architecture, as an appropriate setting for his patrons' affairs, were possible and successful because Camden had prepared the way.

The perfection of this new era of civilization was the coming of the Gospel. Camden here is disposed to accept the chronicle accounts of Nennius and Bede in which the British King Lucius (whom Camden assumes to have been a regional ruler tributary to the Romans) requested a mission from Eleutherius, Bishop of Rome (as Camden is careful to call him), some time in the second half of the second century, at which time large numbers of British were converted. Camden notes the remark by Origen that the British received Christianity so readily because they were prepared for it 'by their Druids . . . who always taught them to believe that there was but one God'.[12] (This testimony, by a Father of the Church, that the religion of the Druids was monotheistic, was a detail which could be exploited by poets and antiquaries alike as evidence that the Druids had knowledge of the 'prisca theologia', and were aware of the true nature of the deity, sharers of that cabbalistic wisdom that circulated orally and secretly among Jews and Gentiles alike in the ancient world.)[13] The tradition of an even earlier contact with Christianity, when Joseph of Arimathea had visited this island shortly after the Crucifixion, is alluded to, but without conviction. As far as Camden is concerned, the shadowy Lucius occasioned the dawn of Christianity in Britain; its full light came with Constantine, the greatest Roman Briton. Constantine, the son of the British Princess Helena and the Emperor Constantius Chlorus in this version of the story, was born in Britain and assumed the purple at York. His establishment of Christianity as the religion of the Empire secured its triumph over the pagan cults. Camden does not glory in this achievement as one might expect; he does not proclaim its providential nature, nor does he interpret it as a peculiar blessing of God upon Britain, as would become the common response in the seventeenth century, but rather, he records it with evidences as a good historian, and allows other authors to make the appropriate speeches of praise. For all this restraint, however, there is a conviction that Constantine was Britain's most important contribution to the destiny of the West.

Although Constantine's religious policy was beyond reproach, his government of the Empire was less than prudent in Camden's view, for by moving the capital to the east, he made it easier for the barbarians beyond the Danube gradually to penetrate the old frontiers. The tone of Camden's narrative darkens, Christianized Britain is soon overrun by the Arian heresy, and Pelagius, who taught that man could assist in his own salvation, and possessed free will which could be directed towards this end, spreads his heresy throughout his native country. The melancholy chronicle of wars, revolts, and eruptions, of a crumbling Empire and a Church riven by doctrinal strife, proceeds until the withdrawal of the legions. By that time, after 476 years of occupation, as Camden

[12] Camden, *Britannia*, col. lxx.
[13] See Frances Yates, *Giordano Bruno and the Hermetic Tradition* (London, 1964), 263, and Stuart Piggott, *The Druids* (London, 1975), 112–19, 160–8.

computes, the Britons and the Romans were so intermingled that they had effectively become one people. If, he teasingly remarks at the close, there are still those who desire a Trojan origin for this country, let them seek it rather through the Romans, 'who doubtless descended from the Trojans' and who so completely made this country their own.[14]

To complete his picture of Ancient Britain, Camden had to pronounce on the Picts and the Scots, and their origins. Rejecting Bede's opinion that the Picts had come from Scythia, he prefers to believe that they were related to the tribes of northern Britain, differing from them only in that they retained their independence from Roman rule, and as a result continued in a state of barbarism. They too, like the British, received their name from their custom of painting their skins, a custom that lingered on far longer in Caledonia than in Roman Britain. As for the Scots who occupied Ireland at the time of the Roman invasion of Britain, Camden is prepared to entertain a Scythian provenance. A chorus of chroniclers and historians, going back at least to Gildas in the sixth century, emphasized the etymological probability that 'Scoti' and 'Scythae' were linked. Scythia in the Middle Ages and Renaissance referred to a loosely defined territory to the north and east of Greece; Greek and Roman historians had described the barbarians who dwelt there in vast numbers as exerting continuous pressure on the civilized world. The area described as Scythia did in fact include the region around the Black Sea, the hearthland of the Celts, who during the first millennium BC spread westwards into much of Europe, including Gaul, Britain, and the Iberian peninsula. The old traditions of a Scythian origin for the Scots had some plausibility, therefore, even to the extent that those traditions, as gathered up by Nennius, had the Scots migrating from Iberia to an uninhabited Ireland. Yet the similarity between 'Scoti' and 'Scythae' was purely coincidental. Camden had no other means of probing the darkness of time beyond the area lit by the ancient historians except by etymology, which really was one of the false sciences. He was right to think of language as an important clue to origins, but he had no sense of the language groups of Europe and Asia, and little understanding of the process of linguistic change. All that he, like

---

[14] Camden, *Britannia* (1695), col. lxxxvii.

all his contemporaries, had to go on was similarity of sound. His frustration at the endless etymological speculation about national origins—endless because there were no known rules to the game—spills over in his discussion of the Scots. After he has summarized a score of scholarly guesses, he exclaims: 'If all this gives no light into the originall of the Scots, [my readers] must apply themselves for it elsewhere, for I am perfectly in the dark in this point; and have followed the truth (which has still fled from me) with much labour to no purpose'.[15]

A similar etymological mist hangs over the Saxons when Camden comes to trace their derivation. He sets himself to analyse their name, instead of their language, artefacts or remains, as the principal clue to their origins. First there is the approach eponymous: did they take their name from their leader in migration, one Saxo? Then there is the approach characterful: did the name derive from the Latin epithet for their stony ('saxea') temper? Perhaps their use of curved swords known as 'saxa' had a particular relevance. Were they related to the ancient tribes of the Saci or the Sassones of Asia?

The early editions of *Britannia* were not enthusiastic about the Saxons, who were not so agreeable to Camden's imagination as the British or the Romans, being a harsh and alien race. By 1607, however, when the last revised edition appeared, he had grown more sympathetic, and the account of the Saxons had been much enlarged. His changed attitude owed much to his improved familiarity with the Anglo-Saxon language, which he had laboured at throughout the 1590s, benefiting from his friendship with William Lambarde, who had been taught by Laurence Nowell, the principal figure in the Elizabethan revival of Anglo-Saxon, and with Robert Cotton.[16] He came to recognize that for all their initial barbarism, the Saxons had been the people who had contributed most decisively to the formation of the English identity by means of language and religion. One can sense the shift to a more positive attitude toward the Saxons in a passage in *Remains Concerning Britain*, the collection of essays complementary to the material of the *Britannia* which Camden published in 1605. 'This warlike, victorious, stiffe, stowt and rigorous Nation, after it had as it were

---

[15] Ibid. col. cxix.
[16] See Stuart Piggott, 'William Camden and the *Britannia*' in *Ruins in a Landscape* (Edinburgh, 1976), 35–6, and Sharpe, *Sir Robert Cotton*, 10–12.

taken root heere for about one hundred and sixtie yeares, and spread its branches farre and wide, being mellowed and mollified by the mildnesse of the soyle and sweet aire, was prepared in fulnes of time for ... our regeneration in Christ.'[17] The astonishing receptivity of the Saxons to Christianity deeply impressed Camden:

No sooner was the name of Christ preached in the English nation, but with a most fervent zeal they consecrated themselves to it, and laid out their utmost endeavours to promote it, by discharging all the duties of Christian piety, by erecting Churches and endowing them, so that no part of the Christian world could show either more or richer monasteries. Nay, even some Kings preferred a religious life before their very crowns. So many holy men did it produce, who for their firm profession of the Christian religion, their resolute perseverance in it, and their unfeigned piety were sainted; that in this point, 'tis equal to any country in the whole Christian world.[18]

The description of individual counties in *Britannia* will bring out the extent of the Saxon religious enterprise, but in his introductory overview, Camden is content to record and admire the enthusiasm for the life of worship and meditation that gave England a comprehensive network of churches and monasteries by the end of the eighth century.

With the ascendancy of Egbert, King of the West Saxons, over the other kings of the Saxon heptarchy, the new name of England became current for the realm, and the name of Britain was lost. Though Camden carries on to deal with the Norman conquest, his deepest concern lies in the ancient phases of history, and this preference becomes apparent when he comes to the topographical body of his book. The relating of history to landscape was a permanent achievement of *Britannia*. Here one can experience Camden's professed intention of 'restoring antiquity to Britain' as he perambulates the counties, tracing the lingering remains of the remote past in the present scene, and evoking the incidents that once occurred there. The land was rich in history, and Camden was for the first time making this richness geographically explicit and available, 'for the honour of his native country', as he announces in his Preface. The ancient British tribal divisions form the background to his presentation of the island, and they shape the method of

---

[17] Camden, *Remains Concerning Britain*, ed. R. D. Dunn (Toronto, 1984), 16.
[18] *Britannia* (1695), col. cxxii.

enquiry, for Camden discourses on the counties as they come within the old tribal areas, beginning with the Danmonii, whose territory is now Cornwall and Devon. This is virtually the only attention the ancient British receive in the topographical part of the book, for Camden does not recognize any earthworks or field monuments as the work of the Britons, nor any artefacts; so they remain an honoured but largely invisible presence in the land. Nor do the Romans feature prominently in the shires. Although the germ of the *Britannia* was the elucidation of the Antonine Itinerary, and the primary intention was to describe Britain as a Roman province, in practice it has relatively little to say about the Roman dimension. Camden does identify place names from the Itinerary and from Ptolemy, but not much else. It is difficult to associate the landscape with specific historic incidents in Roman times, for few are recorded. As he has little archaeological curiosity, Camden pays no serious attention to the remains of Roman towns or camps. He does not attempt to envisage the layout or appearance of a town, or to revive in the imagination the walls, villas, temples, baths, or barracks whose stones lie tumbled about. He is content to establish that, for example, Ringwood in Hampshire was Regnum in the Itinerary, and then to move on. Even in the matter of the Itinerary, Camden does not have a sufficiently clear idea of the course of the Roman roads, so instead of proceeding along the lines of the Antonine routes, as one might expect, he follows the courses of rivers, describing the towns and villages on their banks.

Camden did have a rudimentary archaeological sense, however, as was evident in the antiquarian tour that he made to Hadrian's Wall with his friend Robert Cotton in 1600.[19] There they searched for inscriptions, altars, coins—anything that might help to identify forts and settlements, or to throw light on the times of occupation, the religious cults practised there, and the legions and soldiers who manned the wall.[20] This was a purposeful topographical inspection which yielded a number of inscribed stones and other artefacts,

---

[19] Camden's field trips were as follows: 1578, Norfolk and Suffolk; 1582, Yorkshire; 1589, Devon; 1590, Wales; 1596, Salisbury and Wells; 1600, Carlisle and Hadrian's Wall, with Cotton. In the compilation of *Britannia* he depended much on regional correspondents. See *Remains Concerning Britain*, p. xxi.

[20] See F. J. Haverfield, 'Julius F VI: Notes on Reginald Bainbrigg of Appleby, on William Camden and on some Roman Inscriptions', in *Proceedings of the Cumberland and Westmorland Archaeological Society*, 11 (1911), 343–78.

most of which were sent back to Cotton's house in Conington, Huntingdonshire. The expedition clarified Camden's understanding of the defensive settlements along the Wall, and gave him a pleasurable sense of being closer to the Romans here than anywhere else in the country. The delight in discovery still shines through the workmanlike account of local antiquities, as for example in an incident near Thirlwall in Northumberland: 'An old woman, who dwelt in a neighbouring cottage, shew'd us a little old consecrated altar, thus inscribed to Vitirineus, a tutelar god (as it should seem) of these parts.'[21] Many of the inscriptions gathered in 1600 were printed in the 1607 edition of *Britannia*, under Cumberland, Westmorland, and Northumberland, but Camden did not try to speculate about the implications of these remains; his purpose was simply to record them. It was left to another generation to interpret them. As he wrote in his Preface, 'Somewhat must be left for the Labours of other men. . . . Another age, a new race of men, will produce somewhat new successively. 'Tis enough for me to have broke the ice; and I have gained my ends if I have set others about the same work, whether it be to write more, or amend what I have written.'

To appraise Camden's *modus operandi*, let us look at the perambulation of Wiltshire, a county dense in British, Roman, and Saxon associations. He notes first that the county lies in the territory of the Belgae. There is a preliminary tribute to the famed bravery of the men of Wiltshire, and a brief mention of its many rivers and the abundance of sheep on its plains. Camden then addresses himself to the Wansdyke, one of the county's most impressive topographical features, which he confidently identifies as a Saxon earthwork (helped by the etymological guess that the name means 'Woden's dyke'), and sensibly interprets it as one of the great frontier divisions between the kingdoms of the West Saxons and the Mercians. Various Saxon battles are recalled, and then attention turns to the town of Malmesbury, whose Saxon beginnings are recounted in detail, with praise for the piety of St Aldhelm, and for the vigor of Saxon Christianity. The discussion of Chippenham introduces more Saxon material, with an explanation of the town's name, from Anglo-Saxon 'cyppan', 'to buy', hence the place of a market. Rivers are traced with brief accounts of the

[21] *Britannia* (1695), col. 848.

families whose seats are situated on their banks. Camden speculates that one small river, the Ellan, is the same as one mentioned in this region by Ptolemy as the Alanus. The town of Warminster is proposed as the site of the Roman Verlucio listed in the Antonine Itinerary. When Salisbury Plain is reached, Camden recalls more battles between the Saxon kingdoms, and Alfred's encounters with the Danes. He then investigates the name of Salisbury, eliciting a British meaning, 'dry hill', from behind the Roman name of Sorbiodunum, which in turn he links to the Itinerary. The site of Old Sarum is described, its status in Saxon times emphasized, and its abandonment illustrated with help from a medieval Latin poem. Salisbury Cathedral is briefly admired, with no specific mention of its architecture. The earldom of Salisbury, however, excites Camden's full attention. He narrates its history and celebrates the deeds of its more notable holders, and in the 1607 edition he is able to bring his account up to date by recording that King James has revived the title and bestowed it on Robert Cecil, son of 'the Nestor of our Age', William Cecil, Camden's own patron.

Now Camden sets out for Stonehenge. So uncertain is he of his response to this monument that he first introduces it with a phrase from Cicero, 'insana substructio', rather than in his own words. He describes it as three concentric circles in the form of a crown, and from the 1600 edition onwards used an engraving that gave an exaggerated view of a confused tumble of stones. He accompanies the illustration with some Latin verses by the thirteenth-century poet Alexander Neckham, which tell the legend of Stonehenge's magical transportation out of Ireland by Merlin at the behest of Uther Pendragon. As for its purpose, Camden recounts the traditions that it was either a monument to British chieftains treacherously slain at a meeting with the Saxon invaders, or a memorial to the fifth-century Romano-British leader Ambrosius Aurelianus, killed in a battle with the Saxons. He offers no personal opinion. The brevity of the entry on Stonehenge, the lack of response to the mystery and power of the stones themselves, and the evasive nature of his observations all suggest that Camden never actually visited the most notable antiquity in Britain.[22] He moves

---

[22] Stuart Piggott believes that Camden never saw Stonehenge; see *Ancient Britons*, 102–3. Camden did however visit Salisbury in 1596. Piggott notes that the first person to suggest that Stonehenge was an ancient British monument was Edmund Bolton in *Nero Caesar* (1624).

his narrative rapidly on to Silbury Hill, the great Bronze Age mound, which he interprets as a Roman or Saxon boundary marker, and then passes to Malmesbury, which he identifies with the Roman town of Cunetio. The survey of the county concludes with a history of the ancient earldom of Wiltshire.

To a modern reader, what is remarkable in Camden's report is his inability to recognize any pre-Roman remains in a county that abounded with barrows, earthworks and stone monuments. For all the interest in the Ancient Britons professed in the historical introduction to *Britannia*, he seems unaware that any physical traces of their presence survive. Pre-Roman Britain is a blank. For Camden, the Romans made the first enduring impressions on the English landscape, and he busies himself in identifying the pattern of Roman settlement, mostly on the basis of antique documents and etymology rather than by discovery of visible remains. As for the Saxons, there are more references to events of their era than one might have anticipated from the introductory section, and this fullness is a measure of how much Camden had come to master the history of Saxon times in the years between the first edition of *Britannia* in 1586 and the final revised version of 1607. He was much helped in this matter by access to printed sources, such as editions of Gildas' *De Excidio Britanniae*, Bede's *Historia Ecclesiastica*, and Asser's *Vita Alfredi* which were all in print when he first wrote. Material from the Anglo-Saxon Chronicle, including Athelweard's *Chronicle*, became available through its inclusion in the *Scriptores Post Bedam* by his friend Sir Henry Savile, which appeared in 1596.[23] Above all, he was able to consult a treasury of Anglo-Saxon documents in Robert Cotton's library, relating to ecclesiastical life. His ability to relate all that history to topography is clear by the time of the 1607 *Britannia*.

One feature of *Britannia* that would continue into the numerous topographical books that were its descendants later in the seventeenth century was the prominence given to noble families and their pedigrees. Camden's position as Clarenceux King at Arms after 1597 gave him a professional involvement in the lineage of families, and although he tried to hold this aspect of regional history in check, because it was marginal to his main endeavour, it

---

[23] For a succinct account of early printings of Anglo-Saxon material, see Henry Marsh, *Dark Age Britain* (London, 1970), 197–200.

was hard to exclude, because Elizabethan and Jacobean gentry had a passion for genealogy, and they were the audience for Camden's book. Indeed, major families had a considerable influence over the historical development of their locality, and were a force in the shaping of Britain.

Britannia inspired numerous gentlemen throughout the following century to undertake valuable antiquarian surveys of their own particular counties and to fill out Camden's sketch with the abundant detail that comes from more intimate local knowledge, with the consequence that Britain became the most carefully and historically documented nation in Europe.[24] Equally important was the recognition of *Britannia* as a touchstone of achievement which gave a focus to research into the origins and development of the nation and its institutions, and established a standard for British antiquarian studies in the future. In addition, Camden provided an incentive to further research by including two brief discourses in the introductory matter to *Britannia*, on the degrees of the social hierarchy and on the history of the courts of law.

These discourses would seem originally to have been offered by Camden as contributions to the discussions of the group of historically-minded acquaintances who, in 1586, the year of *Britannia*'s publication, formed themselves into the Society of Antiquaries. One cannot be certain about the chronology for the Society's formation, but it does seem most probable that it was precipitated by the publication of Camden's book.[25] Camden did not work in isolation, and the men who constituted the Society in its early days would have been the principal supporters of his enterprise. Some were close friends, such as the young Robert Cotton, his former pupil at Westminster School, who was already developing into a collector of books and manuscripts; or John Stow, who was working on his *Survay of London*; or the lawyer

---

[24] The principal county topographies published before 1660 were Richard Carew's *Survey of Cornwall* (1602), John Norden's *Speculum Britanniae* (1593) and 1598), which covered Middlesex and Hertfordshire, William Burton's *Description of Leicestershire* (1622), William Dugdale's *Antiquities of Warwickshire* (1656), Richard Kilburn's *Topographie of Kent* (1659), and John Philipot's *Villare Cantianum* (1659). For a comprehensive discussion of seventeenth-century county topographies, see Mendyk, *Speculum Britanniae*.

[25] See Linda van Norden, 'The Elizabethan College of Antiquaries', Ph.D. thesis (University of California, Los Angeles, 1946). Microfilm.

Henry Spelman.[26] Others were officials of Elizabethan London
with a professional interest in the past: heralds such as William
Dethick and Francis Thynne, or keepers of state archives such as
Arthur Agarde or Thomas Talbot. The topics discussed at the early
meetings in the 1580s and 1590s, as printed in the collection
Curious Discourses, edited by Thomas Hearne (1771 and 1775),
show that there was an insistent concern with the beginnings of
institutions and customs. Among the first subjects discussed were
the origin of sterling money, the antiquity of titles of honour, the
origins of parishes, the source of units of land measurement, and
the development of castles. Legal subjects were popular, as for
example the antiquity of trial by jury and of judicial combat. Some
of the most intensely researched papers treated of the history of
officers of state: the Earl Marshal, the Constable, and the High
Steward of England. These discussions were motivated by a
profound curiosity about characteristic features of English society.
They acknowledged that the institutions they examined had an
extremely long history, and were subject to change and development. The roots were almost lost in time, but purposeful research in
state or ecclesiastical records could produce a remarkable amount
of information about origins. The members of the Society were
mostly men who were skilled at delving in the records, and their
contributions to their regular meetings were suggestive rather than
conclusive, so that there was a non-dogmatic air about the Society.
Its meetings continued until 1607 when King James expressed a
dislike of its activities, apparently fearing that its investigations
would look critically on the immemorial rights of his royal
prerogative. There had in fact been a shift toward the discussion of
topics with political implications in James's reign, with subjects
such as the origin and nature of Parliament, and its liberties and
privileges.[27] The antiquaries took the royal disapproval seriously,
and shut down their shop in 1607.

---

[26] Stow provided access to his collection of the papers of the Tudor antiquary,
John Leland, whose ambitious 'Itinerary of England and Wales' was the only
significant forerunner of *Britannia*; but Leland's Itinerary still lay in manuscript, and
its account of England was skeletal in comparison with Camden's.

[27] For the early history of the Society of Antiquaries, see Evans, *Society of
Antiquaries*, ch. 1; May McKisack, *Medieval History in the Tudor Age* (Oxford,
1971), ch. 7; Sharpe, *Sir Robert Cotton*, ch. 1; and Linda van Norden, 'Sir Henry
Spelman on the Chronology of the Elizabethan College of Antiquaries' in
Huntington Library Quarterly, 13 (1949–50), 131–60.

The existence of the Society over some twenty years meant that a number of people could now be identified as antiquaries. Antiquarian research was seen to be a serious and dignified vocation, and enough people were engaged in its pursuits to promise a productive future for the enquiry into the past. Several of Camden's contributions to the Society appear to have made their way into a volume he published (anonymously) in 1605, entitled *Remains Concerning Britain*. Long considered a collection of miscellaneous material that could not be fitted into the *Britannia*, the *Remains* has recently been re-evaluated and shown to be a separately planned work from the beginning, more popular in intent, written in English for an English audience, and more patriotically coloured than the larger work.[28] Some of the contents of the *Remains* are comparable to matter in the preliminary sections of *Britannia*, offering in effect English synopses of those chapters dealing with the character of the island, the first inhabitants (the primitive British—no mention of the Trojans here at all), and the languages of Britain. This last subject is dealt with in an essay which provides the best-informed discussion of the languages of primitive Britain published up to that time. Camden ignores the conventional habit of tracing all languages back to Babel, and concentrates instead on describing first the probable affinities of the British language with ancient Gallic, and then the relationship of the 'English-Saxon tongue' to an extensive family of Germanic languages spread over northern Europe. He is aware of Joseph Scaliger's proposal that these languages might be part of an even larger group, which we would call Indo-European, and notes some of the basic words that indicate the possibility of a link with eastern languages, though he is not yet prepared to give a positive assent to the idea. Camden now shows himself to be an

---

[28] See the edition by R. D. Dunn (Toronto, 1984). Dunn observes that the notes for the *Remains* from the time of its inception (c.1583) were kept in English, while those for *Britannia* were made in Latin. There was however a certain amount of interchange of material between the two books in their various editions: some passages of the chapters 'Britain', 'Inhabitants', and 'Language' migrated into the 1607 edition of *Britannia*, and information about British and Romano-British coins in the 1600 edition of *Britannia*, enlarged in 1607, moved across to the 1614 edition of the *Remains*. See Dunn's Introduction, pp. xvii and xviii. There were editions of the *Remains* in 1605, 1614, 1623, 1629, 1636, and 1637. The first edition was dedicated to Robert Cotton, with whom Camden worked closely and whose library was already indispensable to him.

enthusiastic publicist for Anglo-Saxon as a language that has proved vigorously durable, and he goes to some lengths to explain its characteristics to his audience, showing them that it is both accessible and admirable. At this point he prints an essay by his friend Richard Carew, a panegyric on 'The Excellency of the English Tongue'. Carew (who was Camden's chief informant about Cornish antiquities) writes in a high patriotic strain about the English language, and the claims he makes for its expressiveness, its flexibility, energy, and metaphorical richness, are not exaggerated, for the language was indeed at its zenith. He attempts to convince the reader that its achievements match those of Greek and Latin (though it is surprising to find 'Shakesphear' admired for his Catullan amorousness).

The essays on English surnames and Christian names enable Camden to display his powers of etymological analysis in ways that an English reader would find immediately instructive, and indeed they provide a simple introduction to the art of etymology, which was so much favoured by gentlemen with an antiquarian turn of mind. Collections of proverbs, epigrams, and 'wise speeches' project an enjoyment of the linguistic adroitness of English which is an important part of the book's appeal. The bouquets of medieval Latin verse by English writers that Camden includes appear to represent his personal taste in a little-known literary area; this taste must have been developed by his extensive reading in manuscripts, and the many specimens he quotes, notably in the essays on epigrams and rhymes, would have been quite novel to his readers. He was in fact one of the first English scholars to show an interest in the Latin literature of the Middle Ages, and was able to reveal what a wealth of social detail and historical information was contained in this neglected body of verse. Other topics seem to preserve Camden's views on subjects discussed by the Society of Antiquaries: the brief history of artillery, the account of the development of coats of arms (with its tongue-in-cheek suggestion that the Ancient British might have initiated the custom by being their own painted devices on the battlefield), the survey of the use of money, the sketch of the changing fashions of costume—all have the air of prepared pieces for delivery to an audience.

The essays are economically written, containing great quantities of information in highly condensed form. In most cases, Camden's method is to begin his topic with the earliest reliable records, and to move forward through time, citing examples and embellishing them with brief anecdotes and apt literary quotations. There is something of a holiday air about these essays, a desire to divert the reader with information seasoned with wit and pleasantry. Camden is inclined to indulge himself in the curiosities of antiquarian lore; for example, as he identifies the first use of various kinds of artillery, he regales his reader with details of unusual objects that have been fired against an enemy (such as mill-stones, pigs, and putrefied horses), and he names the first Englishman to be killed by a cannon (Thomas Montacute, in 1425). The sense of intellectual *divertissement* is strong in the essays on word-plays—rebuses, *impresa*, and anagrams (the number of which was increased in later editions). Was Camden perhaps offering this lighter material to a broad audience as an inducement to a more serious study of antiquities?

The essay on epitaphs was possibly the most influential portion of the *Remains*, for it introduced a subject of perennial fascination to antiquarians. Camden's brief discourse begins with Abraham and ends with his own contemporaries. He ponders on the universal impulse to memorialize the dead, and makes short excursions to famous Greek and Roman tombs, before settling down to compile an anthology of epitaphs from British, Saxon, and English sources. He is concerned to demonstrate the continuity of this genre in Britain from antiquity, for he starts with an epitaph of a Briton who died in Rome, then recites the memorial verses to King Arthur, and moves on to epitaphs of Saxon kings and archbishops, then quotes numerous Norman epitaphs that he has recorded in the course of his researches. His aim, he declares, is 'that you may see how learning ebbed and flowed' in England, by becoming aware of the varying levels of eloquence and wit achieved by different generations, but it is clear that Camden also derives great pleasure from the perusal of his 'choice epitaphs'. His essay would be the starting point for many similar collections made in the seventeenth century, notably by John Weever, Henry Holland, William Dugdale, and John Aubrey, and his preliminary observations on burial rites would also inspire a voluminous literature.

Learning is lightly worn in the *Remains*. Its miscellaneous character proved very successful, there being six editions before the Civil War. It acted as a kind of antiquarian *gradus ad Parnassum*, enticing readers towards the pleasures of enquiry into the origins of their race, their language, and their society. For serious readers, that enquiry would be directed to the *Britannia*, and after 1610 that work was available in English in the spirited translation by Philemon Holland. This new edition in folio, enhanced with a splendid engraved title-page, became a common item in gentlemen's libraries, and did more to create a readership for antiquarian writings than did any other volume of the age.

2

Richard Verstegan

'Richard Verstegan, or as some call him, Richard Rowlands, a great reviver of our English antiquities, and a most admirable Critick in the Saxon and Gothick languages, ought with due ceremony to crave a place among these writers . . . because he is little remarked among authors.'[1] So wrote Anthony Wood in his account of Oxford authors, and the obscurity of which he complained in the late seventeenth century has intensified since, so that Verstegan is today almost totally forgotten; yet in his time he was a most innovative antiquary, albeit an unexpected one. The book for which he deserves to be remembered, *A Restitution of Decayed Intelligence in Antiquities* (1605), came from a man whose concerns had previously been almost entirely religious, for he was a recusant and in many ways an outsider to English society. Some biographical details are helpful to explain his unusual situation.

He was born in London about 1550, into a Dutch family which had moved to England about 1500 to escape from the endemic warfare of the Low Countries. His grandfather was a prosperous gentleman called Theodore Rowland Verstegan, and Richard lived under the name of Rowlands while he was in England. He went up to Christ Church, Oxford, in 1565, but being a Catholic he would not take the oath of loyalty to the Church of England, and left without a degree. At Oxford he interested himself in Anglo-Saxon, a language which was then being reconstructed by scholars such as Matthew Parker, John Foxe, John Bale, and their associates, for its value in establishing the antiquity of the English Church. In 1576 he published *The Post of the World*: 'wherein is conteyned the antiquities and originall of the most famous Cities in Europe. With their Trade and Trafficke', dedicated to Sir Thomas Gresham. It is difficult to know what he did for a living in these years, but it is likely that he was involved in the printing trade. As the persecution of Catholics under Elizabeth grew, he became more active in

---

[1] Wood, *Athenae Oxonienses*, i. 427.

the Catholic cause. By 1581 he was running a secret press in London, printing Catholic pamphlets and propaganda, and when this press was seized in 1582 he fled to Paris, where he was soon printing again, issuing booklets that described the vicious persecution of Catholics in England.[2] At least one of these booklets was vividly illustrated by copper plates which he had drawn and engraved himself. His anti-English activities caused the English ambassador in Paris to press for his arrest for defaming the honour of the Queen. His arrest happened at the end of 1583, but he was released shortly afterwards, in January 1584, as a result of the intervention of the papal nuncio. After a visit to Rome, he settled in Antwerp and took the name Richard Verstegan. There in 1587 he published his most notable work of religious protest, *Theatrum Crudelitatum Haereticorum Nostri Temporis*, which was a comprehensive indictment of Protestant cruelty against Catholics, showing the horrors perpetrated on them by French Huguenots, Dutch Calvinists, and English Reformers. This book too was vigorously illustrated, and Verstegan wrote that he hoped the pictures would incite the reader to praise the faithful martyrs and experience a detestation of the Protestant heresy. He called on the Catholic princes to avenge their slaughtered saints.

The *Theatrum Crudelitatum* was probably occasioned by the execution in 1586 of Mary Queen of Scots, for whom Verstegan had a particular veneration. He returned to the theme of the English persecution of Catholics with another martyrology published in 1601, in which his hostility to the Protestant establishment was as strong as ever. Verstegan himself had become part of a network of Catholic agents who were passing news, information, and books between Catholics in England and their countrymen in Europe. His despatches are full of details of imprisonment and torture of members of the Catholic community, and he kept up his role as an intelligencer for a good twenty-five years, from about 1590 to 1615.[3] In 1595 he had visited Spain, and had an interview with Philip II about the situation of the English Catholics. He is last heard of in Antwerp in 1620.

---

[2]   A helpful account of Verstegan is given by A. G. Petti in 'Richard Verstegan and the Catholic Martyrologies of the Later Elizabethan Period' in *Recusant History*, 5 (1959–60). See also Wood, *Athenae Oxonienses*, i. 427–9, and *DNB*.

[3]   See A. G. Petti, 'The Letters and Despatches of Richard Verstegan 1550–1600' in *The Catholic Record Society*, 52 (1959).

It is highly surprising then to find this man, who was so hostile to the English establishment, bringing out a book on English antiquities and dedicating it to King James. One imagines that it was Verstegan's devotion to Mary Stuart that emboldened him to offer it to James, and there was probably an intention to show that one could be an Englishman loyal to the crown and a Catholic at the same time. Verstegan had on several occasions protested that many Catholics under Elizabeth were loyal to the Queen, and were being persecuted for their faith, not for their politics. He no doubt had hopes that James would be more tolerantly inclined (a fair expectation early in 1605, when the *Restitution* was published), but these hopes would be frustrated after the Gunpowder Plot of November of the same year.[4] No doubt too the dedication to the King (even though unapproved) aided the importation of the book from Antwerp, where it was printed, to London, where its real market lay.

The *Restitution* is a book about origins. It is unusual and remarkable in that it offers a credible and varied argument in favour of regarding the English as entirely a Germanic nation, whose real ancestors were the Saxons. Verstegan is indifferent to the ancient British, and dismissive of their Trojan ancestors. Even if the Trojan legends were true, and he professes himself sceptical, the British are quite unrelated to the English. The ancient British are only relevant to the Welsh, who are their descendants. The English, now so flourishing a nation, should ignore the specious ancestry of the Britons and recognize themselves for what they are, a German people. The 'decayed intelligence in antiquities' of the title that needs to be restored is the knowledge of England's Germanic origins, and beyond that, the true origins of the Teutonic people themselves. By history, philology, and legend, Verstegan reinforces his case. This celebration of the Saxons as honourable and valorous creators of the nation was considerably at variance with prevailing antiquarian views in 1605, when attention was usually directed to the British or Roman contribution to the shaping of the national character. Was Verstegan able to offer a different perspective

---

[4] The Gunpowder Plot did call forth from Parliament the requirement that Catholics should take an Oath of Allegiance to the monarch, acknowledging James as the rightful sovereign. Verstegan would presumably have approved of this oath as a way for Catholics to indicate their political loyalty while retaining their religious identity.

because he viewed the scene from the Low Countries, or could it be that he began this work back around 1570, as the product of his enthusiasm for Anglo-Saxon studies at Oxford, and when he had written a book on the origins and antiquities of famous cities? The praise of things Anglo-Saxon would certainly chime with that early Elizabethan vogue when the Church historians were reviving the subject. Perhaps Verstegan's book was begun early but not completed until later, when a new reign had stimulated speculation about the nature of England.

The *Restitution* was ushered into the world by eminent sponsors, mostly Englishmen, and presumably also Catholics.[5] The leading commendatory poem came from Richard White of Basingstoke, who was the English historian and antiquary most widely known on the Continent at the end of the sixteenth century.[6] Like Verstegan, he was an Oxford man and a Catholic, who lived abroad on account of his religion; yet he still retained strong patriotic feelings towards England. He was however in all respects a vastly more distinguished figure than Verstegan. A Professor of Law at Douai University, he eventually became Rector there; his intellectual reputation was crowned when he was made a Count Palatine of the Empire by Rudolph II. His major work was the *Historiarum Britanniae* (1597–1607), a grand compilation of all the legends of Britain's ancient line of kings descended from Trojan Brutus. It presented the whole panoply of British History as derived from Geoffrey of Monmouth in its most complete and polished form, delivered to a continental audience in Latin as an act of tribute to an ancient and glorious nation and it was dedicated to the Parliament and People of Britain. Although now regarded as a

---

[5] The identifiable contributors of commendatory poems were Richard White, Richard Stanyhurst, Francis Tregian, Anthony Greneway, Ralph Radcliffe, and Thomas Shelton. These verses by various Catholic hands serve to remind us of the existence of a tradition of recusant antiquarianism that has been little noticed. Often publishing abroad, or keeping their work in manuscript, these men had as good reason as their Protestant counterparts for exploring the British past; they were proud of the antiquity of their nation and mindful of a rich Catholic inheritance. In this line of Catholic antiquaries, the Benedictine monks Augustine Baker and Clement Rayner should perhaps be noted here. In the early seventeenth century both made collections relating to the history of monasticism in England.

[6] For an account of White of Basingstoke's writings, see J. W. Binns, *Intellectual Culture in Elizabethan and Jacobean England: the Latin Writing of the Age* (Leeds, 1990), 183–5.

monument of misapplied scholarship, in its time it was admired as a *summa historia*, and enjoyed a prestige in Europe greater than Camden's *Britannia*. White commended Verstegan's work in spirited verse, though understandably without endorsing its thesis, for Verstegan paid little attention to the Britons, and concentrated on the Saxons, who held no appeal for White.

The next piece of liminary verse was offered by Richard Stanyhurst, the erudite historian of Ireland and commentator on Porphyry, and another representative of the Catholic community in exile. He too lived in the Low Countries, and was chaplain to the Archduke in Brussels. Stanyhurst was the uncle of James Ussher, who would become the Primate of Ireland; the two men would engage in extensive religious controversy, hurling clumps of historical matter at each other for the honour of their Church. The last poem is by Verstegan himself, writing in the Spenserian manner on the theme of the destructive force of Time, which the antiquary must attempt to reverse. His spur is 'the love to my dear nation due', and the poem concludes with praise of 'Jacobus Magnus' and the fourfold union of his crown.

King James, who was accustomed to derive his lineage from true British stock, and who willingly consented to have Brutus, Cymbeline, and Arthur among his ancestors (as his poets often affirmed), might have been gratified to be hailed as a descendant of 'our English-Saxon Kings'—if he ever read this book at all. Convinced that Englishmen knew nothing of the origin and descent of their nation, and were ignorant of the nature of their own language, Verstegan briskly set about the process of illumination. His main approach would be philological, for he wanted to make it clear that English belonged to a Teutonic language group. To understand the truth of his proposition, the student of English origins should have a broad knowledge of the northern languages: Anglo-Saxon, Old High German, Low German, Danish and Swedish, and even Frankish. On all these languages, Verstegan declared that he had bestowed 'some time of travail', and this gave him exceptional qualifications for the pursuit of his enquiries.

The singling out of language as the clue to national identity takes Verstegan back immediately to the Tower of Babel. According to Verstegan, if not strictly according to Genesis, the Tower was built to preserve men against any future flood, and both Babel and the Flood had their part to play in the creation of the English nation.

After the Lord had visited the confusion of tongues upon mankind for their hubris, he scattered them abroad upon the face of the earth, and Verstegan's book has a neat little vignette on its title-page, showing the various language groups dispersing from Babel. As the familiar Renaissance scheme of the origin of nations begins to unfold, we are led away with the sons of Japhet, in the company of Gomer, in the direction of Europe. Gomer's grandson, 'according to the opinion of sundry very learned and judiciall authors', was called Tuisco, the patriarch and conductor of the Germans, who preserve a memory of their founder in the name Teutsch or Deutsch.

The prominence of Tuisco in Verstegan's narrative gives us a clue to the main source of his fanciful racial ideas. He mentions his indebtedness to Sebastian Munster, whose *Cosmographia Universalis* (1544) he approvingly cites. But behind Munster lay the

2. Vignette from the title-page of Verstegan's *Restitution* (1605), showing the departure of the different nations from the Tower of Babel.

pseudo-Berosus, a much-disputed work which had first put the figure of Tuisco into circulation. The historical Berosus was a Chaldean priest who lived in Babylon in the fourth century BC, and who had compiled in Greek a 'History of Babylonia' which ran from the Creation to his own time. This work had been preserved in fragments by Eusebius and Georgius Syncellus, but in the later fifteenth century the Italian monk Annius of Viterbo claimed to have found a manuscript of Berosus's History, which he published in 1498 along with a version of the Egyptian History of Manetho, another lost work of antiquity which he professed to have discovered.[7] His work was immediately attacked by Italian scholars as a forgery, as indeed it was, but critical hostility did not succeed in suppressing further printings, for the Histories were too attractive to be cast aside. Annius's version of Berosus offered an account of the peopling of the world after the Flood which provided much specific detail about the origins of the different nations after God scattered them from Babel, and his inventions were tolerated for the same reason that Geoffrey of Monmouth's History was retained, because both gave colourful information about tracts of time that otherwise would have been a blank, and both threw a pleasing light on the formation of peoples in earliest antiquity. Annius's Histories were in fact full of aetiological myths which scholars in all countries could exploit for their own purposes.

The pseudo-Berosus added helpfully to the descendants of Japhet, Shem, and Ham by supplying names which had been lost from the record of Genesis. At the same time it drew in classical mythology to the Judaic scheme by declaring that the gods and heroes of the Greeks had been historical figures who were also numbered among the descendants of Noah. Thus for example the Lybian Hercules was one of the progeny of Japhet, and Saturn (who had founded Babylon) derived from Shem. Among the characters now introduced on to the primitive world scene were some who would have a long career in antiquarian circles. Outstanding among them was Samothes, who was a son of Japhet along with

[7] *Commentaria Super Opera Diversor. Auctor. De Antiquitatibus Loquentium* (Rome, 1498). Among other fragments printed in this volume was a section of the Antonine Itinerary relating to Italy, now accepted as genuine. In the words of Thomas Kendrick, Annius's volume 'was undoubtedly the most mischievous study of the remote past published during the Renaissance' (*British Antiquity* (1970), 71–2).

Gomer. Gomer had biblical credentials and was looked upon as an active settler of the western lands (as we have seen in the discussion of Camden), but Samothes rapidly began to rival him as a *pater patriae*. According to the pseudo-Berosus, Samothes was the founder of the Scythians, a race much remarked by the Greek historians for their war-like powers and their wide dissemination, and often mentioned by Renaissance historiographers as having spread into northern and western Europe. In addition, Samothes was deemed to be the progenitor of the Celts, the Gauls, and the Britons. Then there was Tuisco, descended from Shem, who also became a leader of the Celts, and who conducted away from the Tower of Babel the group who became the Germans.

Verstegan makes much of Tuisco in his *Restitution* as he outlines the development of the Germanic race. He notes how the people took the name of their leader, calling themselves Teutsch; he also derives the word Teuton from Tuisco in that loose, intuitive way characteristic of Renaissance etymologists. He claims that Tuisco was venerated as a god, and honoured most after the sun and moon among the German people. Tuisday, or Tuesday, was the day appointed for his adoration. Verstegan is able to make the transition from the specious history of the pseudo-Berosus to the sound historical source of Tacitus by observing that Tacitus had mentioned at the opening of his *De Germania* that the Germans honoured 'an earth-born god, Tuisco', as their founder (though he says nothing about the provenance of this figure). Presumably it was from this solitary reference in Tacitus that Annius of Viterbo had taken the name that he planted in his spurious account of the post-diluvian world attributed to Berosus.

The copious use of this pseudo-Berosan material by Verstegan could be considered as another indication that *The Restitution of Decayed Intelligence in Antiquities* was a book that took shape in the earlier part of Elizabeth's reign, for that is when the influence of the pseudo-Berosus was at its strongest. One mid-sixteenth-century enthusiast, from whom Verstegan drew material, was the Flemish scholar Goropius, whose *Origines Antwerpianae* (1569) played with the story of Tuisco and represented the Dutch (or Teutsch) as the chosen race. In England, Bishop John Bale had extensively exploited the contents of the pseudo-Berosus in several of his own writings of the 1540s and 1550s. Bale was interested not only in filling in the earliest phases of British history, but also in developing the religious implications of the pseudo-Berosan genealogies. It could be maintained, he believed, that the knowledge of God possessed by Adam had been transmitted to his descendants and brought to Britain by Samothes; this strain of the true primitive religion had taken root in Britain and had been fostered by the Druids, who had a profound knowledge of the nature of the soul and of God's purposes towards mankind. Bale hoped to show that the Protestantism of his own time was in part a revival of the Adamite religion of British antiquity, and that true religion had always been present in this island, though long obscured and corrupted.[8]

When Verstegan reaches Tacitus, he gets to firm ground and can recite at length Tacitus's admiration for the Germans. His attempt to promote the Saxons as estimable forebears derives most of its force from Tacitus's account of the German race, in fact. The qualities that Tacitus singled out for praise—their war-like valour, the strictness of their living and their laws, their determination to preserve their freedom—are all seen in retrospect to have a relevance to the English who were descended from the Germanic nation. Unfortunately, Tacitus did not mention the Saxons in his survey of the German tribes, but Verstegan expresses the reasonable belief that they dwelt too far north for Roman knowledge, or that 'Tacitus comprehendeth them under some other name.' He is confident that what Tacitus said about other German tribes remains valid for the Saxons, who came over to Britain in the fifth century.

The viewpoint Verstegan presents us with next is quite exceptional for its time, and important for advancing his case that the Saxons deserve serious attention as the determining factor in the development of the English nation. Instead of taking the conventional view that the Germanic tribes contributed to the decline of civilization in the west, he celebrates them as a reinvigorating force, and the builders of nations. Goths, Franks, Saxons, Vandals, and Langobards were not the destroyers of a high culture and the harbingers of darkness; rather, they are saluted for

---

[8] Bale's views are laid out in his *Illustrium Majoris Britanniae Scriptorum . . . Summarium* (1548), and improved in *Scriptorum Illustrium majoris Britanniae . . . Catalogus: a Japheto per 3618 Annos usque ad Ann.* (1557). See Kendrick, *British Antiquity* (1979), 69–72.

their vitality and courage. Verstegan has virtually no interest in the Romans, so that their prejudices against a fair assessment of the Gothic peoples are not brought into play. There is certainly no bias in Verstegan's acclaim. Barbarians they may have been to the Greeks and Romans, but barbarism is only a phase: it is the vigorous youth of emergent nations. Culture and learning are not resident virtues, but shift with time: 'for where was there ever more learning and scyence than in Greece, and where in the world is there now more barbarism? What most excellently learned men, and great doctors of the Church, had Africa brought forth . . . and with what learned men is Africa in our time acquainted?'[9] Verstegan dismisses the Aristotelian notion that climate conditions culture: 'it is a meer imaginarie supposal, to think that the temperature of the ayr in any region, doth make the inhabitants any more or less learned or ingenious.' The energy with which the old chimeras are driven from the scene is commendable and refreshing.

He sets about writing an ethnographic account of the customs, behaviour, and beliefs of the Saxons, one that is, again, advanced for its time. First there is the problem of their name and its meaning. Once more Verstegan turns to etymology to provide explanations, and proposes that they were called Saxons because their preferred weapon was a kind of curved sword 'anciently written seaxen or seaxes'. He maintains that it was not uncommon for nations to be called after their weapons, instancing the Scythians, whose name clearly derived from the old Teutonic verb 'scytan', meaning 'to shoot an arrow', and the Picards, whose name derived from their role as pikemen. The Renaissance conviction that proper names contained a meaning that described character or origin was responsible for many ingenious feats of etymology, and as we have seen Verstegan was a keen player of this game.[10] Having settled the meaning of the Saxon name, he then attempts to describe 'the ancient manner of living of our Saxon ancestors'. Granted, much is taken from Tacitus's *De Germania*, but Verstegan is genuinely trying to imagine the otherness of the Saxons, and does

[9] Richard Verstegan, *A Restitution of Decayed Intelligence in Antiquities* (Antwerp, 1605), 51.
[10] Verstegan's interpretation of the name 'German' is a good example of his ingenuity. The people were called Ger-mans, or Al-mans, because of their virile character, he maintains. 'Ger' is a variant of 'gar', meaning 'all', so both names are 'as much to say as All or wholly a man'.

not regard them as Elizabethans wearing a different kind of costume, as the playwrights or poets might have represented them. Their food, clothing, and weapons, their marriage and funeral customs, are portrayed; he describes their mode of government, by twelve men in peacetime who elect a king only in time of war. Verstegan is not disposed to draw out the political implications of Saxon rule, as later writers would be. Their laws he cannot retrieve in any detail (a fact that suggests he was unaware of William Lambarde's book on Saxon laws, *Archaionomia*, published in 1568). He is fascinated by the custom of trial by ordeal. He is fascinated too by their gods and their forms of worship. He describes their principal deities, making analogies with Roman gods where he can, but recognizing that he is dealing with an independent religious system.

Verstegan illustrated the *Restitution* with a number of copper engravings which he himself designed and cut. At a time when few Englishmen could draw with any competence, his work is uncommonly skilful and distinctive: an old Netherlandish talent reasserting itself perhaps. It was something of a novelty to have illustrations to an antiquarian book, and Anthony Wood remembered that 'there are several cuts . . . drawn with great curiosity by him which hath advantaged the sale of it much.'[11] He drew the images of the gods to whom the days of the week were dedicated. No visual sources have been found for his designs, so we may tentatively take them as his own inventions, especially as they show a strong influence from contemporary emblem books, rather than from any acquaintance with antique statuary.[12] The sun god is the best of these engravings, with his face surrounded by flames and a wheel of fire upon his chest, but the pedestal shows too much good taste for a Saxon temple, and the niche is improbably adorned with Elizabethan strapwork. The moon goddess, in her short tunic and her hood with ears, is mild and mysterious, set in a landscape where a well-fortified town appears. Tuisco too much resembles a classical statue (even his wild beast's skin hangs like a toga), and behind him rises the Tower of Babel, from which the first Germans are leaving. Woden is altogether too much like a medieval king of the fifteenth century, though he brandishes a Saxon sword, while

[11] *Athenae Oxonienses*, i. 428.
[12] For his information about the gods, he claims to be indebted to Johannes Pomarius, Olaus Magnus, and Saxo Grammaticus.

Thor could be a contemporary monarch, enthroned. Friga, a hermaphroditic figure of war and love, adopts a mannerist pose on her pedestal and bears a sword and bow, 'signifying thereby that women as well as men should in time of need be ready to fight'. Seater is the oddest god.

First on a pillar was placed a pearche, on the sharp prickled back whereof stood this Idol. He was lean of visage, having long haire and a long beard: and was bare-headed and bare-footed. In his left hand he held up a wheel; in his right he carried a pail of water, wherein were flowers and frutes. His long cote was girded unto him with a towel of white linnen. His standing on the sharp finnes of this fish was to signify that the Saxons for their serving him should pass stedfastly and without harm in dangerous and difficult places. By the wheel was betokened the knit amitie and conioyned concord of the Saxons, and their concurring together in the running one course. By the girdle which with the wind streamed from him, was signified the Saxons freedome. By the pail with flowers and frutes was declared, that with kyndly rain he would nowrish the earth to bring forth such frute and flowers.[13]

This is the kind of symbolic figure with interpretation that one finds in Ben Jonson's early masques, and the whole style of presentation derives from the emblem book tradition that was popular all over Europe at this time.

Verstegan is eager to sketch in the ancient history of Britain in order to have a context for the arrival of the Saxons in the fifth century. He thinks it probable that the very first migrants to Britain were led by Samothes, the hero mentioned in the pseudo-Berosus as the leader of the Celts. He then reviews Brutus as a later venturer upon the scene, and is inclined to believe that there was such a figure, who probably gave his name to the country. Folk memory has preserved his name, but was deluded about his origins. Verstegan roundly dismisses the idea that Brutus was from Troy; that was a piece of sheer ignorance or a deliberate desire to emulate Roman origins. None the less Verstegan retains Brutus, but provides a more rational point of departure for him: he must have been a king from Gaul who somehow came to rule over Britain. This explanation opens up a topic that was obviously dear to Verstegan's heart: whether Britain was once part of the continent. If this had been the case, Brutus and his men could easily have

---

[13] Verstegan, *Restitution*, 75.

3. The Idol of the Sun, set upon a fine Mannerist pedestal, from Verstegan's *Restitution*.

4. The Idol Seater, a complex deity of the Saxons, as imagined by Verstegan.

overrun the land without any need of boats. Verstegan's experience of living in the Netherlands, where land had been drowned beneath the sea and also reclaimed from it, had made him conscious of geological change, and he could well imagine that Britain had separated from the continent in fairly recent times. He had seen the remains of fir trees excavated where none now grew, and knew of great beds of shells underground. His sense of the changeable nature of terrain was highly advanced, and in order to persuade the reader of his views, he prints a drawing he has made of 'great bones of fishes found in the earth'. Looking at his accurate drawing, one realizes that he has produced the first depiction of fossils to appear in a printed book. Moreover, he has a clear idea of what they are and how they came to be there. The point that clinches his argument that Britain was joined to the continent until some time after the Flood is ingenious. Wolves still existed in Britain in his day, but 'no man, unlesse he were mad, would ever transport of that race . . . out of the continent into any Iles'; therefore they must have come on foot into Britain after they were dispersed from the Ark, when an isthmus still existed. As for Brutus, he came the same way as the wolves.

Verstegan does not detain the reader long with the Britons, although he briefly narrates their lines of descent according to Geoffrey of Monmouth, to fill in the blank spaces of the past. As he says, they are of no great relevance to an Englishman. The Romans occupy even less space. The 400 years of their occupation are got over in a paragraph, clearing the way for the landing of the Saxons and the founding of the English race. A fine picture of military disembarkation accompanies this moment, showing Hengist and Horsa dressed in short-skirted costumes, with their falchion-like Saxon swords and a crossbow prominently on display. The question of how England came to be so called then has to be settled. Was it from a proper name, or from a region in the Saxon homeland? Verstegan canvasses the possibilities, but as he usually prefers his own opinion, he settles for his own etymology: it comes from the Teutonic word 'Eng', meaning 'narrow' or 'straight', because of the configuration of the island.

There is no need to pursue Verstegan's synopsis of English history in any detail. The Danish invasions do not shake his conviction that Englishmen derive their blood, language, and character from the Saxons, because the Danes were another

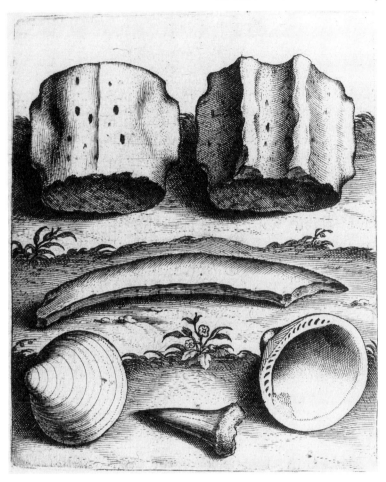

5. Verstegan's accurate and knowledgeable depiction of fossils, 1605.

Germanic people closely akin to the Saxons. Nor does the Norman Conquest mark a radical change, as far as Verstegan is concerned, because the Normans were yet another Germanic race.

Whereas some do call us a mixed nation by reason of these Danes and Normannes coming in among us, I answere . . . that the Danes and the Normannes were once one same people with the Germans, as were also the Saxons; and we were not to be accompted mixed by having only some such joyned unto us againe, as sometyme had one same language and one same originall with us.[14]

The real hero of Verstegan's book is the English language, what he calls the 'English-Saxon' tongue. The Normans may have conquered the land and taken power and changed the laws, but they 'could not conquer the English language as they did the land'.[15] Norman French died out in relatively few generations, and the descendants of the Normans came to speak English, a language that perpetuates the spirit and the character of the Saxons and is an indestructable and victorious force. Anglo-Saxon is the key to the identity of the English. By its means, place names and personal names yield up their meaning, as do titles of honour, which relate to the basic structure of English society. Almost half the book is given over to demonstrating the importance of Anglo-Saxon as an instrument of discovery. Tudor scholars had been quick to see its value for ecclesiastical history, but Verstegan was the first to recognize its larger value to the national historian. He provided a serviceable glossary and did an excellent job of explaining surnames, first names, and place-names, as well as the offices of public life. To contrast with his section on titles of honour, he included a section on names of contempt, believing that these terms were ancient and ineradicable in the race. As Thomas Browne well knew, Thersites will live as long as Agamemnon. To read page after page of Verstegan's linguistic interpretations is to experience a real sense of enlightenment about the English past, to discover a people living in a familiar topography, engaged in known activities, and exercising a known form of government. One must remember that Anglo-Saxon was a language virtually unknown outside a small number of scholars, and that no dictionary appeared until William Somner produced his *Dictionarium Saxonico-Latino-Anglicum* in

---

[14] Verstegan, *Restitution*, 187.   [15] Ibid. 203.

1659. Verstegan's undeniably profitable application of Anglo-Saxon to the English past did much to promote its study and make it a necessary part of an antiquarian's equipment.

In Elizabethan and Jacobean England, languages, like nations and families, required a long descent if they were to command respect. Verstegan shares this prejudice and in an attempt to establish a lineage that gives Saxon a noble antiquity, he considers the possibility that it might have been the original language of mankind. He knows of one scholar, Goropius Becanus, who believed that the Teutonic tongue 'was the first and most ancient language of the world; yea, the same that Adam spake in Paradise'.[16] This opinion was respected by his friend Abraham Ortelius, who had himself written about the early Germans, and who told Verstegan 'that many learned men might peradventure laugh at that which he had written, but that none would be able to confute it'.[17] Verstegan explores this line of enquiry for a little, but comes round to the more conventional view that Hebrew was the true language of Paradise; he is content to trace back the German language to the Tower of Babel, which was antiquity enough. Ortelius was correct in thinking that men might laugh at an attempt to declare German the first language of the world. Ben Jonson, in *The Alchemist*, introduced this notion, probably as a result of reading Verstegan's book, and his satirist's eye saw the potential for ridicule. He makes the credulous Sir Epicure Mammon boast of his ancient alchemical manuscripts:

MAMMON. Will you believe in antiquity? Records?
  I'll shew you a book where Moses and his sister,
  And Solomon have written of the art;
  Ay, and a treatise penn'd by Adam—
SURLY. How!
MAMMON. Of the philosopher's stone, and in High Dutch.
SURLY. Did Adam write, sir, in High Dutch?
MAMMON. He did:
  Which proves it was the primitive tongue.[18]

Verstegan deserves parody of this kind, for there are moments when he is preposterous, usually when he is led astray by his fanciful etymologies. His extravagant claims for the antiquity of the German language are however offset by his intelligent philological

---

[16] Ibid. 190.   [17] Ibid.   [18] Ben Jonson, *The Alchemist*, II. i.

work in identifying the ramifications of the Teutonic language tree, and his explanations of linguistic change and diversification.

Ultimately Verstegan's views on the past history of the German language are not as interesting as his opinions about the present and future state of English, for here he gets involved in the debate about whether English should assimilate foreign words freely or try to maintain a certain linguistic integrity. There was much discussion about the state of the English language at the end of the sixteenth and the beginning of the seventeenth centuries. Figures like Thomas Nashe, Gabriel Harvey, Edmund Spenser, John Florio, Richard Carew—even Shakespeare, in *Love's Labour's Lost*—were engaged in disputing the desirability or otherwise of enlarging the language by loan words. Verstegan is so enthusiastic a defender of Anglo-Saxon that he is convinced that English should uphold its fundamentally Saxon character. Our native English has overcome the challenge posed by French in Norman times; it is a brisk, forthright language, capable of a full and satisfying range of expression; why should it now suffer the change brought about by foreign importations? 'Our tongue discredited by our language-borrowing', runs the marginal note at this point in his book, 'for we have fallen to such borrowing of words from Latin, French and other tongues, . . . beyond all stay or limit'. The native character of English is fast disappearing.

For myne own part, I hold them deceaved that think our speech bettered by the aboundance of our dayly borrowed words, for they being of another nature and not originally belonging to our language, do not, neither can they in our tongue, beare their natural and true derivations: and therefore as well may we fetch words from the Ethiopians, or East and West Indians, and thrust them into our language, and baptise all by the name of English, as those which we dayly take from the Latin, or languages thereon depending.[19]

Verstegan was a proponent of linguistic purity, as he was of racial purity. He never entertained the prospect that the Saxons might have intermarried with the Britons. Equally, he liked to think of the English language as still primarily Saxon, and it is true that his own vocabulary is plain English, with little latinate content. Englishmen should remember their origins, he believed, and keep their language pure and undefiled, and resist miscegenation. His

---

[19] Verstegan, *Restitution*, 204.

book provided an impetus to a movement of linguistic nationalism which would later develop political force, when, in the reign of Charles I, plain, honest, native English virtues were felt to be increasingly threatened by absolutist kingship, which was thought to be Norman in character. Charles's indifference to Parliament, his use of religious controls, and his revival of Norman French laws in favour of the monarch were felt to be striking at English traditions and English rights by exploiting the legacy of the Norman Conquest. Verstegan's account of Saxon kingship, with kings who were elected, not hereditary, and whose power could be revoked by the leaders meeting in consultation, would become influential as the parliamentary cause developed strength. He himself did not intend to make any political point, but by drawing attention to a system of rule that had once prevailed in England, Verstegan was providing material that future supporters of Parliament would find very useful.[20] The study of Saxon laws, modes of government, and religious organization that underlay their concept of the Free-born Englishman would be helped along by Verstegan's presentation of Saxon history and culture.

Support for Verstegan's advocacy of the Saxons came coincidentally from Camden, who published his *Remains Concerning Britain* in 1605, the same year that the *Restitution* appeared. There is no evidence that either writer was aware of the other's intention to publish. (Indeed, the absence of allusion to Camden's *Britannia* in Verstegan's book may be another reason to believe that it was largely written in mid-Elizabethan times.) Camden's work preceded Verstegan's by a few months, as the records of the Stationers' Company indicate. The *Remains* shows that Camden was revising the views expressed in *Britannia* about the importance of the Saxons in the development of the nation, and was also coming to realize that Anglo-Saxon was a far more significant language for antiquarian research than he had appreciated. Camden had become conscious of the vigour of Anglo-Saxon, which had totally overcome the British and Latin languages previously spoken in England, and he came to admire it as a language fully capable of

---

[20] For a development of this theme, see Samuel Kliger, *The Goths in England* (Cambridge, Mass., 1952), 115–25, and J. G. A. Pocock, *The Ancient Constitution and the Feudal Law* (Cambridge, 1957), 30–56, 91–124. Also Christopher Hill, 'The Norman Yoke', in *Puritanism and Revolution* (London, 1958), 58–126.

expressing all the complexity of religious and political life. 'Great, verily, was the glory of our tongue, before the Norman Conquest in this, that the olde English could expresse most aptly all the conceiptes of the minde in their owne tongue without borrowing from any.'[21] Camden, like Verstegan, tried to explicate Christian names, surnames, and titles by recourse to Anglo-Saxon, but not in such detail or order. In this context, he lamented,

I could particulate in many more [instances of Anglo-Saxon derivations], but this would appeare most plentifully, if the labours of the learned Gentlemen Master Laurence Nowell, of Lincolnes Inne, who first in our time recalled the studie hereof, Master William Lambert, Master J. Joscelin, Master Francis Tate, were once published: otherwise it is to be feared that devouring Time in few yeeres will utterly swallow it, without hope of recoverie.[22]

One sees from this how timely was Verstegan's publication and what a stimulus to Saxon studies it must have provided, especially when combined with Camden's newly-expressed admiration for the Saxons. *A Restitution of Decayed Intelligence* was a book of great individuality, and its arguments were fresh and stimulating. It helped to turn the thoughts of English antiquaries away from the ancient Britons, and shifted their attention to a real and retrievable past. It encouraged scholars to pursue Anglo-Saxon studies in order to give the language wider currency. Works such as William Lisle's *Saxon Treatise* of 1623, and more importantly, Henry Spelman's *Glossarium* of 1626, with its extensive legal and ecclesiastical content, helped to enlarge the subject, and Spelman's foundation of a Lectureship in Anglo-Saxon studies at Cambridge eventually resulted in the publication of Somner's great Anglo-Saxon Dictionary in 1659. This in turn prepared the ground for the flourishing of Anglo-Saxon studies after the Restoration, a subject which has been well described by David Douglas in his book *English Scholars*.[23]

The *Restitution* continued to be in demand throughout the seventeenth century. New editions were printed in 1628, 1634, and 1655, and a final one appeared in 1673. This last reprint accompanied a revival of interest in British origins and national

---

[21] Camden, *Remains*, 27.
[22] Ibid. 29.
[23] David Douglas, *English Scholars* (London, 1939), 60–285.

identity brought about by the publication of Walter Charleton's *Chorea Gigantum* in 1663, Robert Sheringham's *De Anglorum Gentis Origine Disceptatio* in 1670, Milton's *History of Britain* in 1670, and Aylett Sammes' *Britannia Antiqua Illustrata* in 1676. Verstegan's views had a bearing on all of these works.

3

Sir Robert Cotton

Without Sir Robert Cotton and his celebrated library, the whole Jacobean antiquarian endeavour would have been much diminished, and would have lacked a centre. For Cotton was the universal facilitator among the antiquaries, the liaison officer, the man one had to know. His library was the meeting place for all who were enquiring into the past, and his open-handed generosity in making his books and manuscripts available probably did more to advance the cause of scholarship than the combined patronage of Oxford and Cambridge. The prefaces of so many books on British historical themes resound with gratitude to Cotton, and authors deep in their books will interrupt their narratives to recall a kindness from him: he is the great provider of essential texts, and the oracle of the antiquaries.[1] Above all, Cotton loved the business of scholarship, the acquisition of books and manuscripts, the discovery of new texts, the evaluation of the status of manuscripts, and the piecing together of the fragments of the past to make it comprehensible. He encouraged all who shared this passion, regardless of age or rank or ideological stance. One of the memorable glimpses of Cotton's irenical domain is given by Father Augustine Baker, the English Benedictine monk who lived a shadowy life in London. In his autobiography, he describes a conversation with Cotton and Camden by the fireside in the room outside the library, a conversation of antiquarian intensity free from the conventional prejudices of the age.[2] Baker was collecting

---

[1] Thomas Smith prints a long list of commendations of Cotton by seventeenth-century scholars in his *Catalogue of the Manuscripts in the Cottonian Library, 1696,* ed. C. G. C. Tite (Woodbridge, Suffolk, 1984), 43.

[2] *Memorials of Father Augustine Baker,* ed. J. McCann and H. Connolly (London, 1933), 112. Baker's researches into charters, chronicles, and monastic documents resulted in six volumes of transcripts, now in the Bodleian Library, some of which were used in the compilation of *Apostolatus Benedictinorum in Anglia* (1626), the work of three Catholic colleagues, Baker, Leander Jones, and Clement

records of the Benedictine order in England, an early venture into monastic history which anticipated the work of Dodsworth and Dugdale, and he was welcomed by Cotton as warmly as the Calvinist Bishop Ussher or the secular-minded Selden.

Cotton was as well furnished with friends as with books, and most of his friends were bibliophiles. Born in 1571 into a Huntingdonshire family, he had been sent to Westminster School where he was a pupil of William Camden, who exerted a defining influence over his life. Several schoolfellows at Westminster became lifelong friends, especially Ben Jonson and Hugh Holland. Jonson was to develop a strong antiquarian strain that would show in his passion for accuracy about Roman politics, customs, and costume, and he would turn to Cotton's library as a source of sound classical detail for the masques he wrote for King James and King Charles; he would send his collaborator Inigo Jones there for the same reason. Hugh Holland became a poet with antiquarian inclinations. After a time at Jesus College, Cambridge, Cotton embarked on the study of the law at Middle Temple, where he was able to consolidate his London friendships.[3] Here he came to know Henry Spelman, John Selden, and the lawyer and poet John Davies. Through Ben Jonson, Cotton came into contact with the poets Samuel Daniel, Michael Drayton, and John Donne; he became an *habitué* of the Mermaid Tavern group of poets, wits, lawyers, and scholars, and he was addressed in the roll-call of that club in Thomas Coryate's letter from India, published in 1616, where that idiosyncratic traveller greeted his old companions in London.

Kinship linked Cotton to the Harington family, so he was related to Lucy Harington, Countess of Bedford, the patron of most of the poets mentioned here. His own early patrons were George Carey, Lord Hunsdon, the Lord Chamberlain after 1597, and then Henry Howard, Earl of Northampton, whom Cotton served in various capacities after 1601. Some time after Northampton's death in 1614, Cotton became the client, friend, and adviser of Thomas Howard, Earl of Arundel. Cotton's proudest connection, however,

Rayner. See M. D. Knowles, 'The Value of 16th and 17th century Scholarship' in Levi Fox (ed.), *English Historical Scholarship in the Sixteenth and Seventeenth Centuries* (London, 1956).

[3] The most comprehensive account of Cotton's friendships is given by Sharpe in *Sir Robert Cotton*, ch. 6. Sharpe's book is the essential accompaniment to any study of Cotton.

was with King James, for both men could trace their descent from Robert the Bruce (they had a common ancestor in the twelfth-century Prince Henry of Scotland) and the King acknowledged Cotton as his cousin. As soon as James succeeded to the throne, Cotton put his antiquarian skills to good use and drew up a 'Discourse of the Descent of the King's Majesty from the Saxons' to justify the King's ancient right to the throne based on firm historical research into genealogies rather than on the fanciful claims of a descent from the Trojan Brutus invented by more poetically-minded celebrants of the new reign. It may have been for this exercise in scholarly loyalty that Cotton was knighted in 1603. Throughout James's reign, Cotton can be considered as a figure close to the centre of national life, with influential connections at court, in legal and political circles, and in the world of letters and scholarship. He lived up to his responsibilities by regarding himself and his library as serving the public good whenever occasion required.

As a result of his familiarity with Camden, Cotton became one of the original members (and very likely the youngest) of the Elizabethan Society of Antiquaries, which had begun to meet about 1586, probably in response to the publication of *Britannia* in that year. Camden communicated his passion for antiquity to him, though given Cotton's early fascination with his illustrious Scottish descent and the concomitant enthusiasm for genealogy, he must already have been highly susceptible to the appeal of the past. Genealogy led him on to heraldry, an interest that strengthened the bond with Camden.

The topics discussed by the Society of Antiquaries in its early years chiefly concerned the origins of English institutions, offices, and titles, although towards the end of the 1590s attention moved towards topographical matters relating to the history of towns and buildings. Cotton's contributions to these meetings included papers on the offices of the Earl Marshal, the Constable, and the High Steward of England, on lawful combats, and on the antiquity of Christianity in England; he also contributed to discussions on the development of castles and on the history of the units of land measurement.[4] For the most part these presentations, in common

---

[4] Sharpe, *Sir Robert Cotton*, 19. Many of the early papers read to the Society were gathered together by Thomas Hearne and published as *Curious Discourses* in 1771.

with the other papers read to the Society, were a raking together of relevant information, and did not attempt to draw conclusions or make a political point. The prevailing mood in the Society in its Elizabethan phase seems to have been one of patriotic contentment as the members began to make systematic searches into the records of the kingdom to illustrate the venerable traditions that had gone into the making of their own England. The Society continued to meet until about 1607, when its gatherings were discontinued. Its members had expected James I, as a monarch proud of his learning, to be a sympathetic patron of their researches into the past of Britain; however, he seems to have taken a dislike to the Society's activities. It has been assumed that the growing interest in parliamentary history and privilege irked the king, who did not like to have the soil around the roots of his prerogative disturbed.[5]

Under Camden's tuition, Cotton learned to extend his researches beyond the national material available in the record offices of London, and to view the development of English offices and customs in the context of European affairs. He began to familiarize himself with the achievements of sixteenth-century French scholars such as Bodin, Hotman, and De Thou, who had a sharper legal and political edge to their work than any English historian. These writers had attempted to reconstruct the ancient constitution of their nation, and were interested in the development of the law and of forms of government in ways which would be followed by politically motivated antiquarians in early Stuart England, notably Selden, Spelman, and Cotton himself. Cotton also began to be caught up in the network of correspondents across northern Europe that Camden had formed: in particular he was in contact with Jan Gruter, the Dutch scholar and expert on classical inscriptions, Francis Junius, the German philologist, and Nicholas Fabri de Peiresc, the scholarly virtuoso of France, to whom no subject was

---

[5] A comment in Fulke Greville's *Life of Sidney* about the unintrusive nature of historical enquiry in Elizabeth's reign gives a clue to what changed in James's time, and why James may have construed the antiquaries as adversaries; the Queen 'did not by any curious search after Evidence to enlarge her Prerogative Royall, teach her subjects in Parliament, by the like self-affections, to make a curious inquisition among their Records, to colour any encroaching upon the sacred circles of Monarchy.' (Quoted by P. Styles, 'Politics and Historical Research in the Early 17th Century', in Fox (ed.), *English Historical Scholarship*, 51.) The most valuable account of the cessation of the Society of Antiquaries is provided by Henry Spelman in 'The Occasion of this Discourse' in *English Works*, ed. E. Gibson (1727).

alien, and whom Cotton met when he came to England in 1606 to visit Camden.

In another way too Cotton benefited from Camden's tutelage. In 1600 the two men made an archeological tour to Hadrian's Wall to inspect the antiquities there at first hand: together they looked at the remains of the forts, gravestones, statues, altars, inscriptions, and coins to sharpen their understanding of the Roman occupation of the north of England. Their discoveries went to enlarge the appropriate section of the 1607 edition of *Britannia*, and numerous artefacts found during their survey were eventually conveyed to Cotton's home at Conington in Huntingdonshire. The visit set an important precedent in the growth of an archaeological attitude to ancient sites. This was a very early example of an archeological tour, as opposed to the perambulation of towns, villages, manors, and castles undertaken by county historians. It can hardly be called an exacting tour, for they did not excavate, measure, or compare, but they traced the patterns of settlement and fortification, talked to regional antiquaries, and tried hard to understand the purpose of the remains they found.[6] However, the historical imagination of Camden and Cotton was not notably creative: they could record and trace and document, and relate what they found to the accounts of the Roman historians, but they could not imagine a society as real as their own working the fields, manning the walls, idling, loving, quarrelling, and practising their customs and religion, as John Aubrey would be able to, fifty years later.

From Camden, Cotton learnt the value of coins as the most useful indicator of settlement and trade in the past. A *denarius* of Vespasian gave a clear date for a Roman presence, as well as being a pretty piece of antiquity in itself. The chronology of the Roman occupation was only just beginning to exercise antiquaries, and coins were of the greatest use in charting the spread of the colonizers. British coins were even more sought after, for they helped to define tribal areas, depicted tribal totems, and provided names for the elusive leaders of the Britons. Their mints must also denote important centres of government. In addition, British coins conveyed a gratifying sense of civilization and commerce, and an assurance of an extensive national life before and during the Roman occupation. As Cotton's seventeenth-century biographer

---

[6] For an account of this northern journey, see Haverfield, 'Julius F VI', 343–78.

Thomas Smith remarked, where there is little or no written history, coins are invaluable, and are rightly to be deemed a literary commodity second in importance only to ancient manuscripts.[7] Cotton built up an impressive collection of coins, and Camden reproduced some of the British specimens in the 1600 edition of *Britannia*, the first social artefacts of the ancient British to be illustrated. Cotton also lent John Speed numerous British and Roman coins to be engraved for *The History of Great Britaine*, where they form the visual backbone of the narrative through British, Roman, and Saxon times. Cotton kept a supervisory eye over Speed's *History*, and letters survive to show that Speed sent his page proofs to Cotton for comment and correction.[8] Speed expressed his gratitude in the Conclusion to 'that worthy Repairer of eating Time's Ruins, the learned Sir Robert Cotton, Kt. Baronet, another Philadelphus in preserving old Monuments and ancient Records; whose Cabinets were unlocked, and Library continually set open to my free access'.[9]

Camden and Cotton remained lifelong friends, and their projects interacted. Camden borrowed manuscripts from Cotton when preparing his edition of old English chronicles, *Anglica, Normannica, Hibernica, Cantabrica a Veteribus Scripta* (1602), a work planned to advance the study of the past of Britain by making available rare historical sources. Camden dedicated his *Remains Concerning Britain* to Cotton in 1605, observing that 'Temples are to be dedicated to the Gods, and Bookes to Good Men.' Cotton for his part was drawn into topographical history by Camden, and began to accumulate material for a History of Huntingdonshire, his own county. At the opening of James's reign they laid plans to collaborate on a great work on the ecclesiastical history of Britain that would be compiled largely from the resources of Cotton's library, but the project was eventually made over to James Ussher

---

[7] Smith, *Catalogue*, 43. Edmund Bolton provided an early example of how coins could be used to supplement the written record in his *Nero Caesar* (1624), where he employed engravings of coins and medals to document the reign of Nero, and, in particular, the Roman involvement in Britain in Nero's time.

[8] See David Howarth, 'Sir Robert Cotton and the Commemoration of Famous Men' in the *British Library Journal*, 18/1 (1992), 26.

[9] 'A Summary Conclusion of the Whole' in John Speed, *The History of Great Britaine* (1614 edn.). Cotton also helped Speed with the account of Roman Britain, and provided him with material for the Life of Henry V. See Sharpe, *Sir Robert Cotton*, 38.

as a more qualified executor. Both Cotton and Camden became involved in supplying documentary material for the reign of Mary and Elizabeth to the French historian Jacques De Thou, who was writing an account of the turbulent decades that followed the Reformation, the *Historia Sui Temporis*.[10] When Camden began to write his own *Annals of the Reign of Queen Elizabeth* (1615), he found Cotton's library a storehouse of essential documents. By the end of his life, Camden had borrowed so many books from Cotton that his will directed that Cotton be allowed to search his chambers to reclaim what belonged to him.

Famously, it was the creation of his library that was Cotton's enduring achievement. His contemporaries admired his learning and respected his political career, but they reserved their acclamation for his library. It was effectively the only serious reference library in London, and Cotton was generous in granting access. Because London had no university, there was no academic library as might be found in most capital cities. The Inns of Court had libraries, but they were not notable, contained mainly legal books, and were restricted to members. The state records were scattered around London in various locations, and were inadequately catalogued; access was often subject to whimsical conditions.[11] The archives of Chancery, the Exchequer, the King's Bench, and the Court of Common Pleas were all separately housed, the Parliamentary records were in the Abbey or the Tower, and the State Papers were often in the possession of the families who held the great offices of state, although there was an effort to centralize public records at Whitehall after 1610.[12] Public and state records

---

[10] Aware that De Thou was going to reassess events in Scotland in the time of Mary, Queen of Scots, King James was anxious that his own views of these events should be adequately reflected in the new history. James appears to have used Cotton as his intermediary in transmitting his advice to De Thou. He was concerned in particular to discredit the highly critical interpretation of Mary's conduct by George Buchanan in his *Rerum Scotiarum Historia* of 1582, and to promote a more favourable view of his mother's reign. See Sharpe, *Sir Robert Cotton* 89–95 and 'Queen Elizabeth's First Historian' in Hugh Trevor-Roper, *Renaissance Essays* (London, 1985).

[11] See R. B. Wernham, 'The Public Records in the Sixteenth and Seventeenth Centuries' in *English Historical Scholarship*, 11–30.

[12] Thomas Powell's *Directions for the Search of Records* (1622) was the first guidebook to the public records and how to consult them, published in response to the increasing number of investigations into the business of state. Powell's book introduces one to scenes of confusion and disorder in all the archival offices: bundles

apart, if one needed to work with historical or ecclesiastical material, it was to Sir Robert Cotton's collection that one went.

The formation of the Cottonian Library and the scope of its contents have been most fully described by Kevin Sharpe in his indispensable book *Sir Robert Cotton*, to which this chapter owes much. He notes the predominance of manuscripts over printed books, and suggests that the majority of the manuscripts came to Cotton as gifts rather than by purchase.[13] The collection began to take shape in the late 1580s, and it was soon notable as a haven for monastic manuscripts, particularly East Anglian ones, which were still drifting around after the storm of the Dissolution. Cartularies, registers of monastic land holdings, saints' lives, and chronicles were early arrivals. Cotton's collecting started in the tradition of Matthew Parker at Cambridge, with the aim of preserving as much as possible of the written record of medieval England, as well as the remains of Anglo-Saxon writings, which were even more valuable because of their antiquity and their unadulterated 'English' character. However, Cotton's close friendship with Camden and his early involvement with the Society of Antiquaries ensured that his interests were broadly and variedly nationalistic, not dominated by ecclesiastical concerns. It would seem that Cotton wanted to build a collection that would be as comprehensive as possible for the study of English history and the laws, institutions, customs, and religion of the land. If the study of English history were to be advanced, as Thomas Smith observed in his biography of Cotton,

and bags of uncatalogued documents, not ordered by date, and often mouse-eaten. Research was an expensive business, and the minions of the dark offices exacted their tolls at every stage of enquiry. Powell cites 10/- for a rummage in the rolls; at the Exchequer, 'for opening the chest', 2/-; 'for the Attorney who sheweth it, 3/4;' nor should one forget to tip the Ussher for opening the doors. ('The Ussher his office consists more in knowing the number than the nature of the Records.') The Domesday Book could be consulted for 6/8 a time; copies of it had to be made by a clerk whose fees were 4d a line for copying 'the old Saxon Letter', and 1/- a page for Latin. Requests for a transcript went down a line of bureaucracy: 'The Foreign Opposer maketh up his Doquet, and delivereth it to the Clerk of the Pipe . . .' One can understand that an antiquarian with protracted business in the records would go to great lengths to obtain exemption from or diminution of these costs by pulling whatever strings he could. An interesting sidelight on the uses of poetry in this period is that even a utilitarian handbook like Powell's *Directions* is prefaced with dedicatory poems to a number of legal knights.

[13] Sharpe, *Sir Robert Cotton*, 57, 62.

recourse must be had to the sources of history; ancient authors must be consulted and compared so that truth should not seem to rely on a single authority; the charters and treaties of kings must be read with care; the archives of monasteries and cathedrals must be examined and the shelves and sacrosanct recesses of libraries explored with imaginative eyes. It is only from public records and original documents that sure and perfect knowledge can be drawn.[14]

What evolved through Cotton's care was effectively the library of the Society of Antiquaries, and from an early stage he entertained the notion of making his books the nucleus of a national collection which might be formed from the combined stock of his and other antiquaries' books, together with the royal library. He addressed a petition to Queen Elizabeth late in her reign proposing this scheme ('at the cost and charges of divers gentlemen'), but she did not respond to it.[15] Undiscouraged, Cotton seems to have felt that he should supply this deficiency in the intellectual life of the nation by making his own library meet the need, and by allowing generous access to his books.

Recognition of his liberal intentions probably moved numerous scholars and gentlemen to make gifts of manuscripts and books to Cotton. Fellow antiquaries such as William Lambarde, George Carew, and John Davies were willing donors, as were the Irish historian James Ware and the Saxon scholar William Lisle. Both William Camden and Arthur Agarde, the Keeper of the Records, left Cotton a portion of their libraries in their wills. Selden gave him the manuscript Annals of Tewkesbury, Ussher presented him with the Samaritan Pentateuch, which had come from Aleppo and was much prized amongst biblical scholars as an extremely early transcript of the Books of Moses. Perhaps Cotton's greatest prize was the copy of Magna Carta given to him in 1630 by Sir Edward Dering.[16] Through the good offices of his friends, the papers of the leading Tudor antiquaries, such as John Leland, John Bale, Laurence Nowell, William Lambarde, and Francis Thynne, came to find a home in his library. They were joined by the collections of

---

[14] 'Life of Robert Cotton', trans. Godfrey Turton in Smith, *Catalogue*, 27.

[15] Sharpe, *Sir Robert Cotton*, 50–1. Sharpe notes the failure of similar schemes for a national library proposed by Leland to Henry VIII, John Dee to Queen Mary, and Matthew Parker to Queen Elizabeth. Cotton's Library eventually became part of the British Museum Library in the eighteenth century.

[16] Ibid. 57–8, gives an extended list of books and donors.

papers read at the Elizabethan Society of Antiquaries, and related documents. Exchange was another means of acquisition and some of Cotton's books and papers testify to profitable deals made with scholars such as the Saxonist William Lisle, the King's Librarian Patrick Young, and the antiquarian Simonds D'Ewes.[17] The traffic was not always one-way, however, for Cotton made presents of books and manuscripts to Sir Thomas Bodley when Bodley was setting up his library, and he promised to make a gift of books to James Ussher for Trinity College, Dublin. (Ussher was particularly keen to have some of Cotton's manuscripts relating to Wycliffe.[18]) He was in the habit of presenting books from his collection to noblemen as New Year gifts: Sir Robert Cecil received a number of such presents, amongst them genealogical works, devotional books, modern histories, and a tract on secret writing.[19] Books and manuscripts were a very acceptable currency in the delicate business of courting favour.

Cotton built up his library over a period of forty years. Kevin Sharpe has estimated that Cotton's income from rents on his estates in Huntingdonshire after 1610 amounted to about £1,000 a year, a comfortable sum for a baronet, and enough to allow him to acquire manuscripts (the cost of which ranged from a few shillings to perhaps £3) steadily from the London bookshops, from friends, from agents abroad, and from the occasional sale of a collector's library. As it grew it developed, as all libraries do, particular areas of strength. Books and manuscripts accumulated around the topics discussed by the antiquaries: there were works relating to state offices, particularly those of Earl Marshal, Chancellor, Admiral, and Constable, and to state ceremonies such as funerals and coronation rituals; there was also much about heraldry, jousts, and duels. In James's reign, Cotton grew more interested in collecting manuscripts that were illustrative of Saxon and medieval history.

The editions made in the early seventeenth century of chronicles relating to the Conquest and to Norman history were all made from

[17] Ibid. 62.
[18] It looks as if Cotton did send Ussher Wycliffe's Homilies, his *Lanterne of Light*, and a manuscript of the examination of the Oxford Wycliffite William Thorpe before Archbishop Arundel. See Colin G. C. Tite, 'Lost or Stolen or Strayed: a Survey of Manuscripts Formerly in the Cotton Library' in *British Library Journal*, 18/2 (1992), 113–14.
[19] Sharpe, *Sir Robert Cotton*, 52n.

manuscripts in Cotton's possession.[20] Until the publication of these chronicles, the study of Norman England was not really feasible, in fact. Cotton's treasury of Norman manuscripts was utilized by Camden, as we have noted, for his volume of chronicles published in 1602. This work printed the earliest account of the Conquest, William of Jumièges' 'Gesta Normannorum Ducum' and a fragment of a life of William the Conqueror (which Camden thought was by William of Poitiers but is now recognized as a piece by Orderic Vitalis). Cotton did eventually acquire a manuscript of William of Poitiers's biography of the Conqueror, which was borrowed by the French antiquary Nicholas Fabri de Peiresc for the edition of Anglo-Norman authors that he prepared with André Duchesne, *Historiae Normannorum Scriptores Antiqui* (1619). Amongst the contents of this volume was the first printing of the *Encomium Emmae Reginae*, an eleventh-century life of Queen Emma, aunt of William the Conqueror, whose marriages to Ethelred and Canute paved the way for the Norman claim to the English throne and the invasion of 1066; this text too was printed from a Cotton manuscript, as was the text of William of Jumièges' 'Gesta', which was now re-edited. One can see here something of Cotton's service to the international community of scholars: Camden's book was published in Frankfurt, Peiresc and Duchesne's in Paris. (The latter volume contained a most florid expression of gratitude to Cotton.[21]) Then there was the edition of the early twelfth-century chronicle, the 'Historia Novorum' by Eadmer, a monk of Canterbury, that was prepared by John Selden in 1623 at the time of his confinement on political grounds. Selden borrowed a thirteenth-century manuscript of Eadmer from Cotton for his edition with notes and commentary, as the title acknowledges: *Eadmeri Historia Novorum . . . in lucem ex Biblioteca Cottoniana . . . Spicelegium.*

The sixteenth century had seen the publication of numerous chronicles relating to Saxon History: Gildas (1525), Bede's *Historia*

---

[20] Elizabeth C. van Houts, 'Camden, Cotton and the Chronicles of the Norman Conquest of England' in *British Library Journal*, 18/2 (1992), 148–62. The details of the printing of Norman chronicles given in the text are derived from this article.

[21] 'Eruditione multifaria, nec non felicissima industria in congerenda antiqua rarissimorum librorum numerorum supellectile, quam pro candore omnibus studiosis libentissime aperit, commendatissimo.' (Quoted by van Houts, 'Camden, Cotton and the Chronicles', 155).

Ecclesiastica (1565), Asser's Life of Alfred (1574), and Geoffrey of Monmouth in several editions (1508, 1517, etc.). Cotton had manuscripts of all these as well as of the valuable narrative of Nennius, written at the end of the eighth century, concerning the history of the Britons, which was not edited until 1691 by Thomas Gale. Cotton also had numerous Saxon charters, lives of Saxon kings and saints, and manuscripts of Saxon laws which were esteemed for the details they gave of the beliefs and practices that prevailed before the Conquest, and which might throw light on the relations between kings and church, on the powers and limitations of kings, on the origins of parliaments and the evolution of the laws. Cotton like Camden grew increasingly interested in the Saxon inheritance of the nation.

Ironically, Cotton's most important Saxon manuscript was one little referred to in his own time, and that was the unique text of *Beowulf*. In the utilitarian atmosphere of the Cotton Library, records of Saxon church councils or details of Saxon lawmaking were more eagerly seized on than poetry that was in a barely comprehensible mode. The *Beowulf* manuscript (Cotton Vitellius A XV) seems to have belonged formerly to the Tudor antiquary Laurence Nowell, for his signature is on the first leaf, and he probably rescued it after it drifted from a monastery at the Dissolution. The first person to notice the significance of the heroic poem was Humfrey Wanley, who described it in the catalogue of manuscripts he prepared for the second volume of George Hickes' *Thesaurus* of Ancient Northern Literature in 1705, and he quoted some fragments from it. This is the only record of the poem before it was badly charred in the fire of 1731, when Cotton's library was stored at Ashburnham House. The Icelandic scholar Grimur Janssen Thorkelin transcribed it as best he could in 1787—an invaluable service, for the manuscript has deteriorated since. His transcription formed the basis of the first printed edition in 1815, but the poem, which like all Anglo-Saxon poems had no name, acquired the title *Beowulf* only in Kemble's edition of 1833. The poem bound with it, the fragment called 'Judith', was transcribed much earlier, by Francis Junius, whose transcript remains in the Bodleian Library.[22] The other precious Anglo-Saxon poetic

---

[22] Junius's grateful remembrance of the Cotton family says much for their long tradition of service to scholars: 'Seeing there is seldom a day that I do not look upon

manuscript that came into Cotton's hands was that of 'The Battle of Maldon' (Cotton Otho A XII). This was transcribed about 1724 by John Elphinstone, and fortunately so, for the manuscript was totally destroyed by the fire of 1731. (A fortunate survivor of that fire were the Lindisfarne Gospels, another manuscript that attracted little attention in the seventeenth century.)

The library preserved several notable medieval poems for posterity. The unique manuscript of *Sir Gawain and the Green Knight* with its accompanying group of poems *Pearl*, *Patience*, and *Cleanness*, now regarded as the supreme achievement of medieval alliterative verse, was catalogued as Cotton Nero A X. The two surviving manuscripts of Layamon's *Brut*, the thirteenth-century alliterative verse chronicle of British history, were both in Cotton's possession (Caligula A IX and Otho C XIII). The mystery play known as the N-Town Play was on Cotton's shelves at Vespasian D VIII. One of the two manuscripts of *The Owl and the Nightingale* was there, bound with Caligula A IX, and there was also the unique text of *Yvain*. The more common medieval poems were also to be found in Cotton's collection. There was a manuscript of *Piers Plowman*, used to effect by John Weever to illustrate social conditions and the corruption of the church in the fourteenth century, and also manuscripts of Chaucer, Gower, Lydgate, and Hoccleve. However, they were not much referred to in early Stuart times, for the campaigning style of antiquarian research in the 1610s and 1620s, when the aim was polemical or political, did not favour the recovery of poetry from its obscure existence in manuscript.

Like most antiquaries raised in Elizabeth's reign, Cotton regarded ancient manuscripts as indispensable material for the religious controversies against the Church of Rome, and for clarifying the antiquity of the church in England. Although he was not himself a controversialist in the wars of religion, he was happy to make his resources available to the defenders of the Anglican Church. In the early 1620s, William Laud contemplated writing an ecclesiastical history of England on the basis of Cotton manuscripts, but he did

---

some Anglo-Saxonicke antiquities, which (by the means and favour of Mr. Selden) I saw and transcribed out of the Cottonian library, I cannot but confesse that an everlasting obligation bindeth me to serve the Cottonian familie in what I can.' (Junius to Dugdale, Jan. 1656, in *Sir William Dugdale*, ed. Hamper, 299.)

not proceed. James Ussher did use the Cotton Library, and all his major works on primitive Christianity in Britain and Ireland, and on the survival of the true church through time, were products of research in Cotton's collection: *De Ecclesiarum Christianarum Successione* (1613), *A Discourse of Religion Anciently Professed by the Irish* (1631), and *Britannicarum Ecclesiarum Antiquitates* (1639). Ussher expressed his indebtedness in the preface to the last-mentioned book in terms that all Stuart scholars could endorse when he described Sir Robert as a great steward and conserver of British antiquity, always ready to advance a serious enquiry into the national past.

What needs to be stressed is that there was always a utilitarian purpose firmly at the centre of Cotton's collecting. His manuscripts were serviceably bound, not decoratively preserved and jealously hoarded. He lent books freely to people who knew how to use them and squeeze their contents into some new work of contemporary relevance. His books were at the service of the nation via its scholars, clerics, politicians, and lawyers. His library lists show a constant succession of loans, some books even going overseas to Continental scholars. Irreplaceable manuscripts were entrusted to servants, or put into carriers' carts, bundled up into ships' holds in the faith that they would come back again. Some were kept by their borrowers for unconscionable lengths of time: the famous fifth-century Genesis went off to France at the request of the antiquary Peiresc, and stayed there for five years, passing from scholar to scholar. Many manuscripts never did return. About 100, a tenth of the total, are estimated to have strayed from the library through the perfidy of borrowers, and are now in other collections.[23] Others have disappeared completely. The most serious defaulter, who inflicted the greatest losses on the collection, was Cotton's friend and patron the Earl of Arundel, who, after Cotton's death, failed to return the superb Carolingian manuscript now known from its present location as the Utrecht Psalter, the most beautiful book of the ninth century, whose illustrations preserve in a haunting way the spirit of late Roman antiquity; he also kept the fourteenth-century Lovel Lectionary, another outstanding illuminated work, now in the Harleian manuscripts in the British Library,

---

[23] Tite, 'Lost or Stolen or Strayed', 130. Tite gives a detailed account of strays from the Cotton Library, with indications of their present locations, as well as a list of losses.

and the celebrated Cotton Genesis, which had to be repurchased by Cotton's grandson fifty years later, and which was later mostly destroyed in the fire of 1731.[24]

The library itself was almost as mobile as its components. Its site changed several times as Cotton moved house in London, and it did not reach its best-known location in Cotton's house at Westminster, adjacent to the Houses of Parliament, until about 1622. The contents by that time were not as large as one might imagine: at its height there were some thousand manuscripts (many of which consisted of several works bound together) and an indeterminable number of printed books, most of which have escaped from the collection. The famous system of shelving, whereby works were numbered by reference to the emperor whose bust presided over them, does not seem to have been instituted until the move to Westminster. Physically, the library was quite small. Kevin Sharpe has discovered a description of the library written in 1692, which is so vivid that it deserves to be reprinted:

I had a short view of Sir R. Cotton's library. It is scituated adjoyning to the house of Commons at Westminster, of a great highth, and part of that old fabrick but very narrow, as I remember, not full 6 feet in breadth and not above 26 in length, the books placed on each side of a tolerable highth so that a man of an indifferent stature may reach the highest. Over the books are the Roman emperors, I mean their heads, in brass statues, which serve for standards in the Catalogue, to direct to find any particular book, viz. under such an Emperor's head such a number . . . I had not the time to look into the books; viz. I saw there Sir H. Spelman's and Buchanan's pictures, well don, also Ben Jonson's and Sir Robert Cotton's and in the stairs was Wycliff's.[25]

What use did Cotton make of his collections? Though he assisted so many people to the press, he himself wrote little and published less. As we have noted, he had a utilitarian view of his library: it was for public service. He saw himself in some ways as a civil servant, providing sound advice to his patrons and friends. He served Parliament with his expertise, and he also aspired to advise

[24] Tite, 'Lost or Stolen or Strayed', 116. The Genesis manuscript (Otho B VI) was one of the rare survivals of a late antique painted book. Cotton had it from Sir John Fortescue, who in turn had been given it by Queen Elizabeth. The book came to England in the reign of Henry VIII, when two Greek bishops offered it to the King as a goodwill gift from the Orthodox Church.
[25] Description by Richard Lapthorne, quoted in Sharpe, *Sir Robert Cotton*, 82.

the King, especially James, his kinsman, in matters touching state policy and in the arts of government. His characteristic approach was to read out the lessons of history, either directly or obliquely. The most elaborate work he composed was *The Life and Reign of Henry III*, a cautionary tale indeed, for it was a thinly disguised parallel with the reign of James I. It can stand as a telling example of how history writing could track contemporary events in a critical way, and is a mixture of political warning with a desire to alleviate state problems. It deserves close attention for it shows how a piece of antiquarian research could be used as thinly veiled political commentary. First published in 1627, anonymously, and apparently without Cotton's permission, it was immediately held to be censorious of King Charles. Cotton was suspected as the author and examined by the authorities, but was released when he persuaded them that he had not approved publication, and that he had written the work in 1614. Certainly, the manuscript of the history in Cambridge University Library carries the note, 'Written by Sir Robert Cotton Knight Baronett in anno 1614 and by him presented to his Majestie the same year.' Given that the *Life and Reign* contains much about the pernicious influence of favourites, which seems to bear specifically upon Buckingham, whose rise began in 1616, it is possible that Cotton later revised it to take account of Buckingham's career. Most likely Cotton did present a manuscript copy to King James, for almost everything he wrote had a specific audience in mind, and he would have regarded it as a piece of wise counsel which showed the application of history to the business of state.

The history is an outline of events in Henry III's reign, interspersed with reflections on the art of government and precepts concerning effective rule. It is written in the sparse economical style that Cotton usually employed, and reads like a précis of an Elizabethan play of the 1590s in which the action is historic but the relevance contemporary. (No playwright chose the reign of Henry III for dramatization, in fact.) It is a cautionary tale. The King ascends the throne when there are few distempers in the state, only the familiar tension between the commons greedy of liberty and the nobility greedy of rule. The King's principal adviser is the well-established Earl of Kent, but the young nobles of the realm come to resent him, chafing to get their hands on power, a situation not dissimilar to that around the Earl of Salisbury in James's reign. The sovereign after some years reveals the great weakness of his rule, a penchant for a favourite, the Frenchman Simon de Montfort. De Montfort is rapidly made Earl of Leicester, the King lavishes money on him, and the business of state begins to run through his hands. The English nobility 'began to grieve' at this deflection of power from them, and Cotton intervenes to comment on the risks of adopting a favourite: 'Great is the Sovereign's error when the hope of subjects must recognise itself beholden to the servant.' The favourite's position is unstable, dependent on the whim of the King's fancy. As the favourite begins to restrict access to the sovereign, and draws bishops to his support, his unpopularity grows, yet he controls more business than ever. 'Thus is the incapacity of government in a King, when it falls to be prey to such lawless ministers, the ground of infinite corruption in all the members of the State.' Alienated peers begin to form a party against the favourite, and hope to persuade the King to a better judgement of state affairs.

The circumstances would fit 1614, when Cotton claimed to have written the piece, for James had then begun to turn away from the advice of his Privy Councillors and Parliament towards a dependence on his favourite Robert Carr, a foreigner in that he was a Scot. At the end of 1613 Carr was created Earl of Somerset, to the outrage of the older nobility. The King was heavily in debt, and paying little attention to business. The Howard faction supported the favourite, the Pembroke faction was deeply critical; the Howards were resisting calling a parliament to resolve the King's financial difficulties, their opponents pressed for one. Parliament was summoned in April 1614.

At a corresponding time in Henry III's reign, a parliament was called, reluctantly, by the Sovereign. Cotton observes that kings who have alienated their subjects never like parliaments, for their critics then can confront them. So they did: they denounced Henry for choosing his principal officers privately without the aid of Common Council, for favouring foreigners above Englishmen, and for delegating power to the favourite. Using language that would be familiar to Stuart readers, Cotton records how Henry's Parliament complained about the granting to favourites of monopolies, which practice alienated the merchants of the realm and depressed trade. Significantly too there were complaints that great lords were exacting money from subjects by activating little-used laws relating to forests. The upshot was that a disgruntled Parliament voted only a pittance by way of supply to the King, and its members departed full of resentment. Cotton's choric voice intervenes: 'Thus Parliaments that before were ever a medicine to heal up any rupture in Princes' fortunes, were now grown worse than the malady, sith from thence more malignant humours began to reign in them, than well composed tempers.'[26]

The Parliament of 1614 refused to vote supply to James. Instead, the members investigated the corruption of offices, and attacked the King's way of raising money by arbitrary impositions. The King defended this right to exact impositions as 'one of the flowers of his prerogative'. Parliament was rapidly dissolved, not to meet again until 1621. In Henry III's case, when deprived of parliamentary support, the King started to sell royal lands and some of his possessions. He even pawned the jewels from Edward the Confessor's shrine to alleviate his poverty. James in 1615 began to sell titles of nobility, a move even more desperate than the sale of knighthoods earlier in his reign, and he also sold the Cautionary Towns in Holland to the Dutch. Thereafter, easy parallels between King Henry and King James were more difficult to make. A date then of 1614–15 would be quite apt for this history, but since the vices and the problems of the Stuarts were of a recurring nature, the history of Henry III, which is so full of warnings of the disastrous consequences that follow from wasteful spending, from surrender of power to favourites, and from reluctance to work with parliaments, also had an uncomfortable relevance to James's position in 1621, on the eve of a new Parliament, when Buckingham was fully in the ascendant and debts were worse than ever. It was equally applicable to the circumstances of 1627, when it was published at the height of the House of Commons' hostility to Buckingham, and when King Charles was already well enmeshed in the familiar Stuart problems.

Cotton narrates the remainder of Henry's long reign, past the crises of debt, favouritism, and parliamentary opposition that make such telling parallels with Stuart politics. It is a tale of disaster followed by reform and recovery. What this history lesson teaches above all is the near-fatal damage done to the Crown by

[26] *The Life and Reign of Henry III* in Cotton, *Cottoni Posthuma*, ed. James Howell (1651), 25.

favouritism: 'Favours past are not accompted, we love no bounty but what is merely future. The more that a Prince weakeneth himself in giving, the poorer he is of friends. For such prodigality in a Sovereign, ever ends in the rapine and spoil of his subjects.' When Henry is finally forced to call another parliament, he is so necessitous and so friendless that he is obliged to render up his royal power to a committee of government, and is reduced to a cypher. England slides into confusion as de Montfort and his allies try to wrest power from the governors, and then their opponents 'invited her ancient enemy to the funeral of her liberty' by calling in the French for assistance. After a military dénouement in which de Montfort is killed and the King restored, Henry attempts to understand why his reign had been so disastrous, 'why that virtue and fortune that had so long settled and maintained under his ancestors the glory of his Empire' had deserted him. Here is history teaching by example in characteristic Renaissance fashion. Henry realizes that 'his wasteful hand' has impoverished him and alienated his people, that by his 'neglect of grace', 'by making merchandize of peace . . . by giving himself over to a sensual security and referring all to base, greedy and unworthy ministers whose counsels were ever more subtle than substantial . . . he had thrown down those pillars of sovereignty and safety: Reputation abroad and Reverence at home'.[27] For Cotton, history is a mirror for princes, and King James would have no difficulty in recognizing himself.

Henry III's response was reform. 'In himself he reformed his natural errors, [for] Princes' manners through a mute law have more of life and vigour than those of letters, and though he did sometimes touch upon the verge of vice, he forebore ever after to enter the circle.' He reformed his court so that it might again be a theatre of honour: where previously 'the faults of great men did not only by approbation but by imitation receive true comfort and authority, now he purged them, for from the Court proceeds either the regular or irregular condition of the State'.[28] He curbed his immoderate liberality, recognizing that 'this bounty bestowed without respect, was taken without grace, discredited the receiver and detracteth from the judgement of the giver, and blunteth the

---

[27] Cotton, *Cottoni Posthuma*, 43–4.   [28] Ibid. 49

appetites of such as carried their hopes out of virtue and service. Thus at last he learned that reward and reprehension justly laid do balance government.' He begins for the first time to live within his means: 'expense of house he measureth by the just rule of his proper revenue.' Equally important is the change of his manner of governing. He dismisses tainted and unworthy ministers, and fills 'the seats of Judgement and Council with men nobly born, (for such attract less offense)'. He sits in Council daily, 'and disposeth of affairs of most weight in his own person'. As Cotton frequently emphasized, the prince must rule: his counsellors 'must have ability to advise, not authority to resolve'. The mood of the nation changed as the people felt the benefits of Henry's reform, and Cotton notes that a prince should 'lay the foundations of Greatness upon popular Love' and that the people 'measure the bond of their obedience by the good they always receive'.

It is not difficult to read these signals. The need for the Crown to be free of debt, the prince to be the source of honour sustaining and sustained by an authentic nobility, and protected by the love of his people, the duty of the king to rule and not be ruled, all these observations point up Cotton's dismay at the course and character of King James's reign. This dismay is coupled with a belief that the kingdom can be saved by the application of known remedies culled from history. Whether the time is 1614, or later in the reign, whether the favourite is Somerset or Buckingham, the pattern of politics remains the same. Such was the fundamental conviction of Cotton, always a conservative thinker.

The directness of the analogies makes it highly unlikely that *The Life and Reign of Henry III* was intended for publication. Offered to the Sovereign privately as a respectful admonition, it could be understood as timely counsel, with the authority of the historical record giving it a power beyond the personal concerns of a subject. Published in 1627, it must have seemed quite derogatory to King James, and unpleasantly critical of King Charles and the current political situation, with the King dominated by the Duke of Buckingham, who was no wise adviser with the well-being of England in mind, but an initiator of reckless and wasteful policies of war against Spain and attacks on France. No wonder Cotton was taken in for questioning. The history was reprinted in 1642, evidently to discredit the Stuart regime, a use that Cotton would surely not have approved.

Cotton did publish a pamphlet under his own name in 1628, one with a similar drift to *Henry III*. This was *The Danger wherein the Kingdom now standeth*, which addressed the crisis of confidence in the King and the Duke of Buckingham that followed the chaotic conduct of the expedition to La Rochelle and the war against Spain. Cotton had no fondness for Buckingham at this stage, for he had been for many years a client of Buckingham's chief opponent, the Earl of Arundel. However, he did not call for Buckingham to be stripped of power or publicly disavowed by the King. The Duke should take his place among the other leading peers in the Privy Council, and he should communicate in some fashion the King's patriotic and Protestant intention to the nation. Cotton wished 'to remove away a personal distaste of my Lord of Buckingham amongst the People' and to change the image of the King to that of 'a zealous patriot'. He was motivated by the enduring principle of his career: loyalty to the monarch as the legitimate centre of power and ultimate guarantor of the nation's stability. History instructs him that if there arises a popular passion to sacrifice any of his Majesty's servants, 'I have ever found it . . . no less fatal to the Master, than the Minister in the end.'[29] He reminds his readers of the fate of Edward II, Richard II, and Henry VI. Moderate policies should prevail, in Cotton's view. But though Charles reluctantly agreed to the calling of a new parliament, and though Buckingham was removed by assassination later in 1628, moderation and mutual assistance did not prevail. Parliament grew more angry with the King as it fought for its rights and liberties, and Cotton was prominent in that debate. His close friendship with the opposition activists John Selden and Sir John Eliot attracted the unfavourable attention of the King, who came to feel that Cotton's library was both the meeting place and the arsenal of those politicans who were hostile to royal policy and royal prerogative. Much of the information about parliamentary rights and precedents and procedures that were invoked against the King seemed to emanate from Cotton's library, so in the summer of 1629 the library was closed by order of the King. Cotton was confined for a while and then released, but he was denied access to his library, which remained locked. In May, 1631, Cotton died, apparently through grief at being parted from his books.

---

[29] Cotton, *Cottoni Posthuma*, 322.

Many of Cotton's tracts were collected and published in 1651 by James Howell, a litterateur of variable allegiance, under the title *Cottoni Posthuma*. Howell's aim seems to have been to illustrate from Cotton's writings the political difficulties of the Stuarts in the first three decades of the century, and to sketch the confrontations that eventually led to civil war. He also wished to present Cotton, with whom he had been friendly, as a figure who attempted to exert a moderating and conciliatory influence on events. Several of these tracts show antiquarian knowledge put to present use: there is a piece on the legality of duelling which offers a history of combats fought in the presence of the King and the Earl Marshal or Constable, probably written for his patron Henry Howard, Earl of Northampton, when he sought to have the office of Earl Marshal bestowed on him in 1608–9. (King James was eager to ban duelling at this time, and the legal status of the duel was much discussed. Selden published a tract *The Duello* in 1610 to establish the antiquity of legal combat and the rights in law of the combatants.) In 1610 or 1611, Cotton probably also wrote for Northampton 'The Manner and Means how the Kings of England have from time to time supported and repaired their Estates', to suggest many ways in which royal revenues might be enhanced, at a time when the proposed Great Contract between King and Parliament had failed. The tract seems to have been a position paper for Northampton to improve his standing with the King, and to open up new sources of money for the Crown. Cotton identified many prerogative rights that had lain in abeyance and that could be lucratively revived, and proposed a new order of knighthood that might be introduced and sold at £1000 a time. James adopted this last suggestion, and Cotton paid to become one of the first of the new baronets.

Cotton offered advice to King James about how to deal with the Jesuit priests who were entering the country in increasing numbers: he recommended imprisonment, not execution, for he recognized the danger of making martyrs. (He also expressed admiration for the tenacity of faith of these Catholics, whom he characterized as patriotic Englishmen for the most part.) There is a history of 'Treaties of Amity and Marriage with Austria and Spain' to help put the proposed Spanish match for Prince Charles into context; he wrote this on behalf of both Houses of Parliament as advice to King James, and warned that the precedents were ominous. Two items relate to the Parliament of 1621, in which Cotton had been active as an ally of Arundel: the impeachment of Bacon had begun, and the Privy Council sent to Cotton to know what Parliament might do by itself without the presence of the King, and what were the powers of the House of Lords as a court. The King himself seems to have asked Cotton to define his role on this occasion too. Cotton's answer was most helpful in clarifying Parliament's scope as a judicial body on the basis of ancient practice. His paper 'That the Sovereign's Person is required in the Great Councils' approved the right of the Commons to hear evidence, and the Lords to pronounce judgement, but the King's presence was required at all stages, and he must approve the verdict. Taken together, the tracts of *Cottoni Posthuma* point up the value set on historical precedent in the Jacobean political world, and present Cotton as a man attentive to the well-being of the state, 'whose main endeavours', as Howell wrote in the Preface, 'were to assert the Public Liberty, and that Prerogative and Privilidge might run in their due channels.'

To regard Cotton as primarily the creator and custodian of a remarkable library, and as a political advisor, is too restricted a view of him. He was a magnificent specimen of the full-blown Jacobean antiquary. He was an expert on Roman and Saxon Britain, a perambulator of the shires, a thesaurus of genealogical and heraldic information, an encyclopaedia of ecclesiastical history, a connoisseur of tombs and the funerary arts, and a collector. He accumulated a fine collection of Roman altars, inscriptions, and coins; his interest in these objects was aroused by his summer on Hadrian's Wall with Camden in 1600. He found, bought, or was given a number of Roman artefacts in Cumberland and Westmorland, and more were sent down to him by friends and correspondents in the north, especially Reginald Bainbridge and Lord William Howard of Naworth. He displayed his collection of altars and inscriptions at his manor house at Conington, where, in the course of rebuilding, he had constructed a terrace joining two octagonal summer-houses as a setting for his antiquities.[30] His cabinet of coins, medals, and seals kept in London was possibly the

---

[30] See Howarth, 'Sir Robert Cotton' 4. The article provides a valuable account of Cotton's antiquarian activities. His collection of altars and inscribed stones was given to Trinity College, Cambridge, by a descendant in 1750, and what is left of them is now in the Museum of Archaeology in Cambridge.

finest in private hands, admired and used as an adjunct to historical research.[31]

The house at Westminster was something of an antiquary's cavern. There were quantities of Roman bric-à-brac sent by friends: for example, 'On Thursday or Friday you shall receive the Roman reliques which were found here in Bocking (Essex) viz. a large brick which covered the Glass, wherein perhaps was ignis perpetuus, for there was olive oil which smelled as fresh as if newly poured in. And also the dish with *Coicilli* written in it. . . . I have also sent you a pott taken up therewith.'[32] That indispensable antiquarian accessory the fossil fish was also to be found in Cotton's chambers: he had one of singular majesty, nearly twenty feet long, found when the fens near Conington were being drained, and mentioned by Dugdale as evidence that the sea had once covered Huntingdonshire.[33] Naturally, Cotton had a collection of portraits of family, friends, and famous men: his outstanding picture was the large canvas of Prince Henry on horseback, now at Parham Park, attributed to Robert Peake, which Cotton was left by the Earl of Northampton. The library had bronze busts of emperors and portraits of great scholars to induce feelings of exaltation and emulation proper to study. A letter survives in the Vatican recording a visit to the library in 1625 by the papal envoy Gregorio Panzani, when Cotton's son Thomas showed him some of the ecclesiastical curiosa that must have appealed to his relic-venerating spirit: part of the skull of St Thomas à Becket, two gospels bound together which were believed to have been given by St Gregory to St Augustine, a Greek Genesis supposed to have belonged to Origen, and a papal bull of the sixteenth century.[34] This was a cabinet of curiosities of the first rank.

Finally, Cotton was not only a preserver of minor monuments, but a maker of them too. In Conington church, about 1613–14, he

---

[31] Howarth believes Cotton's cabinet of coins was exceeded only by that of Prince Henry after the Prince had acquired the superlative collection of Abraham Gorlaeus of Delft in 1611 (a transaction that Cotton seems to have assisted in). (Howarth, 'Sir Robert Cotton', 26, n. 38.)

[32] Letter from John Barkham of Essex, no date, printed in Howarth, 'Sir Robert Cotton', 22.

[33] William Dugdale, *The History of Imbanking and Drayning of Divers Fens and Marshes* (1662), 172.

[34] The letter is quoted by Howarth, 'Sir Robert Cotton', 23, n. 5.

set about raising a number of memorials, to his immediate family, as one might expect, and also, in a fine excess of antiquarian spirit, to his remote ancestors the princes of Scotland. One might think that a church in the Huntingdonshire fens is an odd place to commemorate Prince Henry and Prince David of Scotland, but Prince Henry had been granted the Earldom of Huntingdon and the Lordship of Conington by King Stephen in the twelfth century, titles that were also held by Henry's son David, and both of these princes formed part of Cotton's genealogical tree. Both monuments are classical in style. Prince Henry's reflects Cotton's interest in ancient altars, for it takes the form of an altar with a dedicatory inscription, with projecting pillars.[35] Prince David's cenotaph is a two-tiered structure, the upper storey being a triumphal arch flanked by the unicorns of Scotland. The erection of these memorials, along with ones to his father, grandfather, and great-grandfather, was the result of a flourishing sense of ancestral piety brought about most probably by Cotton's own sense of his increasing station in the world. He had become a baronet, he had political ambitions, and he was enlarging his house at Conington. By emphasizing his Scottish connections he was declaring his closeness to the Stuart regime and gratifying his antiquarian instincts by demonstrating the links between the remote past and the present.

Today, the visitor to Conington church will be attracted to the noble monument to Sir Robert Cotton himself, placed there by his son Thomas. It is a powerfully sculpted bust within a niche, garlanded with laurel. Cotton in his turn has become part of the remote past but his monument, with its enigmatic quotation from Lucan[36] referring back to ancient Rome and looking forward to the end of the world, moves through time to remind us that past, present, and future are all part of the antiquary's vast domain.

---

[35] David Howarth is inclined to attribute this monument to Cotton's friend Inigo Jones. (Howarth, 'Sir Robert Cotton', 13–15).

[36] 'Communis mundo superest rogus.' The phrase is translated by Geoffrey Turton as 'His pyre survives to light the world.' It was added to the inscription by Sir John Cotton, grandson.

4
John Selden

'Mr Selden, the learnedest man on earth' as an admirer described him,[1] might with justice have claimed that title of honour, although his native modesty would have restrained him. His prodigious range of learning was certainly unequalled in Britain, where only Archbishop Ussher could come close to him. Selden's command of the law and legal history, his familiarity with every kind of ecclesiastical document, and his incomparable understanding of the historical development of the European states from classical times, all sustained by a formidable knowledge of western and oriental languages, made him a Renaissance university in himself. He became such by his indefatigable studies, but he owed much to his scholarly friends, notably Robert Cotton, William Camden, and James Ussher. Ben Jonson too had an honoured place as one of his friends.[2] The erudition of men such as these was the product not of university training but of that passion for antiquity that marked the humanist in all the lands of Europe. But antiquity had to be serviceable to the present if it was to be of acknowledged value. For Camden, it had to illustrate the origins and character of Britain, so that Englishmen might truly know who they were; for Cotton the past existed in manuscripts that threw light on the laws and institutions of England. Ussher looked into the clouded perspectives

[1] John Lightfoot, Master of St Catherine's College, Cambridge, 'To the Reader' in *Harmony of the Old Testament* (1647).
[2] Selden's circle of friends was extensive, and included John Donne, Lord Herbert of Cherbury, Michael Drayton, and Samuel Daniel, the poet and lawyer Christopher Brooke, the doctor and magus Robert Fludd, the herald Augustine Vincent, and the collector of travel narratives Samuel Purchas. His legal life and his later political life were both productive of an exceptionally large assortment of friendships. For an account of these, and of his youth and training, see David Berkowitz, *John Selden's Formative Years* (Washington, 1988), 20–32. One should not forget that Selden was also something of a poet, though little of his verse survives, and most of that takes the form of commendatory verses. He was sufficiently respected to be included in Suckling's 'A Session of the Poets', a poem written in 1637 describing the poetic wits of the time.

of ecclesiastical history until he was literally almost blind, but he knew he could trace the stream of true religion running down from the remote past into seventeenth-century Britain. Jonson was inclined to be more pedantic than these other men, but believed that his poetry would have more authority in a learned age if it came freighted with antiquity; in any case he wanted to restore classical standards of value and behaviour to Jacobean England. All were profoundly conscious of living in a country shaped by ancient history and tradition, and took delight in understanding the force of the past working within their own society. As Selden wrote to Cotton in his dedication of *The History of Tithes* (1618), 'the fruitful and precious part of [antiquity] gives necessarie light to the present in matter of state, law, history and the understanding of good authors', and the study of 'the many years of former Experience and Observations . . . may accumulate years to us as if we had lived even from the beginning of Time'.

In attempting an estimate of the polymathic genius of Selden, we find ourselves almost at a loss to know what to single out. We share Jonson's dilemma in the commendatory poem he wrote in praise of Selden that was printed in *Titles of Honor* (1614):

> Which Grace shall I make love to first? Your skill,
> Or faith in things? or is't your wealth and will
> T'inform and teach? or your unweary'd paine
> Of Gathering? Bountie in pouring out againe?
> What fables you have vext! what truth redeem'd,
> Antiquities search'd, Opinions dis-esteem'd,
> Impostures branded, and Authorities urg'd!
> What blots and errours, have you watch'd and purg'd
> Records and Authors of! how rectified
> Times, manners, customes! Innovations spide!
> Sought out the Fountaines, Sources, Creekes, Paths, wayes,
> And noted the beginnings and decayes![3]

That summary is valid for Selden's lifelong dedication to antiquarian research.

Above all, it was on legal antiquarianism that his reputation was raised. He was born in 1584 into the family of a prosperous Sussex yeoman. Although he spent two years at Hart Hall in Oxford, he

---

[3] 'An Epistle to Master John Selden' in *The Complete Poetry of Ben Jonson*, ed. William B. Hunter (New York, 1963), 145–6.

received his real formation at the Inns of Court. He went to Clifford's Inn in 1602, when he was 18, and moved to Inner Temple in 1603. According to Aubrey, he rapidly made the acquaintance of Robert Cotton, and became a copyist for him, soon becoming a close friend with free access to Cotton's library. That library, along with the records of Chancery, would be Selden's major resources throughout his life. In the course of the next ten years, he wrote a series of works in which he perfected his characteristic working methods and established his position as one of England's outstanding scholars. During the year 1610, his star rose above the horizon with the publication of his treatise on the history of the law in England, *Jani Anglorum Facies Altera*, and a short tract on the history and legal status of the duel. Most of his early antiquarian enquiries were concerned to trace the origins of the law in England, to discover the circumstances in which they were made, and by what parties. In particular, these early works were curious to establish the status of the king or tribal leader in the lawmaking process of primitive times: did he impose laws or was he a consulting party in their formulation? Could it be determined whether laws existed before kings? It would seem to be the case that Selden was prompted to these enquiries by the arrival of a king who had exceptionally strong views about his own relationship to the laws, and who believed in the dependency of the law upon the king as a matter of demonstrable historical fact. We shall return to King James's pronouncements on the law very shortly.

A useful introduction to Selden's attitudes may be gained from his earliest piece of legal antiquarianism, the Latin treatise *Analecton Anglo-Britannicon*, which he wrote in 1607, although it was not published until 1615, in Frankfurt. A somewhat rudimentary work, it none the less offers a number of clues to his working methods and to his intentions as a scholar. The title *Analecton* literally means 'a gathering of crumbs' and hence indicates a collection of fragments rather than a formally composed work, a detail that probably explains the delayed publication of the piece. Dedicated to Sir Robert Cotton, whose library furnished much of Selden's material, it is a compilation of extracts from old authors that sketches in a history of the government of Britain from legendary times to the Norman Conquest. Selden's design is to survey the many kinds of political authority that governed the land in antiquity, and to deduce what might have been the ancient political rights of the British and the Anglo-Saxon people before their liberties were suppressed at the Conquest. There is no specific application of the findings, for Selden does not like to make overt political statements: what he prefers is to put evidence on record in accessible form, and to make certain that the evidence he thus makes available points in a particular direction. So, in the *Analecton*, he recovers appropriate historical material from recondite sources, and prints it with minimal commentary: the extracts for the most part speak for themselves. They tell of a primitive Britain governed by an aristocracy, then falling into a colonial condition under the Romans, during which time native constitutional forms were suppressed. In the course of the Saxon centuries, a mixed government of aristocracy and kings developed, only to be overthrown by the Conqueror in 1066. But even then, Selden suggests by his research among contemporary documents, there is evidence for the persistence of certain Saxon laws and institutions.[4] One can detect here an attempt to document a persisting history of government by means of assemblies rather than by kings or by other absolute authorities.

Selden's drift becomes clearer in his substantial work *Jani Anglorum Facies Altera* of 1610. The inelegant title translates as 'the other face of the English Janus', a conceit that plays with the idea of the Janus of English Law looking backwards and forwards from the Norman Conquest. Selden is mainly concerned here with the view backwards into antiquity, but he does carry his work through to the reign of Henry II. In his Preface he expresses the wish 'that the ancient original and procedure of our Civil Law might more fairly and clearly be made out', and insists that it would be wrong to refer the original of our laws to the Conquest, for they are of far more ancient date. Selden then soberly proceeds to set down an account of the primeval inhabitants of Britain, beginning not with Trojan Brutus but with an even earlier founder figure,

---

[4] J. G. A. Pocock suggests that Selden's title *Anglo-Britannicon* indicates an indebtedness to the work of the Huguenot scholar François Hotman, whose *Franco-Gallia* (1573, 1576, and 1586) was an enquiry into the history of the ancient laws and liberties of the French nation. The pattern of development in Hotman's book is similar to Selden's thesis: 'The original freedom of the Gauls . . . virtually destroyed by the Romans, was restored by the life-giving incursions of the Franks, and for centuries thereafter, until the successful usurpation of Louis XI, the assembly of the nation was supreme if not sovereign.' Pocock, *Ancient Constitution*, 20.

Samothes, the son of Japhet and brother of Gomer (whom we have encountered in the researches of Camden and Verstegan). Samothes, as already noted, had been put into circulation by Annius of Viterbo in the late fifteenth century in his fraudulent history of Berosus. There, Samothes was identified as the father of the Celtic nations, and he had been seized on by John Twyne and Richard White of Basingstoke, among others whom Selden cites, to supply the generations of inhabitants before the arrival of Brutus. Selden allows him to flourish in Albion, then brings in Brutus from Geoffrey of Monmouth and from Ralph Higden's *Poly-Chronicon*, and settles the Trojans comfortably in this island. He cites some of the laws of the legendary British lawgiver Dunvallo Molmutius from Geoffrey. What is disconcerting about Selden's procedure is the absence of any avowed argument. All this fabulous nonsense is narrated in a straight-faced way, and it looks as if he is going to continue into the history of the Roman occupation without any change of manner. But suddenly Selden stops, and overthrows the whole British apple-cart. Samothes is brushed away, Berosus is denounced as a fabrication of Annius the deceiver, and the Brutus story is dismissed as 'a poetic fiction of the Bards, done on purpose to raise the British name out of the Trojan ashes'. He then introduces his trusted principle of 'synchronism', 'the best Touchstone in this kind of Triall' as he called it elsewhere,[5] to discredit these fables. 'Synchronism', a principle already announced and practised by Camden in his prefatory essays to the *Britannia*, entailed the use of sources as close as possible to the events described, collation with comparable documents, and the matching of events with a reliable chronology. Under such scrutiny, the figures of Samothes, Brutus and their descendants faded away like ghosts at cock-crow.

Selden was in fact giving a startling demonstration of his chosen historical method, dependency on verifiable records, for he had lured his unsuspecting reader along the familiar paths of fabulous history, and then told him he was in never-never land. Selden was conscious of employing a new style of historical research in this book, and wanted to accentuate it as sharply as possible. Only historians whose accounts are wholly credible when exposed to

[5] Selden, 'From the Author of the Illustrations' in Michael Drayton, *Poly-Olbion*, in *The Works of Michael Drayton*, ed. J. W. Hebel (Oxford, 1933), vol. iv, p. viii*.

rational scrutiny are acceptable, and original documents, the integrity of which he can guarantee. Under these conditions, Caesar and Tacitus stand out as uniquely reliable reporters, both as contemporaries and even eye-witnesses of the events they described. Selden follows Camden's suggestion in the *Britannia* that it is possible to deduce from these historians that the Gauls and the Britons shared similar customs, forms of government, laws, and rituals, and that many details of Ancient British society can be reconstructed by applying information from classical reports about the Gauls and the Germans to the British tribes. Selden experiences such a wave of gratitude towards Camden for leading him to a fruitful understanding of British society in antiquity, that he interrupts his staid narrative to apostrophize him: 'Quem te memoram Camdene!' and there follows a brief Latin poem in praise of Camden. A moment like this suddenly reveals the emotions that lie beneath the surface of antiquarian research: the excitement of seeing a new way forward—or backwards—into a subject, the delight of working with difficult material, and the admiration for a great scholar who has opened up a new terrain. Selden's expostulation is almost a prayer of thanksgiving to strengthen him in his purposes. With the help of Camden, and the Roman historians, he is able to reconstruct in some degree the polity of the Ancient Britons. They appear to have met in assemblies to discuss public affairs and to decide on matters of war and peace, and these assemblies were effectively the centre of government. As Paul Christianson, who has written so understandingly of Selden, points out in his discussion of *Jani Anglorum*, the evidence that Selden draws together from ancient sources suggests a considerable dispersion of political power in pre-Roman Britain, and Selden 'has no sense that kings initiated civil society or ordained its ancient laws'.[6] British society derived its unity from the binding power of a common law and a common religion, and not from any single political authority. It is important that kings should not have been pre-eminent in the making of laws, for Selden's undeclared aim is to find the source of the laws of Britain and the centre of its government in assemblies, not in kings.

All his life Selden was motivated by his intense commitment to

---

[6] Paul Christianson, 'Young John Selden and the Ancient Constitution' in *Proceedings of the American Philosophical Society*, 128/4 (1984), 275.

the common law of England, and to the sovereignty of Parliament. Yet he lived at a time when the King insisted on his right to be a 'free monarch', above the law and above Parliament, and Selden seems to have used his antiquarian scholarship to assert the antiquity and authority of the law over the entire community of the state against the perceived threat of claims for royal absolutism. King James had published *The True Law of Free Monarchies* in 1598, at Edinburgh, and it had been reprinted twice in London in 1603 when he became King of Great Britain. Besides expounding the principle of the divine right of kings, which he derived from Old Testament statements about David and Solomon, those antetypes of Christian kingship, he also argued from biblical sources that the king must be the father of the nation. In the matters of the king's relation to the law, and the grounds of allegiance of the subject to the king, James played the antiquarian himself, and looked to 'the time of the first age' in order to set down 'the first manner of establishing the laws and forms of government among us'. He emphasized that kings in Scotland were not chosen out of a society for valour and virtue to rule over that society: on the contrary, the first king, Fergus, came from Ireland to occupy Scotland, which was 'scantily inhabited' and barbarous. So he and his successors

made and established their laws from time to time, and as the occasion required. So the truth is directly contrary in our state to the false affirmation of such seditious writers, as would persuade us, that the laws and state of our country were established before the admitting of a king: where by the contrary you see it plainly proved, that a wise king coming in among barbares first established the estate and form of government, and thereafter made laws by himself, and his successors thereto.[7]

He goes on to insist that all subjects are his vassals, holding all their lands from him as their overlord, that Parliament is the servant of the king, to be summoned and dismissed as it pleases him, and 'that the King is above the law, as both the author and the giver of strength thereto'.[8]

The ideology for an absolute monarchy is present in *The True Law*, and although James when King of England was more conciliatory than his book augured, for he bound himself to uphold the rule of law, and worked reasonably well with Parliament, yet he

---

[7] *The True Law of Free Monarchies* in *The Minor Prose Works of King James VI & I*, ed. James Craigie (Edinburgh, 1982), 70. [8] Ibid. 72.

remained jealous of his prerogative, and the threat of a movement towards absolutism became part of the political consciousness of the age. It may not have been a coincidence, as Christianson has pointed out, that *Jani Anglorum* was dedicated to Robert Cecil and published in 1610 just after the breakdown of the Great Contract, the proposed deal between Parliament and the King, brokered by Cecil, that would have granted the King a regular income raised from taxation, in return for his restraining his expenditure and relinquishing certain parts of his prerogative.[9]

Jani Anglorum is a puzzling work to read because Selden did not explicitly declare what his argument was. The reason for this reticence would seem to be that it was implicitly directed against the King. The material that he draws together in this treatise develops an understandable rationale if one recognizes that it was written against the King's position. The work demonstrates to lawyers, constitutionalists and to the free citizens of the nation— and also the King—that the origins of the laws and government in what is now England were quite differently derived from those of Scotland as described by James. From Caesar and Tacitus, Selden drew a picture of a society dominated by a primitive aristocracy, given to consulting in assemblies from which kings derived their authority, which was thus a limited power.

Besides these assemblies, which Selden likens to rudimentary parliaments, he identified an alternative source of law in the Druids. Using Caesar's account, Selden represents the Druids as the guardians of the laws and of religion and of morals. He also notes that they had a place where they met regularly to make, interpret, and preserve the laws for all Britain. Their laws were not written down, but were based on custom, and were transmitted from generation to generation.[10] Here seemed to be the origins of the customary law in Britain, of which Selden and his fellow common lawyers were the remote inheritors. Selden was keen to demytho- logize the Druids: there was no reason to believe that they were the possessors of a supernatural wisdom, nor was there any credible evidence that they had contact with Pythagoras and his teachings about the transmigrations of the soul (a notion derived from a

---

[9] Christianson, 'Young John Selden', 274.
[10] See *Jani Anglorum Facies Altera* (English translation, 1683), chs. 9 and 10. Also Christianson, 'Young John Selden', 275.

suggestion made by Lucan). He even attempts to provide a reasonable explanation for that puzzling statement by Caesar (in *De Bello Gallico*, vi. 14) that the Druids used Greek for writing letters and for their public transactions. Caesar must have been mistaken, he believes, for the Druids could not possibly have known the Greek language. Either they used the Greek alphabet to write their Gallic language (as the Syriac New Testament is printed in Hebrew characters), or Caesar mistook 'the rude Gothic characters' of their own script for Greek.[11] Selden puts the Druids plainly before the reader as priests and lawgivers and guardians of the law, quite unmysterious. There were no royal lawmakers in his version of ancient Britain.

Selden chooses to linger over another feature of ancient British society that may have a bearing on his attitudes towards the rule of James I, and that is the prominence of women in British affairs. He notes from Plutarch that the Breton Gauls admitted women to their councils, and deduces that the British must have done so too. Tacitus had observed that the Britons were willing to go to war under a woman. Selden pauses in his narrative to defend the right of women to rule, as they were permitted to do in England by ancient custom, and contrasts this situation with French political conventions, where women are denied rule by the prevalence of Salic Law. In an unexpected digression, Selden praises the qualities of women as leaders and vindicates their legal and customary rights to supreme authority in a state. Boadicea of the Iceni and Cartismunda of the Brigantes were the first known female wielders of supreme power in a tradition that culminates in Elizabeth.[12] What motivated this eulogy is unclear, for Selden always avoided

[11] Selden instances the fact that Caesar while in Gaul sent an important letter to a colleague in Greek so that it could not be understood if intercepted, as proof that the priests of the country did not know Greek.

[12] Did Milton have this passage in mind when he was writing *The History of Britain* (1670), and interrupted his narrative of ancient British politics in Book II to express his personal opinions about the unseemliness of women in power? Selden's praise of female authority was evidently a noted feature of *Jani Anglorum* in the seventeenth century. The preface to the English translation of 1683 by Redman Westcot (the pseudonym of Adam Littleton) advertised this feature, although it is trivialized by the patronizing manner of the translator. Selden, he writes, has 'pleaded the excellencies and rights of that Angelical Sex (if Angels have any sex) to the abasement and overthrow of the Salick Law'. Women should be aware of their entitlement, remarks Westcot, and this is one reason for making the book available in English.

declaring that he had any contemporary targets in view, and he
habitually professed to set down merely a factual statement of
historical detail or events. But there would appear to be some
covert criticism of James here as he praises the excellence of
Elizabeth, and the date of his treatise, 1610, coincides with the rise
of adverse opinions about the quality, style, and direction of
James's governance of the state, in tandem with an increasingly
nostalgic view of Elizabeth's reign.[13] Elizabeth, a strong and
successful queen, had known the proper limits of royal prerogative
and understood the need to consult with parliaments; she knew
how to bind the nation to her in loyalty and affection.

In his account of the early history of Britain, Selden spends little
time over the centuries of the Roman occupation. He assumes that
ancient British society was broken by the invaders, and that Roman
law was imposed over the conquered island. Yet he finds no reason
to believe that Roman laws and forms of government had any
lasting influence after the Romans withdrew. Nor can he determine
whether the ancient British polity reconstituted itself after the
departure of the Romans; there is no reliable evidence, but he is
doubtful that any recovery could have occurred after four hundred
years of occupation. The Saxons who gradually occupied the
country from the fifth century onwards brought with them
constitutional forms that were not greatly dissimilar from those
that the ancient British had known, and their legacy has survived, in
Selden's view. The Saxons had a true monarchy, yet their monarchs
made their laws in council with the advice of their chief men. Selden
quotes the preamble to the laws of Ina, King of the West Saxons in
the early eighth century, where the King stated that he framed his
laws 'by the advice and order of Kenred my father and of Hedda
and Erkonwald my bishops, and all of my aldermen and of the
elders and wise men of my people'. From such statements Selden
can infer a Saxon constitutional process wherein the laws derived
from a king consulting in a primitive parliamentary forum, a forum
that he refers back to the assemblies of the German tribes described

---

[13] See, e.g. Anne Barton, 'Harking Back to Elizabeth: Ben Jonson and Caroline
Nostalgia' in *English Literary History*, 48 (1981), 706–31, and Roy Strong, *Henry,
Prince of Wales and England's Lost Renaissance* (London, 1986). Around 1610
began a movement to acclaim Prince Henry as the inheritor of the Elizabethan
qualities of leadership, valour, and Protestant integrity, in contrast to his father,
whose personal shortcomings were by now well registered by his English subjects.

by Tacitus. He then proceeds to detail the many ways in which Saxon customs, institutions and offices have impressed an enduring pattern on English life. He notes the Saxon origin of many of the offices of state, such as those of chancellor, treasurer, constable, justices, and sheriffs (offices whose history had been the subject of discussions at the Society of Antiquaries early in James's reign). He shows too how bishops soon acquired a place in the regular councils of the Saxon kings. Running over the many collections of Saxon laws that had survived (many of which had been published by William Lambarde in his *Archaionomia* of 1568), he delivers an admiring account of 'a flexible effective constitution, adjusting to new circumstances by dropping old laws and making new'.[14]

Selden now approaches the great divide of English history, the Norman Conquest. Was this an absolute break with the past, or was there continuity of a kind in laws and government? William was undoubtedly a 'free monarch' at the time of the Conquest, but by his affirmation of the laws of Edward the Confessor he acknowledged the validity of the common law of England, and bound himself to accept that law. Selden portrays the Conquest as an overlaying of Norman authority upon surviving Saxon traditions of custom and law. New customs were brought in, of course, and new laws; the lands were redistributed and the system of feudal tenure introduced. The Norman kings were more free to act without constitutional restraint. Selden ends his book in the reign of Henry II with a demonstration that, in Christianson's words, 'the feudal law blended with Saxon custom to produce a potent, vital polity.'[15]

Jani Anglorum is an important work because it first showed Selden's scholarship fully developed to trace a subject over a great span of time: in this case he traced the common laws of England back to their earliest documented sources. It exhibits his favoured method of research: to go back to the remotest times and move forward, rejecting all information and historical report that does not hold up under the tests of 'synchronism'. Legends and fables are

---

[14] Christianson, 'Young John Selden', 278.
[15] Ibid. 281. For recent discussion of Selden's constitutional views, see Pocock, *Ancient Constitution*, 280–305, and Richard Tuck, 'The Ancient Law of Freedom: John Selden and the Civil War', in *Reactions to the English Civil War 1642–1648*, ed. John Morrill (London, 1982).

particularly mistrusted. Characteristic too is the absence of a specific application of his research to contemporary concerns. This silence seems to have been a tactic on Selden's part to avoid the perils of censorship, for if the King or the Privy Council or the bishops felt the matter was too sensitive and impinged on their honour or their privileges, or questioned the bases of their authority, the book was liable to be stopped in the press and the author called in for questioning. King James, for example, did not encourage research into legal or constitutional origins, and his frowns caused the Society of Antiquaries to cease meeting in 1607 because he felt some disquiet at their activities. Ecclesiastical antiquarianism was for the most part welcome, because it could be used in the defence of Protestant doctrines and Church discipline, but investigations that let in light on the dark places where the roots of his prerogative lay were another matter. Selden's impassive way of conducting an antiquarian enquiry, with its bald recitation of factual detail and undeclared aims, was the consequence of working in a perilous political climate. Stuart readers of his works who were politically astute could draw the conclusions to which Selden's accumulation of verified material pointed, but this oblique strategy has meant that his works have never been particularly accessible to later generations.

Jani Anglorum Facies Altera was effectively the first attempt to trace the development of the laws and constitution of England. It is a presentation that accommodates the major breaks of national history, caused by invasion, within the framework of a continuing customary law. Selden has a sense of the enduring character of the nation that finds its natural expression in some form of mixed monarchy, with king, noblemen, and religious leaders sharing sovereignty and involved in the making and changing of the laws. The work showed how one of the essential characteristics of English law was its flexibility, its capacity for change, and its openness to continuous interpretation by lawyers, a feature that gave it a particular efficacy as an instrument of social control. A circumstance that may have been relevant to its composition was the desire expressed by King James at the beginning of his reign to codify the laws of his kingdoms, to put them in a fixed form as in Roman law. Selden's demonstration of the continually growing and changing nature of English law could be regarded as a work of resistance to any proposed attempt to freeze the law into a formalized code. The accompanying demonstration of the existence of some kind of consultative assembly from immemorial times that participated in the process of lawmaking and had a voice in the exercise of power gave Selden a lifelong belief in the rights of Parliament to share in the sovereignty of the country.

The arguments of *Jani Anglorum* were repeated and abbreviated in the English tract he composed in 1610 entitled *England's Epinomis* ('On the Laws of England'), and he returned to the issue in the annotations he wrote for an edition of *De Laudibus Legum Angliae* ('In Praise of the Laws of England'), a work by Sir John Fortescue, Chief Justice in the reign of Henry IV, much valued by students of the law for its statements about the Common Law and its immemorial antiquity. The little book is cast as a dialogue between the Chancellor of England and Prince Edward, son of Henry VI, so its standpoint is that of a lawyer instructing the prince in the importance of the law. Selden translated the book from Latin, added extensive notes, and published it anonymously (though dated from the Inner Temple) in 1616. That was the year when King James's *Works* were first published as a complete body of writings. Did Selden bring out his edition of Fortescue to reinforce the reputation of the common laws of England at a moment of monarchical assertiveness?

Selden cannot agree with Fortescue that England's laws are the most ancient in the West, for he believes that 'All laws in generall are originally equally ancient', dating back to the beginning of civil society in every nation. Civil law arises out of the laws of nature, the natural need for justice and arbitration that men in all societies feel, but additions and variations occur 'according to the several conveniences of divers states'.[16] Selden expresses his sense of the combination of continuity and change that characterise the laws of England with a most serviceable image: 'In regard of their first being, they are not otherwise than the ship, that by often mending hath no piece of the first material, or as the house that's so often repaired, *ut nihil ex pristina materia superstet*, which yet (by the Civil Law) is to be accounted the same'.[17] His notes confirm even more strongly than in his previous work the conviction, based on copious research, that the laws of England survived the various

---

[16] Sir John Fortescue, *De Laudibus Legum Angliae*, ed. J. Selden (1616), 17.
[17] Ibid. 19.

invasions of the country and are an integral part of national identity. The unspoken conclusion is that they must not be bound or encoded, but must be allowed their customary role in upholding the liberties of Englishmen and interacting with the sovereign power of the monarch.

Selden engaged in a more conventional antiquarian enquiry when he was invited by his friend Michael Drayton to provide a prose commentary for his topographical poem *Poly-Olbion*, the first part of which was published in 1613. In general outline, this work is a versification of Camden's *Britannia*; its subtitle reads 'a Chorographicall Description of Tracts, Rivers, Mountains, Forests, and other Parts of this renowned Isle of Great Britain'. The title is a characteristic piece of Renaissance word-play. Olbion is a variant of Albion, the old Greek name for the mainland of Britain, and the prefix 'Poly' generates a meaning something like 'the Variety of Britain'. That verbal construction is close to the Greek 'polyolbos', meaning 'rich in blessings', so the title that Drayton invented conflates the name of Britain with the abundance of blessings it enjoys. Drayton's method of progression in *Poly-Olbion* is similar to that of Camden in *Britannia*, for he traces the rivers of each county, narrating the events that have occurred on their banks and describing the towns and countryside and commodities of each region. Unlike Camden, however, Drayton was firmly committed to the British History, and the figures of Brutus and his descendants recur frequently throughout the poem. The First Song of the poem is wholly given over to Brutus and his wandering Trojans, their arrival in Albion and their victories over the resident giants. *Poly-Olbion* is what Polonius might have described as 'epical-pastoral', and Brutus and the British heroes are an essential part of the legendary machinery of the work, providing opportunities for colourful action and bestowing a splendid aura on the beginnings of the nation.

Drayton may have been moved to invite Selden to furnish notes or 'illustrations' to his poem by the example of Ben Jonson's treatment of some of his early masques, several of which he published with a formidable apparatus of notes to vindicate his claim that his 'transitory devices' for the Whitehall stage 'were grounded upon antiquity and solid learnings', and that there was a high seriousness behind their festive outward show. Drayton no doubt wished to adhere to the Renaissance critical commonplace that poetry should be a vehicle for learning, mixing pleasing images and expression with sound instruction; but his preface also indicates that he had anxieties over his readership, for he hoped that the poetic descriptions would engage his female readers, while the more searching male audience would find plenty of solid matter in the notes. The poetry and the notes do not happily co-exist, however, for Selden could not bring himself to humour the fictions of the British History, and takes the opportunity to denounce the whole Trojan charade as an intolerable imposition on the modern reader. He admits in his prefatory note that he lacks the 'Historicall Faith' of his friend Drayton in the matter of the 'first Inhabitants, Name, State, and Monarchique succession', which are all derived from Geoffrey of Monmouth. He declares that 'touching the Trojan Brute, I have (but as an Advocat for the Muse) argued; disclaiming in it, if alleg'd for my own Opinion'.[18] In fact, he does his best to discredit the legends by attacking them with all the resources of his great learning. As a man of scrupulous scholarship, he is outraged at the survival of this extravagant story, so full of 'intollerable antichronismes, incredible reports, and Bardish impostures, as well as from Ignorance as assum'd liberty of Invention in some of our Ancients'. He reminds us that 'untill Polybius, ... no Greeke mentions the Isle; untill Lucretius, no Roman hath exprest a thought of us; until Caesars Commentaries, no piece of its description was known, that is now left to posterity. For time therefore preceding Caesar, I dare trust none; but with Others adhere to Conjecture'.[19] Yes, he will help out his friend by identifying the sources of the specious history of Britain, but 'I importune you not to credit' the events, he urges his readers; 'I discharge my selfe; nor impute you to me any serious respect of them.' He declares himself to be a true follower of Camden, whom he praises as 'that most Learned Nourice of Antiquitie'. Selden is an avowed modernist, proud of belonging to 'this later age (wherein so industrious search is among admired Ruins of olde Monuments)', and regards it as his critical duty to dispel the old mythologies of history wherever they prevail. He does acknowledge the power of 'that universall desire, bewitching our Europe, to derive their bloud from Trojans',[20] but modern scholarship must establish a

---

[18] *Poly-Olbion*, in *Works*, vol. iv, p. viii*.   [19] Ibid. pp. ix*–x*.
[20] Ibid. 22.

new clarity in antiquarian studies, and cherished fictions will have to go. All the fabled founders of the western nations are losing their credibility, and even Romulus may be only an imaginary ancestor of the Romans.

The clash between poem and notes makes for interesting reading. What Drayton versifies, Selden cannot or will not substantiate. The poem runs on in a pleasantly pastoral manner, with Drayton pointing out the beauties of the countryside in an amiable, undemanding way; then Selden weighs in with his dense, ingrown prose charged with historiographical information and prodigious learning in several languages. There is much harsh pedantry in these notes; Selden overstretches himself to display his erudition, and his prose must be amongst the most graceless and convoluted of the century. It comes as no surprise to find that the second part of *Poly-Olbion*, published in 1622, carried no more instructive illustrations from Mr Selden. What Selden's notes to the first part did achieve, however, was the effective discouragement of any further elaboration of the history of Trojan Brutus in imaginative literature.

In *Poly-Olbion*, Bards and Druids are frequently alluded to whenever ancient British scenes are described, for Drayton evidently was fascinated by these figures, and it is by means of his Bards and Druids that he managed to wring a few concessions from Selden concerning the credibility of the British History.[21] Camden had mentioned both these groups in *Britannia* without giving them any unusual attention; his account of the Druids is restrained by the reports of Roman authors about their abhorrent rites of human sacrifice, and of the Bards he had little to say. Drayton, however, magnified the Bards, representing them as the repositories of the ancient history of Britain, the guardians of the national memory. Passing down their songs from generation to generation, they recollected the great deeds of the heroes, preserved the genealogies of the race, and praised the beauties of their land. (The fact that each section of *Poly-Olbion* is called a Song suggests that Drayton saw himself directly in the line of the ancient Bards.) The Bards were closely associated with the Druids, who were also the exponents of an oral tradition of knowledge and wisdom. Why

---

[21] For an extended account of Drayton's use of these figures, see Geoffrey G. Hiller, ' "Sacred Bards" and "Wise Druids": Drayton and his Archetype of the Poet', in *English Literary History*, 51 (1984), 1–16.

should not the true history of earliest Britain have been preserved orally by these groups, and why should men doubt that Geoffrey of Monmouth had had access to these traditions persisting in Wales in the twelfth century? People doubt the existence of the British kings and heroes because Caesar made no mention of them in his Commentaries, but if their history was transmitted by an oral tradition, it is not surprising that he said nothing about them, for how would he have been aware of them? In any case, Drayton argued, Caesar knew virtually nothing of Britain, so superficial was his contact with the island:

> Unskilfull of our tongue but by Interpreter,
> Hee nothing had of ours which our great Bards did sing.[22]

As well as the Romans, the Picts, the Saxons, and the Danes had all stormed through Britain, all eager to destroy the native culture. No wonder there were so few records left.

Selden in his notes agrees that there may be some justice in Drayton's complaint. Since classical authors had written respectfully of the Druids and Bards, Selden feels obliged to address the question of what they knew. One can sense how he begins to fall under the spell of these potent enchanters as he begins to corroborate the claims of Drayton's verse. He is prepared to entertain the possibility that the Bards had orphic powers to charm and sway their hearers, and considers that the Druids may indeed have been ancient magi, the transmitters of religious mysteries by means of an oral tradition that could be considered comparable to that of Moses and the Cabalists. He is even prepared to believe, from a suggestion by Pliny, that they worshipped 'one All-healing or All-saving power'.[23] Monotheists, then, they might have been. They were also, he is certain, the administrators of the law in ancient Britain: 'They sate as Judges, and determined all causes emergent, civill and criminall', and their practice was evidence of the existence of a common law in pre-historic times. He is inclined to overlook the barbaric aspect of druidic culture, 'I omit, therefore, their sacrificing of humane bodies, and such like . . .' and ultimately becomes so caught up in the attempt to

---

[22] *Poly-Olbion*, Song VI, ll. 320–1.
[23] Ibid. 193. The notes to Songs IV and IX are particularly significant for Selden's observations about the Bards and the Druids.

restore the reputation of the Druids that he confides to his readers
that he knows of some surviving representations of these priests:

Conrad Celtes observes [in his *Tractatus de Hercynia Sylva*] to be in an
Abbey at the foot of Vichtelberg hill, near Voitland, six Statues, of stone,
set in the Church-wall, some VII foot every one tall, barehead and foot,
cloakt and hooded, with a bagge, a booke, a staffe, a beard hanging to his
middle, and spreading a Mustachio, an austere looke and eyes fixt on the
earth; which he conjectures to be Images of them. . . . I once thought that
Conrad had beene deceived. But I can now upon better advice incline to his
judgement.[24]

Later in the century, Aylett Sammes would include an illustration of
a Druid in his *Britannia Antiqua*, based on this source.

So Drayton and Selden co-operate amicably for a while, but their
relations are strained again in the Tenth Song, where Drayton has
the River Dee sing a defiant vindication of Brutus and the descent
from Troy, to which Selden coolly responds. As the poem moves
away from Wales and into England, Selden is able to deal more
fully with Saxon and Norman matters, and address subjects that
have a fuller documentation than the ancient British stories. He can
engage in miscellaneous antiquarian enquiries over points of legal
history, the origins of county and civic offices, heraldry and titles of
honour. Much of the material he had already gathered for *Jani
Anglorum* finds a place here, and he is also able to infiltrate into his
notes his interest in the development of the law, the growth of
representative assemblies, and the rights of the subject in a free
state. For example, Song XVII inspires a lengthy discussion of
Magna Carta, where he asserts that this covenant was effectively a
restoration of liberties enjoyed in Saxon times, but eroded under
the Normans. *Poly-Olbion* also allowed Selden to expound his
principles of 'synchronism' as a valuable method of determining the
credibility of ancient records, and it gave him an opportunity to
emphasize the importance of philology in studies of the past as a
means of tracing the origin and development of terms and customs
not only through time but also across different societies. Selden's
marginal references to his notes indicate a familiarity with a
remarkable range of modern European scholarly writings, as well
as a more predictable knowledge of English medieval material,
chronicles, charters, and legal documents, and of the whole body of

---

[24] Ibid. 197. Illustrations to Song IX.

classical literature. The application of this battery of scholarship to Drayton's pastoral poem resulted in one of the oddest combinations in the literature of the seventeenth century.

Selden's most disciplined application of his antiquarian learning was made in *Titles of Honor* (1614), his least contentious book. This volume might properly have been dedicated to the King (for amongst many other topics it traces 'the particular right of the title of Emperor anciently in the Kings of this Isle'), but Selden evidently did not feel the need to ingratiate himself, and it was offered as a testimony of affection to Edward Heyward, 'My most beloved Friend and Chamberfellow'.[25] Selden also prefaced his book with a poem in Greek addressed to William Camden, 'that singular Glory of our Nation, and Light of Britaine'. Camden as herald must have been delighted with this scholarly elucidation of the origins and development of the many ranks and offices of the western world; as author of the *Britannia* he would have recognized that here was a definitive work of social history and an important addition to his own achievements in describing the process whereby the Britain of his own times was tenuously descended from the Roman world. *Titles of Honor* was probably the most advanced work of historical scholarship yet published in England. Using the whole spread of the surviving Roman record as his quarry, and drawing on ancient Greek and Byzantine sources, as well as every kind of medieval documentation, he traced out the slow evolution of degrees of rank and title in all the nations that had once belonged to the Western and Eastern Empires of Rome. Nor was his ambition limited to the world once ruled by Rome, but his curiosity reached out to

---

[25] *Poly-Olbion* too was a work one would have expected to honour King James in various ways, but its oppositional aspect has been credibly identified by Richard Helgerson in a recent article. Helgerson remarks how writers who were disaffected with the King were increasingly inclined to praise the country but not its monarch, and topographical poems such as *Poly-Olbion* and William Browne's *Britannia's Pastorals* gave opportunities for patriotic expression that did not involve direct praise of the King. Helgerson notes how Drayton breaks off the list on English monarchs with Elizabeth in the Seventeenth Song, omitting to draw James into the illustrious record; even the praise of the Stuart line in the Fifth Song fails to mention James. Drayton belonged to the circle of poets and scholars around Prince Henry, and *Poly-Olbion* was posthumously dedicated to the Prince. Selden's presence as the poem's annotator would have been a sign, to some readers, of the work's coolness towards King James. See R. Helgerson, 'The Land Speaks: Cartography, Chorography and Subversion in Renaissance England' in *Representing the English Renaissance*, ed. S. Greenblatt (Berkeley, Calif., 1988), 327–62.

the honours of African and Asian nations, to degrees amongst the Turks, and even 'to the bounds of utmost Tartary'. The structures of the ancient societies encountered in the Bible were particularized in minute and comprehensible detail, as were those of the Persians and the Greeks. The hierarchies of the world from the beginning of time are paraded before us in splendour, and the universal passion of mankind for the differentiations of rank is analysed as never before. Predictably, the honours of Britain have a central place in Selden's concerns, and in describing the introduction of the Norman social structure after the Conquest he is led into a much fuller understanding of the origins of the feudal system than he had attained in *Jani Anglorum*, and he is now able to chart its spread across western Europe in the Middle Ages with a confidence based on a sure knowledge of its operation. He also documents the foundation of the many orders of chivalry in Europe, and outlines the history of such honour-groups in the West (from which he excludes Arthur and his Round Table as merely fabulous). *Titles of Honor* was the supreme achievement to date of the kind of historical enquiry that the Elizabethan Society of Antiquaries had aspired to, but of far greater scope and with a profundity of learning in many languages that was quite beyond the members of that body.[26]

Selden was indeed a formidable linguist who had command of an exceptional range of oriental languages: Hebrew, Syriac, Chaldean, Samaritan, Aramaic, Arabic, Persian, and even Ethiopic are all cited in his works. Where and how he acquired these skills is unclear, but some conjecture may be allowed. He might have made a beginning at Oxford, where Hebrew was taught, a chair having been founded in the 1540s. There was also informal teaching of Syriac and Chaldean in the colleges, with the aim of producing linguistically profound biblical scholars.[27] But Anthony Wood in his account of

---

[26] Selden's model for *Titles of Honor* was possibly Jean du Tillet's *Recueil des Rangs de Grands de France* (Paris, 1602). Selden was heavily indebted to French scholarship for his work, and drew particularly on the published researches of Jacques Cujas, Joseph Scaliger, Jean Bodin, François Hotman, and Pierre Pithou. A French work that seems indebted to Selden was André Favyn's *Théâtre d'Honneur et de Chevalerie* (Paris, 1620). For Selden's relations with continental scholars, see Woolf, *The Idea of History*, 207–14. Woolf's book contains an illuminating chapter on Selden.

[27] For an account of the provision of oriental-language teaching at Oxford in the later sixteenth century, see S. L. Greenslade, 'The Faculty of Theology' in *The*

Selden in *Athenae Oxonienses* wrote that Selden got his great knowledge of oriental languages after he fell to the study of the law, so perhaps we should look to London as the place where he learnt most. The chief promoter of the study of oriental languages in the reign of James I was Lancelot Andrewes, whom Selden soon came to know in London. Andrewes was especially interested in the works of the Greek Church fathers, which he found serviceable in the defence of the Church of England, for they provided an alternative tradition of theology to the Latin fathers. He was also concerned to study as many early versions as possible of Old and New Testament texts in Semitic languages in order to establish as exactly as possible the words and meaning of the Scriptures. The new translation of the Bible that was being carried out between 1604 and 1611 gave an impetus to the study of those languages associated with Hebrew amongst the scholars engaged on that project. Selden probably learnt his Hebrew, a language in which he became exceptionally proficient, in this ethos of biblical scholarship around Andrewes. Andrewes also believed that the study of Arabic should be promoted in England for patristic reasons, as many of the Greek fathers had been translated into Arabic, and information about their lives and theology could be gained from such sources. (There was also pressure from the medical profession to know more about Arabic medicine.)

Andrewes' most successful protégé in this area was William Bedwell, who became the leading Arabist of Jacobean England, and who was also a friend of Selden in London. Bedwell was probably Selden's most important mentor, and could have supplied a course of reading, and offered practical help and guidance in negotiating the scripts and grammar of the family of Semitic languages. The biographer of Bedwell, Alastair Hamilton, has given an account of the books printed on the continent that could have provided the apparatus for mastering the oriental languages; amongst these were Arab grammars, Syriac and Chaldean grammars, and New Testaments, and the polyglot Bibles from Spain and the Netherlands which printed the texts in Latin, Greek, Aramaic, and Syriac.[28]

Oxford History of Oxford, iii. ed. J. McConica (Oxford, 1986), 295–334, and especially 315–17.

[28] Alastair Hamilton, *William Bedwell the Arabist, 1563–1632* (Leiden, 1985), 8–13.

Bedwell managed to extend his interests to Persian and Ethiopic, and his influence helped shape the great Polyglot Bible that was published in London in 1657 under the editorship of Brian Walton, printing texts in nine languages. Selden was one of the men who helped advance that great work. Bedwell and Selden lent each other oriental books, and were obviously on good terms.[29]

A dazzling display of Selden's polymathic diversity is his study of the deities of the Middle East in biblical times, *De Diis Syriis*, published in 1617 (though according to the Preface it had already taken shape as early as 1605). This was the first study of comparative religion by an Englishman. The work would seem to be the product of Selden's intensive engagement with oriental languages—he made use of Greek, Hebrew and Syriac in his researches—and arose from a desire to understand the religious cults of the peoples surrounding the Israelites so that one could appreciate more fully the development of monotheism in a polytheistic environment. *De Diis Syriis* seems to be a work of disinterested intellectual curiosity, devoid of any religious or political sub-text, and as such, something rare in Selden's œuvre. The movement of curiosity away from the humanist preoccupations with Greece and Rome was in itself a novelty, as was the shift in focus from Jewish beliefs and practices to heathen cults. Classical writers and the books of the Old Testament remained the principal guides to the false gods of Syria. False gods they were, but not by any means illusory. Selden assumes that the gods worshipped by the neighbours of the Israelites were demons, and were gods of power. He does not speculate about their origins, unlike John Milton, whose 'Nativity Ode' and Book I of *Paradise Lost* were indebted to *De Diis Syriis* in the matter of names and characteristics of the heathen gods. Milton had no doubt that they were fallen angels who tyrannized mankind until the birth of Christ put an end to their sway. The Syria of the title is effectively Mesopotamia, where religious influences from Egypt, Persia, and later Greece, mixed with indigenous forms of worship to produce a rich confusion of cults which Selden tries to clarify and explicate. Thoth, Osiris,

---

[29] See, for example, the letter from Selden to Ussher of 24 Mar. 1622 reporting that he and Bedwell were both making use of Ussher's copy of a Nubian Geography (James Ussher, *A Collection of Three Hundred Letters* (1686), 78). Selden must also have known Edward Pococke, the brilliant orientalist who was a generation younger than he, and who was a pupil of William Bedwell.

Mithra, and Baal had their altars and their followings from Assyria to the fringes of Arabia. Milton caught their exotic barbarism in his description of Satan's companions, transformed

> Oft to the image of a brute, adorned
> With gay religions full of pomp and gold,
> And devils to adore for deities.

Their gaudy, blood-stained images remain for ever in the memory, in verse of mesmerizing power:

> Next Chemos, the obscene dread of Moab's sons,
> From Aroar to Nebo, and the wild
> Of southmost Abarim; in Hesebon
> And Horonaim, Seon's realm, beyond
> The flowery vale of Sibma clad with vines,
> And Eleale to the Asphaltic Pool.
> Peor his other name, when he enticed
> Israel in Sittim, on their march from Nile,
> To do him wanton rites; which cost them woe.[30]

Selden reviewed all these gods, and defined their particular powers and province of authority. He explored how important cults such as those of Baal and Ashtoreth developed local variants in response to pre-exisiting beliefs and ceremonies. He enumerated the many permutations of the cult of Hercules to show how one new religion made its way across the region, benefiting from the readiness to accept new deities in the eastern Mediterranean world. The worship of Dagon, the fish-god of the Philistines, was of unusual interest to Selden: he was puzzled as to its origins, although he recognized that it must have been associated with a maritime, seafaring people. (Milton would find the information about Dagon helpful when he came to write *Samson Agonistes*.) There is a memorable chapter on the dirt-gods of the region, Baal-Zebub, Lord of the Flies, Belus Stercoreus, and Jupiter Stercoreus, and the stinking Ashmodeus. Selden was enough of a proto-anthropologist to recognize that these deities were held to be preservers against disease and insect plagues; Milton, however, remembered only his account of the repulsiveness of their rites when he came to evoke the loathesomeness of the fallen angels in *Paradise Lost*.

The similarities Selden observed in the character and power of

---

[30] *Paradise Lost*, i. 406–14.

certain gods led him to discern the same god behind several names. He recognized the common identity of Osiris, Adonis, and Thammuz, and from the legends connecting them with types of Venus and Proserpina, he knew their worship was associated with fertility and seasonal festivals. Selden ventured on to the path that would eventually lead to *The Golden Bough*. As a scholar, Selden was disposed to take a morally neutral view of what he was describing. Although he noted from time to time that he was writing a history of demons, and maintained the assumption throughout *De Diis Syriis* that the religion of the Jews was the worship of the one true God, his absorption in his subject was so intense that his moral guard dropped intermittently. He conveys the impression that all religions are equally interesting, if not equally true. The phrase he placed at the end of his book, to avert the evil eye, as it were,—'Soli Deo Unico et Triuno Honor et Gloria'—has the effect of calling attention to his restrained reverence for Jehovah as he moves among the heathen gods. There was always something of the secularist about Selden.

De Diis Syriis was admired and respected by humanist scholars all over Europe,[31] but Selden's next antiquarian treatise, *The Historie of Tithes* (1618), proved immensely provocative to many of its English readers, in spite of its sober air of impartial enquiry. He seems to have embarked upon it as a contribution to the debate about tithes that had been running through the second decade of the century. The title and subtitle of a book by George Carleton, Bishop of Chichester, gives the general sense of the main issue: *Tithes Examined, and Proved to be due to the Clergy by Divine Right* (1611). Henry Spelman had composed an eloquent account of the sacred origin of tithes and the honourable duty of Christians to maintain the clergy by means of 'God's portion' in his *De Non Temerandis Ecclesiis* of 1613, and Selden's work may have been begun in response to Spelman's claims that tithes were due both by the laws of God and the laws of nature. Other strenuous defences of tithes by clergymen had followed.[32] Tithes were vital to the

---

[31] There were editions of *De Diis Syriis* published at Leiden in 1629, Leipzig in 1662, and Amsterdam in 1680. The work was dedicated to the Dutch classical scholar Daniel Heinsius.

[32] Foulke Robertes, *The Revenue of the Gospel is Tythes* (1616) and Roland Gostwyck, *The Anatomie of Ananias: or God's Censure against Sacrilege* (1616, repr. 1618). Spelman's *Larger Treatise Concerning Tithes* may have been written

maintenance of the clergy, and yet increasingly tithes were being alienated from the clergy into secular hands.[33] To limit the spread of lay impropriations and to affirm the sanctity of tithes by arguing that they were due by the law of God was the aim of many clergymen who felt that the steady despoliation of Church properties and revenues that had gone on since the Reformation must be stopped and reversed. But Selden as a common lawyer was not friendly towards any revival of ecclesiastical power, and was, as we have noted, essentially a secularist, wary of all divine-right arguments, whether they related to kingship, episcopacy, or tithes, because he believed they had no demonstrable legal basis, and tended towards the advancement of arbitrary power. He intended in his *Historie* to set down the known facts about tithing: its origins, its spread, its status in different societies and the transmission of the practice down to modern times. He was careful in his Preface to insist on his neutrality in a subject clouded by 'malice, ignorance and jealousy'. He protests that his book was not written 'to prove that tithes are not due by the law of God, not to prove that lay hands may still enjoy appropriation; in summe, not at all against the maintenance of the clergy'.[34] His aim, he declares, is 'but to give other light to the practice and doubts of the present' by a recitation of factual detail. He has no intention of disputing the divine right of tithes: that is 'wholly a point of divinity', only 'fit to be meddled with by professed divines'. Too often, he claims, these divines overlook the historical part while arguing about the biblical precedents. His book (dedicated to Cotton) will 'remaine as a furnisht Armorie for such as inquire about this Ecclesiastique Revenue'.[35]

There was something slightly disingenuous about this presentation, for to lay out the historical data concerning tithes was in effect to damage the strength of the clergy's case by showing up the disparate customs and discontinuous practice of tithing. The subject was ideally suited to Selden's kind of antiquarian research,

around this time too. D. R. Woolf believes that Selden was inspired by the model of Joseph Scaliger's discourse on tithes, *Diatriba de Decimis*, published in *Opuscula Varia*, ed. Isaac Casaubon (Paris, 1610). Woolf, *The Idea of History*, 217.

[33] See Christopher Hill, *The Economic Problems of the Church* (Oxford, 1956), 77–167, for an account of the loss of tithes to the Church in the early seventeenth century. [34] Selden, *The Historie of Tithes* (1618), A3v.

[35] Ibid. p. vi.

for it involved forays into that no man's land between history and traditional beliefs, and touched on the customs of nations and conflicts between civil law and canon law. It enabled Selden to engage in his favourite method of trawling through a subject from the earliest possible time down the centuries to the present in order to document its growth and change, and establish facts and practices that would be at variance with what was commonly believed in his own time. This method entailed the careful use of chronology, and chronology would be aided by his principle of 'synchronism' which would ensure that documents studied belonged to the relevant period and so might be relied on for evidence. Selden was also able to apply his skills in philology, the precise scrutiny of key words and terms in their original language and linguistic context in order to determine as far as possible their exact meaning. Philology is not here the handmaiden of antiquarian studies, as Camden might have believed, but 'the only fit wife that can be found for the most learned of the Gods' (Mercury), a wife who, attended by 'Curious Diligence and Watchfull Industrie, discovers to us often from her raised tower of judgement many hidden Truths'.[36]

Selden asserts his scholarly authority immediately in his opening discussion of the biblical basis of tithes, which can be traced back to Abraham's tribute to Melchizedek upon the redemption of his nephew Lot. The simple statement of Abraham's payment, 'And he gave him tithes of all' (Genesis 14: 20), is subjected to intense linguistic and legal scrutiny. What does 'all' comprehend, in the context of the events of Genesis? The spoils of war, or his possessions? If the latter, does it relate only to living, growing things that come from God? Selden moves into Hebrew in order to get a better grip on the phrase, and then brings in Jewish commentators on the passage. He looks at Syriac and Arabic translations and their implications. The brief verse is open to a bewildering range of interpretation, and the argument is carefully moved by Selden away from the simple claims of divine right to the customary laws of nations.[37] He enquires into the practice of

---

[36] Selden, *The Historie of Tithes*, p. xix. The marginal note here directs the reader to the fifth-century writer Martianus Capella, 'De Nuptiis Philologiae et Mercurii', and also to Quintilian's 'Orator'.

[37] Selden argues that it is not at all clear that tithes were imposed upon mankind by divine law. The duty of tithes was not plainly enjoined by God as one of his

tithing in the nations of the ancient world, and discovers it to be widespread but various. He probes into such questions as to whom tithes were paid, and for what purpose, and whether voluntarily or by law. Tithing is shown to be not necessarily a religious custom, for states have received tithes as well as churches. The bad news for the clergy is that Selden can find no evidence that tithes were paid to the Church in the first four centuries of its existence. The Church fathers of the fourth and fifth centuries, Ambrose, Augustine, and Jerome, put the case for tithes as a proper way of maintaining churches, but in late antiquity the custom was only fitful and intermittent, and very often, these taxes were paid voluntarily. As a coherent system of financing the clergy, tithing did not develop until the time of Charlemagne, and then gradually spread across northern Europe during the next four hundred years. In this period, the claim that tithes were due by divine right came to be repeated until it achieved a status in canon law. Selden presents the universal system of tithing that developed throughout Europe after 1200 as a triumph of papal policy then beginning to enlarge its domination over all the nations of the West. Selden's argument here has been deftly summarized by Paul Christianson: 'tithes belonging of right to the parish priest had spread across Europe as a well-planned programme of legal innovation by the papacy, involving conversion of tithes from voluntary to ones due by customary right, and pressure on lay rulers to embed the general collection of tithes into secular law'.[38]

In the case of England, Selden can attest that tithes were well established by mid-Saxon times, and he provides an extended account of pronouncements concerning them, their scope, and their application to churches and monasteries. To this end, he uses a number of Saxon manuscripts of charters and chronicles from Cotton's library, working easily with the language as he shows the intermittent prevalence of tithes and notes when regulations relating to tithes begin to appear in the civil law of the Saxon kingdoms. (In an act of scholarly benevolence, Selden includes a

commandments, or as a direct order such as 'Thou shalt not suffer a witch to live', and the other laws and ordinances given by God to Moses in Genesis 21–3.

[38] Christianson, 'Young John Selden', 303. Another helpful examination of Selden's *Historie of Tithes* appears in Woolf, *The Idea of History*, 217–35.

valuable digression on the origins of parishes in Saxon England.[39]) However, Selden can demonstrate that the regular parochial payment of tithes only began in the reign of Henry III, and so was a fairly recent development in historical terms, in spite of the conventional clerical assumptions that tithing was an immemorial custom that had grown up with the Church in the West.

Selden wrote as a common lawyer entering the grounds of canon law, and he had a cynical view of canon lawyers. He regarded them as motivated by ecclesiastical priorities, and devoted to the enlargement of Church influence, Catholic or Protestant. Too often they invoked the cloudy privileges of divine law in defence of their actions, privileges that the sceptically-minded Selden considered chimerical. In his long study of medieval legal practice in Chapter 7, he had viewed the struggles between common lawyers and canon lawyers and seen that now one side prevailed, now the other. He observed, for example, that the ecclesiastical lawyers of the later twelfth and thirteenth centuries, supported by intensifying papal pressures, had been so much in the ascendant that they had managed to insinuate the payment of tithes as a regular duty into the common laws of the realm; but the case could be altered as the balance of power shifted. 'The laity at pleasure commonly limited the canon law, especially where it toucht their dignities and possessions.' Since tithes had got into the common laws, they could be 'altered by any change of regulations enacted by statute'. He concluded that canon law 'in such things as are not merely spiritual, is always governed and limited (as with us) by those common laws'. So, in Selden's judgement, the clergy had no right to tithes by divine law, but were entitled to them by the common law of the land, which could be varied or rescinded by the authority of the King in Parliament, like any other laws. The drift of Selden's book was towards Erastianism, the conviction that the secular powers of the state should have effective control over ecclesiastical affairs.

---

[39] This section, chapter 9 of the *Historie*, provides an excellent example of the importance of philology to Selden's analysis of historical change. He shows how the word 'parochia' originally meant a province or a bishop's jurisdictional area, to which tithes were sometimes paid in late antiquity. The term gradually became applied to parishes in the modern sense as these developed in mid-Saxon times, as churches became more numerous, and priests became resident. 'If parishes themselves developed historically, and the word "parochia" had changed its meaning, how then could tithes have always been paid parochially?' (Woolf, *The Idea of History*, 228).

The outrage amongst churchmen that greeted the publication of *The Historie of Tithes* was tremendous and heartfelt. Selden was hauled up before the Court of High Commission, and summoned before the King to explain his intentions in casting doubt on tithes by divine right. His old friend Lancelot Andrewes came to his defence, but to no avail; the book was suppressed, and the author obliged to issue a letter of apology for his 'error' in publishing it, and in questioning the sanctity of tithes. Coals of fire were heaped on Selden by churchmen as they reaffirmed their convictions about tithes due by divine right: three books appeared within three years in which Selden was denounced for his sacrilegious attitudes.[40] He was bound by the terms of his apology not to respond, and James warned him that he would be thrown into prison if he retaliated. Selden had remarked in his Preface to the book that there is a tendency in society to oppose the extension of knowledge 'by such as laboured that Ignorance might still continue in her Triumph', and now he saw his opinion proved correct.[41] The combined opposition of the King and leading churchmen on a sensitive issue concerning divine right sharpened his natural dislike of prerogatives and of ecclesiastical influence in what he considered to be civil matters. Anthony Wood, writing a brief account of Selden much later in the century, thought that 'he never came off in any of his undertakings with more loss of credit' than in his débâcle over *The Historie of Tithes*, and 'he did never after affect the bishops and clergy, or cordially approve their calling, though many ways were tried to gain him to the church's interest'.[42] Selden had effectively

---

[40] These were James Semphill, *Sacrilege Sacredly Handled* (1619), Richard Tillesley, *Animadversions upon Mr. Selden's History of Tithes* (1619), and Richard Montagu, *Diatribae upon the First Part of the Late History of Tithes* (1621). William Sclater's *The Quaestion of Tythes Revised* came out in 1623, and Stephen Nettles' *An Answer to the Jewish Part of the History of Tithes* followed in 1625. Richard Perrot followed up with *Jacob's Vowe, or the True History of Tithes* (1627). Woolf remarks that '*The Historie of Tithes* set off the biggest historical controversy in England since Polydore Vergil had called Geoffrey of Monmouth a liar' (230). The controversy descended at times to scurrility: Dr Tillesley provoked Selden by remarking that his name spelt backwards was 'needless'. Selden retorted that it was 'needles' to prick doctors with, and that the anagram of Tillesley's name was, 'I tell lies'. (George W. Johnson, *Memoirs of John Selden* (1835), 60.)

[41] *The Historie of Tithes*, p. xvi. Selden notes in this context the hostility that greeted Erasmus's publication of the New Testament in Greek. 'Light from Antiquitie' is not welcome to people who dwell in the penumbra of common and received opinions.   [42] Wood, *Athenae Oxonienses*, ii. 181.

hit the rock of Church censorship with this book, and the Church establishment prevailed over him.

The rebuff he had received seems to have deterred him from publishing further antiquarian research for several years. He attempted to put his learning at the service of the King and nation in 1619 by writing a history of maritime jurisdiction that argued the rights of nations to exercise dominion over their territorial waters, a work intended to counter Hugo Grotius's *Mare Liberum* of 1609, which had asserted the freedom of the seas to ships of all nations. British protectionist policies concerning shipping and fishing as they developed in the 1610s required a legal defence for sovereignty over home seas, which Selden supplied, under the title 'Mare Clausum'. But James and Buckingham decided for reasons of international policy not to approve it for the press, to Selden's irritation, and it remained in manuscript until 1636, when, reworked, it was published with a dedication to Charles I at a time when Selden wished to ingratiate himself with the crown, and when King Charles needed a tough statement of maritime rights as he tried to strengthen the navy.[43] Selden's interest in maritime law may have been aroused by his friendship with Samuel Purchas, who had gathered together narratives of travels and voyages of the English nation to form an extension to the work of Richard Hakluyt.[44]

Given the character of his friends, it is not altogether surprising to find that Selden became a member of the Virginia Company, and that his legal expertise was called on to provide advice about fishing rights and the maritime rights of the colony. Indeed, he was eventually asked to join the committee charged to draft a constitution for Virginia.[45] His involvement in the Company as

[43] *Mare Clausum* was translated into English by Marchamont Nedham in 1652 for the benefit of the Commonwealth regime, under the title *Of the Dominion, or Ownership of the Sea*. Some of Selden's assertions of maritime sovereignty were incorporated in the Navigation Act of 1651.

[44] It was from Purchas that Selden acquired the greatest treasure in his library, the Codex Mendoza, a Mexican pictographic manuscript that had been prepared for the Emperor Charles V. This had been captured by French privateers; Hakluyt eventually obtained it from the French King's geographer royal, and he willed it to Purchas when he died in 1616. Purchas left it to Selden in 1626, and it finally went with Selden's books and manuscripts to the Bodleian Library. See Berkowitz, *Selden's Formative Years*, 29.

[45] The other members of the committee were Thomas Roe, Christopher Brooke, Edward Herbert, and Philip Jermyn. The constitution was issued in 1621. For

a legal consultant seems to have been a principal cause of his imprisonment in 1621, when King James moved to restrain the Virginia Company's activities, the climax of a protracted confrontation between the two parties. Once in prison, Selden turned to antiquarian research for solace. He spent his time editing and commenting on the *Historia Novorum* of Eadmer, the Canterbury monk whose chronicle, written in the early twelfth century, provided a valuable account of English affairs from 1066 to 1120, and contained information about the Danish invasions of the ninth century. This edition, published in 1623 as *Spicelegium in Eadmer* and dedicated to John Williams, Lord Keeper of the Privy Seal, filled a notable gap in the published chronicle literature between Bede and William of Malmesbury. Also during his sojourn in prison, Selden turned his attention to a scarcely known area of scholarship, Byzantine history, and translated the *Alexiad* of Anna Comnena.

Scholarship could bring tribulation, or allay the miseries of captivity; it could also be accompanied by excitement. The most animated book that Selden wrote was the one he least expected to write, *Marmora Arundelliana* (1628), which was precipitated by the unanticipated arrival in London of a consignment of Greek statuary and inscribed stones, gathered by the Earl of Arundel's agents in the eastern Mediterranean. The Earl was the leading aristocratic collector of paintings and antiquities in England, his collections even surpassing those of the King's until Charles acquired the Mantua treasures in 1627.[46] He had been the pioneer collector of classical statuary, and already by 1619 had a sufficiently impressive number to commission Inigo Jones to design an Italianate gallery for their display. Arundel's passion for antique marbles caused him to employ English diplomatic representatives and merchants to scour the Greek islands and the coast of Turkey for statues and other pieces of antiquity that could be brought home. The cargo that arrived in January 1627 was the reward of his long-distance prospecting. Arundel was a close friend of Selden, as also of Cotton. Antiquarian interests bound them together, and

Selden's involvement in the Virginia Company, see Berkowitz, *Selden's Formative Years*, 55–61.

[46] For Arundel as a connoisseur and collector, see David Howarth, *Lord Arundel and his Circle* (New Haven, 1985).

Arundel, as the senior earl of England and Earl Marshal, naturally valued the expertise in genealogy, heraldry, and titles that the others possessed. Politically too they were allies, often to be found in opposition to Buckingham's policies and out of favour with the King. Arundel acted as Selden's political patron and protector, and on two occasions Selden sat as an MP in seats controlled by Arundel.

It is understandable, therefore, that Selden was one of the first to be alerted to the thrilling appearance of these Greek remains in London. The Latin of the Preface to *Marmora Arundelliana* still rings with the memory of how Cotton had rushed round to Selden at night to tell him of the arrival of the shipment, urging him to come and help unriddle the secrets of these stones, 'ad Graeca illa arcana eruenda'. So, at daybreak on the morrow, there was Selden in the gardens of Arundel House where the treasures lay: 'Illucescente die crastino, convenimus triumviri in hortis Arundellianis.' The other scholars whom Arundel and Cotton had called up were Patrick Young the royal librarian and Richard James, who was Cotton's librarian and a poly-linguist, 'vir multi-iugae doctrinae studiique indefatigabilis', as Selden describes him. In that cold dawn they went over the broken inscriptions and 'first obtained a knowledge of the Decrees of the Smyrnans and their treaty with the Magnesians'.[47] But the great prize was a large fragment, now known as the Parian Marble, bearing an extensive chronological inscription relating to Athenian history. Selden and his friends soon realized that some of the events detailed on this stone could be cross-referenced with biblical events, and that they now had information that would enable them to begin the task of synchronizing long stretches of Hebrew and Greek history.

One of the great dilemmas of Renaissance scholarship was the difficulty of establishing a reliable chronology for the nations of the ancient world, and correlating the histories of the significant peoples. Even with the wealth of detail given in the books of the Old Testament, it was hard to put together any firm chronology for Jewish history. When did Abraham live, when was the building of the Temple, when was the captivity in Egypt, and who was then the Pharaoh? Greek historians were highly specific in their detailing of events in the literate centuries, but this clarity shaded into

---

[47] Preface in *Marmora Arundelliana* (1628) (my translation).

vagueness before 500 BC. The Greek states interacted with Persia from time to time, but the Persian dynasties were obscure. The Egyptians were even more obscure, and their language impenetrable. How did early Roman history match with Greek and Jewish events? The situation was complicated because different nations had different ways of computing time, and linked their dates to reigns, or to tenures of priesthood, to archonships, Olympiads, or senatorial periods. The whole scholarly endeavour to recover the ancient world in all the diversity of its interacting states was prejudiced by the lack of properly synchronized histories. The most eminent master of chronology in Britain was James Ussher, whose computations are described elsewhere in this book, and Selden consulted steadily with him over the problems raised by the data of the Parian Marble, but the achievement of clarifying the chronology of Greek history and correlating it with biblical events was essentially Selden's, and he presented it in *Marmora Arundelliana*. He established a 'Canon Chronicus' of Greek history, beginning in 1582 BC with Cecrops, King of the Athenians, and terminating in the reign of Philip of Macedon. He was able, for example, to propose a date of 1529 BC for the Flood of Deucalion, King of Lycoria, which he regarded as the Greek record of Noah's Flood. As one looks at Selden's tables, the sense is very strong of the jigsaw of antiquity fitting together at last.

As a humanist scholar, Selden was characteristically attracted to the inscribed stones among the Arundel Marbles; he expressed little interest in the statues. *Marmora Arundelliana* is a general descriptive catalogue of the collection of antique statuary, carvings, and inscriptions that Arundel had assembled in the gardens of his residence on the banks of the Thames, but it was the inscriptions and their historical implications that occupied most of Selden's attention. The decipherment of ancient inscriptions had a long and illustrious history, to which he was honoured to add, and his book transcribed and commented on twenty-nine Greek inscriptions and many in Latin, as well as a group of Romano-British inscriptions, some of which had been given to the Earl by William Camden. A particular curiosity to which he drew attention was a number of stones inscribed with Hebrew found in the repairing of Aldersgate and now in Arundel's possession. To a less sober mind than Selden's, these would have been seized on as evidence of the presence of Noah's offspring, or declared to be a sign that the Phoenicians had founded London. Selden, however, was prepared to take a shorter view, and suggested that they were part of a synagogue, or fragments of a Jewish grave, from the late twelfth or early thirteenth century, evidence of a colony of Jews in Norman times.

Marmora Arundelliana was aimed at a European audience of classical scholars, and it was received with widespread admiration, adding to the international reputation Selden had already established with *De Diis Syriis*.[48] The book also advanced the Earl of Arundel's reputation as a collector, antiquary and patron. In the 1630s the Earl would form plans to issue a great catalogue of his collections of paintings, statuary, and *objets d'art*, with engravings of the principal treasures, but this project was never carried through, and Selden's volume remained the chief vehicle of Arundel's fame to the world of scholars and virtuosi.[49]

During the 1630s, Selden's antiquarian interests were directed increasingly towards the laws and government of the Jews. He published a long sequence of works concerning their social institutions, legal codes and practices, and their religious discipline.[50] He became one of the great European Hebraists, an international authority on ancient Judaism. His most important work *De Jure Naturali et Gentium Juxta Disciplinam Ebraeorum* (1640) presented Selden as a legal philosopher concerned to investigate the origins of civil society. He argued that the laws of

---

[48] The great French antiquary Nicholas Fabri de Peiresc noted in a letter of 1629 that *Marmora Arundelliana* was already circulating in Rome, and that he had read it in Paris as soon as it came out. While admiring Selden's scholarship, he regrets a certain lack of compassionate appreciation in the author towards those who had retrieved the marbles, feeling that Selden should have paid due tribute 'à celuy qui les avoit arraché des mains des barbares avec tant de sollicitudes et de dangers', i.e. William Petty and his associates. *Lettres de Peiresc*, ed. P. Tamizey de Larroque (Paris, 1888–98), v. 328.

[49] Selden's book on the Arundel Marbles was a timely act of preservation, for a generation later Francis Junius was complaining to Dugdale that many of the pieces had been stolen or cut up in the Commonwealth years, a 'desperate losse of such inestimable antiquities' (Letter of 21 Apr. 1656 in *Sir William Dugdale*, ed. Hamper, 307.) The Parian Marble was broken up, and part of it was used to patch a chimney at Arundel House in the time of the Civil War. (William Hales, *A New Analysis of Chronology* (1830), i. 128.)

[50] Selden's later works were *De Successionibus ad Leges Ebraeorum in Bona Defunctiorum* (1631); *De Successione in Pontificatum Hebraeorum* (1638); *De Jure Naturali et Gentium Juxta Disciplinam Ebraeorum* (1640); *Uxor Ebraica* (1646); *De Synedriis et Praefecturis Iuridicis Veterum Ebraeorum* (1655).

nature formed the basis of the civil law amongst the Hebrews, and dwelt at length on the origin and nature of authority and the limits of obedience, in a way not dissimilar to Thomas Hobbes's project in *Leviathan* (1651), though he centered his work much more than Hobbes in the paradigmatic experience of the Jewish nation. These later works of Selden lie beyond the scope of this book. They show, however, a continuing belief that the record of ancient societies furnishes material of permanent value in the unending search to know the nature of the laws that operate through all societies, and the extent to which men are bound by them.

In the end, it was as a common lawyer that Selden wished to be remembered. 'I. Seldenus I. C. hic situs est' is the only inscription on his tombstone in Temple Church (I. C. for Jurisconsult), and the lack of any Christian sentiment may be indicative of his secular cast of mind. As Anthony Wood remarked, when Archbishop Ussher preached his funeral sermon, he 'did not, or could not, say much of his sound principles in religion'. The Master of the Temple said on that occasion, 'if learning could have kept a man alive, our brother had not died.'[51] Selden went to unusual depths to escape from the world when he died in 1654, ordering his grave to be dug ten feet deep or more, and his coffin covered with 'a huge black marble stone of great thicknesse', over which was turned an arch of brick, and then earth piled on that, with a memorial slab on the surface. It was almost as if he doubted the Last Judgement, and feared only the lawlessness of men.

---

[51] Wood, *Athenae Oxonienses*, ii. 181.

5
James Ussher

Selden's funeral sermon was preached by his lifelong friend James Ussher, the Irish theologian and antiquarian, who declared that 'he looked upon the deceased as so great a scholar, that himself was scarce worthy to carry his books after him.' In truth, however, they were of a similar stature, towering figures of scholarship, 'the great Goliaths of Literature' as Anthony Wood called them.[1] What Selden was to legal antiquarianism, so Ussher was to ecclesiastical antiquarianism, each a master of prodigious learning, and as familiar with the most ancient sources of his subject as of its subsequent development through the ages until his own time. But the current of Selden's researches flowed towards a more secularized world, whereas Ussher primarily directed his energies to consolidating the position of the reformed Church in a world where religious issues remained paramount. Ussher's work was in fact the last great flowering of Reformation scholarship in Britain, in the tradition of John Foxe, John Jewel, and Matthew Parker, and like them, he was concerned to demonstrate the truth and antiquity of the Protestant religion against the arguments of Roman Catholic antagonists. He was a major participant in the intellectual war between the Roman and Protestant Churches that persisted for a century after the Reformation, and for that reason, much of his writing was in Latin, for he addressed an international audience. Yet it was his distinction to remain an admired and respected scholar even amongst his Catholic opponents, for the integrity of his beliefs and the quality of his scholarship alike impressed themselves on his contemporaries of all parties.

Ussher had been born in Dublin in 1581, into a family divided by Protestant and Catholic allegiances. His grandfather and an uncle were among the initiators of the new university in Dublin, Trinity

---

[1] 'Life of Gerard Langbaine' in Wood, *Athenae Oxonienses*, ii. Selden had earlier acclaimed Ussher as 'usque ad miraculum doctus' ('learned to a miracle') in the Preface to *Marmora Arundelliana*.

College, founded in the 1590s to provide a firm Calvinist education for the Irish gentry; another uncle, Richard Stanyhurst, was converted by the Jesuits, and became a prominent Catholic controversialist, based in the Spanish Netherlands. Eventually, Ussher's mother converted to Catholicism. Being himself one of the earliest students at Trinity, he grew up in an atmosphere of religious debate, fostered by the strenuous Protestantism of the new college and by the divisions within his family. According to his most detailed biographer, Charles Richard Elrington, the Professor of Divinity at Trinity College who edited his works over the period 1847–64, Ussher's intellectual career was shaped by his need to respond to certain provocative theological works that he read during his student years. Foremost among these were *A Fortresse of the Faith* by the English Catholic Thomas Stapleton, published in 1565, *De Quattuor Summis Imperiis*, 'Of the Four Great Empires' (1556), by the German Protestant Johannes Sleidanus, and his uncle Richard Stanyhurst's 'Historie of Ireland'. Stapleton's book attempted 'to establish the antiquity of the Romish faith and the novelty of the reformed Church, which he professed to maintain by the whole current of tradition transmitted through the works of the Fathers'.[2] Stanyhurst had written about the early Christian history of Ireland, laying out how St Patrick had brought Ireland to the faith of Rome; his 'Description of Ireland' and 'Historie of Ireland' had been printed in the first volume of Holinshed's *Chronicles* in 1577. Sleidanus had described the grand millenarian scheme favoured by Protestants in which the course of history would run through the four monarchies of Assyria, Persia, Greece, and Rome, as the prophet Daniel and the Book of Revelation foretold, and culminate in the fifth monarchy of Christ which would endure for a thousand years, when he would reign over the true faithful, who had been gathered into the reformed churches of Europe. Stapleton had constructed the most substantial case for the Roman Church as the only authentic guardian of the true religion, preserved in all its integrity since the time of Christ; his work had been specifically directed to English Protestant readers to break their confidence in their new national Church. Reaction to the various themes of these

---

[2] C. R. Elrington, *The Life of the Most Rev. James Ussher, D.D.* (Dublin 1848), 8–9, and Hugh Trevor-Roper, 'James Ussher, Archbishop of Armagh' in *Catholics, Anglicans and Puritans* (London, 1987), 126–7.

books would shape Ussher's researches for years, for he had a mind that relished the challenge of controversy.

Ussher was an instinctive scholar, a notable linguist, and a passionate bibliophile; he was fascinated by the study of religious antiquities from an early age. While he was an undergraduate, he applied himself determinedly to Greek and Hebrew. During the same years he developed an enduring curiosity about the time-scale of divine history, and in order to satisfy it, compiled a chronology of the Old Testament, in Latin, as far as the Book of Kings. Questions of chronology would preoccupy him all his life, motivated as he was by a scholarly desire to clarify the dates of ancient history in relation to the biblical record, and to a lesser degree to provide reliable data for the computation of the timetable of the latter days.

Shortly after graduating in 1597, he embarked on the daunting task that he set himself as a necessary preparative to a life of controversy as a defender of the Protestant faith: to read through the entire works of the Church Fathers. He carried out this programme of study over eighteen years, but he was never able to realize the ambitious scheme that developed from this mission, the publication of the whole corpus of patristic writings in a 'Biblioteca Theologica'; other projects demanded his time. A minute knowledge of the history, theology, liturgy, and canons of the early Church was indispensable if one wished to make an appearance on the polemical scheme in the sixteenth or early seventeenth century, for the argument from antiquity was the one that was held to be most compelling in any debate about the succession of the true Church or in questions about the approximation of contemporary religious practice to that of primitive Christianity. Ussher was ordained in 1601, and preached his first sermon on the day that the Protestant forces defeated the Spanish invasion of Ireland at Kinsale. The threat of the Catholic Counter-Reformation was not just a war of ideas; it was prosecuted with swords as well as words.

A most unexpected consequence of the English victory at Kinsale and the suppression of the Irish uprising that accompanied the Spanish landing was that, out of the booty taken, the army leaders gave £1800 to Trinity College for the purchase of books to strengthen that academic 'Fortress of the Faith'. Ussher and a colleague were sent to London to buy books, and on this occasion he met Sir Thomas Bodley who was engaged on a similar enterprise, laying in books for his new foundation at Oxford. The London booksellers held considerable stocks of manuscripts in those days, as well as books published on the Continent and out-of-print works. Possibly Ussher also made the acquaintance of William Camden and Robert Cotton on this first visit to London; he certainly was familiar with them in 1606, the next time he came, and from then on, their antiquarian interests bound them together in friendship and co-operation. It seems to have been in 1606 that Camden and Cotton suggested to Ussher that he might take up the task of writing an ecclesiastical history of Britain that would demonstrate the ancient independence of the Church in Britain from that in Rome, a work that the English antiquaries had been contemplating for some years. Ussher seems willingly to have engaged himself, with consequences we shall trace.[3] Camden also asked Ussher to furnish him with material relating to Ireland for his revision of *Britannia*, especially information about St Patrick's mission, about the foundation and history of Dublin, and about the antiquities of the country as a whole. Ussher responded copiously, and also sent Camden details of manuscripts of the early chroniclers Gildas and Nennius that were unknown to Camden, along with some account of their lives. Information about ancient Ireland was hard to come by, for there were few scholars or gentleman antiquaries over there, and Camden expressed his gratitude to Ussher in the 1607 edition of *Britannia*, praising his 'diligence and learning' and admiring 'a degree of knowledge and judgement above his years'. It was no doubt his association with the eminent Camden that gave an edge to his curiosity about Irish antiquity, a curiosity already aroused by the writings of his uncle, Richard Stanyhurst. The first fruits of his independent researches was a treatise that clarified the meaning and legal status of an obscure form of land tenure in the Celtic Church, and its relation to obsolete ecclesiastical offices. 'Of the original and first institution of Corbes, Herenachs and Termon Lands' was the kind of compilation that would have entranced the members of the Society of Antiquaries in its early phase, when it was much preoccupied with the origins of ranks, titles, offices, and customs. The treatise may indeed have been read at the Society before its suspension, though we have no record of this: only the title suggests that it was a work

---

[3] See Sharpe, *Sir Robert Cotton*, 33–4, and 107–8.

written with the Society in mind. Ussher later sent it to Sir Henry Spelman who incorporated its substance in his *Glossarium* (1626), offering the usual complimentary credit to the author: 'Literarum insignis Pharus'—a lighthouse indeed shining in the dark places of Irish antiquity.

With his regular visits to England, Ussher became widely known in antiquarian and ecclesiastical circles. John Selden and Sir Henry Savile came to be amongst his close friends. (Savile, the Provost of Eton College, had produced an outstanding edition of the works of St Chrysostom (1612), a paradigm of what Ussher himself hoped to do for all the Church Fathers.) He was in demand as a preacher in London, and soon came to the attention of King James, who, understandably, looked on him with great favour for his learning, and for his sound Calvinist beliefs. James promoted him in the Church, raising him ultimately to be Archbishop of Armagh, the Primate of Ireland, in 1625. James set a high value on scholarly debate as a means of vindicating the Protestant position against Catholic attacks that insisted that the reformed churches were novel and erroneous in doctrine, schismatic in tendency, and no part of the true Church. Ussher's erudition could be marshalled both for attack and defence, and James urged him to take the field against the Catholics. He was even willing to relieve Ussher of his episcopal and professorial duties in Ireland to allow him to labour in English libraries for the defence of the faith. In 1621, the King wrote to the Lord Deputy and Council of Ireland to announce that he had granted Ussher an indefinite sabbatical for research purposes. James wished 'to employ him in the collecting of Antiquities of the British Church before and since the Christian faith was received by the English nation . . . which being published might tend to the furtherance of belief and good learning'.[4]

One result of this encouragement was the lengthy harangue *An Answer to a Challenge made by a Jesuit in Ireland* (1625), a broadside attack on Catholic doctrine. More significantly for the advancement of antiquarian learning was *A Discourse of the Religion anciently professed by the Irish and British* (1623 and 1631). This was in part an attempt to wrest control of Irish history from the hands of the Jesuits, such as Stanyhurst, Campion, and

---

[4] Quoted in Elrington, *Life*, 63.

O'Sullevan,[5] partly too a demonstration of the pure Christianity that was early carried to Ireland and remained unvitiated by Romish corruptions, virtually until the Norman conquest in the twelfth century. 'Though the saving truth of God was delivered by the prophets and the apostles' many Irish still

embrace and with a most strange kind of credulity entertain those lying legends wherewith their monks and friars have polluted the religion and lives of our ancient saints. I do not deny ... that corruptions did creep in little by little, before the devil was let loose to procure that seduction which prevailed so generally in these last times, but as far as I can collect by such records of the former ages as have come into my hands (either manuscript or printed), the religion professed by the ancient bishops, priests and monks and other Christians of this land was for substance the very same with that which now by public authority is maintained therein, against the foreign doctrine brought in thither in latter times by the Bishop of Rome's followers. I speak of the more substantial points of doctrine, that are in controversy between the Church of Rome and us at this day, by which only we must judge whether of both sides hath departed from the religion of our ancestors.[6]

This statement clearly shows how Ussher intended his antiquarian research to bear upon the live issues of faith in his own day. In addition to strengthening the intellectual foundations of the Church in Ireland, he hoped to persuade the educated Catholics, most notably the priests, and then the Irish gentry, that their position was untenable. The ideal reader for this kind of treatise was someone like John Donne, who for a decade at the end of Elizabeth's reign and the beginning of James's read through a vast body of divinity to

[5] Stanyhurst's 'Description of Ireland', included in Holinshed's *Chronicles* of 1577, was on the whole supportive of the Elizabethan colonial enterprise, and moderately censorious of the Gaelic Irish and their ways. In 1584, he published *De Rebus in Hibernia Gestis* in Antwerp, where he was a religious exile. This later work displays a much greater sympathy with the native Irish, and emphasizes the importance of the Catholic faith to the Irish identity. Stanyhurst's 'Description' was heavily indebted to the 'History of Ireland' written by the English Jesuit Edmund Campion, who had lived in Dublin for a period in the early 1570s with Stanyhurst, his friend from Oxford days. Campion's work was published by James Ware in 1633, but Ussher might have seen it in manuscript. Philip O'Sullevan Beare's *Historiae Catholicae Ibernica Compendium* was published in Lisbon in 1621, and his hostile *De Religionis Ibernicae Casibus, de Anglo Haereticae Ecclesiae Sectus* in 1629.
[6] *The Whole Works of the Most Rev. James Ussher*, ed. C. R. Elrington (Dublin, 1847–64), iv. 238–9.

decide on the conflicting claims of the churches to preserve the light of the true faith in their sanctuaries. Donne was susceptible to the appeal to antiquity: as he wrote in Satire III, 'though truth and falsehood be | Near twins, yet truth a little elder is; | Be busy to seek her', and that search involved tracing the streams of religion back to the source to see which flowed from the most ancient springs. He would have applauded the careful tracing of the course of doctrine and liturgical usage through the centuries. Donne did in fact change his religion as a result of the evidence put forward by the Church of England, but how many readers like Donne were there? Only a few hundred in the British Isles, one imagines. The important task, as far as Ussher was concerned, was to convince the leading men of the state and the clergy, who by their influence or their eloquence could make a larger alteration in society. English Protestants looked with admiration at the feat of William Laud in out-arguing the Jesuit Fisher in 1619, and so winning the assent of the Marquis of Buckingham to the doctrine of the Church of England. Triumphs such as these were rare, but they were famous victories when they occurred, and raised morale immensely. But for every soul gained for Protestantism by open debate, ten were won to Rome by the whispered conferences of the Jesuits, who worked so well in private. In spite of this discouragement, Protestant divines remained convinced that the case for the reformed churches rested on historical foundations. Conformity with ancient practices had to be established, for the whole justification of reform was that it recovered the purity of faith and worship that the primitive Church conserved after the death of Christ and when the Holy Ghost was a sustaining presence in the councils of the Church. Faith and the forms of worship were inextricably involved.

Ussher enlarged his potential audience by demonstrating at the outset of his treatise that the religion of the ancient Irish 'differed little or nothing from that which was maintained by their neighbours the Britons'. Using the earliest possible sources, notably Gildas and Columbanus from the sixth century, Adamnanus from the seventh, and Sedulius Scotus, a ninth-century Irish scholar who knew Greek and who seems to have based his worship on the Greek New Testament rather than the Latin Vulgate, Ussher drew a picture of a Church using the Holy Scriptures in an almost uncontaminated form, adhering to the doctrines concerning predestination, grace, mercy, faith, works, justification, and salvation that were close to the pronouncements of St Augustine of Hippo, the touchstone of orthodox theology, and using a liturgy and celebrating communion in ways that were similar to the practice of the Church of England in the seventeenth century. He was able to print a specimen of the ancient Irish liturgy, 'so I have seen it set down in an ancient fragment, written well nigh nine hundred years since, remaining now in the library of Sir Robert Cotton, my worthy friend, who can never sufficiently be commended for his extra-ordinary care in preserving all rare monuments of this kind.'[7] The specimen differed greatly from modern Roman usage, but was not dissimilar to the Church of England's practice in Ussher's time. The administration of the sacrament of baptism in Ussher's Church was the same as in the ancient British Church, and as in the old Gallic Church, but the Roman practice had diverged much from the primitive forms. Ussher cited Gildas (also from a fragment in the Cotton Library) to prove that 'Britons were contrary to the whole world, and enemies to Roman customs, as well as in their mass as in their tonsure.'[8] Unlike the Church of Rome, the ancient Church in Britain and Ireland permitted a married clergy; indeed, Ussher admits, the clergy was sometimes polygamous. The monastic life in Ireland, according to Gildas, was holier, more austere and abstinent than that practised by the orders that came in later under papal authority. The distinctive identity of the early Celtic Church in Britain and Ireland is built up in great detail by Ussher.

Ussher refuted the cherished fable of St Patrick's Purgatory which held that the saint had experienced a vision that assured him that all those who visited a certain sanctuary in a spirit of penitence and faith would be granted indulgence for their sins. By close reading of the earliest writers, he deduced that the doctrine of purgatory did not exist in the first centuries of Christianity. Not all was sweetness and light, however, in those early days. Heresy had made an unwelcome appearance *circa* 400 from a home-grown source: 'the greatest depressers of God's grace, and the advancers of man's abilities, were Pelagius and Celestius, the one born in Britain, the other in Scotland or Ireland.'[9] Their 'venomous doctrine' asserted that 'in attaining of righteousness everyone was governed by his own will, and received as much as he did merit', and it flourished in

---

[7] *Works*, ed. Elrington 274.   [8] Ibid.   [9] Ibid. 259.

the fifth century and again in seventh-century Ireland until eradicated by firm bishops. Pelagianism had much in common with the Arminianism that was spreading over England in Ussher's own time, and which he detested; it would be comprehensively discussed in his next book on British antiquities. Sufficient for this treatise was the account of how the heresy was defeated by the assertion of the 'sound doctrine' of the first Christian evangelists to Ireland. The remainder of the book describes the steady extension of the spiritual and temporal power of the Pope into Ireland after the eleventh century, although Ussher denies, with evidences, the right of the Pope to any temporal jurisdiction in the country: papal claims to dominion were based on forged documents, he insists. To conclude, in a 'Postscript to the Reader', Ussher declares that his intention has been to 'produce such evidences as might show the agreement that was between our ancestors and us in matters of religion'. He believes that, as a result of his researches, the Church of Rome can no longer sustain its claim to a continuous existence: its doctrine is full of novelties and corruptions, and the reader must recognize that the spirit of the early Church is most responsibly preserved by the present Church of Ireland. To confirm the link between Church history and royal authority, he ends his discourse on the ancient religion of the Irish with an avowal that his research has been done for the approbation of King James, 'to support the rights and pre-eminence united unto his imperial crown'.

Confident of his achievement, Ussher wished to put on record the body of evidence he had used in support of his case. Printed books were available for inspection by those scholars who disagreed with him, especially Catholics; they might check his facts readily. But manuscripts were rare and inaccessible. So in 1632 he published an invaluable collection of letters and documents relating to the early Irish Church that he had discovered in the course of his investigations. Much of the material in *Veterum Epistolarum Hibernicarum Sylloge* had never been published before, and it remains an important source book for the study of early Irish history. The great majority of these documents come from 'the rare treasury' of Sir Robert Cotton's library. Here, *inter alia*, are the Letters of St Patrick, extracts from Nennius and Giraldus Cambrensis relating to Ireland, and rare letters from the seventh century relating to the controversy over the date of Easter that was one of the significant divisions between the Celtic and the Roman churches. The *Sylloge* was also intended to give substance to the tradition, as old as Bede, that Ireland had been a place of learning and literature in the seventh, eighth and ninth centuries. The old trope of Ireland as 'the land of saints and scholars' was better illustrated by Ussher than by any of the patriots of the nineteenth century.

Ussher continued to explore the conditions of the primitive Church in Britain, and his treatise on Irish Christianity was a prelude to a much more ambitious work, *Britannicarum Ecclesiarum Antiquitates,* published in 1639. The vehicle is Latin, no doubt to carry this celebration of the British Church to a Continental audience, but also because so much of the source material used here is in that language. This volume was the culmination of the research that King James had encouraged Ussher to undertake, now dedicated to King Charles. Charles, unlike his father, had little interest in ecclesiastical antiquities, but as the Supreme Governor of the Church of England he was the natural dedicatee of the most scholarly, extensive, and coherent account of the origin and spread of Christianity in Britain that had yet appeared. It was the masterpiece of that kind of nationalistic Church history that Matthew Parker had aspired to write in mid-Elizabethan times, but Ussher had access to a much greater range of documents and sources than Parker, and his sense of the capillary progress of Christianity through Britain was quite unprecedented. He understood the pattern of development across the British Isles as a whole, thanks to his intensive study of the Celtic Church. Ussher took his account up to the end of the seventh century, and he could show that by the time of the arrival of Augustine's mission at the end of the sixth century, the British Isles were thoroughly Christian, and the Celtic Church was animated by an apostolic spirit. He characterized the mission of 597 as one directed primarily to the pagan Saxons of Kent. The *Antiquitates* is a much vaster work than the earlier treatise on the ancient religion of Britain; it goes over the old ground, but gives much greater documentary detail about the growth of the Church and its organization in mainland Britain. Ussher carefully sifts the fables relating to the first contact with the gospel, inclines towards an acceptance of Joseph of Arimathea's mission shortly after the death of Christ, and accepts as genuine the story of King Lucius's conversion in the late second century. He vividly evokes the persecution of the British Christians in the time of Diocletian. By the time of Constantine, he believes the Church was broadly networked across Britain. He applies his scholarship to determine how the various episcopal sees were formed in Britain, and, from the record of Church councils, gives the fullest account yet made of the bishops of the fourth and fifth centuries.

The tone of the book is markedly less anti-Catholic than his earlier study. Now the object of his odium theologicum is the Pelagian heresy, to which he devotes no fewer than six chapters. Pelagius, a fourth-century British Christian based in Rome, had originated a complex of doctrines that spread rapidly amongst the Christians of the fifth century, and proved remarkably tenacious, persisting even as late as the ninth century. Britain was particularly susceptible to this heresy, the features of which were a belief that an individual's will and desire to be saved were instrumental in attaining salvation, that good works as well as faith were efficacious means of salvation, and that Christ's grace was available to all men. St Augustine had refuted Pelagius's liberal dispensation, and had formulated his strict code of predestination which denied that the individual's will had any place at all in the scheme of salvation, the fate of all men having been immutably fore-ordained by God. Augustine's rigid code formed the keystone of Calvinist theology, which had firmly shaped Ussher's own beliefs.[10] In the seventeenth century, the doctrines preached by the Dutch theologian Arminius, which found many followers in England and France, looked to their opponents very much like a revival of Pelagianism. Ussher viewed the spread of Arminianism in England with horror. It had permeated the ecclesiastical hierarchy by the 1630s, encouraged by Archbishop Laud, and it was gaining adherents in the universities. King Charles himself was favourably inclined towards the Arminians, in total contrast to his father. For Ussher, the Arminian threat was more acute than that of Catholic subversion in the 1630s, and his book *Antiquitates* was vehement against it, attacking its original form, Pelagianism, as a most pernicious doctrine. Ussher would have found it difficult to confront the main proponents of Arminianism directly, for he was moderately friendly with Laud and King Charles, and he did not wish to increase the divisions of the Church by a great quarrel

---

[10] Ussher appears to have shifted his ground in the later years of his life towards the liberal position he had so long denied, acknowledging the possibility of universal redemption. See the testimonies to this effect gathered by Elrington in *Life*, 290–6.

among the bishops. In the later 1630s, however, he must have found it hard to celebrate the Church of England as the upholder and preserver of ancient Christian virtue when its topmost branches were infected with the ancient heresy. Antiquarian research gave him the chance to anatomize that heresy, to explicate its errors in detail, recognize the power of its attraction, and demonstrate that the heresy could and must be suppressed by the rigour of orthodox arguments if the Church was to survive as a conduit of the true faith. The ancient British Church had succeeded in freeing itself, and the implication was that the Church of England would not be sound until Arminianism had been driven out.[11]

These historical works of British and Irish antiquity should be seen in company with Ussher's grand surveys of the progress of the true Church in the world. True to his Elizabethan upbringing, he held the conviction that there had always been a visible Church surviving through even the darkest periods of Romish domination. This belief formed part of the panoramic historical scheme, subscribed to with variations by most of the apologists for the reformed Church in the sixteenth century, that interpreted the progression of Christianity in the light of the Book of Revelation. For Ussher, the binding of Satan (Rev. 20: 2), which removes his influence from the world and allows the Church a favourable age in which to develop, occurs with the coming of the Gospel, and may be dated from the birth or death of Christ, or from the ending of the Jewish dispensation with the destruction of the Temple in 70 AD. 'The coming of Antichrist occurs at the end of the first six centuries, and the loosing of Satan at the end of ten centuries', in the reign of one of the eleventh-century popes.[12] Satan loosed and free to deceive the nations once more raged on through the Middle Ages, but the true Church emerged again after 500 years at the time of the Reformation, and its saints would defeat Antichrist, bind Satan again, and prepare the way for the return of Christ and the inauguration of the Millennium. Ussher worked out his version of this scheme in a lengthy book which he published in 1613, at the beginning of his career, and dedicated to King James:

---

[11] See Trevor-Roper's discussion of this theme in 'James Ussher', 144–7.

[12] Elrington, *Life*, 36. Elrington gives a detailed account of Ussher's historical scheme. Antichrist's appearance at the end of the sixth century could be related to the birth of Mahomet or to the mission of St Augustine to England, if one chose to read history in such terms.

De Christianarum Ecclesiarum ... Successione. This treatise supplies the framework within which many of his other writings can be set, dealing as they do with the condition of the primitive Church, the growth of Roman errors over purer doctrine, the triumph and decline of papal power, and the establishment of an accurate chronology by which to date the divine plan.

De Successione seems to have been in part the result of Ussher's engagement to Camden and Cotton to compose a work illustrating the history of the true faith independent of the influence of Rome. It owes something to the historical scheme of the German Protestant Sleidanus whose work Ussher had admired from an early age, but its ultimate drift is to place the reformed Church in England in the line of those manifestations of pure doctrine and true faith that have persisted from antiquity. As the title suggests, the work is concerned to trace the descent of the primitive Church in visible form from the time of the apostles to the Reformation, answering in a way the formidable question of the Catholics: 'Where was your Church before Luther?' Ussher declares in his preface that his book is in effect a continuation of Bishop Jewel's *Apology of the Church of England* (1562), which had spelt out the continuity of the doctrines of the Anglican Church with those of the Church in the first six centuries, with the difference that Ussher intends to push the lines of continuity right through to the Reformation.[13] He sets up his chronological scheme of Church history bedevilled by Antichrist and Satan, and through its apertures we are shown the recurring manifestations of the faithful in their precarious and persecuted Churches: the Albigensians in south-west France, the Waldensians of southern France, Savoy and Piedmont, the Wycliffites of England, and the Hussites of Bohemia are among the most luminous. The documentation is intensively supplied, for this work was intended to be a bastion of Protestantism, with all its outworks solidly built against Catholic attack. There must be no doubt that the true faith had been kept down through the centuries; the Reformation was no sudden phenomenon, but the culmination of a long process of testimony that was in line with biblical prophecy.

---

[13] In fact, Ussher pushed his scheme through only to the late thirteenth century. His work can be also be seen as a vast elaboration of the historical scheme outlined by John Foxe at the beginning of *The Acts and Monuments.*

As Ussher grew older, he became more concerned with establishing a universal chronology through which the whole spread of human history could be viewed and understood in its comparative relationships, and into which the religious events and movements that he had studied in such detail could be keyed. An accurate account of time had fascinated him from his student days when he had compiled a chronology of the Old Testament. His interest was renewed when Selden asked for his help in clarifying the Greek chronology for his book *Marmora Arundelliana* in 1628. To help set Greek history in line with Hebrew history, Ussher sent Selden a letter of impressive erudition discussing the disparities between the chronology that could be derived from the Hebrew version of Genesis and that derived from the Pentateuch written in the Samaritan language (which gave slightly different ages for the patriarchs), along with a digest of the opinions of the ancient chronologers Eusebius, Syncellus, and Julius Africanus.

The art of chronology, according to an eminent nineteenth-century exponent, lies in 'computing, adjusting and verifying the whole range of dates, according to certain cardinal epochs, eras and periods, to produce one entire uniform and consistent system in which sacred and profane history shall be brought to harmonise or correspond with each other'.[14] This synthesis was a *summum desideratum* of Renaissance humanist scholarship, to facilitate a proper understanding of the temporal relationships between different ancient histories. When did Alexander invade India, and where did this event fall in the history of the eastern monarchies and in the history of the Israelites? When did Moses lead the Israelites out of Egypt, and in what Pharaoh's reign? The problem of dating events in the ancient world was a difficult business because of the absence of any generally accepted chronological era. In the case of Hebrew history, there were very few references to events in the Old Testament in the surviving records of other nations, and the biblical record itself is often vague. Some help was provided by chronological lists from Assyrian and Persian sources that lit up occasional passages of Israelite history, but whole eras remained as dark as Egypt's night. As well as a humanist desire for

[14] Hales, *New Analysis*, i. 3. Hales notes that at the time of writing, he was aware of 130 chronologies that essayed to establish the date of Creation, and 'the number might be swelled to 300, with industry'.

synchronism to provide a firm framework for historical studies, there was a concern on the part of many religious scholars to relate the scheme of Providence to an accurate calendar of events. God's will worked through history: events were not accidental, but determined. The course of world history was prefigured in the Book of Revelation in a mysterious system of episodes, periods, and numbers that evidently related to time in the Christian era, although in ways that were almost infinitely debatable. It was a duty of theologians and scholars to attempt to understand the divine scheme, especially in its operation in the Latter Days that were assumed by Protestants to have begun with the Reformation. But understanding was contingent upon chronology. Events in Christian time had often been foreshadowed by events in Old Testament time. The prophecies of Daniel bore on the Latter Days, but to understand them one needed to know what units of time Daniel was referring to when he used events of his own time as a measure. There may be a parallelism of events too: many thought the earth might be destroyed, or the Saviour might appear, at the same point after the birth of Christ as the Flood was after the Creation of the world. But when was the Flood?

Since Ussher's Chronology was regarded as his most celebrated achievement in the seventeenth century, it may be helpful to outline the state of the art when he came to it.[15] Various scholars in antiquity had compiled chronological lists for their own nation and the nations with which it interacted, notably the Alexandrian Greek Eratosthenes in the mid-second century BC and Dionysius of Halicarnassus. The Roman scholar Sextus Julius Africanus seems to have made the first-known chronology for Christian purposes about 220 AD, and he attempted to work back through the books of the Old Testament to establish the dates of the patriarchs, and ultimately the date of Creation, subjects of no concern to classical chronographers but of surpassing interest to Christians. A much more thorough chronicle had been put together by the Church historian Eusebius which went down to the time of the Emperor Constantine in 325, and paid much attention to events of relevance to the Church. His work had also synchronized biblical history with Graeco-Roman history, and confirmed the much greater

---

[15] The following account is largely derived from Alden A. Mosshammer's work, *The Chronicle of Eusebius and Greek Chronographic Tradition* (Lewisburg, 1979).

antiquity of the former. Eusebius's Chronicle had not survived in its original form or language (Greek), but it was known to western scholars through the Latin translation that St Jerome had incorporated into his own Chronicle, which he took up to the end of the fourth century. Jerome's chronology was transmitted down through the centuries until the Renaissance as the definitive record of world history, backed by his immense authority as the maker of the Vulgate Bible and by his exalted status as one of the major fathers of the Church.

Eusebius had done the hard graft behind Jerome, in fact, though Jerome received the credit. Eusebius, who was able to draw upon a long tradition of chronological tabling, had worked out the cross-cultural referents, and had related Hebrew history to Athenian, Persian and Assyrian history via the Book of Ezra in which the rebuilding of the Temple in Jerusalem can be dated to the second year of Darius, and he had exploited the work of the Alexandrian Eratosthenes, who had related Greek history to the Persian king lists that he had access to, using the expedition of Xerxes against the Greeks as the nodal point. Eusebius was able to tie in the Persian king lists to biblical dates via the Babylonian captivity. He had used the dating lists of Dionysius of Halicarnassus to relate the Athenian, Spartan, and Roman histories. He had also discussed the conceptual problems behind the making of a chronology that stemmed from the various methods of computing time in different societies, such as the four-year Olympiad for the Greeks, the tenure of Ephods among the Spartans, and the consular and imperial measures among the Romans.

The oldest date that could be assigned with any confidence, thought Eusebius, was the birth of Abraham, which he used as his base Year One. He did not propose a year for the Creation. It was difficult to ascertain the dates of Moses, but he was definitely before Deucalion, Europa, and the birth of Apollo (the Greek gods and heroes were regarded as transfigured recollections of historical personages). For Eusebius, the critical dates (which he called the epochal dates, because they marked the opening of an epoch) were the birth of Abraham, the Exodus, the Fall of Troy, the first Olympiad, the rebuilding of the Temple, and the death of Christ. He built his chronology around these dates, as he determined them, and he transmitted to posterity a synchronistic format that allowed for a presentation of universal history and comparative chronology.

A succession of medieval historians had continued to update the Jerome–Eusebius Chronicle, but no major revision took place until the French Huguenot scholar Joseph Scaliger undertook to reconstruct the ancient chronology in the light of several texts that had surfaced during the Renaissance, notably the Greek manuscript of the *Chronographia* by the late eighth-century Byzantine scholar George Syncellus that derived from sources independent of Eusebius's Chronicle. Scaliger published his *De Emendatione Temporum* in 1598, a work in which he laid down his principles of chronology and discussed its challenges; *Thesaurus Temporum* followed in 1606, with comprehensive chronologies of the ancient world. His work was corrected and extended by the French Jesuit Dionysius Petavius in *De Doctrina Temporum* (1627).

It was against this background that Ussher worked. He was convinced that he had an important contribution to make. He believed that Scaliger had miscalculated the birth of Abraham, and in consequence the whole sequence of primeval dates was thrown out. Selden's work on the Greek chronology in *Marmora Arundelliana* needed to be incorporated into the comparative sections, and adjustments made. Ussher had also grown interested in astronomy in its practical and historical forms, and had come to realize that in Macedonian times the length of the months had been changed from lunar to solar, and this discovery had a bearing on secular and ecclesiastical history. All this needed setting out, and towards the end of his life he issued a succession of chronological books. In 1648 he laid out his discoveries about the changes in Macedonian dating, and applied the Julian calendar to a revised sequence of Greek dates. In 1650 he unveiled the first part of his perfected system in *Annales Veteris et Novi Testamenti*, running from the first age to the time of the Maccabees, with much Asiatic and Egyptian matter; the second part (1654) took the tables up to the destruction of the Temple in AD 70. He did not finish the final part, which would have taken the sequence up to the beginning of the fourth century. An English translation, *The Annals of the Old and New Testament or The Annals of the World deduced from the origin of Time*, was published in 1658.

Labouring in the mines of ancient chronology, Ussher names his almost forgotten predecessors who undertook the same work: Julius Firmius Maternus, Æsculapius, Annubius, Ptolemy. In the opinion of these pagans, the course of time could be traced, but its origin would for ever elude detection. Censorinus doubted 'whether time had a beginning, or whether it always was; the certain number of years cannot be comprehended.' It was not strange that heathens should despair, when even many Christians could not certainly conclude when the world was created. 'The sands of the sea, the drops of rain, the days of the world, who can number?' Not Philastrius Brixiensis, nor Lactantius Firmianus, nor Theophilus of Antioch, who all failed to identify 'the geniture of time'. Dionysius Petavius, with the experience of his own immense endeavours in chronology, believed that the secret of the date of Creation could only be known by divine revelation. Ussher, however, was convinced that 'the Holy Ghost has provided against this doubt' by furnishing the narrative of the Old Testament with sufficient precision for a patient, studious, and mathematical mind, like his own, to identify the very beginning of time. If one is learned in 'sacred and exotic history', astronomical calculation, and the old Hebrew calendar, 'one may attain, with difficulty, not only the number of years, but even of days, from the creation of the world'. A rare voice from the past encouraged persistence: St Basil the Great was certain it was possible to discover when the foundations of the world were laid, and 'when time had its first motion'.[16] Ussher persevered.

He describes the complexities of the task: the need to correlate 'political years' in a nation's calendar with astronomical years, the need to work with the most accurate annual unit, which he takes to be the Julian year, and to calibrate all relevant national calendars with this measure. It is essential also to establish the number of equinoxes that have elapsed since the Creation of the world. Equinoxes were the stepping-stones across the current of time. By heroic acts of computation, 'collating the Hebrew Calendar with the Chaldean History and the Astronomical Canon', Ussher deduced that Creation began on the 23rd day of October, 4004 BC. How could he be so precise? Ussher found that the dates of the Old Testament time scheme required an autumnal start,

but for as much as the first day of the world began with the evening of the first day of the week, I have observed that the Sunday which in the year [4004] aforesaid came nearest the Autumnal equinox, by astronomical

---

[16] Quotations here from 'The Epistle to the Reader' in Ussher, *The Annals of the Old and New Testament* (1658).

tables, notwithstanding the stay of the sun in the days of Joshua, and the going back of it in the days of Ezekiah, happened upon the 23rd day of the Julian October; from thence concluded, that from the evening preceding . . . both the first day of Creation and the first motion of time are to be deduced.[17]

As the Jewish Sabbath was the Christian Saturday, and the Sabbath began at 6 p.m. on the day preceding, Ussher assumes that Creation 'fell upon the entrance of the night preceding the 23rd of October' (which in modern time would be 6 p.m. on Saturday the 22nd), in order that God might be able to rest on the Sabbath of the first week.

Ussher is a strict literalist in timetabling the Creation. A day is a day is a day, not a thousand years in the sight of God. On the first day, therefore, 'God, together with the highest Heaven, created the Angels, and the wonderful fabric of this world.' On the second day, Monday, October 24th, 'a separation was made of the waters above, and the waters here beneath enclosing the earth'. The dry land appeared upon the third day, Tuesday, October 25th, the sun, moon, and the stars were made on the Wednesday, the fish and flying fowl appeared on the Thursday, and on Friday the 28th were created the animals and man. Ussher remarks that when man was created in the image of God, this 'consisted principally in the divine knowledge of the mind' and 'in the natural and proper sanctity of the will'. Friday was a crowded day, for then Adam named the animals, and Eve was created. Then God rested on the first Sabbath, October 29th. According to Ussher's reading of Genesis, God 'brought the new-married couple into the Garden of Eden' after the first week had ended. He warned them not to eat of the Tree of Knowledge of Good and Evil, but the temptation took place and they fell, and they were driven out of Eden lest they should eat of the Tree of Life, 'whence it was very probable that Adam was turned out of Paradise the self same day that he was brought into it, which seemeth to have been on the tenth day of the world (answering to our first day of November)'.[18]

So Ussher, unlike the poetic historians of Paradise, most notably Milton, has no period of timelessness in Eden when Adam and Eve could enjoy the garden and develop those rich ancestral memories

---

[17] Ussher, *The Annals of the Old and New Testament* (1658).
[18] *Annals*, 2.

of an unfallen world; they are in and out in a day. Nor for Ussher did time begin with the Fall, but it was running steadily from the first moment of Creation.

The *Annals* proceeds through the long years of the patriarchs, maintaining a brisk narrative pace. The Flood occurs 1656 years after the Creation of the world. The birth of Christ Ussher believes to have been commonly miscalculated: 'the true nativity of our Saviour was full four years before the beginning of the vulgar Christian era, as is demonstrated by the time of Herod's death.' Confidently interweaving the sacred and secular histories of the ancient world, Ussher presented a compendious scheme into which all known events were firmly slotted. His success was complete, in the Protestant world at least. The *Annals* was rightly considered a triumph of scholarship, and dominated the field of chronology as long as the Bible was held to be unassailably true as a historical text. So incontestable were Ussher's findings regarded that his dates were thenceforth printed in the margins of bibles to mark the progress of the divine history. Even today, Ussher is remembered by many who have no other knowledge of him for his exquisitely precise dating of the Creation.

The accomplishment of this grand design had involved research in many oriental languages, in Hebrew, Samaritan, Chaldean, Syriac, Persian, and even Arabic and Ethiopic. Like his friend Selden, Ussher had industriously taught himself to read these languages in some measure, the first four of which were essential to a biblical scholar if he were to evaluate the earliest texts of the Old Testament. The Protestant faith, founded as it was on the rock of the word of God, needed that word to be as precise as possible, and early translations into neighbouring languages of the Pentateuch, the five books of Moses, might in particular preserve a more accurate record of the original divine expression than the surviving Hebrew texts or the Greek Septuagint.[19] Variant readings, as in the Samaritan Pentateuch that Ussher acquired, could affect the dating by attributing slightly different ages to the patriarchs, for example.

[19]   The Septuagint is the translation of the Hebrew Testament into Greek made by seventy Jewish scholars on the orders of Ptolemy Philadelphus (mid-third century BC), who wished to have a copy of the Hebrew Law for his celebrated library at Alexandria. The Septuagint differs in many respects from the Hebrew Bible: in the order of the books, in including more books, later assigned to the Apocrypha, and in details within books.

Ussher was an active collector of oriental manuscripts, with agents in the Middle East who searched for rarities, the chief of whom was the chaplain to the English merchants in Aleppo, a Mr Davies. He it was who found the Samaritan Pentateuch and the Syriac version of the Old Testament that Ussher so much valued. The Archbishop was liberal in lending such manuscripts to scholars working on the Polyglot Bible, the finest achievement of English scholarship in the biblical languages, which was being prepared under the direction of the Laudian clergyman, Brian Walton. Ill health prevented Ussher from a full participation in this project, which reached publication in 1657.

James Ussher and William Laud both built up notable collections of oriental manuscripts, gathering these antiquities for the benefits of English biblical scholarship. Eventually their collections enriched the libraries of their respective universities. Ussher's progress in the eastern languages was aided by the skills of his younger brother Ambrose, who was an extremely able orientalist, but who died at a fairly early age. Like Selden, Ussher soon fell into companionship with William Bedwell, the most knowledgeable man in the kingdom for Arabic and the biblical tongues, exchanging books and correspondence with him. Eminent orientalist though he became, however, Ussher sadly considered, towards the end of his life, that he had spent too much time for too little profit on these studies. He told John Evelyn in 1655 'how great the loss of time was to study much the eastern languages; that, excepting Hebrew, there was little fruit to be gathered of exceeding labour ... the Arabic itself had little considerable'.[20]

If the East disappointed, the North had its compensations in illustrating the history of his own region. Ussher was a competent Saxonist, and collected Anglo-Saxon manuscripts. He owned the unique manuscript of the scriptural poems attributed to Caedmon, which was edited in 1655 by Francis Junius, the linguist and antiquarian who had been librarian to the Earl of Arundel. Ussher lent his support to Abraham Wheelock, who occupied the first lectureship in Anglo-Saxon at Cambridge, encouraging him in the 1630s to establish the language firmly in the university.[21] Ussher

---

[20] John Evelyn, *The Diary of John Evelyn*, ed. E. S. de Beer (6 vols.; Oxford, 1955), 21 Aug. 1655.
[21] Wheelock was also an orientalist, as well as an Anglo-Saxon scholar, and was involved in the preparation of the Polyglot Bible. He planned to write a refutation of

also made some headway in Gothic, carrying on a correspondence with Wheelock about a version of the Lord's Prayer in an ancient Gothic version of the Gospels he possessed.

One question concerning language remains. Could Ussher speak Irish? Though learned in so many languages, he may have been ignorant of the native tongue of his own country. Irish was a barbaric language in the opinion of the English settlers, and the language of the Catholic peasantry. Ussher as Primate of Ireland was adamant against the translation of the Gospels into Irish, against the use of an Irish liturgy, and against sermons in Irish. In this, he was false to the spirit of Protestantism that had always demanded access to the Gospels in the vulgar tongue. But to concede this right to the Irish seemed to him a concession to barbarism: the Irish must come to the Church of Ireland through the medium of English; the Church would not accommodate itself to them. In this regard, Ussher's role in the colonial overlordship of Ireland is apparent, for the imposition of the Protestant religion was also the imposition of English authority. Ussher's refusal to use Gaelic was the common practice of the English settlers, who regarded the native language as an expression of the incivility from which the Irish had to be redeemed.[22]

Such was the immensity of Ussher's scholarly ambitions that, inevitably, much remained unfinished. His projects were on a vast scale, many of them involving the conduct of an argument across many centuries with ponderous documentation. His final project, the *Annals*, took the whole span of human history as its theme. The activity of the first two generations of Reformation scholars, particularly those in France and the Netherlands, had raised a new mountain range of learning, which had to be climbed by the men of Ussher's generation before they could begin to build their own towering structures. Ussher belonged to the heroic age of scholarship, when in principle, several lifetimes should be spent in mastering the Alexandrian Library of the ages, and several more

the Koran, but was dissuaded by Samuel Hartlib. See J. C. T. Oates, *Cambridge University Library: A History* (Cambridge, 1986), i.

[22] See J. T. Leerssen, *Mere Irish and Fior-Ghael* (Amsterdam, 1986), 39–53, for an account of English hostility to Gaelic both as a barbaric language and as a subversive language. Official opposition to Gaelic dated from the Parliament of 1366 held at Kilkenny, when rulings were made to stop the English in Ireland from adopting local customs.

in responding to current controversies and in advancing knowledge. In practice, only fifty crowded years were available at most.
Some time before he died, he was asked what could best be done for

the advancement of solid and useful learning, both sacred and profane. He
answered thus: (1) by learned notes and illustrations of the Bible; (2) by
considering and enquiring into the ancient councils and works of the
Fathers; (3) by the orderly writing and digesting of ecclesiastical history;
(4) by gathering together whatsoever may concern the state of the Jews
from the destruction of Jerusalem to the present age; (5) by collecting all
the Greek and Roman histories, and digesting them into a body.[23]

What Francis Bacon would have thought of this programme is
imaginable: so much of it by his lights was the spinning of cobwebs
over the furniture of the past, industry to little or no purpose. But
for Ussher, driven by the Reformation imperatives of buttressing
the work of reform by scholarship, and purifying the scriptures by
indefatigable textual research, and seeking the providence of God
in history, his scheme represented the best application of the human
mind.

Because he composed most of his works in Latin to reach a
European audience, his writings, like those of his contemporaries
and correspondents Joseph Scaliger, Isaac Casaubon, and Gerard
Vossius, are now neglected and not readily accessible. His works
were reprinted in the 1840s and 1850s when the Church of Ireland
was under attack and in danger of being disestablished,[24] but since
then he has been largely overlooked, and even the scholarly reprint
vogue of the 1960s and 1970s all but passed him by. So much of his
work was committed to the now dead controversies of the Counter-
Reformation, or advanced subjects whose value has not outlived
the seventeenth century. Ussher's contribution to the place of the
Church in the reconstructed society of the 1640s and 1650s, when
he attempted to justify the continuance of episcopacy in a modified
form, now attracts more attention than his volumes of antiquarian
research. His case exemplifies, perhaps more than any other, the
strain of theological antiquarianism which perished with the issues
that had given it life.

When Ussher died in 1656 (a year many thought, on the basis of
his own *Annals*, might be the terminal date of the world, because

---

[23] Elrington, *Life*, 300–1.
[24] See Trevor-Roper, 'James Ussher', 123.

of its parallelism with the Flood), he was honoured as a celebrated scholar and a man of moderate religion who had kept the respect of royalists and parliamentarians throughout the Civil Wars. The Lord Protector, Cromwell, gave him a public funeral and burial in Westminster Abbey, and as a tribute to the integrity with which he had maintained his defence of a limited episcopacy, allowed the liturgy of the Church of England to be used at his funeral. After his death, his chaplain Nicholas Bernard published a biography of the Archbishop, and printed a number of his miscellaneous tracts, one of which discussed the meaning of Babylon in the Apocalypse. Ussher's friend Gerard Langbaine, the Provost of Queen's College, Oxford, attempted to transcribe and publish the great exordium to the 'Biblioteca Theologica' which had remained a continuing interest of Ussher's over much of his life. This was an immense prologue to the study of the Church Fathers, the eventual publication of whose works would be the glory of English scholarship. 'Dr. Langbaine set to work most laboriously, copying out the manuscript, and endeavouring to fill up the quotations in the margin, which had been eaten away by rats. Devoting himself with indefatigable industry to the task during a severe winter, he caught cold in the Bodleian Library, and died within a year of the Archbishop.'[25] This tale of heroic fortitude deserves to be recorded in the 'Acts and Monuments' of seventeenth-century scholars, and it gives the measure of Ussher's superior intellectual stamina in the quarries of learning, that the quantity of material he extracted should overwhelm those who tried to carry it to the public forum.

Like all the other antiquaries of the seventeenth century, Ussher encouraged other men to the task of investigating the past in adjacent fields. So vast were the tracts of antiquity, so few the explorers; in the absence of a society to co-ordinate and advance knowlege, mutual assistance was the best way to stimulate enquiry. Ussher was the undisputed master of Irish ecclesiastical antiquities, but he never had time to undertake a full antiquarian survey of his country. He did, however, urge James Ware to apply himself to the discovery of Ireland's past. Ware, born in 1594, had been a student at Trinity College, Dublin, where Ussher recognized his genius for antiquities. Industrious, and zealous for the honour of Ireland,

[25] Elrington, *Life*, 320.

Ware combined his career as an administrator (which led to his becoming Auditor General of Ireland in 1632, and later a member of the King's Privy Council in Ireland) with a busy life of research. He wrote a Latin history of the bishoprics of Ireland which appeared in 1622 and 1628, then compiled a biographical register of Irish writers, *De Scriptoribus Hiberniae* (1639). Like Ussher's discourse on primitive Irish religion and the *Sylloge* of early texts that he published in 1632, Ware's book is inclined to make much of the fecundity and scholarship of the early Irish writers. It is surprising how many works from the fourth, fifth, and sixth centuries Ware can describe; unfortunately, only the titles have survived and the texts have disappeared. The impression of splendid achievement remains, however, in spite of the material losses, but it becomes clear from the references how much of this illusory splendour is reflected from the compilations of John Bale, the mid-sixteenth-century Bishop of Ossory, who had drawn up a vast catalogue of early British writers. None the less, in so far as a nation's reputation is partly made by its authors, Ireland fares well in Ware's estimate of the literary record, for he retrieves from the shadows an impressive number of religious and historical writers and poets from early medieval times to his own age.

The early history of Ireland was a relatively neglected subject, so Ware was eager to enlarge the body of available information and opinion. To this end he put into print in 1633 three works that added considerably to the store of knowledge: Meredith Hanmer's 'History', written in the early seventeenth century, Edmund Campion's brief but picturesque account of Irish origins, manners, and customs written in 1571, and Edmund Spenser's 'View of the State of Ireland', which he had written in the 1590s, and which Ware now dedicated to the Earl of Strafford as Lord Deputy, who was best fitted to receive this piece of political and cultural intelligence. Ware also published in this volume Henry of Marlborough's 'Chronicle of Ireland', covering the years from 1285 to 1421; the whole volume, entitled *The Historie of Ireland*, was dedicated to Strafford, who had just taken up his post in Dublin.

Captured in the Civil War, Ware led a subdued life in London during the 1650s, when he met with a number of notable antiquaries: Selden, Dugdale, Ashmole, Francis Junius, and Sir John Marsham. He also spent time in Paris, where he developed a friendship with the French antiquary, Samuel Bochart. Devoid of office, he had the leisure to put in order the Irish collections he had made over the years, publishing *De Hibernia et Antiquitatibus* in 1654 (with a second edition in 1658). This is a grand survey of ancient Ireland in which the Elizabethan and Jacobean preoccupation with origins mixes with a good deal of fresh observation of field antiquities. Ware parades the familiar received wisdom concerning the first inhabitants, assuming that Ireland must have been first settled by the descendants of Japhet. The old philological trails are followed, so he derives the Scoti, who occupied Ireland in Roman times, from Scythii, and imputes a Scythian origin to the Irish, as had been the normal view in the sixteenth century.[26] Some of Ware's topics merely involve a relocation westwards of ancient British matter, as with his discussion of Druids, whom he represents as figures comparable to the Magi of Persia or to the Chaldean philosophers among the Assyrians, but when he considers the role of the Bards in ancient Irish society, he describes them as more significant than their British counterparts. He painstakingly puts together all references to Ireland in the classical writers, and as he moves into the early Christian period, his sources multiply, so that he is able to construct a serious and credible account of the development of Irish society, with its particular manners and customs, up to the Norman Conquest. He explains at length the origins of the leading Irish families, and the meaning of Irish names, reports the superstitions of the country and the natural phenomena, and gives a knowledgeable description of Irish costume and of the characteristic Irish weapons and ways of fighting. Particularly valuable are Ware's accounts of the forms of government that existed in Gaelic society and of the code of law known as Brehon Law, which prevailed before the Norman occupation. He is able to explain the complexities of the system of land tenure known as tanistry, peculiar to the ancient Irish, by which the successor to an

---

[26] The story was at least as old as Nennius. (Spenser's tract had offered a similar derivation.) Ware notes, but rejects, another old foundation story that the Scoti were descended from Scota, the daughter of the Pharaoh in the days of Moses, who had migrated westwards via Spain with her followers (bringing to Ireland, no doubt, an early contact with monotheism). In addition, other legends suggested that the Roman name Hibernia retained a recollection of the Spanish Prince Iberus or Hiberus who was fabled to have made a later settlement of Ireland in the middle of the second millennium BC.

estate or to a title was elected during the lifetime of his predecessor, thus making it possible that the strongest or worthiest man might inherit. As to the Irish language, Ware thinks it was related to the ancient British, or Welsh, indicating that there might have been a settlement of colonies of Britons at some unidentifiable time in the past. He instances the use of coracles in both Ireland and Wales as a sign of a shared, prehistoric, common culture—but he also believes that coracles might have been the craft that brought the Scythians to Ireland in the dawn of time.

Ware was concerned to trace the growth of Christianity in Ireland, following the footsteps of his patron Ussher. He gives extensive histories of the cathedral churches of the country, laying emphasis on the long tradition of episcopacy. Some of his observations about the early Church are quite intriguing, as when he proposes that the round towers often found near Irish churches were 'for the reception of a sort of Anchorite Monks', and he goes on to speculate about the existence of a tradition of Irish stylites, or 'Aerial Martyrs' in the early centuries of the Celtic Church.[27] All in all, with its copious detail and broad description of the antiquities and traditions of Ireland, *De Hibernia* is an impressive work which finally brought the country out of the shadow of Britain and characterized it fully to a scholarly European audience. Ware must have known that he had amply fulfilled Ussher's expectations of him as his successor in Irish antiquities.

---

[27] James Ware, *The Antiquities of Ireland* in *Works Concerning Ireland*, ed. Walter Harris (Dublin, 1739), 129–35.

6

Sir Henry Spelman
and William Somner

In his biography of Sir Henry Spelman, published in 1698, the Oxford scholar Edmund Gibson expressed his admiration for 'the knowledge of the Laws and Antiquities of our Nation' that Spelman exhibited. 'Those, for a good part of his life, he seems to have studied for the service of his country, and for his own diversion; but not with an eye to any particular undertaking.'[1] From our more distant viewpoint, we can recognize that Spelman did have a great project in mind, but that, like most ambitious antiquarian schemes, it was only partially fulfilled. He desired to strengthen the whole fabric of the Commonwealth by firming the foundations in the deep past. The laws, rights, and entitlements of Church and state were his preoccupation; all these powers and privileges should mutually support and be consolidated by the monarchy. The frontispiece that he designed for his history of Church councils, *Concilia*, exemplified the structure of the stable state: it showed the king as the keystone of an arch upheld by the pillars of the secular and ecclesiastical powers.[2] Spelman's sense of the interdependence of Church, state, and monarch is everywhere apparent.

A temporal Prince cannot properly dispose of the matters of the Church if he have not Ecclesiastical Function and Ability as well as Temporal: for I doubt not but that the Government of the Church, and of the

---

[1] Edmund Gibson, 'Life of Sir Henry Spelman' in Spelman, *Reliquiae Spelmanniae* (2nd edn., 1727), a2. The *Reliquiae* were bound together with Spelman's *English Works*, and the volume was first published in 1698.

[2] B.M. Add.MSS 34600. fo. 134. A variant of this motif was used by Thomas Fuller as the frontispiece of *The Holy State* (1642). Note that in the engraved title-page to Dugdale's *Monasticon Anglicanum* (1655), a work much influenced by Spelman, the keystone of the arch is missing, because there was no king in 1655. A broken pediment remains, and the scenes pictured on the arch are of social breakdown and collapse.

6. Sir Henry Spelman's 'Arch of State' as appropriated by Thomas Fuller for his book *The Holy State* (1642). The pillars of both Church and State are based on books: the Old and New Testament, and the Statutes and the Laws. The monarch is the keystone of the arch.

Commonwealth, are not only distinct Members in this his Majesty's Kingdom, but distinct Bodies also under their particular Heads, united in the person of his Majesty, yet without confusion of their Faculties, or without being subject the one to the other.[3]

Clarifying the rights and limitations of the three co-operative powers of the nation as they had accumulated through time was Spelman's true vocation, and, given the scale of the undertaking, it is understandable that his achievement was partial and unfinished.

Spelman was born in the mid-1560s to a well-established Norfolk family. He attended Trinity College, Cambridge, and then went on to study law at Lincoln's Inn. His antiquarian interests asserted themselves at an early age, for he became a member of the group of lawyers and heralds who made up the Society of Antiquaries in the late 1580s.[4] For many years he led an active public life as a Norfolk gentleman: he was a JP, and Sheriff of Norfolk in the early years of the seventeenth century, as well as MP for Castle Rising and then for Worcester in the parliaments of James I. He served on royal commissions, and undertook legal work for the Council of New England. About the age of 50, he retired from public responsibilities to devote himself to the study of antiquities, in particular 'to search into the Reasons and Foundations of the Law, which he knew were not to be learnt, but from the Customs and Histories of our Nation in elder Ages'.[5]

He had already become exercised by an issue that would concern him until the end of his life, the despoliation of Church property and the subsequent impoverishment of the Church of England. After the Dissolution, huge areas of monastic land had been sold to private buyers, and during the reign of Elizabeth, and later, land and buildings belonging to the Church of England continued to be bought and sold on the market, especially glebe land which had originally been devoted to the maintenance of a vicar, but which proved in practice to be easily detachable from the vicarage. The patronage of livings as well as the ownership tithes continued to pass into lay hands: Spelman estimated that 3,845 out of 9,284

---

[3] Spelman, *Reliquiae Spelmanniae*, 148. This passage is highlighted by F. M. Powicke in his valuable article 'Sir Henry Spelman and the *Concilia*', a lecture of 1930 reprinted in *Studies in History*, ed. Lucy Sutherland (London, 1966).

[4] Spelman's name appears on the list of the Society drawn up by Arthur Agarde, probably in 1591. See Evans, *Society of Antiquaries*, 12.

[5] Gibson, 'Life' in Spelman, *Reliquiae Spelmanniae*, a2.

livings in England and Wales were under lay control by 1613.[6] 'We have got the Houses of God into our Possession, his Churches, his Lands, his Offerings, his holy Rights; we have gotten them, and lead them away captive, bound in chains of Iron; that is, so conveyed and assured unto us, by Deed, by Fine, by Act of Parliament, as if they should never again return unto the Church.'[7] This impropriation of Church property was leading to the secularization of the Church and bringing about an economic decline, endangering the Church's function in the land and its part in a Christian commonwealth. The rapacious attitudes in Tudor and Stuart times towards Church property raised the serious issue of sacrilege.

The problem came home to Spelman in a personal way when his uncle Francis Sanders, who had bought a parsonage and its glebeland in Norfolk, tried to build on the land and encountered unusual difficulties and obstructions. He asked Spelman for an opinion of his rights in the matter, and Spelman worked up his answer into the tract *De Non Temerandis Ecclesiis* (1613), or 'Churches not to be violated'. Spelman concentrated his attention not so much on the legal rights of the particular case as on the larger question of the status and sanctity of Church property. All 'spiritual Livings' 'composed of Land, Tithe and other Oblations of the People' are 'separate and dedicate to God . . . for the service of his Church there and for the maintenance of the Governor or Minister'. Oblations or gifts to the Church are gifts to God, and cannot be alienated, by canon law. God is the ultimate owner of these spiritual offerings, as of Church lands, buildings, and tithes: the minister is only the usufructuary, who enjoys their benefit or use. Spelman reviews the biblical authority for tithes and for the privileges of land offered to the service of God or to the maintenance of priests. He draws arguments from the law of nature that requires God to be honoured, and from the custom of nations that approves the setting apart of property for religious purposes and for the maintenance of clergy. He cites too the rulings of several Church councils, going back to the sixth century, about the impiety of alienating Church lands. He concludes that it is undeniably an act of sacrilege to take into private ownership things that have been

    [6] 'Apology of the Treatise *De Non Temerandis Ecclesiis*', in *English Works* (1727), 35.   [7] Ibid. 8.

given to God, and fears that only rapid restitution of such property can avert the judgements that will surely fall on the guilty possessors. Spelman sent off his opinions to his uncle, but his uncle died the very day the messenger arrived, no doubt reassuring Spelman that he had an accurate view of the subject. In fact he himself was not guiltless. He had earlier acquired the leases on lands belonging formerly to the abbeys of Wormegay and Blackborough in Norfolk, and his experience of the legal complications and misfortunes that they brought him underlay the conviction that the impropriation of Church property was ill-starred.[8]

Spelman's discussion of tithes in this tract had important consequences, for his claim that they were due to the Church by divine right may well have provoked John Selden into investigating the whole question of the status of tithes throughout recorded history. Spelman had written that 'the Law of Nature teacheth us that God is to be honoured, and that honour due unto him cannot be performed without ministers.' The law of nature does not determine that any fixed proportion of our goods should be devoted to the maintenance of God's ministers, 'but the wisdom of all the Nations of the World, the practice of all the Ages, the example of the Patriarches Abraham and Jacob, the approbation and commandment of Almighty God', all direct that one tenth is the right sum. To counteract such broad affirmations of universal practice in favour of the Church, Selden compiled his *Historie of Tithes*, denying that tithes were a sacred duty or that they had been regularly paid in Christian societies.

In 1616 a second edition of *De Non Temerandis* was published. The tract was itself an oblation, being dedicated 'Deo et Ecclesiae', to God and the Church. Spelman noted at the end that he had been reluctant to reissue the work, for it had large implications, and he knew that it would raise the hackles of many gentlemen whose families had acquired Church lands since the Reformation. However, the subject was important, and involved the well-being of the national Church. The relevance of the issues raised by the tract did not abate, but became more urgent when politics entered a more radical phase under the Long Parliament. Spelman died in 1641,

---

[8] Spelman records his own miseries caused by lawsuits arising from disputed leases of manors and lands that had once belonged to monasteries in *The History and Fate of Sacrilege* (1888 edn.), 144–6. 'Hereby he first discerned the infelicity of meddling with consecrated places.'

but in 1646 a new edition of *De Non Temerandis* came out, with a long preface by Clement Spelman, the author's son. The Church was once again in danger of despoliation, he pointed out, because of measures before Parliament: 'the great dissolution of Bishopricks and Deaneries is only threatened, not acted,' and the arguments of the tract might avert further misadventure. Clement Spelman reinforced his father's belief that 'Sacrilege is the diversion of holy and ecclesiastique things to prophane and secular use', and that the penalty of sacrilege is divine displeasure. He asserted again that 'No statute or humane Law doth or can take away the Dedication or Consecration of Abbies, Monasteries, etc. discharge or annul the interest which God and his Church hath in them.' He then enlarged the scope of the tract beyond its original limits by calling into question the legality of the dissolution of the monasteries by Henry VIII. Whether the abbeys yielded their property to the Crown by surrender or by statute or by threat of arms, the whole process was illegal, uncanonical, and impious. Reformation of doctrine and discipline was in order, but despoliation was an offence against God.

Clement Spelman then embarked on a reading of national history seen as the consequence of sacrilege. Here he was drawing on the large collection of examples that his father had gathered throughout his life on a subject he felt passionately about. The list begins with William the Conqueror, who had fired St Peter's Church at York and rifled abbeys, and whose family suffered a series of brutal mishaps, with three of his issue murdered. These happenings were causally related in Spelman's mind, and the pattern of English history throughout the Middle Ages confirms the belief that sacrilege incurs divine punishment on the transgressors. Henry VIII, whose crimes outdid all those of his predecessors, clearly shows the law of divine revenge at work. In the first half of his reign, he was a God-fearing King, and all was honour, prosperity, and success; but when he turned against the Church, rebellions and turmoil afflicted his realm, and childlessness his person. Spelman makes a good deal of the childlessness of all his children, which he is convinced was a judgement against his sacrilegious policies. 'His Family is extinct, and like Herostratus, his name not mentioned, but with his crimes.'[9] The eloquent defence of the sanctity of Church property

---

[9] *De Non Temerandis Ecclesiis* (1646), Epistle to the Reader, c4.

by Spelman expressed and intensified a line of High-Church sentiment that increasingly vilified Henry VIII. Charles I 'scarce ever mentioned Henry VIII without an Abhorrency of his Sacriledge', related one of his biographers;[10] Dugdale gave him a place of dishonour on the title-page of the *Monasticon Anglicanum*. The theme of the fruitlessness of sacrilege is vigorously pursued in Clement Spelman's epistle. Did the immense wealth that Henry gained from the monasteries benefit him or the nation? No. It sifted away uselessly, so much so that 'about the 36th year of his reign, of all the Kings of England, he alone coynes not only base Tinne and Copper, but leather Money'. In spite of Henry's vast spoils of land and money, his daughter Elizabeth had to live off an impoverished treasury, and 'the Crown Lands are now so wasted as they will scarce defray the ordinary charge of the King's Household'.[11] Clement Spelman goes so far as to declare that 'the Nationall Warre and generall Ruine' of the 1640s must ultimately proceed from Henry's sacrilegious actions at the Dissolution, 'made lawful by our acts of parliament'. He pleads with Parliament not to make any more depredations on the Church, for that can only imperil the fortunes of England. Parliament did not listen, for Spelman's voice was only too recognizable as a High-Church cry of pain.

Another work of Spelman's in defence of the Church was published posthumously in 1646. This was *A Larger Work of Tithes*, edited by Jeremy Stephens, his assistant and collaborator in his later years. It was a book of predictable orthodoxy underpinned by antiquarian learning, and may originally have been written as a retort to Selden's *Historie of Tithes* in the second decade of the century. Once again, 'he asserts Tithes to the Clergy, from the Laws of Nature and of Nations; from the Commands of God in the Old and New Testament, and from the particular Constitution of our own Country.'[12] In his prefatory reflections on the maintenance of the clergy, Stephens noted that Spelman's earlier work *De Non Temerandis* had had a beneficial effect on its readers, and gave details of numerous gentlemen who had restored their impropriations to the Church, or who had repaid the Church the interest they

---

[10] Richard Perrinchief, 'Life of Charles I', in *The Works of King Charles the Martyr* (1687), 62.

[11] *De Non Temerandis* (1646), d2v.

[12] Gibson, 'Life' in Spelman, *Reliquiae Spelmanniae*, b3.

had gained from such possessions.[13] Stephens also prepared for the press Spelman's fullest work on violations against the Church, *The History and Fate of Sacrilege*. Compiled during the 1620s and 1630s, this work was sent for publication in 1663, 'but that work sticking long in the Press, both the copy and the sheets printed off, perished in the grand conflagration of London, 1666.'[14] The long delay suggests that influential men might have had an interest in obstructing its publication, for this was a book that was severe against those families that had benefited from the sale of Church property at the Dissolution, and documented with an undeniably vindictive pleasure the misfortunes that had subsequently befallen them. Many guilty families were held up to obloquy, and Spelman's insistence that providence would punish the progeny of these families must have made it a widely unpopular book. Even Edmund Gibson regarded it warily when he came to publish Spelman's works in 1698, and omitted it from the folio. It was, however, published later in the same year by a less discreet though unknown editor, probably by a member of the High-Church party in reaction to the Revolution settlement after 1688.[15] *The History of Sacrilege* amplifies those themes already familiar from Spelman's earlier exercises in denunciation. It is a largely uncritical work, a one-eyed view of history, remorselessly repeating the theme that sacrilege provokes judgements, not only on the perpetrators but on their descendants. The theme is argued with a degree of feeling that is not encountered elsewhere in Spelman's writings.[16] Sacrilege is the

[13] One of these gentlemen was Lord Scudamore, who also generously restored and beautified the church at Abbey Dore in Herefordshire in 1633–4, creating one of the most satisfying Laudian interiors of the south-west.

[14] Wood, *Athenae Oxonienses*, ii. 230. Wood provides an informative sketch here of Stephen's career as a scholar and high-church apologist.

[15] See Philip Styles, 'Politics and Historical Research in the early 17th Century' in Fox (ed.), *English Historical Scholarship*, 68. H. A. Cronne's essay in the same volume on the study and use of charters contains much valuable information about Spelman, particularly in relation to the *Concilia*.

[16] The subject is naturally productive of strong feelings. The editors of the 1888 reprint end their introduction with a tirade against those descendants of families that benefited from the Dissolution whom they know to be among their readers: 'You share in these sins, for you have denied restitution. . . . You have three centuries of legalised guilt to answer for. It is to you that the festering mass of corruption and guilt in our manufacturing districts is owing; to you that draw your thousands from the revenues of the Church, and subscribe your annual guinea to some benevolent society . . .' etc.

same crime in all nations, in all religions, at all times. The stage is set for one of those encyclopaedic discourses so numerous in the seventeenth century, that begin in paradise and end in the present day. The accumulation of examples has already become tiresome by the early ages of the world, but Spelman perseveres through history until he reaches his real target, the Dissolution of the Monasteries. 'I am now come out of the rivers into the ocean of iniquity and sacrilege, where whole thousands of churches and chapels dedicated to the service of God were by King Henry VIII ... sacked and razed as by an enemy.'[17] After the familiar comments on the ephemeral benefits Henry gained, and the extinction of his line in one generation, Spelman goes on to survey the history of the chief families that participated in the spoil of the monasteries, and who approved of the Dissolution in Parliament. God's judgements are everywhere seen amongst them—even in playground accidents: 'George Lord Dacres, being but seven years old ... broke his neck by a fall from his vaulting-horse at Charterhouse, and his barony and family extinct.' A surprisingly large number of compromised families are now extinct, Spelman notes with considerable satisfaction. He had put his finger on a striking social change, but he drew the wrong conclusion, as he sought to show a relation between sacrilege and misfortune. As Christopher Hill more accurately saw, Spelman's attempts 'to show that individual families inheriting monastic lands came to bad ends are beside the point: it was the traditional social order, handed down from the Middle Ages, that was destroyed. . . . Those landed families which survived did so by moving over to a kind of economic activity very different from that which had predominated before the dissolution.'[18] Though unusually aware of the process of social change in his political writings, Spelman did not wish to look beyond his own narrowly and obsessively held thesis in matters of reverence and respect towards religion.

Spelman's concern over the misuse of Church land showed up again in an informative little tract published in 1641, just after his death. This was *De Sepultura*, a piece which provides a new angle on that subject of perennial fascination to seventeenth-century antiquaries, burial rites. In 1630, Spelman had been appointed one

---

[17] Spelman, *History and Fate of Sacrilege*, 99.
[18] Hill, *Economic Problems*, 163.

of the Commissioners to enquire into 'the Oppression of Exacted Fees', and his report considers the legality of selling land for burial in churchyards and inside churches. The enquiry was part of a movement to bring greater propriety into Church affairs that would accelerate once Laud became Archbishop. The question was well suited to the kind of legal antiquarianism that Spelman excelled in: it involved evaluation of evidence from the Bible, canon law, and common law. How far could custom and precedent prevail against biblical authority and the pronouncements of the early Church? The custom of charging for graves was well established, but charges had increased steadily, so that 'No ground in the Kingdom is now sold so dear as a Grave. That poor little Cabinet, that is not commonly above five foot long and a foot and a half in breadth, where there is no room to stirre either hand or foot . . . is sometimes sold to the poorest man for 16 pence, sometimes for 2s. 8d.' And there is no tenure of a grave, only leasehold. Land may be sold for burial, as Genesis 23 gave precedent to, but whether a church may sell and resell the same land for graves is another matter. Burial fees had become a valuable perquisite of the clergy, but what was their justification? 'Why should the dead pay for going into the Grave, any more than the living do for going into the Church?' In particular, the fees exacted for privileged burial in the Church, encroaching on sacred space, seemed to mingle simony with impiety. The whole question of what was legal and allowable in English churches was extremely tangled. Spelman goes through the rulings of the ancient Church councils that relate to charges for graves and to burial fees and finds that while most of their canons deny the right to sell graves, custom, however, approves of the practice. The Archbishop of Canterbury has the right to determine the issue, but appears never to have done so. Spelman explains how distinctions have become blurred by time by quoting an Anglo-Saxon ecclesiastical law of Canute that decreed that money for praying for the soul should be paid at the opening of a grave; after the Reformation, this prayer money had been commuted to a burial fee. He himself is firmly against the sale of graves and the charging of fees, as a form of simony, yet for all his researches he cannot produce clear legal support for his position, sufficient to stand against custom.

Another occasion on which Spelman was asked to exercise his skills as a legal antiquarian related to the embarrassing plight of

Archbishop Abbot in 1621. Abbot had shot and killed a warden while out hunting, an accident unfortunate for a layman but discreditable to an archbishop. King James had asked a group of bishops and lawyers for their opinion of the case. Was the Archbishop guilty of an irregularity by hunting, or was hunting a permissible sport for prelates? Here was a field day for casuists. Spelman believed that the canons of the Church should be binding in this matter, and identified the fourth Council of Orleans, held in the later fourth century, as the source of the most explicit pronouncements on the subject. Its decree 'De Clerico Venatore' provided guidelines against which Archbishop Abbot's misdemeanor could be measured. This canon forbade hunting to ministers of the Church 'voluptatis causa', but not 'recreationis causa' or 'valetudinis causa'. As Abbot maintained that he was out hunting on the advice of his physician, to avoid the stone or gout, he seemed to be on the right side of the law. Moreover, he was hunting quietly, and not engaged in 'clamosa venatio' that was also forbidden to clerics. But, Spelman reluctantly admitted, Continental canon law was not applicable to English bishops, 'who by favour of Princes and the State have Baronies annexed to their Sees'. He then raised a pertinent question: why do the great prelates have deer parks as part of their lands if hunting is forbidden them? In the end, he judged that the Archbishop was not behaving irregularly, and the rest of the committee shared his opinion. It proved very hard to know what laws or canons bore upon the case. 'Because the Canons and Decrees themselves are so general and so ready to entertain Distinctions and Limitations, the Doctors and Glosses so differing, etc., we could not return a unanimous opinion.' The committee recommended that a dispensation be granted to Abbot, and the King followed their advice.[19]

Spelman's experience of the confused state of the law in relation to the Church of England must have helped to strengthen his determination to address the large problem of the constitution of the Church, and the true scope of ecclesiastical power. Hooker had surveyed the body of belief and doctrine that the Church assented to, and defined the limits of Anglican faith, expounded the meaning of the sacraments, and defended the liturgy and ceremonies of the reformed Church. But what was its inheritance of canon law?

[19] 'An Apology for Archbishop Abbot', in *English Works* (1727), 109.

Canon law is made in the councils of the Church, so Spelman conceived a plan of documenting all the councils that had been held in Britain since the earliest days of Christianity, and all the general councils of the Church catholic and universal that British representatives had attended. It was a monumental task. As a lawyer and a scholar with strong Anglican sympathies, Spelman believed that it was essential to clarify the ideological development of the Church in Britain from its first plantation. Such a work would give the Church a firmer intellectual structure and consistency, a legal integrity, and a sounder credibility as a venerable institution with an unbroken history since Roman times. To illustrate Spelman's intentions, one might elaborate the image of 'The Arch of Government' that Spelman devised for his title-page. In Jacobean times this arch was similar to those Roman remains that one sees in seventeenth-century Italian paintings and drawings: only the head of the arch protrudes above ground. Spelman's ambition was to excavate the arch to its foundations and show that it had a firm and continuous structure.

This ambition was also held by several divines who were concerned with the intellectual dignity of the Church. In his Preface to the *Concilia*, Spelman recalls that Lancelot Andrewes had seen the need for a work on Church councils, and had encouraged his protégé Matthew Wren, a much younger man, to take up the project. Wren informed him that Spelman was already gathering materials to this end. Andrewes died in 1626, so Spelman must have started his collections in the early 1620s. Councils were a preoccupation of European Church circles in the later sixteenth and early seventeenth centuries, and Andrewes himself had pointed out how backward English scholars were in documenting their conciliar history in contrast to Italian, German, and French scholars.[20] Support for Spelman's project also came from James Ussher, the

---

[20] In the century before Spelman's work appeared, the following continental collections had been published: *Concilia Omnia*, edited by Peter Crabbe (Cologne, 1538), four volumes on councils by Laurentius Surius (Cologne 1567), five volumes edited by Dominico Nicolini (Venice, 1587), a collection of Spanish councils (Madrid, 1593), *Generalia Concilia*, edited by Severinus Bini (Cologne 1606), and a series of works published in Rome (1608–12) under the auspices of Pope Paul V. (Details from Powicke, 'Sir Henry Spelman and the *Concilia*', 214.) The intense interest in councils was part of the post-Reformation scholarly activity devoted to the retrieval and ordering of Church history; the enterprise was a case of humanist scholarship providing material for ecclesiastical polemics.

Archbishop of Armagh, who was himself engaged in documenting the early history of the Church in Britain; in the 1630s Laud became one of the great encouragers of the work.[21]

The names of the backers of this project should make us realize how much the *Concilia* was a product of what we now loosely call the Laudian movement in the Church of England. That movement most fully expressed the change of attitude towards the status of the Church of England that developed during the reign of James I, primarily under the influence of Lancelot Andrewes. The Elizabethan attitude to the Church as an instrument of government in the sovereign's control, essentially an Erastian attitude, began to give way to a new sense of the Church as a divine institution that needed to resist the secularizing tendencies of the state. The Church should define its identity and its rights more vigorously, and intensify its mission to serve and honour God in traditional ways. Laud's promotion of the rights of the Church of England during the 1630s, his emphasis on the sanctity of the Church as an institution and as a building, and his encouragement of greater beauty and order in worship, represented a sustained attempt to impose this new perception of the Church's role upon the nation. Spelman was an important contributor to the intellectual structure of Laudianism. His defence of the special status of Church property and revenues, his vindication of tithes, and above all his work *Concilia, Decreta, Leges, Constitutiones in Re Ecclesiarum Orbis Britannici* (1639) helped to fortify the Laudian dispensation.

The book was dedicated to King Charles, after much consultation with Ussher, Wren, and Laud about the phrasing of the dedication so that it would not provoke hostility from the advocates of plain religion. When Spelman opens his narrative, the first business he has to settle is the date when the Gospel came to Britain. Claiming to follow the testimony of the sixth-century chronicler Gildas, whom he regards as the earliest reliable guide, he asserts that the faith came soon after the passion of Christ, brought by Joseph of Arimathea. He cites a Vatican manuscript that gives a date of 36 AD for this event, and quotes both Origen and Theodoret to the effect that Christianity reached Britain shortly after Christ's death. So Glastonbury is the holiest place in Britain, for it has a

---

[21] Laud arranged for Spelman's assistant to become a prebendary of Lincoln Cathedral as a reward for his work on the *Concilia*.

direct association with Christ. Moreover, Spelman believes that the church raised there by Joseph must have been the very first church built for the worship of Christ in the world. Such pre-eminence deserves to be illustrated, and he commissioned an engraving to show how it probably looked, made of woven twigs with a roof of straw.

Before he prints his collections of the proceedings of early councils and synods, he gives a résumé of the early history of the Church in Britain, mainly taken from Bede. Amongst the numerous events of the early centuries, he notes the coming of Augustine's mission from Rome in 597 and the conversion of King Ethelbert and the Kentish Saxons, but the incident occupies only a few lines of text. Augustine's purpose was to convert the Saxons; the British had long been Christianized, and the Roman intervention occurred in an angle of the island occupied by an invading race. Augustine succeeded 'in kindling their brutish minds to prayer by his august services', but his achievement is not further commented upon. The British Church had existed for centuries before his coming, and it is part of Spelman's plan to ensure that the origins of the Church of England completely by-pass Rome and date back to apostolic times.

The documents that Spelman prints at the beginning of the *Concilia* are as doubtful as his acceptance of the Glastonbury legend. The letter from King Lucius to Eleutherius, Bishop of Rome in the late second century, requesting instruction in the Christian faith, was already looked on askance by antiquarians. None the less, he reproduces the text from the Cotton Library that purported to be an accurate transcription of the letter, offering a mild reservation: 'Nusquam (quod sciam) extat haec epistola, de ea autem sic Beda meminit.' ('Nowhere, as far as I know, is this letter extant, but Bede recalled it.') Spelman had little or no sense of monastic forgeries, and much preferred to include doubtful material to swell the earliest records rather than to exclude it on the grounds of scholarly scruple. He reaches safer ground when he prints the proceedings of the first council attended by British bishops, that of Arles in 314, the details of which he is able to take from Bini's *Generalia Concilia* of 1606.

A fundamental problem facing Spelman was the difficulty of discovering the details of English councils and synods and royal formulations of ecclesiastical laws. The work of continental

The first Church of the Christians In Britaine.

7. Christian primitivism: the first church at Glastonbury, from Spelman's *Concilia* (1639).

scholars meant that there were accessible accounts of the General Councils of the Church that British bishops had participated in, and that were binding on the Church in Britain, but the records of English councils were elusive. Cathedral muniments had to be searched, and the Cotton Library consulted. The college libraries at Oxford and Cambridge preserved numerous relevant manuscripts from pre-Conquest times. The work of locating manuscripts, and then deciphering them, took many years. During this time, Spelman developed a considerable proficiency in Anglo-Saxon, with the help of William Somner of Canterbury, an antiquary whose relations with Spelman are described later in this chapter. Somner furnished Spelman with much material from the archives of Canterbury Cathedral. Another major source of assistance was James Ussher, who gave Spelman the benefit of his knowledge of the conditions of the early Church, and provided him with information about St Patrick. The compilation of the *Concilia* took fifteen years, but the result was by far the fullest account in existence of the constitution of the pre-Conquest Church. The book is an archive of information about the business of the Church as discussed and pronounced upon for 700 years. The practices and customs of the Church, its internal discipline, its rights and privileges and duties in society, the manner of its financing, are set out, layer upon layer as they changed in time. Pronouncements concerning the scope of every ecclesiastical office, from archbishop to deacon, are included. The relationship between the monarch and the Church was determined as far as possible from original documents for different phases of Saxon history. Rulings concerning doctrine were recorded. Spelman was able to print the most comprehensive collection yet seen of Anglo-Saxon laws concerning the Church, derived from a wide variety of manuscript sources. The laws of Alured, Edward the Elder, Athelstan, Edmund, Edgar, Ethelred, Canute, and Edward the Confessor were now made available. The volume is in fact an inventory of Church practice and procedure, but Spelman did not venture into interpretation or application. He did not attempt to decide whether one canon superseded another, or to indicate the superior status of one king's laws over a predecessor's. The extent to which any decrees of the old English Church may be considered binding on the seventeenth-century Church is left open: that is a matter for divines and Church lawyers to resolve.

The first volume of the *Concilia* extended up to 1066. Spelman had projected three volumes: another from the Conquest to the Reformation, and a third that would detail the records of the Church from the Reformation to the reign of Charles I. He had made some collections towards the second volume, which was eventually brought to completion by Sir William Dugdale and printed in 1664. Dugdale took up the work at the Restoration, urged on by Archbishop Sheldon and Lord Clarendon. Their concern to see the *Concilia* finished is clear evidence of how strongly the governors of the Church in the seventeenth century felt the need for supportive documentation of the Church's legal and dogmatic inheritance. Andrewes, Ussher, Laud, and Sheldon backed this undertaking as a necessary specification of Anglican identity, one that would both strengthen and defend the Church's position in society and against Catholic or Puritan criticism.[22] Undoubtedly, the *Concilia* helped to root the Church of England more firmly in antiquity, and justified the hierarchy and spiritual

---

[22] As the Anglican and royalist writer Francis Wortley observed, a True Protestant 'is one who professeth the Doctrine and Discipline of the Church of England, established by the General Councils and Synods, and after confirmed by the known law of the Kingdom'. An Anabaptisticall Independent 'cannot bear to hear of Councils and Synods, and is much troubled that [St Paul] approves of the Altar' (*Characters and Elegies* (1646), 11, 14).

discipline of the Church from ancient precedents. The compilation of the *Concilia* advanced Spelman's own position in society too: it probably explains why he is buried in Westminster Abbey and not in the parish church of St Margaret's.

We may turn now to the antiquarian research that Spelman carried out into secular matters, his uncovering the foundations of the other pillar of the Arch of State. His ambition here was to write a definitive book on the origins and growth of the English law, a counterpart to his work on ecclesiastical origins. He soon found, however, that his enquiries were hindered by the difficulty of knowing what the legal terms used in Anglo-Saxon and Norman documents meant. There were so many words and phrases of which the meaning and implications were unclear 'that he despaired of his design, for want of understanding the language'. He recognized that further progress would be impractical, unless a firmer definition of terms were available, and terms needed to be understood in the context of their use in Saxon and medieval times. So he conceived the idea of a Glossary, in which 'by collecting obsolete words and variety of instances' he would be able 'to give a tolerable conjecture at the true signification'.[23] The dimensions of this project, at first sight a modest exercise in philology, became prodigious. The subtitle of his work, which he entitled *Archaeologus*, indicates the scope: 'Latino-Barbara, Peregrina, Obsoleta et Novatae Significationis Vocabula, quae post labefactas a Gothis, Vandalisque; Res Europas, in Ecclesiasticis Profanisque Scriptoribus; variorum item Gentium Legibus Antiquis, Chartis et Formulis occurunt.'[24]

Spelman was old enough to have been a close friend of Camden, and in preparing his Glossary he benefited from the international connections that Camden had established in his long career. Antiquaries all over Europe were excited by Spelman's design, especially those whose bias was legal or philological, for its contents would be of use to all who had to make sense of the records of the emergent society of the early medieval world. Those

[23] Gibson, 'Life' in Spelman, *Reliquiae Spelmanniae*, a2.
[24] The title may be translated as 'A list of words that are of Barbarous Latin origin, or foreign or exotic; obsolete terms and neologisms, that came in after the collapse of the European polity caused by the Goths and the Vandals; words that occur in writers ecclesiastical and profane, and also in the ancient laws of the nations, in charters and formulaic phrases.'

acknowledged in the Preface include scholars from France, Germany, and the Netherlands, with Peiresc, Bignon, Rigault, and Salmasius the most notable. The English scholars he names, not so numerous as the Continentals, are Camden, Cotton, Selden, Ussher, and John Williams, and the Scottish scholars Cowell and Skene. He pays tribute to them all in an engaging phrase: 'ex operibus suis re antiqua splendidis, saepe mihi ramum aureum ad tartareas istas regiones peragrandas.' ('From their works, refulgent with the matter of antiquity, I have often plucked the golden bough that will preserve me in the dark regions through which I have to venture.')[25] The dark regions that he penetrated with their help were indeed an unknown country, for in recovering the meanings of archaic words, Spelman was also recovering the structure of societies that had been lost to memory. By following up the conclusions of Verstegan and Camden that the Englishmen of Saxon times belonged to the Teutonic peoples and that English was related to the family of Germanic languages, he understood that Anglo-Saxon law and customs were part of a larger system of laws, customs, and social organization common to the barbarian races of northern Europe. Upon these extensive tribal groupings the Normans, themselves of northern origin, impinged, imposing their more complex and hierarchical social structure. One can understand why scholars in lands where these Teutonic nations had settled were interested in Spelman's investigations.

The Glossary turned out to be not a dictionary of definitions (though many words were simply defined) but a series of dissertations on key terms. It is now a commonplace of historical opinion to say that as a result of reconstructing the legal framework of Saxon and Norman societies, Spelman arrived at the first coherent understanding of the feudal system that the Normans introduced and perfected in the two centuries following the Conquest.[26] Spelman's disquisitions on such titles as 'Baro' ('Baron') or 'Dux' ('Duke') uncovered the historical origins of these ranks, their powers and duties, the terms on which they held their land, their relationships to the monarch, their obligations in war, and their privileges in law. Under the heading 'Feodum, exteris Feudum'

---

[25] Preface to *Archaeologus* (1626).
[26] The definitive account is by Pocock in *Ancient Constitution*. See ch. 5: 'The Discovery of Feudalism: Sir Henry Spelman'.

Spelman was able to explore the system of land tenures and obligations that was fundamental to the Norman state. By clarifying the status of the term 'allodium', as relating to estates held not of a superior but in absolute ownership, the Glossary helped one to understand the nature of the transformation in land ownership that the Normans brought about. Concepts of hereditary tenures, knight service, feudal dues and homage, the obligations of wardship and relief, became comprehensible as part of the rigorous feudal structure of Norman society. The laws of England had obviously changed to serve the interests of the new system. By examining the scope of the key term 'felo' ('a crime') as it changed in application from the tenth to the twelfth centuries, Spelman was able to throw light on the social expectations of England before and after the Conquest. Legal words such as 'judicium' yielded information about the outreach of the law, the structure of the legal system and the nature of punishments; 'Cancellarius' provided an opportunity to explore the administrative structure both of government and the law. The limits of secular power against ecclesiastical power could be defined by explicating the meaning of words that occurred frequently in border disputes between the two estates.

In Elizabethan times, the feudal system had disintegrated so extensively that its character was barely understood. Its origins were simply not known. The differences between Saxon and Norman society were imperfectly grasped, and the status of the law in each society had never been properly defined. The common lawyers of England were confident that their laws could be explained entirely by reference to the English past, uncritically imagined, and that they dated back to time immemorial, broadening out from precedent to precedent as they descended through the ages. Spelman put the study of English law on a comparative basis, and displayed its affinities with the laws of the Germanic peoples. He demonstrated that the Normans had introduced the mature feudal system into England at the Conquest, and that although feudalism had its origins amongst the Germanic nations, it was not present in any significant way in Saxon England. The whole system of land tenure had been altered at the Conquest, and the laws of England thereafter were intimately bound up with the imported system, a change which could be documented by reference to charters and the terms of land grants. Contrary to the belief of most lawyers, the common law was not some sacrosanct accumulation of the rights and limitations of free-born Englishmen that had come down from Saxon times and before, with minor modifications after the Conquest, but it had a history and a chronology that showed it underwent great change at the hands of foreign invaders. The law was less ancient and less venerable than the lawyers wished it to be; it was utilitarian and shaped by identifiable historical forces, and served the interests of the ruling class. It was not necessarily older or superior to the powers of monarchy, and indeed the Conquest had shown the law to be subject to the king's will.

The first part of the *Archaeologus* or Glossary was published in 1626.[27] It stopped at the letter L. The remainder was completed by Dugdale and published in 1664. Edmund Gibson in his short biography of Spelman suggested that the work broke off at that point because Spelman did not wish to provoke controversy by his discussions of Magna Carta and Parliament. This, however, would seem to be an unworthy accusation, for Spelman habitually dealt with controversial subjects; the Glossary was a slow business, and his attention was caught by Church matters. His health was also troubling him, as the Latin poem he attached to the end of the first part indicates. This unexpected introduction of a personal note brings out quite poignantly the sheer stress of protracted antiquarian research, so toilsome and wearing.

> Iam mihi pars operis multo sudoris peracta,
> Prima iacet: superest multo peragenda secunda.
> Utque; viae in medio fregit quae praeterit aegrum,
> Sic ea quae sequitur terret: pars ultima vitae,
> Ultima nec videat timeo monumenta laboris.
> O qui principio medium, medio adijce finem.

(The first part of the work, accomplished with much sweat of mine, now lies complete: the second part remains, to be accomplished with much more. And as the part which has gone by broke [the health of] him who, a sick man, [stands] in mid-journey, so that which follows terrifies him: for I

---

[27] Spelman offered the Glossary to the King's printer 'desiring only £5 for his labour, and that to be paid in books'. The printer declined the offer, as he considered the book unsaleable, and Spelman had to bear the whole charge of printing the work himself. The incident casts light on the small audience for antiquarian works in Stuart times, when the subject was not national, county, or family history. See Gibson, 'Life' in Spelman, *Reliquiae Spelmanniae*, a2v.

fear lest the last part of my life see not the final monuments of [my] labour. O add the end to the middle, [thou] who [added] the middle to the beginning!)

Unquestionably, the origins of Parliament did interest him, and work on the Glossary had given him a new perspective on the question. J. G. A. Pocock puts the matter succinctly: as

the relationship of the barons to the crown from the eleventh to the thirteenth centuries is to be understood in terms of vassalage and its obligations, the appearance of county freeholders in Parliament, where they were not obliged to attend by their tenures, could come about only in a society where feudal relationships were beginning to lose their exclusive importance.[28]

The growth of Parliament had to be understood as a feature of the decline of the feudal system. The common lawyers' reverence for Saxon parliaments and witangemots as the early formal expression of the Englishman's right to determine political developments and to advise his sovereign, whilst limiting his power, is quite misdirected, according to Spelman's conclusions. Parliament as the seventeenth century knew it had begun to take shape in the thirteenth century, and had evolved gradually from that time.

This idea of gradual evolution of institutions, of history as slow process, rare elsewhere in Stuart historical thinking (which was overfond of identifying origins, naming names, and seeing change as a series of climacterics) is a feature of several papers that Spelman wrote on the development of Parliament, and that were eventually published in the *Reliquiae Spelmanniae* of 1698. These pieces are not easy to date. 'Of Parliaments' begins with the teasing observation that he has 'seen so many Parliaments miscarry in the last sixteen years' that he hesitates to open up the subject. A date in the late 1620s would sort adequately with this claim. In his survey, he is concerned to locate the presence of representatives of the commons in councils of state. He can find no evidence at all to suggest that the common people had any say at all in the government of the country in Saxon times. In Norman times, he is unable to find any evidence to support Polydore Vergil's claim that Henry I held a Parliament of three estates in the sixteenth year of

---

[28] Pocock, *Ancient Constitution*, 119.

his reign. Even in King John's time, the only knights who were summoned to parliamentary consultation were those who held lands immediately of the king, and who were therefore obliged to attend. The first appearance of men who represented the freeholders of a county, or of burgesses, is hard to specify, but Spelman points to the tenth year of Henry III as a possible beginning of a commons presence. 'Of Parliaments' is not a treatise written with any conclusiveness, but it is evident to Spelman that the commons are late-comers on the parliamentary scene, and that kings did not stand in need of parliaments until long after the Conquest, and that kings summoned only those lords and knights who were bound in fealty to attend and advise. The implications for the political conflicts of Charles I's reign were highly favourable to the King, for they suggested that the King had powers that greatly antedated parliaments, and the common law which was often invoked against the royal prerogative was not an unchanging institution deriving from Saxon times or earlier that could reliably be used against the crown because it could claim a greater antiquity and authority than the prerogative of kings.

In another tract, 'Of the Ancient Government of England', he struck a blow against the belief in the immemorial antiquity of the common law by reporting on his researches into Saxon records. Gathered into seven kingdoms, the Saxons had the same language and customs, but each kingdom had its laws; when they came together into one monarchy in the ninth century, the common law was that which was indeed common amongst the older kingdoms, but at the same time laws individual to a particular kingdom were abolished. As a scholar first and then a lawyer, Spelman admits that although we have many collections of laws from Saxon England, ratified and promulgated by kings, we have little understanding of how they were applied, and equally little understanding of how the government of Saxon England was actually carried out. Even the change-over of the laws at the Conquest was unclear and ill-documented. Spelman states his conviction that the slow processes of transition make definite pronouncements of the questions concerning the laws, customs, and government of the remote past difficult in the extreme.

To tell the Government of England under the old Saxon laws seemeth an Utopia to us at present; strange and uncouth: yet there can be no period assigned, wherein either the frame of those laws was abolished, or this of ours entertained; but as Day and Night creep insensibly, one upon the other, so also hath this Alteration grown upon us insensibly.[29]

This sense of slow gradual change had much in common with Selden's thoughts on the evolution of the institution of government.

Conscious that he has made a number of advances in clarifying the early history of law and government, Spelman signals that his treatise is a contribution to the ambitious project that he entertained for much of his career, the discovery of the rights and privileges of Church and state. He invokes the image of the Arch of State which he favoured as the emblem of his task: 'The Common Law is but the half Arch of the Government, tending only to the temporal part thereof, and not unto the Ecclesiastical.' He acknowledges his bias in politics when he confesses that the Crown must be supported by both estates, and the Crown must reciprocally confirm the integrity of both its supports. 'As therefore each side of an Arch descendeth alike from the Coane or top-point, so both sides of that their Government was alike descended from the King.'[30]

During his lifetime, because so many of his writings on secular subjects remained unpublished, Spelman was known primarily as a defender of ecclesiastical rights. His views on Church affairs were vigorous and strongly held, while on secular matters he valued scholarship more than polemic, and probably the recognition that many of his delvings were tentative and inconclusive may have deterred him. In addition, a certain political wariness may have kept him from making public his views on the law and government. Though he was an early and distinguished exponent of painstaking methodical enquiry into the incunabula of national institutions, and aware of the need for a comparative approach to English problems, he did not thrust his findings at the world, and he was not eager for disputation. He never drew his writings into a coherent corpus, nor for that matter did he write a keystone work which would have held his various researches together and served as an ideological centre for his concerns.

Spelman valued friendship and co-operation above the rancorous exchange of political beliefs, and in a way, he was fortunate to die in 1641. Antiquaries attracted relatively few elegies, but on

---

[29] 'Of the Ancient Government of England' in Spelman, *Reliquiae Spelmanniae*, 49. [30] Ibid.

Spelman one survives from the hand of the royalist Sir Francis
Wortley, which was printed in a collection of poems devoted to
those men who served the royal cause well. It registers in a fairly
simple way the appreciation of his defence of the Church, and
shows how much Spelman was considered to be one of the
intellectual heroes of the age.

> There's none I know hath written heretofore,
> Who hath obliged this Church and Kingdome more.
> Thou hast deriv'd, nay prov'd, our Church as high
> As Rome can boast, and giv'n her pride the lie.
> Thou hast the series of her story shown,
> So hast o'er us her Hierarchy o'erthrown.
> I read thy books, and I admire thy soule,
> Thy daring soule that durst proud Rome controule:
> Thou with their own Authorities, dost prove
> That which they would, but never shall remove:
> Thou prov'st that Gregories Monks found Bishops here
> Durst check his pride, who after Martyrs were:
> Who held the Rites and Customs of the East
> Which Polycarpus durst approve the best,
> Who twice to Rome as an officiall came
> To fix that Feast, which now we must not name.
> Thou prov'd our Church as glorious as Romes
> For Doctrine, Discipline and Martyrdomes.
> Thou prov'd to us the mighty power of Kings
> In calling Councells even in spirituall things;
> And temporall rights the Churches Pedigree,
> Her frequent Councells even in Brittany;
> As a choyce piece of evidence a story
> Which we may style great Brittaines chiefest glory,
> The Brittish Church, our Kings owe this to thee;
> Shall we not reverence then thy memory?
> Hadst thou been Romes, thy supererogation
> Had raised a stock of merits for our Nation.
> But thou art ours, I joy I live to know
> I had a friend good men shall reverence so.[31]

---

[31] Wortley, *Characters and Elegies*, 48–9. The feast that men must not name in
1646 is Easter. Another elegy for Spelman was composed by William Cartwright,
the Caroline playwright and dramatist who had an interest in philology. He
applauds the integrity of Spelman's scholarship, and singles out the *Concilia* and 'De
Sepultura' for particular praise. The tenor of his judgement can be gauged by the
following lines:

It will be evident from this account of Spelman's career that he must have been a competent Anglo-Saxon scholar, for a great deal of his primary material was in that language. He was well aware that 'the knowledge of the Saxon language was so far necessary as without it the Antiquities of England be either not discovered or at least imperfectly known.'[32] He effectively taught himself the language, receiving help from other antiquaries such as James Ussher and Francis Junius, and depending heavily on the interlineated manuscripts in the Cotton Library and the Saxon–Latin word lists in the same collection.[33] He also used texts with Latin translations parallel to the Saxon, such as Lambarde's *Archaionomia*. Already in his *Concilia* of 1639, he was encouraging other scholars by printing a guide to Anglo-Saxon characters at the front of the book.[34] In the last decade of his life he became friendly with a younger antiquary, William Somner, who was in the process of making himself the most proficient Anglo-Saxonist of the century, and who eventually occupied the lectureship that Spelman founded at Cambridge in 1638 for the advancement of the subject. Somner's career has many affinities with Spelman's, for in both cases their High-Church antiquarianism was supportive of the Laudian movement and of the privileges of the Church and the clergy, and both advanced the knowledge of Anglo-Saxon England considerably. Somner's achievements and his contribution to antiquarian life deserve to be better known.

Canterbury was the theatre of his activities. He was born there in

> Thou didst consult the Ancients and their Writ,
> To guard the Truth, not exercise the Wit;
> Taking but what they said; not, as some do,
> To find out what they may be wrested to;
> Nor Hope, nor Faction, brought thy Mind to side,
> Conscience depos'd all Parts, and was sole Guide.

(*The Plays and Poems of William Cartwright*, ed. G. B. Evans (Madison, Wis., 1951), 550.)

[32] Kennett, 'Life of Somner' in Somner, *Treatise*, 24.

[33] Junius also had plans to compile a Saxon dictionary. 'I keepe myself busie with referring the most antient Gothicke dialect, occurring in the Codex Argenteus, to that collection of an Anglo-Saxonike Dictionarie I have been long gathering for mine own private use.' (*Sir William Dugdale*, ed. Hamper, 302.) Junius's Dictionary was published in 1743 by the Rev. Edward Lye.

[34] Spelman also designed the Anglo-Saxon type for the Cambridge University Press edition of Bede prepared by Abraham Wheelock that was published in 1643. See Oates, 'Abraham Wheelock', i.

1606, the son of the Registrar of the Courts, and he himself came to hold various offices in the ecclesiastical courts of that city. He was singled out for advancement by the Archbishop, William Laud, and his first publication was *The Antiquities of Canterbury* (1640). Not surprisingly, given his patronage, this work was dedicated to Laud. The Epistle Dedicatory reminds the reader of Laud's encouragement of antiquarian studies, praising 'His Grace's extra care and cost for the collection of Antiquities of all sorts from all parts, crowned by singular piety and nobleness in disposing of them to the good and service of the Publick'. (Somner may well have had in mind here Laud's patronage of the orientalist Edward Pococke, who was a tireless searcher after Greek and Arabic manuscripts and coins in the Middle East; Laud made generous gifts of these manuscripts to the Bodleian Library.)

Growing up in a historically rich city undoubtedly fostered his antiquarian curiosity. From his youth, he was eager 'to know the genealogie of houses, walls and dust'. As his biographer, White Kennett, remarked, 'when he refreshed himself in the fields, it was not merely for digestion and for air, but to survey the British Bricks, the Roman Ways, the Danish Hills and Works, the Saxon Monasteries, and the Norman Churches.'[35] The 'curious and observant eye' that these comments suggest gave his work on Canterbury its particular distinction. It was the first book devoted to the intensive study of an English cathedral. There is the predictable account of its foundation, endowments, and growth, illustrated from charters, the expected history of its archbishops and their actions, all worked up from the cathedral muniments; there is the conventional record of the monuments and their inscriptions, with notices of the worthies buried within; what is unprecedented, and in advance of the age, is the responsiveness to the architecture and the real interest in style. 'Somner walked often in the Nave, not in that idle and inadvertent posture, nor with that common and trivial Discourse, with which those open Temples are vulgarly prophaned', but observantly, 'to distinguish the age of the building, to sift the ashes of the Dead'.[36] Not only is Somner appreciative of the beauty of Canterbury's architecture, something that other antiquaries (Weever, for example) ignore, he tries to work out the chronology of the building by reference to stylistic

---

[35] Kennett, 'Life of Somner' in Somner, *Treatise*, 9–10.   [36] Ibid. 9.

change. He attempts 'a History of the Fabrick'; his understanding may be rudimentary in comparison with later ages, but he has a genuine sense of the development of architectural forms. When trying to determine the age of the choir, for example, he knows it must be no older than the Conquest, 'because the building of it upon arches, a form of Architecture though in use with and among the Romans long before, yet after their departure not used here in England till the Normans brought it over with them from France'.[37] He is well aware of the limitations of Saxon building, and knows the Saxons were not capable of raising arcades of arches in two or three tiers. He believes, from the evidence of charters, that most Saxon monasteries had been built of wood, and knows that the Normans introduced a new style of stone architecture, quoting William of Malmesbury: 'video . . . in vicis et urbibus Monasteria novo aedificandi genere consurgere.' He even knows that the Normans brought stone from Caen for their new buildings.

The *Antiquities of Canterbury* is a real guide book, in a recognizable modern sense, even in the encouraging tone of voice towards the reader:

Next observe we the first cross-iles (wings some call them) of the Church, those (I mean) between the nave and the quire, which by the work seem of like age with the body, saving that the North-Ile (the goodly and glorious window at the head thereof, a piece in its kind beyond compare) was a gift of Edward IV, as may be seen upon it.[38]

He can identify the coats of arms that are so numerous in carvings and windows, something that modern Church historians have great difficulty in doing. Most exceptionally, he is interested in the stained glass of the Cathedral, and devotes a long appendix to a detailed description of the biblical scenes in the choir, with the texts accompanying them.

'Now must I play the Mystagogus, and shew you the Monuments,' he announces as he begins his tour of the realms of the dead. From tomb to tomb he goes, noting the inscriptions and reviving the memory of old names. He makes considerable use of Weever, who had gone over the same ground a generation before. Somner breaks off to admire the new font, the gift of Dr Warner, now Bishop of

[37] William Somner, *The Antiquities of Canterbury* (1640), 168.
[38] Ibid. 166.

Rochester. It is a rare piece, 'a monument of the operative and exemplary piety' of the donor, and moreover, Somner pointedly remarks, 'it is the first thing of worth, that by any private hand hath been offered to this Church in latter times.' The contrast with the centuries of benefactions that the book has already described could not be starker, and we are made aware that the hundred years since the Reformation have been a bleak age for the Church. We can understand too why Somner was so admiring of Laud in his attempts to reintroduce 'the beauty of holiness'. The font is illustrated: it is a recognizably Laudian piece in a freely-handled classical style, a four-pillared base carrying a scalloped basin, very much of the 1630s. Underlying the whole book is an anxiety that the Cathedral might not survive unharmed for much longer. Greece, which created so much that was beautiful, slid into a state of barbarism, Somner warns the reader in the Preface. He wants to be sure that the record is as complete as he can make it in case times turn against the Church. Canterbury did suffer in the Civil Wars. As White Kennett recalled, the 'popular phanatique fury . . . stormed and pillaged the cathedral, the beautified Windows were broke, the Tombs of Princes and Prelates were ravaged, and every graceful ornament despoiled.'[39]

Somner makes it clear in his introduction that he has compiled the history of the Cathedral, the city, and its parish churches almost single-handed. Previous collections of Canterbury antiquities, such as those of John Twine, who had been mayor of the city in the 1550s, have been scattered and lost. In constructing his account, Somner has had the greatest trouble with the misty origins of Canterbury. Convention demanded that noble cities have named founders, and the British history furnished one in Rud-Hudibras, an early King. Somner shows the usual indecision about accepting the British history: he notes Camden's scepticism, but adds that 'divers men of judgement and good Antiquaries too' accept it, citing Lambarde, Holinshed, Stow, and Speed. He leaves the question open, and hastens on. As for that great crux in divinity, the first planting of the Church in Britain, Somner is happy to waive Canterbury's title to be the nursery of the Church in favour of a far earlier source. St Augustine founded the abbey at Canterbury after the conversion of King Ethelbert, but Somner comments that he

---

[39] Kennett, 'Life of Somner' in Somner, *Treatise*, 15.

came to convert the Saxons, who were 'idolaters', 'but the Britaines were Christian almost from the time of our Saviour's death, and so they continued, though at this time living with their Bishops in the remote parts of this Island.'[40] This is the standard, indeed the necessary, Anglican position.

The chief consequence for Somner of his work on Canterbury was a determination to master Anglo-Saxon and end the inaccessibility of that language for scholars. He had worked on Saxon charters and laws for the *Antiquities*, and had received a good deal of assistance from Meric Casaubon, who was a prebendary at Canterbury, and the son of the defender of the Jacobean Church, Isaac Casaubon. The younger Casaubon had already published a small book, *De Lingua Saxonis*, but he realized something more ambitious was needed to bring about a revival of Anglo-Saxon studies in England, and urged Somner to compile a truly serviceable dictionary and grammar.

Looking back over the century, White Kennett could say that by Tudor times 'the Saxon Language was extinct, and the monuments of it so few and so latent, that it required infinite courage and patience to attempt to prosecute the knowledge of it.'[41] Certainly, the language was restored and kept alive by a handful of scholars, and in the view of George Hickes, the great Oxford Saxonist who flourished at the end of the seventeenth century, 'since the Conquest, only two foreigners and about twenty natives had by their own industry attained to the knowlege of this tongue.'[42] The circle around Matthew Parker had made a start in recovering and reading Anglo-Saxon manuscripts: Laurence Nowell, John Josselin, and William Lambarde were the most proficient of these scholars in the early years of Elizabeth's reign. Lambarde published his collection of Anglo-Saxon laws, *Archaionomia*, in 1568, and this

[40] Somner, *Antiquities of Canterbury*, 4.
[41] Kennett, 'Life of Somner' in Somner, *Treatise*, 22.
[42] Ibid. 31, quoting the Preface to Hickes' *Institutiones Grammaticae Anglo-Saxonicae* (1689). According to Hickes, 'Jocelin, Somner, Marshall, and Junius published all their Saxon purely and correctly,' but Selden, Spelman, and even the Cambridge professor Abraham Wheelock put theirs before the world 'with faults and imperfections'. Kennett drew attention to the survival of 'lectures in the Saxon Tongue' at Tavistock Abbey until the Reformation, mentioned by Camden under Devonshire. This local knowledge of Saxon persisted, Kennett thought, because 'interest did oblige them to understand the language of their original charters' (ibid. 28).

remained the principal work of Anglo-Saxon scholarship until Jacobean times. Camden made progress in the language, but it was Verstegan who made the fullest case for its value to antiquarians, as we have seen. Selden and Ussher managed to teach themselves the language very competently. When William Somner set about compiling a full dictionary, he was able to build on materials assembled by all these men. He used the Saxon vocabulary put together by Nowell which had come into the hands of John Selden, who lent it to Somner. A similar vocabulary had been made by Josselin (who had been Archbishop Parker's secretary); this was transcribed by the antiquary Sir Simonds D'Ewes, who also lent it to Somner. Principally, however, Somner used two ancient Saxon–Latin glossaries in the Cotton Library. He found the word lists in Verstegan's *Restitution* most helpful, and he annotated this book thoroughly. Casaubon, Junius, and Ussher all provided help and advice, and the impression one has is of a concerted collaborative effort on the part of Stuart antiquaries to propel Somner towards his goal.

Throughout the 1640s and 1650s Somner worked on his project, against we know not what disorders in his professional life as an ecclesiastical officer in the Civil War years and during the Puritan supremacy.[43] His philological enquiries for the better understanding of Saxon took him into the Irish and Scottish languages, Danish, Sclavonian, Gallic, and Gothic. He was able to pour some of his linguistic expertise into the glossary of obscure words that he supplied for the collection of early English historians published in 1652, *Historiae Anglicanae Scriptores Decem* by Sir Roger Twysden. He furnished Saxon charters from Canterbury to Dodsworth and Dugdale for their *Monasticon*. Formal encouragement came when he was appointed to the Cambridge lectureship in Anglo-Saxon that had been founded by Sir Henry Spelman in 1638. Abraham Wheelock the orientalist had been the first holder, and he had made the transition to Anglo-Saxon studies with considerable success. When he died in 1653, James Ussher recommended Somner to Roger Spelman, who had the nomination rights, and Somner was installed.

---

[43] Somner did not hide his royalist loyalties: he published a poem, 'a Passionate Elegy', entitled 'The Insecurity of Princes' on Charles I in 1649, and wrote verses evoked by the frontispiece to *Eikon Basilike*.

The *Dictionarium Saxonico-Anglicum* was finally published in 1659, at Oxford. Its appearance was also the result of a collaborative effort, for the expenses of printing were paid for by a group of supporters who are named in the book. They included Thomas and John Cotton, Thomas Barlow the Bodleian librarian, Dugdale, Ashmole, Simon Archer, John Marsham the orientalist, Thomas Stanley the philosopher-poet, Orlando Bridgeman the eminent lawyer, William Lilly the astrologer, and John Warner, Bishop of Rochester, the donor of the Canterbury font. The Dictionary, in thick folio, provided the first comprehensive explanation of Anglo-Saxon vocabulary, with specimen phrases and English and Latin equivalents. After the lexicon, Somner also printed the Anglo-Saxon Grammar by Ælfric the Grammarian as a way of communicating the structure of the language. Ælfric had written his Grammar at the beginning of the eleventh century in the manner of Priscian's Latin Grammar which was the widely-used textbook of the early medieval world.[44] Francis Junius had discovered in the library of Peter Paul Rubens in Brussels an ancient manuscript copy of the Glossary that Ælfric had compiled as a companion to his Grammar, and Somner was able to print this text together with the Grammar to round off his book.

In contrast to the grave erudition of its contents, the Dictionary was prefaced by a number of commendatory poems notable for their cheerfulness and wit. They still transmit the rejoicing in the antiquarian camp at the achievement of a remarkable deed in unpropitious times. Anglo-Saxon had been securely restored:

> A language lost from th'Archives, and from Thee
> Receives a happy Palingenesy.
> Thus from thy teeming head, and fertile braine,
> Minerva-like, the Saxons live again.
> Welcome great Hengist, and thy brother too,
> 'Tis no Invasion, but a Visit now.[45]

John Boys, a gentleman of Kent and Somner's neighbour, asked:

> Shall Paper live,
> And Inke, when Brasse and Marble can't withstand

---

[44] Priscian wrote his *Institutio Grammatica* in Byzantium at the beginning of the sixth century.

[45] 'To the much admired Antiquary, William Somner, the great restorer of the Saxon Tongue', by William Jacob, physician.

This Iron Age's violating Hand?
Or that thy Title, Dictionarium
Saxonico-Latino-Anglicum
Will sell thy Book? . . .
So that thy trade is out of fashion, Friend.
Loe, 'gainst Antiquities we now contend.
Our Quarrel is against the former Age
'Gainst our dead Fathers we dire Warre do wage.

It was true that the prevailing mood of the Commonwealth years was hostile to antiquarian research. It was not a time to show reverence to 'our dead fathers', and, of course, the majority of antiquaries were royalists and Anglicans. The upheavals of the 1640s did not favour sustained research, and the urgency of resolving present issues prevailed over slow-paced scholarship directed to the past. That hostility lessened somewhat under Cromwell, but the booksellers were not eager to publish Dugdale, for example, and authors often had to buy their way into print. Throughout the 1650s, the market slowly but steadily improved.

At the Restoration, the antiquaries were back in fashion. Somner at this time was extremely busy recovering Church lands and possessions for Canterbury Cathedral. He did, however, help Dugdale to complete Spelman's *Concilia*, and he tried to make progress with a book on the Antiquities of Kent that he had been working on for many years. As part of this work, he published a treatise on *Gavelkind* in 1660, an enquiry into the peculiar Kentish system of inheritance whereby if a man died intestate, all the male heirs shared equally in his estate. It is a Spelmanesque work, expounding the nature of feudal tenures and giving definitions of land-use terms. Scholarship here prevails over regional pride and romantic views of the past, as Somner exposes as a 'monkish figment' the legend perpetuated in Kent's coat of arms that the county remained 'invicta' (unconquered by William), and therefore had not been subject to the tenures of villeinage. The only other section of the book on Kentish antiquities to appear in print was the *Treatise of the Roman Ports and Forts in Kent*, which was eventually published in 1693, under White Kennett's editorship, Somner himself having died in 1669. This was an exercise in historical geography in the tradition of Camden, identifying the location of antique military stations and giving some account of archaeological discoveries relating to them. It was also the occasion of Kennett's excellent memoir which preserves such a valuable record of Somner's career. Without that memoir, the merits and enterprise of a remarkable man might have been quite forgotten.

7

John Weever

John Weever was an unexpected antiquarian. He published *Ancient Funerall Monuments* in 1631, a year before his death, without having given any previous indication of interest in the subject. Thirty years earlier, he had tried his hand at a literary career, publishing five short volumes of verse, variously satiric, erotic, and religious, around the turn of the century, and had then fallen silent. What little we know of him has been pieced together in a recent biography by Ernst Honigmann, from whom we derive a picture of a fretful, irascible Cambridge scholar of Lancashire origins, tranquillized by money from a successful marriage, who turned in middle life to the study of church antiquities. At his own expense he travelled all over England for many years, compiling a record of monumental inscriptions and a register of who is buried where. It seems to have been a solitary, self-imposed task, carried out haphazardly, that began to acquire some method only after he gained the acquaintance of the major London antiquaries in the early 1620s. He claims our attention, however, for several reasons. His hopelessly ambitious task was characteristic of the kind of comprehensive, nation-wide survey of an antiquarian subject inspired by the example of Camden's *Britannia*, and it was carried forward by a rather simple-minded patriotism that desired to honour the memory of worthy men and women, wherever they were buried. He brought a note of literary richness to antiquarian studies, writing often with an eloquence suitable to his subject of mortality and commemoration. Weever also exemplifies the antiquarian as consolidator: he wrote to strengthen the social fabric of the Church in England by reminding his readers that the Church, whether Catholic or Protestant, has always had a role in preserving and protecting the honourable dead of the nation, and he was motivated in part by an anxiety that this historic function was in danger of being negated by the growth of Puritan narrow-mindedness which had no sympathy with the Church as a repository of accumulated social history.

8. Portrait of John Weever meditating upon death, by Thomas Cecill, from *Ancient Funerall Monuments* (1631).

Weever's book dealt with a subject that has always fascinated the English: tombs and memorials. In every century since the Norman Conquest, down to the First World War, the generations of the English have recorded their estimate of the prominent families of the time by means of innumerable memorials on the walls of local churches. The greater families raise their monuments as far eastwards as they can within the chancel; the lesser breeds are content to hang their tablets on the walls of aisles. On every side prose and verse offer lapidary praise to the deceased. Besides cataloguing the many virtues that have passed into the grave, these memorials preserve a wealth of information about family lineage, and in many cases are the only surviving records of marriages and affiliations. (Many of these monuments also represent the best of English sculpture in their time, but that was not a matter of interest to seventeenth-century antiquarians.) Churches carry this freight of history through time, and although much damage had been done at the Reformation, much survived, and the Elizabethans had applied themselves vigorously to the filling of vacant spaces. Even as Weever wrote, in the 1620s, the passion for raising monuments was attaining an unprecedented intensity as Jacobean notables crowded into the vaults and their families, in a competition between old blood and new money, strove to advertise their merits in alabaster and jet. This pride in secular accomplishments often antagonized the godly members of a church, who, with a severe reformist outlook, believed these images had no right to invade the House of the Lord.

In this atmosphere of rising tension, Weever went the rounds of the churches diocese by diocese, an early funereal Pevsner, gathering information for his book. He set out his intentions in 'The Epistle to the Reader', in a mildly confused way that was typical of him. He wished to defy oblivion, the antiquaries' perennial enemy, by recording memorials before time or religious change could deface them. He claimed to be offering a work of public usefulness, and justified his activities by reference to the proclamation issued by Elizabeth in the second year of her reign 'Against the Breaking and Defacing of Monuments of Antiquitie'. Weever clearly felt that this proclamation needed to be invoked again in his time to remind men of the social value of memorials, for he feared a new outbreak of iconoclasm in England. He quotes with approval how the loss of these monuments would extinguish 'the honourable and good memory of sundry vertuous and noble persons deceased' and also that 'the true understanding of divers Families in these Realms (who have descended of the bloud of the same persons deceased) is thereby so darkened, as the true course of their inheritance may be hereafter interrupted, contrary to Justice.' His book is in fact complementary to Elizabeth's proclamation: the one forbids the defacing of monuments; the other gathers and preserves the information on those monuments, and puts it into the possession of a national rather than a parochial readership. In an age when titles were being sold for money, older, well-established families might like to fall back on their ancestry for reassurance of their superior estate, and conversely, new gentry might be able to discover traces of eminent ancestry that would give some depth to their recently acquired status.

Although in principle Weever's collections might serve to clarify lines of descent, in practice he was not particularly interested in genealogy. In this regard, he was out of step with most of his antiquarian contemporaries, who had a firmer grounding in heraldry than Weever possessed. It is fair to say that he ignored half the value of a memorial. An Elizabethan or Jacobean funeral inscription was most particular to record the parentage of the deceased and of his or her spouse, as well as the names of children and their marriage partners, if any, so that the memorial could be used with certainty as a document of family relations. In addition, any coats of arms belonging to the family would be prominently displayed, for that was a definitive way of establishing identity in Renaissance society. Yet Weever virtually ignored coats of arms, and displayed little knowledge of heraldry, a serious disadvantage in an antiquary. Rather than produce a genealogical handbook, Weever wished to compile a book of worthies, 'to revive the memories of eminent worthy persons', as he stated in the Preface, by annotating the names he traced in the dust of tombs, reminding the reader of almost-forgotten deeds and accomplishments that he knew of from his wide knowledge of chronicles and old verse. A patriotic compulsion to show that valour and honour and piety and learning had always flourished in England from earliest times drove him to set down all that he could about the occupants of the tombs he inspected, with the result that his book is surcharged with historical detail and anecdote. One can appreciate why his progress is so slow through Canterbury Cathedral and Westminster Abbey, where the density of famous men is such that every grave deserves a eulogy.

Besides the remembrance of ancient virtue, the other important concern of *Ancient Funerall Monuments* was to rehabilitate the Christian zeal of the Middle Ages. Weever wished to 'extoll the ardent piety of our forefathers', especially 'in the erecting of Abbeyes, Priories, and such-like sacred Foundations'. This desire would often lead Weever to praise the Christianity of the Saxons, but it would also make him assert that the Catholic Middle Ages could show many admirable examples of piety, and that monasteries were often the home of good Christians and learned men. He knew that his favourable opinion of the Catholic centuries would be 'unpleasing to some', but he insisted:

I hold it not fit for us to forget that our Ancestors were, and we are of the Christian profession, and that there are not extant any other more conspicuous and certaine Monuments of their zealous devotion towards God, then these Monasteries with their endowments, for the maintenance of religious persons, neither any other seed-plots besides these, from whence Christian Religion and good literature were propagated over this our Island. Neither is there any other act of pietie more acceptable to the sight of Almighty God than that of building Churches, Oratories, and such like sacred edifices, for the true service of his heavenlie Maiestie.[1]

These positive sentiments towards the monastic life are part of a broadening sympathy for monasticism that was generally shared by the early Stuart antiquaries. It found its first expression in the Preface to Camden's *Britannia*, and it reached its fullest expression with the publication of the *Monasticon Anglicanum* in 1655. It is not hard to divine that many of these scholars must have looked back to the monasteries as congenial preserves of learning, and could easily imagine themselves installed in a scriptorium, sustained by the routines of a regular and economically sheltered life.

Ancient Funerall Monuments contained the first broad expression of approval of the medieval Church to appear since the Reformation. Writing in the 1620s, Weever was sufficiently distant from that event to be able to recognize some of the finer qualities of medieval piety. He was inclined to be tolerant, for as far as he was concerned, Catholicism was no longer the main enemy of the

---

[1] The Epistle to the Reader in John Weever, *Ancient Funerall Monuments* (1631), A–Aiv.

Church of England. He regarded the Puritans with much greater apprehension, sensing that their demands for a plainer religion carried implications of renewed iconoclasm in the manner of the Henrician or Edwardian reformers. Radicalism in religion was usually indifferent to the inheritance of the past. As Matthew Parker and his associates had responded to the dispersal of manuscripts in that first phase of reform by making collections of all they could, so Weever made haste to collect the memorial inscriptions of England before they vanished. His instinct was just, for the great majority of epitaphs and inscriptions he preserved have now disappeared, removed if not by Puritans, by later generations of Anglicans to make way for their own declarations, or tidied out of existence by improving parish councils.

To establish his credentials, Weever introduced his work with a long 'Discourse of Funerall Monuments'. It is a typical seventeenth-century antiquarian discourse, beginning in the dawn of time and progressing through the societies of the ancient world, dispensing esoteric information in a grandiloquent style. Assuming that all civilized societies seek to protest against what Thomas Browne would later call 'the iniquity of oblivion', and raise monuments to defy time, Weever began to unfold a comparative account of funerary customs and memorials in antiquity. Here he was on a Renaissance highroad, frequented by a number of European scholars before him.[2] He relies almost entirely upon literary sources, quoting much from Virgil and Lucan in particular, with some allusions to Homer. Although he mentions that he has been to Rome, he has derived no evident benefit from that experience, for he makes no mention of the ancient tombs that were such an attraction to visitors. He offers a brief description of Egyptian and Hebrew burial customs, deriving much of his information from George Sandys' *Relation of a Journey* (1615). His knowledge of his subject is patchy and ill-informed, and anachronistic. He soon makes his way to the topic of burial practices in Britain in antiquity, and here again he is not very reliable. He characterizes ancient British burials, for example, as being usually 'on the ridges of hills, or upon spacious plains, fortified or fenced about with Obelisks,

---

[2] Weever was aware in particular of Onophrius Panvinius's *De Ritu Sepeliendi Mortuos* (Venice, 1558) and Johannes Kirchmann's *De Funeribus Romanorum* (Frankfurt, 1625).

pointed stones, Pyramids, Pillars or such like monuments'.[3] Stonehenge is for him, as for most English historians of the time, a monument to the Britons slain in a treacherous rendezvous with the Saxons in the fifth century. The barrows and burial mounds observable all over the country he assumes to be of Saxon date. After much rumination on the universal instinct to preserve the bones and ashes of the dead ('for the soul, knowing itself by divine instinct immortal, doth desire that the body (her beloved companion) might enjoy the like felicity') he reaches the topic of compelling interest, English memorials, and the larger subject that he introduces by means of those memorials, the history of Christianity in England.

Weever's patriotic piety is happy with the customary view that the gospel was first brought to Britain by Joseph of Arimathea shortly after the Crucifixion, in the reign of Aviragus, son of Cymbeline. The general conversion of the island took place, he accepts, in the second century during the reign of Lucius, who 'was the first Christian King of this Island, and indeed of the World'.[4] The sources for these convictions are the medieval chroniclers Robert of Gloucester and John Hardyng, both of whom were retailing the British History of Geoffrey of Monmouth. He admits that their views on early Christianity are 'questioned in divers points by some of the learned Senate of our Ecclesiastical Historians', but 'I will adhere to the common received opinion.'[5] He believes that the tradition of Christian worship was never extinguished in Britain, but continued unbroken into Saxon times. The mission of St Augustine was necessary because the persecution of Christians by the pagan Saxons was so intense that the faith was almost eclipsed in the main parts of the country, though it survived in Wales and Cornwall. The reconversion was a success because of the natural disposition of the British, and latterly the Saxons, towards Christianity, as Camden had noted. Weever was not inclined to distinguish between British and Roman forms of Christianity in the early centuries. He paints a picture of religious life under the Saxon kings of the seventh century that made England a holy isle of unspotted faith and tireless works, 'a wonderful order of piety both in priest and people'. The early

---

[3] Weever, *Ancient Funerall Monuments*, 6.   [4] Ibid. 414.
[5] Ibid. 413.

monastic foundations were places of humility, faith, and learning. This state of primitive religion, though disrupted by the Danish invasions, persisted up to the Conquest, culminating in the saintly Edward the Confessor.

Even after the Normans had extended papal influence the length and breadth of the country, a vigorous piety thrived. In his overview of the state of religion in England during the Middle Ages, Weever is anxious to balance the favourable against the unfavourable. He reminds us of the continuing foundation of religious houses during these centuries, the coming of new orders with a fresh commitment to holiness; he instances many acts of piety by kings and clerics. But he also dwells on the tendency to backsliding that occurs in most religious orders, and ultimately the familiar picture of dissolute, luxurious monks given over to worldly pleasures prevails. He introduces stories of monastic lewdness and malpractice, such as the Abbot of St Albans seducing a townsman's wife and then imprisoning the husband for slander, or the Prior of the Crutched Friars being found 'in bed with his whore both naked about xi of the clocke in the forenoone upon a Friday' (which was supposed to be a day of abstinence from flesh). Anecdotes like these set the stage for the dissolution of the monasteries and the Reformation. As he takes the reader through the Henrician Reformation, with much quoting of documents, Weever is at pains to show his approval of royal supremacy in matters of Church government, and he tries to show that this practice was indeed long established in England by printing the whole of the charter of the foundation of St Albans Abbey by King Offa, from which he deduces that the king's supremacy in ecclesiastical matters was the norm in Saxon times.

What gives Weever's history its peculiar interest, and lifts it above the run of Jacobean reviews of the Middle Ages, is his use of medieval literature to illustrate his contentions. He remarks in the Preface how much 'good literature' had been produced in the monasteries, and he proves his point amply as he quotes throughout his book from medieval poems and chronicles in English, using them both as specimens of literary worth and as a kind of sociological evidence for currents of opinion in past times. He is eager to arouse an interest in Middle English literature, poetry in particular, and one of his motives for writing *Ancient Funerall Monuments* seems to have been to provide an occasion for bringing some of the neglected literature of the Middle Ages to public attention. By linking poets and metrical chroniclers to the vigorous life of medieval England that is evoked in his book, Weever does his best to make these writers attractive to an historically-minded audience. His model for this kind of interpolation would appear to be Camden's *Britannia*, for Camden from time to time introduced lines of chronicle verse or of monkish Latin poetry to give imaginative colour to his narrative; Weever, however, goes far beyond Camden in this trait, and makes his book a florilegium of English medieval verse. He frequently quotes Chaucer, usually to illustrate the scandalous behaviour of the clergy and the lamentable state of the Church. (His most pungent quotations are taken from 'The Summoner's Tale' and 'The Friar's Tale'.) With firm Protestant satisfaction, Weever reminds his readers that 'Chaucer writes much against the pride, covetousnesse, unsatiable luxuries, hypocrisie, blind ignorance and variable discord amongst the Churchmen and all other votaries.'[6] He recommends a perusal of Chaucer's Life, 'written at large, by Thomas Speght, (who, by old copies, reformed his workes) which the Reader may see a little before the beginning of his books', and when he arrives before Chaucer's grave in his perambulation of Westminster Abbey, he is able to quote the poetical tributes of a number of Chaucer's followers: Thomas Hoccleve, John Lydgate ('his Prologue of Bocchas'), and 'that excellent and learned Scottish Poet, Gawayne Dowglas, in his Preface of Virgil's Aeneid'.

A favoured text for evidence of corruption amongst the medieval clergy is *Piers Plowman*, a poem which Weever also exploits generally for details of social conditions in the fourteenth century. Weever introduces him thus: 'In this King's raigne [Edward III] Robert Longland a secular Priest, borne in Shropshire, at Mortimers Cliberie, writ bitter invective against the Prelates, and all religious Orders in those dayes.'[7] In spite of the harsh matter that Weever extracts from Langland, he writes appreciatively of the quality of his verse, and responds warmly to the personality of the poet. The sense of intimacy he shows here may well have been the result of working from the manuscript in Sir Robert Cotton's library (acknowledged in the margin) rather than from the printed text of

---

[6] Weever, *Ancient Funerall Monuments*, 73.   [7] Ibid. 72.

Robert Crowley's edition of 1550. The manuscript that Weever must have been using was bound up with the Middle English metrical chronicle of Robert of Gloucester, and is identifiable as Cotton Caligula A XI, now in the British Library. (This is a manuscript with an illustrious pedigree, as it was acquired by John Stow, who gave it to Cotton, and it bears many annotations in the hand of John Selden.) Robert of Gloucester was a source particularly dear to Weever: he reaches for him time and again to bring to life some forgotten worthy whose epitaph he has encountered. 'His lines you will say are neither strong nor smooth; yet perhaps they may give your palate variety: and as you like them, you shall have more hereafter,' Weever advises his reader.[8] To intensify their flavour, he prints the lines in black letter.

Robert of Gloucester enjoyed a brisk vogue at the beginning of the seventeenth century, as the manuscript of his Chronicle was handed round a circle of antiquarian friends. Written in the late thirteenth century, it ran from the Trojan dawn down to his own time, and was heavily dependent on Geoffrey of Monmouth, Henry of Huntingdon, and William of Malmesbury; its attraction lay in the exceptionally fresh and detailed accounts it gave of the reigns from Henry I to Henry III. Stow had first drawn attention to Robert of Gloucester in his *Summarie of Englyshe Chronicles* in 1565, and Camden had used this Chronicle for much the same illustrative purposes as Weever in his *Remains* of 1605 (though sparingly); Selden too found it a valuable storehouse, discovering in it much material relevant to *Titles of Honor* and to *The History of Tithes*. (In this last work, he notes the existence of a copy of the manuscript in Cotton's collection and one in the library of Thomas Allen at Oxford.) When Selden came to annotate Drayton's *Poly-Olbion*, he drew extensively on Robert of Gloucester, and the poet William Browne seems also to have been familiar with the manuscript in the Cotton library, for he introduces Robert into the fourth song of the second book of *Britannia's Pastorals*, his historico-topographical tour of the country published in 1613 and 1616. Robert of Gloucester was then picked up by Weever, who clearly found much pleasure in his rough measures as well as in his informational content. This active exploitation of a single manuscript for so wide a variety of purposes—historical, legal, military, topographical,

---

[8] Ibid. 60.

and biographical—provides useful evidence for the vigour of antiquarian studies in the early years of the century.[9]

Clearly Weever felt he had a mission to alert his reader to the merits of the neglected literature of Middle English. An example of his enthusiasm is the manuscript he found in the Earl of Exeter's library 'by one Richard a religious Hermite' that we now know as the English Psalter by Richard Rolle, written in the fourteenth century. Weever quotes at length from this, remarking that 'my Reader might palliate his taste with an Essay of our Ancestors old English, as well in the curte composition of their prose, as in the neatness of their holy meeters, which howsoever abounding with libertie, and the character of the times, yet have, I confesse, my admiration.'[10] He calls attention to the expressiveness of many fifteenth-century epitaphs, and takes every opportunity to introduce Gower or Lydgate on topics relevant to his discourse, or to familiarize his audience with the chronicles of Hardyng or Fabian. His method is always to quote the text rather than to paraphrase, so that he can convey something of the character of the worthies of old England in the language of old England. He noticeably refrains from quoting from the Elizabethan and Jacobean poets on historical matters, even though he was well acquainted with Shakespeare and knew Daniel and Drayton. (It would, in any case, have been most surprising if Weever had quoted from Shakespeare's history plays when surveying the monuments of English kings, for drama did not possess the respectable status of poetic history.)

When one comes to place Weever's *Ancient Funerall Monuments* among the antiquarian productions of Stuart England, one realizes what an odd miscellany of a book it is. Its fascination with the dimly-glorious generations of Englishmen who need to be rescued from oblivion has a patriotic, late-Elizabethan air, reminiscent of John Stow. In its obsession with the splendours associated with the grave and the rituals of burial, it is a truly Jacobean work. Weever frequently describes himself moving amongst the tombs that gave him so much pleasure, and the engraved portrait at the front of the book imposes an image of a man haunted by death: he stares out gloomily, with his hand on a skull and a pile of books before him,

---

[9] The Chronicle of Robert of Gloucester was first edited and published by Thomas Hearne in 1724.

[10] Weever, *Ancient Funerall Monuments*, 154.

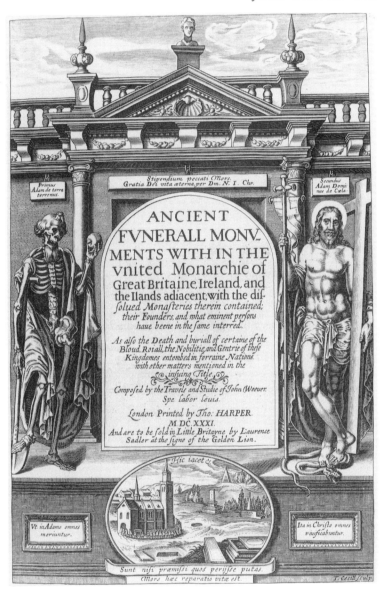

9. Title-page of *Ancient Funerall Monuments*, engraved by Thomas Cecill, showing the figure of death counterbalanced by the resurrected Christ.

looking the complete Jacobean mortalist, a creature of the shades. The numerous passages in favour of the renovation of the Church of England look forward to the reforms of the Laudian movement in Caroline times.

Ancient Funerall Monuments is a personal and idiosyncratic work, and its peculiarities no doubt stem in part from the relative isolation in which Weever carried out his researches. There are few references to him in his own lifetime. He seems not to have been associated with the Society of Antiquaries before its demise in 1608, and he does not appear to have made fruitful contacts with other antiquarians until the early 1620s. His mentor was Augustine Vincent (?1584–1626), who was Windsor Herald and Keeper of Records in the Tower, whom he met around 1620, and 'who persuaded me to go forward as I had begun, and withal gave me many church collections, with divers memorable notes, gathered by himself and others; and by his means I had free access to the Heralds' Office'.[11] Vincent in turn had been a protégé of Camden, whom he had defended against the attack by Ralph Brooke, York Herald, who claimed to have found a number of serious genealogical errors in *Britannia*. Vincent lacked the stamina needed for large antiquarian projects, but he was generous in his help to other scholars. He made collections towards a History of Northampton-shire, his native county, but it remained unfinished; he did, however, offer a good deal of material to William Burton when he was working on his *Description of Leicestershire*. His ambition was to produce a Baronage of England, another project that faltered to a halt; in this case, William Dugdale was able to use his papers for his own successful history of the Baronage. The assistance he gave Weever is another example of the co-operation between antiquaries that was such a feature of the Stuart scene. Their fields of interest lay close together, for Vincent had compiled a manuscript on 'Funeral Rites, Ceremonies, and Solemnities . . . according to the antique and modern customs of sundry nations and times' that has many similarities with the prefatory chapters of Weever's book.[12]

---

[11] Weever, *Ancient Funerall Monuments*. See also Ernst Honigmann, *John Weever* (Manchester, 1987), 60–3, for an account of Weever's relations with Vincent. For a review of Vincent's career, see Nicholas, *Augustine Vincent*. Nicholas notes that Vincent inherited his father's genealogical collections, and these may have included gleanings from church monuments that could have been passed on to Weever.

[12] The manuscript remains in the College of Arms, Vincent MS 87.

Weever was fulsome in his gratitude to Vincent, expressed in his 'Epistle to the Reader', where he confesses that Vincent saved him from discouragement as well as augmenting his stock of materials. Vincent also performed the invaluable service of introducing him to Sir Robert Cotton. Once into Cotton's library, Weever was able to pull his collections together, for now he was able to illustrate his accumulation of inscriptions and epitaphs with material extracted from the charters, chronicles, and poems that he found on Cotton's shelves. The great majority of his numerous quotations acknowledge a Cottonian source. Through Cotton, Weever met Sir Henry Spelman (who was also interested in funerary customs, and who wrote a tract on the subject, 'De Sepultura') and John Selden and Sir Simonds D'Ewes, all of whom offered help and encouragement. At last, Weever was caught up in the network of antiquarian scholars who gave him the necessary impetus to prepare his papers for the press. Sadly, he did not come to meet William Camden, who was ill for the last few years of his life before he died in 1623, but Camden's inspiriting essay on epitaphs in *Remains Concerning Britain* must have been one of the germs of Weever's later work.

Tokens of gratitude to those who favoured him may be found in the few illustrations to *Ancient Funerall Monuments*. In general, Weever was indifferent to the design or decoration of the monuments he described, but, nearly five hundred pages into his book, he unexpectedly introduces full-page woodcuts of the fifteenth-century brass to William Cotton and of the tomb of his wife Mary at St Margaret's, Westminster. These illustrations are faithfully done, conveying the style of the period in carving and dress with some accuracy, and they may well be by Weever himself. They are evidently placed in the book in honour of Sir Robert Cotton, whose relationship to Robert Bruce and the Scottish kings is then detailed, and Bruce's descent from 'the Stemme Royall of the Saxons' set down. This genealogical flourish enables Weever to draw attention to Cotton's relation to King James 'of happy memory', who, Weever maintains (following Verstegan's lead), has restored 'the lyneall Royall race and bloud of the Saxon Monarchie. In him uniting the Briton, Saxon, Norman and Scottish Royall bloud, and by him restoring not only the name, but the ancient dignity of the Britaine Empire.'[13] Cotton died as Weever's book

---

[13] Weever, *Ancient Funerall Monuments*, 496.

was being prepared for publication, so Weever was able to insert a Latin elegy of his own composition into the Preface, summing up the many achievements of 'this worthy Repairer of eating-time's ruines, this Philadelphus, this Treasurie, this Store-house of Antiquities, Sir Robert Cotton'.

Ancient Funerall Monuments is a discursive, not to say rambling book which retains its value as a record of burials and inscriptions, many of which no longer exist materially. It has some significance too as an index of a broad antiquarian sentiment that was becoming a feature of a gentleman's outlook by the 1630s. As a miscellany of information and curious detail relating to Church history and burials, and as a panorama of English social life from early Saxon times, it had its appeal in an age appreciative of magpie learning. In our day, the book has developed a new interest unintended by Weever, for it carries a revealing personal commentary on Church matters and social fashions, delivered in asides and protestations, that must exemplify in some degree the attitudes of those in the reign of Charles I who wished to see the dignity of the Church increased, and who would have supported the Laudian movement of the 1630s.

Weever's defence of the Church of England takes the form of a profound dislike of Puritans, a note struck time and again in his book. Their hostility to images threatened the raw materials of an ecclesiastical antiquarian, and their levelling spirit disapproved of monuments as works of pride and authority. He hears of Puritans 'forswearing to build Churches; swearing to pull down crosses, and to deface or quite demolish all Funerall Monuments, swearing and protesting that all these are the remains of Antichrist, papisticall and damnable'.[14] He deplores

the contagious broode of Schismatickes, who, if they might have had their wills, would not only have robbed our churches of all their ornaments and riches, but also would have laid them level with the ground, choosing rather to exercise their devotion and publish erronious doctrines, in some emptie barne, in the woods or common fields, then in those Churches, which they held to be polluted with the abominations of the whore of Babylon.

The growth of these 'schismatickes' provides some justification for his task of preserving memorials. When he surveys the ancient

---

[14] Weever, *Ancient Funerall Monuments*, 37.

penalties for desecrating monuments, his mind is on the present as he reminds his reader that death, banishment, cutting off of hands, or condemnation to the mines were once the lot of those who destroyed tombs. He hopes that the Romans were right when they believed that the violators of monuments 'should be struck to death by lightning from heaven; and after death that they should be frightened, tost up and down, and tormented in hell with burning torches by the hands of the Furies'.[15] He can imagine that the violence and the disrespect for hierarchy of the radical Puritans might have the power to disrupt the kingdom like another Peasants' Revolt, wherein 'we may clearly behold the hideous face of Anarchie, or government without Prince or ruler, as also the distorted image of Plebeian fury'.[16]

Understandably, Weever believed that churches should be handsomely maintained and adorned, and his book helps us to understand why Laud's campaign for greater decency and order in churches was necessary. The neglect that many churches suffered from is sadly and sometimes bitterly registered. Dirty and unkempt churches abound, and on one occasion he remarks on the shabbiness of furnishings that is all too common: 'a little small silver chalice, a beaten-out pulpit cushion, an ore-worne Communion cloth and a coarse surplice: these are all the riches and ornaments of the most of our Churches.'[17] When he does meet with a well-kept church, he is quick to praise it, as with Stone in the diocese of Rochester: 'The whole Fabricke of this Church is upholden in wondrous good repair, her inside is neatly polisht, and the Monuments of the dead (which are ancient and many) very faire, and carefully preserved.'[18] All too often, however, the comments speak of ruin and of monuments 'cut almost in pieces, dismembered and shamefully abused, so that neither reading nor traditions can give us any true notice of their names'.[19] The pessimistic mood lightens occasionally, as Weever reflects that the Church is in good hands, and there is hope for improvement: in his Preface, he praises King Charles (to whom the book is dedicated) for proposing to renovate St Paul's, and also William Laud, Bishop of London since 1628, for contributing to this great work of renewal.

---

[15] Ibid. 47. [16] Ibid. 747. [17] Ibid. 49.
[18] Ibid. 333. [19] Ibid. 312.

Weever has much to say about the working conditions of a church antiquary. They are not good. Local officials were not always welcoming to a stranger who came to take notes on the church: 'I have been taken up in divers Churches by the Churchwardens of the Parish, and not suffered to write the Epitaphs, or take view of the Monuments as I much desired, for that I wanted a Commission.'[20] He predictably goes on to envy Leland for the immense advantage he enjoyed by having a licence from the King to pursue his enquiries. Tombs were his business, but they were often an unsavoury business, for he found that tombs made good pissing-places in churches 'a custom (to our shame) too commonly used of us in these days'. Not only did this habit dishonour the church, but it was also an insult to the dead, 'for indeed such as had their graves, tombes, statuas or representations thus stained and defiled, were thought to have passed out of this world with shame and ignominie'.[21] St Paul's was a national scandal, for 'beastly and uncleane persons . . . pollute and bedaube the doores and walls of the place where God is to be worshipped, with pisse, or some other more nasty excrements'. Such 'atheisticall uncleannesse' might cause the nation to be punished by God, he darkly hints. And, while on the subject of impious practices, he continues, 'It could be wished, that walking in the middle Isle of Paules might be forborne in the time of Divine service.'[22]

As one might expect from a man who lived so long amongst tombs and epitaphs, Weever has much to say about the culture of death in his own time. Even though he lived in an age of splendid funerals, and when tomb-makers were at the peak of their art, he has his discontents. Distinction of rank is not sufficiently observed in death, and he looks wistfully back to late medieval and Tudor times in several digressions of feudal titles in order to emphasize how precisely defined the hierarchy of society once was. 'Sepulchres should be according to the quality and degree of the person deceased, that by his tomb everyone might be discerned of what rank he was living.' Now money can push itself forward, and purchase posthumous glory that was once reserved for persons of honour or nobility. In an outburst of satire against the vanity of his age, he denounces the gilded mercantilism of Jacobean England, the

[20] 'To the Reader', ibid.   [21] Ibid. 47.   [22] Ibid. 373.

preposterous fashions that excessive wealth was wasted upon, and adds a protest at the un-English appearance of the latest tombs:

More honour is attributed to a rich quondam Tradesman, or griping usurer, then is given to the greatest Potentate entombed in Westminster: and their tombes are made so huge great, that they take up the Church, and hinder the people from divine Service. Besides if one shall seriously survay the Tombes erected in these our dayes, and examine the particulars of the personages wrought upon their Tombes, hee may easily discerne the vanity of our mindes, vailed under our fantasticke habits and attires, which in time to come will be rather provocations to vice, then incitations to vertue; and so the temple of God shall become a Schoolehouse of the monstrous habits and attires of our present age, wherein Taylors may find out new fashions. And which is worse, they garnish their Tombes, now adayes, with the pictures of naked men and women; raising out of the dust, and bringing into the Church, the memories of the heathen gods and goddesses, with all their whirligiggs.[23]

This last enormity 'is more the fault of the Tombe-makers, than theirs who set them aworke', he admits, but it is an undeniable sign of the degeneracy of the times.

The magnificence of funerals has gone, he laments. 'Great men of birth or qualitie' are no longer 'carried in Chariots drawn with horses, trumpets and several sorts of musicall instruments sounding before the corpse'. Catafalques no longer stand a year in the church in memory of the deceased. Man is no longer pompous in ashes and splendid in the grave. But Weever was surely doing his age an injustice, for the streets of London were full of sombre pageants of mortality as frequent hearses made the slow journey to the Abbey or St Paul's, or to the innumerable parish churches, and the nobility, gentry, and merchants of London overstrained their resources in expensive funerals and costly monuments. It may be that the full formal pomp of funerals was no longer so splendidly maintained as in Elizabethan days, with all the elaborate rituals prescribed by the College of Arms and executed by heralds, but in other respects the ceremonies of death were attaining an un-precedented lavishness, with long processions clad in black, churches draped in black cloth, memorial gifts given to mourners and the poor, elegies written and pinned to the hearse, hatchments hung aloft, and funeral sermons of chilling length and eloquence

---

[23] Ibid. 10–11.

pronounced from the dark pulpits. From the 1580s onwards, English churches were acquiring more inscriptions, epitaphs and monuments than ever before.[24] Yet Weever seemed unaware that he was living in a golden age of mortality, for his preliminary Discourse swells with discontents about the decline in the rituals attending death in his days. His study of antiquity sharpens the edge of his dissatisfaction. In contrast with the hecatombs of sacrificial victims, the huge pyres and half-acre monuments of the dead, funeral games and banquets, and the heroical grief of the bereaved, modern mourning seems shallow and undistinguished:

Funerals in any expensive way here with us, are now accounted but as a fruitlesse vanitie, insomuch that almost all the ceremoniall rites of obsequies heretofore used, are altogether laid aside: for we see dailie that Noblemen and gentlemen of eminent ranke, office and qualitie, are either silently buried in the night time, with a Torch, or two-pennie Link, and a Lanterne; or parsimoniously interred in the day-time, by the helpe of some ignorant country-painter, without the attendance of any one of the Officers of Armes, whose chiefest support, and maintenance, hath ever depended upon the performance of such funerall rites, and exequies.[25]

A stately funeral strengthens the community of the living, and those most able to provide this amenity, the aristocracy and the gentry, were, in Weever's estimation, failing in their duty to consolidate the society they headed. (They were also failing to employ Weever's friends, the heralds, a point of personal irritation with him.) His perception that 'the procuration of funerals, the manner of buriall, the pompe of obsequies bee rather comforts to the living then helpers to the dead' is a just one, and his desire to see a decorum in funerals that would extend a steadying influence into the conduct of the participants was of a piece with his love of order and ritual that disposed him to High-Church practices in religion and to a conservative view of morality. Reverence for the dead should be a paramount duty for the Christian citizen, but he regrets this ideal has expired. The period of mourning is no longer a whole year, but has been abbreviated to months, even to days. Many people can hardly disguise their eagerness to find new

---

[24] The decline of 'grandiose funerals' seems to have occurred in the latter part of the century. See Michael Maclagan's views on this subject in 'Genealogy and Heraldry in the 16th and 17th Centuries' in Fox (ed.), *English Historical Scholarship*, 33–4.   [25] Weever, *Ancient Funerall Monuments*, 17.

partners. With a Hamlet-like bitterness he complains that 'husbands can burie their wives, and wives their husbands, with a few counterfeit teares, and a sowre visage marked and painted over with dissimulation; contracting second marriages, before they have worn out their mourning garments, and sometimes before their cope-mates be cold in their graves'.[26]

Weever seems to deplore the zeal for life shown by the survivors. Heirs hasten to spend their inheritances, parents lie forgotten in the dust, monuments are left unbuilt to save money for the vanities of this world, and life sweeps on. With his protests about 'the decline of funeralls', one would hardly guess that Weever was a contemporary of Donne, whose funeral sermons were the most eloquent accompaniments to interment ever uttered in England, or that he was writing at a time when the funeral elegy was an art universally practised by educated gentlemen, or that the tombmakers of Southwark were delivering their masterpieces to towns and villages throughout the country. This was the time when Maximilian Colt, Cornelius Cure, Gerard Christmas, Nicholas Stone, and Epiphanius Evesham were carving their incomparable effigies and giving a new inventiveness to memorial designs. Two of the most sumptuous tombs in Westminster Abbey were being built as Weever wrote his 'Discourse of Funerall Monuments', those of the Duke of Buckingham and the Duke of Lennox. Weever's own book, coming out in 1631, seems a timely expression of an intense national consciousness about the importance of memorializing the dead.

The task Weever set himself, of surveying the whole country, proved beyond him. He only managed to publish his collections for the dioceses of Canterbury, Rochester, London, and Norwich, in a plump folio volume. It would seem as if he intended to issue three volumes in all, but his notes for the rest of the country remained undigested in manuscript.[27] 'Much more might be said' he admitted at the end of his book, 'but I am called for myself to the press.' An even more imperative summons called for him in 1632, and in typical seventeenth-century style, his book became his monument.

---

[26] Ibid.
[27] These notes are preserved in the library of the Society of Antiquaries, MS 127 and MS 128.

In his concern with epitaphs, Weever was perpetuating interest in a topic that had risen to prominence around the year 1600, when the Society of Antiquaries devoted several meetings to this subject, possibly related to Camden's and Cotton's tour of Hadrian's Wall, which had focused their attention on Roman gravestones, cenotaphs, and memorial inscriptions. In April 1600 the Society discussed the topic 'of the antiquity, variety and ceremonies of funerals in England' and in June the subject was 'the antiquity and variety of tombs and monuments in England', followed by 'the antiquity and selected variety of epitaphs' at the November meeting.[28] Camden's contributions to these debates may survive in the section entitled 'Epitaphs' in his *Remains* of 1605. As mentioned earlier, this essay may have been the genesis of Weever's work, for it throws out many suggestions that Weever enlarges upon. For example, Camden anticipates Weever in some ways by his proposal to print 'a century of choice epitaphs of our nation for matter and conceit, some good, some bad, that you may see how learning ebbed and flowed; most of them recovered from the injury of time by writers'. There are other similarities. Camden opens with a brief survey of funeral customs in antiquity, lingering on some of the more picturesque national habits, such as those of the Scythians 'who carried about the cleansed carkases to the friends of the deceased for forty days with solemn banquets'. He furnishes a short history of epitaphs, tracing them back, in Renaissance fashion, to a named originator who may be identified as the inventor of an object or a genre or a tradition—in this case to the disciples of the Greek poet Linus who composed verses for their master which were sung at his burial and then engraved on his tomb. Camden then turns to the nationalist aspect of his topic, as he demonstrates how Britons have been commemorated in epitaphs since antiquity, beginning with a Briton who died at Rome and was remembered in the Latin of the imperial era, and going up to Elizabethan times, when Renaissance Latin again has a classical ring to it, and when English has also achieved a copious eloquence. Camden is appreciative of Saxon learning until its collapse after the reign of Alfred when, in Camden's opinion, 'between Thames and Trent there was scant one found which could understand Latin'. The revival of learning in England in the twelfth century is highlighted

---

[28] Subjects listed in Hearne, *Curious Discourses*, pp. cxix–cxx.

by means of some excellent epitaphs. Camden uses his examples to make the point that throughout the Middle Ages there was a tradition of learning and good letters in Latin. He also chooses his examples from the tombs of princes, bishops, and knights who made some stir in the world, to remind his reader of the long succession of worthies who have added lustre to the name of England, a strategy that Weever would also adopt.

Camden also published a little guide book to the tombs in Westminster Abbey, *Reges, Reginae, Nobiles et alii in Ecclesia S. Petri Westmonasterii Sepulti* (1600). The several reprintings of this piece provide some indication of the growing interest in tombs and inscriptions in the early seventeenth century. Admittedly, Westminster Abbey with its array of royal and noble sepulchres had long been a favourite loitering-place for the historically minded and for those who liked to savour the aroma of ancient greatness—Lady Anne Clifford, for instance, noted in her diary that as a child in the 1590s she loved to meditate on the glory that was England among the monuments in the Abbey—and Camden's little book, written in Latin, presumably helped foreign visitors to contemplate the scene. Camden's method is factual and succinct, giving a brief account of the incumbent of a tomb, followed by the epitaph. His abstract of the history of the Abbey insists on the antiquity of Christianity in Britain, claiming that King Lucius built a church on this site in 170 AD when he was converted. Camden also pays particular tribute to the Christian spirit of the Saxons who built the first monastery and renewed and endowed it.

St Paul's Cathedral received a similar treatment in 1614 with the publication of *Monumenta Sepulchraria Sancti Pauli* by Henry Holland, the son of Philemon Holland who was responsible for the English translation of *Britannia* in 1610. This collection of 'the Monuments, Inscriptions and Epitaphs' of those buried in the cathedral is essentially a guide book for the curious, with a Latin introduction no doubt for the foreign visitor, containing directions to the sites of particular monuments and printing the epitaphs without comment. The only departure from this rule of plain information comes when Holland describes the monument of Sir John Beauchamp, son of the Earl of Warwick 'as appeareth by his arms upon his Tombe', which is commonly believed 'by ignorant people' to be the grave of Humphrey, Duke of Gloucester. Holland is so struck by the customs that have grown up around this tomb in recent years that he interposes a note 'from the Collector to the Reader' in order to record the appearance of new social rituals:

> Divers men of late yeares, and those no worse than Citizens and Tradesmen, forsooth, on St. Andrewes Day before Christmas, after they have met and foole-wisely in the morning come and presented themselves before his Monument, they have had a great feast prepared, and assumed unto themselves to have offices under the said Duke Humphrey.
>
> Secondly, on May Day, a certaine rude company of Tankerd-bearers have used to come betimes in the morning, and there as idle as the others, have presented themselves before the same Monument, and strewen hearbes and sprinkled water upon it, terming themselves Duke Humphrey's servants in several offices. . . . But thirdly, there are another sort of sworne servants and resident attendants on this deceased Nobleman, who do daily give their attendance, and offer their hungry devotions unto his shrine: and you shall be sure to find some or other of them every day throughout the yeare waiting, betwixt the houres of twelve and one at noone.[29]

This peculiar custom of a community forming around a tomb, professing service to the nobleman mistakenly thought to be buried there and assuming offices in his imaginary household, and the daily gathering there of the hungry and the unemployed, are phenomena to be remarked. The ceremonies of festive misrule, and the beggars' feast at which they feed on empty air seem to suggest an instinctive belief that the dead could provide dignity and food for the living. Nor was 'Duke Humphrey's' the only monument that was the focus of odd ceremonies in St Paul's. Holland notes that the tomb of the Bishop of London who procured the Charter of London from William the Conquerer used to be the site of rituals at Christmas, 'when the Mayor and Aldermen would go about the monument and say "De profundis" '. Now the ceremony continues, but in the post-Reformation scene, 'the popish order is quite abolished.' The assumptions underlying these practices indicate that tombs and memorials help bind together the generations of the living and the dead and in their way make a contribution to the idea of community.

Holland's book was reissued in 1633 under a new title *Ecclesia*

---

[29] Henry Holland, *Monumenta Sepulchraria* (1614), E2. 'To dine with Duke Humphrey' was an Elizabethan phrase that signified going hungry, presumably for lack of employment. The nave of St Paul's was used as an informal employment exchange for porters and other unskilled labourers at this time.

Sancti Pauli Illustrata, with its contents enlarged and brought up to date. Holland had also developed something of an ideology by the time of this second edition, coming out strongly in favour of William Laud's plans to bring more order and beauty into churches. The book is dedicated to Laud as Bishop of London (he would be translated to Canterbury that same year); Holland praises Laud's project, supported by King Charles, for the restoration of St Paul's, whilst expressing the fear that 'in repairing the same, some Monuments of the dead might be defaced, if not quite razed', and so his book appears to ensure that the funerary contents of the cathedral will be preserved 'to Memory and Posterity'. He notes with evident approval the additional beauties that the Cathedral has already acquired under Laud's stewardship: the new glazing of the chancel windows, 'the hanging of the Quire and high Altar place with red cloth of tapistrie, and . . . beautifying and repairing the Quire and the Entrance to the Quire, erecting the statues of 6 Kings and 3 Bishops, with Pillars and Pillasters of black Touch or Marble, which Kings and Bishops had been Builders and benefactors to the Church'. He also approves of 'the sumptuous new repairing and guilding of the Organes'.[30]

In this second edition of his book Holland shows much more interest in the literary quality of the epitaphs he prints, showing himself to be appreciative of modern wit in the genre. He recommends the metaphysical virtuosity of the Latin epitaph for Bishop John King, Laud's predecessor in the see, and applauds the ingenious anagram of King's name that also contrives to contain a chronogram of King's age at death, 62: 'Ionnes KIngVs PraeLatVs = en apertVs Ionas AngLIcVs'. Equally, a chronogram devised for the year 1621, when King died, gave him much pleasure: 'eCCe CVpIo DIssoLVI aC ChrIsto aDgLVtInarI'.[31] In keeping with this fondness for the wit of funeral inscriptions, Holland commends to his reader the most recent addition to the monuments in St Paul's, that of 'Deane Donne, which is, appearing out of his winding-sheete, done in white Marble, standing upon an Urne.'

Holland refers to John Weever's book as potentially a rival work,

[30] 'To the Reader' in Holland, *Ecclesia Sancti Pauli Illustrata* (1633).
[31] A chronogram is a verse or inscription in which the value of the Latin numerical letters (MDCLXVI) adds up to a significant number or date.

and hastens to assure the reader that his is no mere copy or extract of Weever, but a true original collection:

I am not ignorant also that Mr. John Weever his laborious collected volume of *Funerall Monuments* is lately published: wherein I see and haply you may find many and most of my collected Epitaphs, done, doubtless, by his owne industry. But considering the Premises, viz. that most of mine were published nineteene years agone, I hope both the Readers thereof and all other, unto whose hands this my collected Pamphlets shall happen to come, will hold me excused and vindicate me from robbing him or ploughing with his Heifer, this small piece of ground. Whose collections also of Epitaphs in this Church, as in others, is onely of Auncient Monuments, mine, of all, modern as well as auncient, unto this very yeare and day. And I was importuned to publish this my Collection the second time, I professe, before I ever looked on his labour.[32]

Holland need not have worried. He was clearly an early worker in this particular graveyard, and a conscientious one, whereas Weever appears not even to have noticed the existence of *Monumenta Sepulchraria*. It is a measure of Weever's isolation that he seems largely unaware of how much his collections reduplicated the work of other antiquaries, especially in the London churches. He does acknowledge the existence of Camden's *Remains* in his marginal notes (though he never refers to Camden's guide to Westminster Abbey) and he also mentions Stow, but it does not occur to him that the combined endeavours of Stow, Camden, and Holland have rendered his long chapter on the diocese of London almost redundant. John Stow in particular had covered the ground in his *Survay of London* (1598, 1603, enlarged by Anthony Munday 1618, reprinted 1633); he had painstakingly recorded the memorials in all the churches of London, and revived the memory of those buried there in terms that had done much to intensify the sense of London's distinction through the centuries.

For all his repetition of material already published, however, Weever's account of London memorials holds its own by the delight and restless curiosity he shows in his subject. His utilitarian task was to preserve the location of monuments and transcribe their inscriptions: but these memorials were gateways into the past, and the past has no boundaries. The spectres of the dead crowd around him, soliciting his attention, and one step beyond the gateway, he

---

[32] 'To the Reader' in Holland, *Ecclesia Sancti Pauli Illustrata*.

hardly knows which way to turn. He had no method as such to guide him, but was impelled by fancy or suggestion. Characteristically he would trace the foundation of a church back to Saxon times, and then cross the dim border between history and fable, and end up among the Trojans. He is attracted to the legends that declared Brutus to have been the founder of London under the name of Troy Novant, and is pleased to believe that St Paul's stands upon the site of a temple first built by Brutus. In spite of the modern scepticism about the Trojan stories, which he acknowledges, Weever cannot bring himself to deny the British History, because it threw so much light into the dark tracts of the past, and provided a firm succession of personages and events where otherwise there would be nothing. Camden had been also unwilling to deny the British History outright, and his reluctance to offend conservative sensibilities allowed that fantastical version of antiquity to persist well into the seventeenth century. So Weever can accept without criticism the claim made on an inscription in St Peter's Cornhill that the church was founded by King Lucius in the second century, and that it was originally an archiepiscopal see until St Augustine bestowed the primacy upon Canterbury. He is happy to recount that Elvanus, the second holder of the see, 'built a librarie near unto this church, and converted many of the British Druids to Christianitie'.[33] His patriotic imagination is aroused as he describes the site of the grave of Nennius, 'Duke of Logria', near Bishopsgate. Nennius ('if we give credit to our ancient Chronicles') was the brother of Lud and Cassibelaunus, 'who in the warres between Julius Cesar and the Britains, fought courageously in the defence of his country, causing Cesar to flie back with the losse of his sword, which Nennius took from him in single encounter'. He died of wounds received from Caesar in that attack, and was buried with Caesar's sword in his grave, 'which sword was called Reddeath, or rather Readiedeath; wherein had anyone been never so little wounded, he could never escape with life'.[34] *Ancient Funerall Monuments* contains an abundance of such romantic material mixed in with considerable factual detail and sound history, and

[33] Weever, *Ancient Funerall Monuments*, 414. Weever has taken his information from Stow's *Survay*.

[34] Ibid. 420. Robert of Gloucester is the source for these details, supported by Hardyng.

this combination places the book as a typical piece of early Stuart antiquarianism, where a strong regard for tangible evidence is modified by an uncritical fondness for the venerable legends of the nation.

Weever's concern to record memorials before destruction over-took them was prescient. Nine years after the publication of his book, the Long Parliament assembled with a strong Puritan representation, determined to shake the fabric of the Church and state. William Dugdale had a premonition of what the effects of that 'fateful convention' might be in the realm of antiquities, foreseeing 'the subversion of the religion established . . . whereby nothing less could be expected than the profanity of all places of God's publique worship, destruction of Monuments in Churches, and defacing of whatso ever was beautiful and ornamentall therein'.[35] He set off on his emergency tour to record as many tombs and inscriptions as he could in the travelling season, effectively to extend the work begun by Weever. Later antiquarians would see him as a model of comprehensiveness in his chosen field. Aubrey in his 'Perambulation of Surrey' felt he was following in Weever's footsteps; Robert Plot had an ambition to complete Weever's work, though he failed to do so.[36] Thomas Browne was updating Weever when he compiled his 'Repertorium' of the tombs in Norwich Cathedral, and he managed to emulate the engaging tone of his original in that piece as well. When Jeremy Taylor composed his *Holy Dying* (1651) he understandably appropriated phrases from Weever's mournful eloquence about mortality,[37] and Thomas Fuller compiled his folio of *The Worthies of England* (1662) in a Weeverish manner, providing an anecdotal treasury of local notables in a way that *Ancient Funerall Monuments* had pioneered. Many strands of learning are twisted together in Weever's book, and one can well appreciate why it became one of the most frequently mentioned antiquarian works of the century.

[35] *Sir William Dugdale*, ed. Hamper, 14.
[36] See Mendyk, *Speculum Britanniae*, 194.
[37] For Taylor's borrowings from Weever, see *Holy Dying*, ed. P. G. Stanwood (Oxford, 1989), 250, 251, 262, and 268.

8

Sir William Dugdale

The recovery of the Middle Ages, including the rehabilitation of medieval institutions, was an enterprise that many seventeenth-century antiquarians were engaged in, with Selden and Spelman in the vanguard; but the most persistent attempt to clarify the development of medieval institutions was carried out by Sir William Dugdale in a career of sustained research extending from the 1630s to the 1680s. Dugdale had an unprejudiced view of the Middle Ages, and did not believe that the centuries before the Reformation were sunk in ignorance and monkish superstition. He recognized that medieval society had been dominated by disciplined institutions, which had conditioned the growth of the nation, and that he and his contemporaries lived in a world that had been shaped by the social structures that had evolved in a time of feudalism and universal faith. Curiosity about the origins and growth of offices and institutions had been one of the unifying concerns of the Elizabethan Society of Antiquaries, whose investigations often took the form of short exploratory forays into the past. The greatest obstacle to a proper understanding of the structures of medieval society was the confusion of the surviving records, civil, ecclesiastical, and familial. These were so dispersed, disordered, and neglected that any hope of their profitable reintegration must have seemed almost unimaginable to an Elizabethan scholar; but the patient industry of the Stuart antiquarians did impose order, and out of order came understanding. Dugdale's great sequence of books, *The Antiquities of Warwickshire, Monasticon Anglicanum, The History of St. Paul's, Origines Juridiciales*, and *The Baronage of England*, represents a lifetime of assiduous work among the records. These firmly documented definitive studies are a permanent contribution to the scholarship, the basis of all future work in their respective areas. Dugdale's folios stand as an heroic achievement. The retrieval of documents, the ordering and comparison of them in an objective

10. Portrait of William Dugdale by Wenceslaus Hollar, from *The Antiquities of Warwickshire* (1656). The antiquarian dressed for study, and surrounded by a confusion of manuscripts.

and non-partisan manner, and their final printing for public use amounted to a victory of persistence and method.

The outline of Dugdale's life, though not of his opinions, is available from the brief autobiography that he wrote towards the end of his life. His friend Anthony Wood, the cantankerous Oxford antiquary, had access to this document, for he printed much of it in his notice of Dugdale in *Fasti Oxonienses* of 1692, adding material to extend it to Dugdale's death in 1686.[1] It is a fairly plain account of Dugdale's career, but it is of great interest for showing how his antiquarian curiosity was aroused. It also reveals how a network of local antiquarians had developed in England in the first thirty years of the century, and makes clear that by 1640 this network had spread all over the country. Dugdale was born in 1605, the son of a Warwickshire gentleman. His birth was marked by a swarm of bees in his father's garden, which happy incident, according to William Lilly, 'the famous Figure-flinger' or astrologer, augured 'the infant would in time prove a prodigy of industry.' (Lilly made this observation with the full benefit of hindsight.) After some time at a grammar school in Coventry, his father brought him home to coach him in the Law, and married him off at the unusually early age of 17. He never went to university. From his youth he was naturally disposed to the study of history and antiquities, and this tendency was encouraged by a kinsman Samuel Roper, who was a barrister at Lincoln's Inn. His ambition to undertake some work of note was aroused by reading *The Description of Leicestershire* by William Burton, the brother of Melancholy Burton, and a near neighbour of Dugdale's. The two soon met, and Burton encouraged the younger man to develop his plans for a similar work on Warwickshire. To this end, Burton put Dugdale in touch with Sir Simon Archer of Tamworth, who had already made considerable historical collections relating to the county. In turn, Archer introduced Dugdale to most of the gentlemen of note in Warwickshire, who seem to have been universally favourable to Dugdale's design, as tending to the honour of their own families and of the county at large. They were very willing to give him sight of 'their ancient deeds and evidences'. All this took place in the early 1630s, and in 1638 Archer took Dugdale to London and introduced him to Sir Henry Spelman, then nearing 80. Spelman approved highly of Dugdale's skill as a

---

[1] See a reprint of the autobiography in *Sir William Dugdale*, ed. Hamper.

collector and organizer of antiquarian material, having looked over his Warwickshire papers with their emphasis on the lineage of county families, their landholdings and deeds. Spelman determined to advance Dugdale's fortunes, and his great influence and reputation drew Dugdale out of the county arena in which he had hitherto functioned, and pushed him on to the national scene. He recommended him to Thomas, Earl of Arundel, the Earl Marshal, as a person worthy to serve in the Office of Arms as a herald. He also brought about the connection that would ensure Dugdale's lasting reputation, by suggesting that he engage in research into the monastic foundations of England. 'He told him that one Roger Dodsworth, a Gent. of Yorkshire, had taken indefatigable pains in searching the records and other ancient memorials relating to the Antiquities of that County, but especially touching the foundations of Monasteries there, and in the northern parts of the Realm.'[2] Spelman mentioned that he himself had made transcripts of the foundation charters of many monasteries in Norfolk and Suffolk and he urged Dugdale to join with Dodsworth in this vast and necessary work of preserving the monastic records. Dugdale met Dodsworth shortly thereafter, and they agreed to co-operate, with the understanding that the Warwickshire project should not be neglected.

During this same stay in London in 1638, Dugdale was introduced to Sir Christopher Hatton, whose father had been Elizabeth's Lord Chancellor, and who was 'a person highly affected to Antiquities'. He arranged for Dugdale to have access to the records in the Exchequer and in the Tower of London, two of the major depositories of ancient documents in the country. The plea-rolls and leiger books that he found there were indispensable to an understanding of land ownership, tenures, and finance in the Middle Ages. Another antiquarian sanctuary, the library of Sir Robert Cotton, was opened to him by an introduction to Cotton's son brought about by his kinsman Samuel Roper. Roper also arranged for him to have special access to the Domesday Book in the Exchequer, with its invaluable accounts of land-tenure at the Conquest. This astonishing transformation of Dugdale's prospects was completed when Sir Christopher Hatton reinforced Spelman's appeal to Arundel to make Dugdale a herald. He was created

---

[2] Anthony Wood, *Fasti Oxonienses* in *Athenae Oxonienses* (1692), 694.

Blanch Lyon Pursuivant in 1638, and was advanced to Rouge Croix Pursuivant the next year. These appointments gave him a lodging at the Office of Heralds in London, and a modest income, augmented by funeral fees.

When the political climate rapidly began to worsen in 1641 as a result of the activities of the new Parliament, the duties of an antiquarian in a time of crisis were clear to Dugdale. He was keenly aware of the vehement feelings of the Puritan party against what they deemed to be the trappings of popery in the established Church: ornaments, images, stained-glass windows, and monuments that seemed too pagan for a church; even cathedrals themselves as the seats of the hated bishops came under threat. What the Puritans liked to destroy was the working stock of the antiquarians: coats of arms, inscriptions that carried details of kinship lines, and Church records of every kind, besides the aforementioned decorations. Churches were the documentary centre of parish and county life: all families of any note had an interest in them through burials. The records were of stone and glass and brass, as well as paper, and all were menaced with destruction. So, urged on by Sir Christopher Hatton, Dugdale

did in the summer time 1641, (taking with him one Will. Sedgwick, a skilful Arms painter) repair first to the Cathedral of St. Paul within the City of London, and next to the Abbey Church of Westminster, and there made exact draughts of all the Monuments in each of them, copied the Epitaphs according to the very letter; as also of all Arms in the windows or cut in stone. All of which being done with great exactness, Mr. Dugdale rode to Peterborough in Northamptonshire, Ely, Norwich, Lincoln, Newark upon Trent, Beverley, Southwell, Kingston upon Hull, York, Selby, Chester, Lichfield, Tamworth, Warwick, and did the like in all those cathedral, collegiate, conventual and divers other parochial churches, wherein any tombs and monuments were to be found, to the end that the memory of them (in case if that ruin then imminent might come to pass) ought to be preserved for future and better times.[3]

This was a prodigious undertaking, and the sight of Dugdale on his emergency mission should dispel any notions of the antiquary as a human spider lodged in some dim study. When the Civil War broke out, he was active as a heraldic officer on behalf of the King, demanding declarations of loyalty from a number of towns; he

---

[3] Ibid. 695.

caused Banbury to disarm, but Warwick and Coventry defied him. He was present at the Battle of Edgehill, mindful of the historic nature of the conflict, and afterwards went back to record the disposition of the armies, and the places of burial of the dead. War put all records at risk, so Dugdale beavered away in the Bodleian and in the college libraries while he was at Oxford with the King, and made sorties to Worcester and Lichfield to work on the cathedral registers for his book on Warwickshire and to gather material for the *Monasticon*. He also began to extract material for a history of the nobility of England. Dodsworth in Yorkshire was also stepping up his work on the monasteries, and had managed to transcribe the charters and grants kept in St Mary's Tower in York before it was blown up in the siege of 1644. Dugdale pays tribute to Thomas, Lord Fairfax, the besieger of York, as a preserver of antiquities, recalling that 'he showed himself very generous to all such Soldiers at York who could retrieve any of the said Charters that were so blown up.' (We should remember too that Fairfax also protected York Minster from looting and so saved the medieval stained glass. Dodsworth eventually gave his manuscript collections to his patron Fairfax, who deposited them in the Bodleian Library.)

With the collapse of the royalist cause, Dugdale went to France in 1648, where he spent his time investigating the records of French religious houses that had dependencies in England, accumulating new material for the *Monasticon*. Returning to England, he and Dodsworth made a final assault on monastic records that they had not yet explored in the Tower and the Cottonian Library, and brought the huge work to the press. At this point, August 1654, Dodsworth died. Dugdale was left to carry the whole cost of the printing, and to negotiate terms with the booksellers for the sale of the edition. He was forced to borrow money to see it through the press, and then the reluctance of the booksellers to take it up caused him to stop the publication after the first volume. At the same time, Dugdale was bringing his *Warwickshire* to completion, and for this work, 'he was at the whole charge of Printing, and Paper for publishing the same, and continued in London to correct the Press himself, by reason that the ordinary Correctors were not skilled at all in the Pedigrees.'[4]

Even as this work was coming off the press, an acquaintance

---

[4] Wood, *Fasti* 696–7.

drew his attention to some old manuscripts relating to St Paul's in his possession. Following up this trail, Dugdale was taken to Scrivener's Hall and shown 'many other Manuscript books, original Charters, old Rolls and other very antient writings in bags and hampers, relating to the said Cathedral of St. Paul. All which [were] freely lent to Mr. Dugdale (amounting to no less than ten Porters' burthens) to be carried to his lodgings.'[5] Conscious that St Paul's was being daily mutilated by its occupation by soldiers ('for it was made a Horse-garrison by the Usurpers'), Dugdale was moved by the spirit of conservation that was his personal daemon to compile a history of the Cathedral with a register of all its monuments and inscriptions, and because of the endangered condition of the building, he decided to have it plentifully illustrated with engravings. This volume came out in 1658.

The Restoration brought Dugdale back into public life. The new Chancellor, Clarendon, had been impressed by *Warwickshire* and the first volume of the *Monasticon*, and persuaded the King to promote Dugdale to Norroy King of Arms. The second volume of *Monasticon* came out to a warmer reception than the first, in 1661. Clarendon and the new Archbishop of Canterbury, Gilbert Sheldon, began to importune Dugdale to complete the unfinished works of Spelman, who had died in 1641, and so, repaying his indebtedness to the man who had furthered his career so much, Dugdale set about the task of completing the *Concilia*, the account of the Saxon Church Councils in England (the first part of which had appeared in 1639), where much doctrine that would be relevant to the Church of England had been decided. Once more into the Cottonian Library went Dugdale, transcribing records in order to round out Spelman's scheme.[6] He also undertook to finish Spelman's Glossary of words and terms in Anglo-Saxon and Norman law. Now at last he was able fully to exercise his knowledge of Anglo-Saxon, which he had been cultivating since his early days, ever since Spelman had lent him an Anglo-Saxon psalter for that purpose in the 1630s. He received much help from William Somner, the maker of the Anglo-Saxon Dictionary that

---

[5] *Sir William Dugdale*, ed. Hamper, 27.

[6] The *Concilia* was a work which enjoyed the encouragement of archbishops in all its stages. William Abbot first showed it favour, Laud and Ussher urged it forward, and Sheldon both encouraged its final stages and welcomed its completion.

appeared in 1659. The two completed works of Spelman were published in 1664.

Dugdale now gave his attention to a substantial history of the law, lawyers and the Inns of Court, which he entitled *Origines Juridiciales* (1666), a book whose fate exemplifies the hazards that antiquarian research laboured to overcome, for hardly had it gone on sale than most of the stock was burnt in the Great Fire (a fate shared by the unsold copies of the Glossary and the *Concilia*). The other great work of these later years was *The Baronage of England* (1676), the history of the aristocracy and its deeds since Saxon times, a project which had exercised his imagination since the early 1650s, when the aristocracy was frozen under the Republic.[7] This volume has been described by a present-day member of the College of Heralds as 'a landmark in the history of English genealogical scholarship. . . . Here for the first time is a vast and solid work of scholarship, almost every statement in which is directly referred to an original source. Modern scholarship may have revised some of Dugdale's judgements [but] our *apparatus criticus* stems back to the massive marginalia of this great work.'[8] Dugdale was promoted to Garter King of Arms in 1677, and knighted. He brought out a third volume of the *Monasticon* in 1673, containing a considerable quantity of documentation that had come to light since the publication of the second volume in 1661.[9] Dugdale's vigorous old age finally came to an end in 1685, when he died in his chair of a great cold, appropriately enough on St Scholastica's Day, as Wood noted with appreciation. He left his manuscript collections to his son-in-law, Elias Ashmole, who had antiquarian tendencies of his own.

---

[7] Dugdale made considerable use of papers that Dodsworth had gathered for an identical work. See Douglas, *English Scholars*, 53–4. Dodsworth mentioned his collections towards a Baronage of England in a letter to Dugdale dated 29 May 1650. Augustine Vincent, Windsor Herald, whom we met in conjunction with John Weever, had also been engaged on a Baronage of England from the time of the Conquest. It was completed by his son John, but never published, a fact which once again points up Dugdale's ability to finish a work and get it into print. See Wood, *Fasti*, 700.

[8] Michael Maclagan, 'Genealogy and Scholarship in the 16th and 17th Centuries' in Fox (ed.), *English Historical Scholarship*, 45–6.

[9] Anthony Wood had furnished several monastic charters and other evidences to this volume; knowing Dugdale's propensity to assimilate others' work without recognition, he made certain that his own contributions were precisely recorded in his account of Dugdale in his *Fasti*.

What are we to make of Dugdale's prodigious output? Almost all of it was information retrieval, the recovery of factual matter relating to the development of great institutions during the Middle Ages: the monasteries, the legal system, and the aristocracy. The scale of his operations was grander than any previous endeavour, and its achievements were astonishing, especially when one considers the disorder of the records he worked from. The monastic charters and deeds were scattered everywhere after the Reformation; legal and state records lay in utmost confusion, and often in mouldering neglect. Family records had to be solicited from interested parties. Churches all over the country had to be painstakingly visited and their inscriptions and coats of arms transcribed. It is true that Dugdale benefited to some extent from other men's labours without giving them sufficient acknowledgement. This was an accusation which was lodged against him in the eighteenth century, but it is beside the point, and characteristic of a more jealous age of scholarship.[10] He did use the documentary collection of Roger Dodsworth as the chief foundation of the *Monasticon*, and similarly developed his *Baronage* out of Dodsworth's papers, but in the seventeenth century, antiquarian research was a co-operative endeavour, and scholars were desirous of having their protracted schemes brought to fulfilment by a fellow antiquary if age or death curtailed their designs. Dugdale was in fact doing his senior collaborator the ultimate service of bringing a lifetime's work to publication.[11] *Warwickshire* benefited from the

[10] The accusation was expressed in a letter sent by the herald John Anstis to the Master of University College, Oxford, in 1713, in which he described Dugdale as 'that Grand Plagiary', declaring that he could 'trace the fellow's guilt through every book he hath printed . . . getting a good estate and character among such as did not know his talent of stealing, with his grave countenance.' (Letter from John Anstis to Dr Arthur Charlett, in *Sir William Dugdale*, ed. Hamper, 497.) The controversy was revived by David Douglas in his book *English Scholars*. In relation to the *Monasticon*, it should be remarked that John Marsham's Latin preface clearly indicated the division of labour: 'Mr. William Dugdale had the supervising of it, and added so much of his own, that he has well deserved the name of an Author; but the chief praise is due to Mr. Roger Dodsworth, who gathered these precious Remains of Antiquity from the dark recesses where they were buried, and spent 30 years in this commendable employment.' (Dugdale, *Monasticon Anglicanum* (English translation, 1718), p. v.)

[11] Dugdale described Dodsworth as 'a person of wonderful industry, but less judgment; was always collecting and transcribing, but never published anything.' (Dugdale to Sir Simonds D'Ewes, 20 Jan. 1649, in *Sir William Dugdale*, ed. Hamper, 220.) For details of Dodsworth, see N. Denham-Young and H. Craster, 'Roger Dodsworth and his Circle' in *Yorkshire Archaeological Journal*, 32 (1934), 5–32.

material gathered by Sir Simon Archer, whose contributions were effectively lost in the vast expanse of the volume, and Dugdale certainly received all the credit for the achievement of that book, but antiquaries in that age were more concerned to rescue evidence from oblivion than to attain a personal glory through scholarship.

One of the depressing features of antiquarian studies in the seventeenth century was the large number of collections of historical material made by individual gentlemen that remained in manuscript because the author was not sufficiently concerned or organized to get them into print. Often these collections were of a parochial nature, and needed to be part of a larger work to be of value. Dugdale was a master compiler of composite antiquarian studies, he was the river into which these rivulets flowed, and the evidence of his life and letters suggests that his contemporaries were happy to give him their collections and remain his friends. What impresses about Dugdale is his relentless energy in extracting information from the deteriorating residue of medieval documents in scattered repositories, and his constructive determination to carry through a project when older colleagues faded or died, or simply gave him their papers because they knew he would see them into print.

For the most part, Dugdale's work appealed to the landed gentry of England, for it was their origins, actions, interactions, tenures, and acquisitions that he touched on in book after book. These concerns are most obvious in *Warwickshire*, but they run through everything Dugdale wrote. It would be hard to say that any of his books had a thesis, an argument to unfold, or a point to prove. They are objective, factual compilations. They share the common antiquarian attitude of wishing to honour our forefathers for their achievements by preserving the memory of their deeds, and they are written in a spirit of admiration for the English nation, or at least the active part of it that made history, the gentry and aristocracy, for the sheer volume of the records indicates what a stirring nation England had been, and what a talent for raising strong institutions Englishmen had long possessed. Dugdale's lifelong ambition was to get the record of the past straight, and to preserve it without prejudice. That meant getting it off perishable manuscripts and into durable print, and it meant ordering the chaos of the past. For these purposes his methodical, patient working habits were admirably suited. Hard graft for twenty years was not uncommon for a book by Dugdale, but he did bring his projects to completion, and the results still stand.

Though Dugdale may have had no thesis to defend, inferences could be drawn from his compilations, notably from the *Monasticon*, which was the most contentious of his works, because the very choice of subject suggested that the monastic movement deserved respect and even admiration. A large body of Protestant believers in England had held the opinion that medieval monasticism was a totally corrupt form of religious life, evasive, lazy, and oftentimes luxurious. Monastic ruins were the most visible reminder of the Reformation that had created modern England and that had given Protestant Englishmen their identity: they acted as markers that differentiated the old order from the new. The upholders of the new order, the Protestant gentry, did not want any formidable reminders of the Catholic past, nor did they wish to have a printed record of the titles to their estates before the Dissolution, for so many of them had benefited from that change. Throughout the reigns of Elizabeth and James there was silence about the role of the monasteries in the national life.[12] It was only when Laud rose to prominence and showed a greater tolerance of Catholic elements remaining in the Anglican Church that a more appreciative view of monasticism could develop, and it is no surprise that Roger Dodsworth and later Dugdale began to show an interest in monastic records when official attitudes to the Catholic past were softening: the 1620s in Dodsworth's case, the 1630s in Dugdale's. Dugdale's antiquarian friend Sir Roger Twysden, one of the great restorers of medieval history who put into circulation many of the minor medieval chroniclers in his *Historiae Anglicanae Scriptores Decem* (1652), was also developing a sympathetic attitude towards the monastic movement in the 1630s.[13] He expressed the opinion that two monasteries should have been preserved in each county for

[12] ' 'Tis well known that Mr. Camden and Mr. Weever were forc'd to apologize for barely mentioning the Monasteries.' (Preface to Thomas Tanner, *Notitia Monastica* (1695).) Tanner is referring to Camden's comments in his Preface to *Britannia*: 'There are some, I hear, who take it ill I have mentioned Monasteries and their Founders. . . . Perhaps they would have it forgot that our Ancestors were, and we are Christians, since there were never more certain Indications, and glorious Monuments of Christian Piety and Devotion to God, than those; nor were there any other Seminaries for the Propagation of the Christian Religion and good Literature.'

[13] Among the ten historians whom Twysden put into print were Ailred of Rievaulx, Simeon of Durham, and Gervase of Canterbury.

purposes of devotion and scholarship. John Aubrey looked back nostalgically to the time of monasteries from the 1650s, certain he would have found a congenial lodging in them where he could have pursued his antiquarian researches undisturbed. Although a Puritan-dominated regime was in power when the *Monasticon* came out in 1655, there was a considerable readership for it among Anglicans, royalists, and recusant gentry who shared a more tolerant understanding of the virtues of monasticism. None the less, booksellers were reluctant to take on a book so opposed to the prevailing spirit of the time, and sales were slow. Some Puritan critics murmured that the *Monasticon* was published to make Catholicism more acceptable, an accusation that followed the book through all its phases: when the third volume came out in 1673, there were complaints that it was published purposely to promote popery.[14]

The challenge to conventional Protestant opinion was made in the Propylaion or Preface to the *Monasticon* that was written (in Latin) by Dugdale's friend and fellow antiquarian Sir John Marsham.[15] He gave a highly favourable account of the rise of monasticism, laying emphasis on the vigour of the institution in Anglo-Saxon times. He has praise for the Middle Ages too:

It cannot but be the greatest Satisfaction to see the History of Ancient Christian Discipline reviv'd, or the Originals of Monasteries rescued from the Death of Oblivion. As our pious Ancestors, Kings, Noblemen and others, were magnificent to a Miracle, in building of Churches, and founding, endowing, enriching and privileging of Monasteries, so neither were the Monks unworthy of praise, for having with religious Care and industrious gratitude committed to writing the benefits received of them. . . . This is a plentiful addition to English History, . . . relating to the Church and State, whose Affairs are commonly so interwoven, that they can scarce be rightly understood asunder. The ancient Structure and Polity

---

[14] *Sir William Dugdale*, ed. Hamper, 25.

[15] Marsham was a lawyer, and like most antiquarians, a royalist. He was unusual, indeed almost unique, in addressing himself to Egyptian history and antiquities, and most particularly to establishing the sequence of Egyptian history. His achievement is best seen in *Diatriba Chronologica* (1649) where he discussed the major difficulties of Old-Testament chronology, and more fully in *Chronicus Canon Aegypticus, Ebriacus, Graecus et Disquisitiones* (1672). He left unfinished a work on the chronology of the Persian empire. Sir Henry Wotton wrote of him that 'he was the first who made the Egyptian antiquities intelligible'. Marsham was the uncle of Thomas Stanley, who dedicated his *History of Philosophy* to him in 1655.

of our Church is imperfect without the History of Monasteries. The Monks were formerly the greater part of the Ecclesiasticks, and the Walls of Convents were for a long time the Fences of Sanctity, and the better sort of Literature. . . . Were it not for the Monks, we had certainly ever been mere Children in the History of our Country.[16]

Marsham then takes the offensive, and complains about the unchristian spirit that prevails in the country as he writes in 1654: 'Alas, we see the most august Churches, and the stupendious Monuments dedicated to the eternal God, than which nothing can be more defac'd, under the specious Pretence of Superstition, and expecting utter Destruction. Horses are stabled at the Altars of Christ and the Relicks of Martyrs are dug up. There are certain Zealots, so religiously mad,' he declares, that they respect nothing from the past, and will wish to consign the *Monasticon* to the flames.[17] The antiquarian fraternity, however, vastly admired the book. None was more enthusiastic than Dugdale's predecessor in his heraldic offices, Sir Edward Walker, the exiled Garter King of Arms. He wrote from Amsterdam, 'I shall say no other but that our times are not worthy of it, and that (it being lent me but for three days) I have almost made myself blind perusing it.'[18]

The *Monasticon* consisted predominantly of charters, but it also gave an account of the various monastic orders in England, with histories of the great abbeys and the names of their abbots. Most importantly, the foundation charters and charters relating to the growth of the monastery were printed in full, and all known details of the territorial benefactions made to the monastery were set down. Details were also given of all the smaller houses, chapels, and churches in which the monasteries had an interest, so that the picture of the network of abbeys and their dependencies, which covered the whole country, was recreated with an account of the administrative system that held it together. The dealings of kings, noblemen, and gentlemen with this state within a state were documented, so that men in the seventeenth century might know how much more balanced were the relations of Church and state in the Middle Ages. The *Monasticon* established for the first time the importance of charters as a primary source for the writing of

[16] John Marsham, Preface to Dugdale, *Monasticon* (1718), p. v.
[17] Ibid. p. vi.
[18] Walker to Dugdale, 6 Aug. 1655, in *Sir William Dugdale*, ed. Hamper, 293.

medieval history, and as a source for understanding the legal practices of earlier centuries and aspects of the feudal system relating to conditions of tenure. Not all the charters printed were from the original deeds; many were copies, and Twysden wrote to Dugdale to warn him about monkish forgeries that attributed greater antiquity or privileges to an abbey.[19] But the very fact of printing so many charters was important. They were preserved permanently, and from now on they could be subjected to criticism and revision.

The English abridgement of the *Monasticon* in 1693, made by Joseph Wright, the historian of Rutland, offers a succinct explanation of its value in the Preface to the Reader. It records 'the divers sorts of Liberties and Immunities' that were granted to Church lands, which include 'Courts of Pleas, Markets, Fairs, Commons, Free Pastures, Estovers, Exemptions from Tithes, Tolls, Taxes and Contributions'. These privileges were passed on by the statutes of Henry VIII to those who received Church lands after the Dissolution, so that 'such Persons as enjoy any of those Lands are intituled to many of the same Liberties and Franchises as were at first given with the said Lands.' Wright notes that the *Monasticon* has been admitted as good evidence in the courts of Westminster. He also points out its value to students of the common law, for what it tells of

the commencements of Tenures, the nature and manner of Appropriation and Endowment . . ., the old ways of Tithing, Conveyancing and something of Pleading. . . . It is also useful in History, giving us a lively Idea of the manner of our Forefathers' way of living, their Zeal for God's publick worship, as then profest, and the Simplicity of their Devotions; and of their great Charity to the Poor, and Hospitality and Beneficence to all comers, maintained and exercised in the Monasteries. . . . This book is also of great use in matters of Heraldry and Genealogies.[20]

Wright makes it seem as if the *Monasticon* was a Restoration tax-evaders' guide amongst other things, and no doubt it was used to that end by some, but its appeal was primarily historical. It has however been suggested that an underlying reason for Dugdale's

---

[19] Letter to Dugdale, Mar. 1658, ibid. Twysden also complained that the lay-out of *Monasticon* was unsatisfactory, and that it was difficult to consult. It is true that the book is not user-friendly.

[20] J[ames] W[right], *Monasticon Anglicanum Epitomized in English* [1693], 'To the Reader'.

care in documenting the former possessions of the monasteries was a desire to see some of the property restored to the use and support of the Church. It is true that he expressed concern at the inadequate level of maintenance that the Church of England enjoyed after the Reformation, since so many Church lands had been impropriated or annexed by laymen, and so many tithes due in law were not paid. If the Anglican Church ever revived, and was enabled to recover its property, the *Monasticon* would be a valuable register of its former possessions.[21] But in the 1650s, under the Republic, the restoration of the Church of England must have seemed an improbable event, and it is unlikely that Dugdale or Dodsworth had any realistic hopes of a recovery.

Dugdale's opening tactic is of some interest. He chooses to start with an account of Glastonbury Abbey, whose foundation he traces back to Joseph of Arimathea. This is not what one expects of a serious historian in the 1650s, but the intention was undoubtedly to show a conviction that the planting of the Church in England occurred in apostolic times and long antedated the mission sent from Rome by Pope Gregory. The Church's roots are in primitive soil, and no matter what corruptions may have afflicted it later, it is a true, independent, apostolic Church in origin. Only after he has firmly established the primacy of Glastonbury does Dugdale turn to Canterbury, the scene of the Roman mission.

The engraved frontispiece to the *Monasticon* provides some clear indications of Dugdale's attitudes towards the medieval Church in England, the Dissolution, and the current state of religion in the country. It was the normal practice of authors in the seventeenth century to design their own title-pages or frontispieces as a visible statement of intent, and we may assume that Dugdale was responsible for this introduction to his first printed book. Close inspection reveals it to be a highly polemical frontispiece, as a recent study has shown.[22] The theme is the sanctity of religious endowments, and the betrayal of his ancestors' vows by Henry VIII. The top central panel shows the confirmation of Magna Carta by Henry III, with a page reference to Matthew Paris's Chronicle. The page in question tells of the King's affirmation that the Church will

---

[21] See Margery Corbett, 'The Title-Page and Illustrations to the *Monasticon Anglicanum* 1655–1673', in the *Antiquaries' Journal* (1986), 102–9.
[22] See ibid. for a detailed interpretation of the title-page.

be free and have 'its rights and liberties unimpaired', and his agreement to the excommunication of 'all those who knowingly and maliciously deprived the Church of her rights'.[23] The scene can be read as a warning to the contemporary successors to the temporal power, the Commonwealth government, 'of the illegality and sinfulness of their proceedings both enacted and contemplated against the Church'.[24] The vignette on the left plinth shows a medieval king making an act of donation to an abbey, while the right hand one shows Henry VIII reneging on his predecessors' vows at the Dissolution. At the top left is shown the piety of the early Church, which has resulted in the building of an abbey (possibly Glastonbury), while the counterpart engraving presents the figure of Antiquity, half hidden in darkness, on whom light shines from an Anglo-Saxon book. The book has been identified by Margery Corbett as the Textus Roffensis, a collection of laws with the charters of Rochester Abbey, which documented 'the primitive church rising to maturity, independent of Roman influence'.[25] The presence of the Anglo-Saxon text, as well as the concern with sacrilege in the title-page, might be an allusive tribute to Sir Henry Spelman, the effective patron of Dugdale in his early years and the good genius of the *Monasticon*. Two standing figures flank the arch that forms the main feature of the design: St Augustine, who led the Roman mission to the Saxons of Kent and who was a member of the Benedictine order, and St Gregory, who sent Augustine to England. Gregory wears a mitre, not the papal tiara, for Protestants refused to recognize the Pope as anything other than the Bishop of Rome. The total effect of the engraving is to stress the antiquity and tradition of the Church in England, planted in the earliest times of Christianity, forming part of the Church catholic and universal for many ages, enjoying the support and protection of kings, then undergoing destruction at the hands of a wilful and law-defying monarch. That process of destruction is still being perpetuated in the 1650s, but it is sacrilege, the despoiling of a true Church.

The *Monasticon* had copious illustrations, among which were the most accurate engravings of Church architecture that had ever appeared in an English book. These were drawn and etched by

---

[23] Corbett, 'Title-Page', 106, quoting Matthew Paris, *Historia Major* (1640 edn.).   [24] Ibid. 107.   [25] Ibid. 108.

11. Title-page of *Monasticon Anglicanum* (1655), by Wenceslaus Hollar. The inscription is evidently incomplete, perhaps reflecting Dugdale's hesitations over the question of authorship.

Wenceslaus Hollar, originally from Bohemia, who was the fore-most copperplate artist working in England. He had done much work for the book trade in London, but Dugdale came to know him through his dealings with the Earl of Arundel, the Earl Marshal, in whose household Hollar had lived and worked for several years.[26] Dugdale employed Hollar to illustrate most of his works, and the two men became quite friendly, for there are many affectionate references to Hollar in Dugdale's correspondence. Hollar was an ideal illustrator of antiquarian books, for he had a wonderfully sharp eye and an understanding of architectural styles, and he drew with an exquisitely delicate hand. In addition, his soft lines and gentle touch contribute noticeably to an indefinable sense of nostalgia which seems thoroughly appropriate to his subject matter.

All these qualities are notably absent in the other artist whom Dugdale employed on the *Monasticon*, Daniel King, whose crude, ill-drawn, and two-dimensional views are a disgrace to the art of etching. He may have been a pupil of Hollar, though he can hardly be said to have benefited from the training he received, and his pitiful work shows only too plainly the gulf between the skills of the native and Continental etchers in the 1650s. King seems to have enjoyed the patronage of Lord Fairfax, and it is likely that Fairfax recommended him to Dodsworth as a suitable illustrator for his monastic collections. This speculation, that he was an inheritance from an earlier phase of the collaboration between Dugdale and Dodsworth, and came with the backing of the influential Fairfax, would explain why King contributed so many plates to the first two volumes. King gathered together the etchings he had made for the *Monasticon* and published them as a picturebook without text in 1656, under the title *The Cathedrall and Conventuall Churches of England and Wales Orthographically Delineated*, a venture which suggests that there might have been a market for views of

---

[26] For details of Hollar's English career, see Graham Parry, *Hollar's England* (Salisbury, 1980), and Richard Pennington, *A descriptive catalogue of the etched work of Wenceslaus Hollar* (Cambridge, 1982). Also my articles 'Wenceslaus Hollar, the Antiquarians' Illustrator', in *Ariel* (Apr. 1972), 42–52; and 'Wenceslaus Hollar and the Earl of Arundel', in *Long Room: the Bulletin of Trinity College, Dublin* (1981), 6–13.

cathedrals in the decade of the 1650s: the customers were presumably of a royalist and Anglican disposition.[27]

Hollar's plates greatly enhance the preservationist spirit of the *Monasticon*, for they provide a record of what the great churches looked like in the mid-seventeenth century, when their continued existence was no longer certain. St Paul's and Lichfield Cathedrals in particular were considered in danger of destruction in the 1650s, through Civil War violence and subsequent mistreatment, and both were well illustrated in the 1655 volume.[28] Hollar's etchings are the visual complement to Dugdale's historical text: both provide reliable records and accurate transcriptions. Dugdale himself had little interest in the appearance of the buildings he documented, and never mentions an architectural detail, but it was an admirable move to engage artists to depict the major churches. He was motivated by the fear that, under the new regime of the English Republic, the cathedrals, the seats of the reviled bishops, might go the same way as the abbeys. The functions of the Church of England had been suspended, its bishops deposed, its clergy purged, and its services banned.[29] The spirit of plain religion was in the ascendant, and who knew what would happen to the great churches, which no longer had any function, and were reminders of the ancient ceremonious religion that was now despised?

Dugdale defrayed the cost of the illustrations by seeking sponsors for them at £5 a plate. Friends, acquaintances and antiquarian well-wishers rallied to the cause, and Dugdale's correspondence contains

---

[27] There was a second edition, enlarged, in 1672. No views could be less orthographic, in fact. Daniel King also published *The Vale-Royall of England* in 1656, a collection of antiquarian descriptions of his native Cheshire written by several hands, but rather misleadingly represented as King's own work.

[28] Hollar's principal view of Lichfield seems to have been directed away from the *Monasticon* into Thomas Fuller's *Church History of Britain* (also published in 1655) by Elias Ashmole, a protégé of Dugdale and later his son-in-law. Ashmole contributed this plate to the *Church History* with an inscription mourning the fate of Lichfield, and Fuller observed, 'But alas it is now in a pitiful case indeed, almost beaten down to the ground in our civil dissentions. I have at the cost of my worthy friend exemplified the Portraiture thereof; and am glad to hear it to be the design of ingenious persons to preserve ancient churches in the like nature, (whereof many are done in this, and more expected in the next part of *Monasticon*), seeing when their substance is gone, their verie shadows will be acceptable to posteritie.' (iv. 175)

[29] The ban on Anglican services became final on 25 Dec. 1655. Evelyn's Diary for that day notes, 'I went to London where Dr. Wild preached the funeral service of Preaching, this day being the last day; after which, Cromwell's proclamation was to take place, that none of the Church of England should dare either to preach, or administer Sacraments, teach school, etc. on pain of imprisonment, or exile.'

numerous letters from men who wished to support the *Monasticon*
by paying for a plate. It was an act of solidarity of Anglicans in
winter. The sponsors had their coat of arms engraved on the plate,
and were allowed to express some brief sentiment in Latin in their
cartouche. Almost all these inscriptions are elegiac, lamenting the
ruin of the church they depict. Most express the desire that
posterity should know how splendid the monuments of the Church
of England had been ('ut posteris innotescat splendida maiorum
pietas' reads Thomas le Gros's plate of Norwich, for example—
'that posterity should not be ignorant of the splendid piety of our
forebears'), and many play with the Horatian topos of 'aere
perennius', that these paper illustrations will outlive brass and
stone, and that the etchings will long survive the buildings they
describe. Some plead for an end to the desecration of churches, as
does John Rushworth, Spelman's executor, on his plate of Ripon:
'Maneat usus, tollatur abusus' ('Let the use continue, the abuse
cease'). Occasionally a more defiant note is struck: 'Resurgat
ecclesia, et resplendescat in eternum' ('Let the Church revive and
shine eternally') was the wish of William Cole on the plate of
Sherborne Abbey. There are even instances of forlorn wit. Thomas
Davison inscribes on his Durham plate, 'In occasu religionis et
pietatis, orientalem faciem ecclesiae Dunelm. illustrat' ('As religion
and piety set, [Thomas Davison] shows the east end [the rising face]
of Durham'). The prevailing sentiments of the illustrations are,
however, deeply pessimistic.

The same spirit of preservation that inspired the *Monasticon* lay
behind *The History of St. Paul's Cathedral* (1658), which was a
rapidly compiled book, written to take advantage of the great
quantity of charters and other documents that came into Dugdale's
possession in 1656. *St. Paul's* was much more fully illustrated than
the *Monasticon*. This time Hollar was the only artist engaged, and
his work has a special value because of the complete destruction of
the Cathedral in the Great Fire of 1666. Hollar's etchings are the
only records we have of the interior of St Paul's: the solid Norman
nave, the screen at the crossing, and the lofty Gothic choir are
clearly depicted, though we get no sense of the disorderly public life
that filled the western half of the church. Equally valuable are the
views from every angle of Inigo Jones's refacing of the Cathedral,
which he carried out in the 1630s. This had resulted in a neo-
classical casing on three sides, which went rather incongruously

with the rest of the Gothic fabric. The monumental portico that
Jones erected at the west end was considered one of his most noble
designs, yet without Hollar's views of it, it would scarcely be
known.

Although Hollar's etchings give the book its permanent value as
a visual record of the earlier Cathedral, there is a puzzle about how
much of the work is his own. There is a large folding plate, present
in some copies, which seems to have been sold separately as a
broadsheet, although it has an obvious association with Dugdale's
book.[30] This plate has a frame of miniature etchings of some of the
illustrations that appear full-size elsewhere in *The History of
St. Paul's*, but in this frame they are signed by Daniel King. To this
architectural synopsis is added a small copy of Visscher's view of
London, executed by King and David Loggan. Inside the frame are
verses 'On St. Paul's Cathedral represented by Mr. Daniel King', by
the royalist and Laudian poet Edward Benlowes. There is also a
Latin elegy, 'Threnodia Aedis Paulinae', by Benlowes (who signs it
with an anagram of his name, Benevolus), which laments the
degradation of St Paul's and the loss of the Church of England and
of the King. There is praise for the royal name of the engraver, who
is now the only king to preserve the church in these grim days. By
way of thanks, the artist includes a small wreathed head of
Benlowes in the margin. The verse tribute to Daniel King makes it
clear that he must have drawn the architectural illustrations for the
book, and that he was the principal recorder of St Paul's. There is
no mention of Hollar. One might guess that Dugdale called in
Hollar to prepare the plates from King's drawings because he was a
far finer etcher than King, and the folding plate might have been
published to put the record straight and ensure that King's role as
the original illustrator was not overlooked. At any rate, the sheet
survives as evidence of some forgotten dispute among artists. The
situation is complicated by a note in the book itself, in the section
entitled 'A View of the Monuments', stating that they are shown 'as
they stood in Sept. 1641'. Thus it would seem that Hollar, when he
etched the illustrations for the tombs, was working from old
drawings, presumably those made by William Sedgwick on the eve
of the Civil War, which Dugdale referred to in his Diary.[31] So, if the

---

[30] See Harold Jenkins, *Edward Benlowes* (Cambridge, Mass., 1952), 258–60.
[31] Such is the freshness of a few of the designs, however, that one feels Hollar
must have gone to the site and made new sketches in several cases. These apparently

claims made on King's broadsheet are accepted, Hollar's role in *The History of St. Paul's* appears to have been largely that of a brilliant copyist, although through the centuries he has enjoyed sole credit for these famous illustrations.

As with the *Monasticon*, the dedications of the plates express a mixture of forlorn sadness at the ruin of the church and defiant belief in its powers of recovery. The former greatly predominates and there is in these descriptions a strong sense that the Church of England has gone for good. St Paul's stands for the condition of the Church as a whole. William Backhouse inscribes his plate 'Ne labantis Ecclesiae vestigia dispereant' ('Lest the remains of the collapsing church perish'); Margaret Clapham (wife of Sir Christopher Clapham, a Yorkshire gentleman) dedicates the plate of Donne's tomb to the memory of that 'mellifluous and extraordinary man' ('melliflui et eximii doctoris'), while 'sighing at so much profanation and ruin of the church' ('gemens talis et tantae ecclesiae profanationem et dilapidationem'). Sir Aubrey de Vere, on his plate of the Chapter House, shows it as it used to be, 'in qua ordo et disciplina Dei servientium', not as it is now, 'ubi sterquilinia et stercora equorum aceruari solebant' ('full of dunghills and piled with horse manure'). Henry Compton, youngest son of the Earl of Northampton, calls for divine revenge against those who have committed this outrage against the church, with quotations from Homer and Virgil. Thomas Barlow, Bodley's librarian, strengthening his imprecations, invokes Horace to condemn his contemporaries if they do not repair the temples and tottering shrines of the gods, and Lucan to lament the desecrations brought about by civil war. Hollar himself expressed his sentiments on a plate showing the nave of St Paul's: 'Wenceslaus Hollar Bohemus huius ecclesiae (quotidie casum expectantis) delineator et olim admirator, memoriam sic preservabit' ('Wenceslaus Hollar the Bohemian, illustrator of this church (which daily expects its fall), and once its admirer, will thus preserve its memory'). He ends with a hope that the church will live again and its destroyers perish. A resolutely optimistic note is struck by Wingfield Bodenham in dedicating his plate of the shrine of St Erkenwald: 'This has withstood fire, riot and the ravages of a thousand years, and will survive this present neglect.' It did not.

new sketches are inscribed, 'W. Hollar del. et sculp.' Those he copied are marked, 'W. H. fecit.'

The plate inscriptions show how *The History of St. Paul's*, like the *Monasticon*, became a rallying point for Anglicans and royalists at the time of their eclipse. A group of plates subscribed by John Robinson even extolled the memory of William Laud, whose action in rebuilding the Cathedral in the 1630s made him 'vir ultra marmora perennandus' ('a man more lasting than marble'). Robinson was Laud's nephew, and so had an interest in Laud's reputation, but his open praise would have found an echo in many of the subscribers' hearts.

Dugdale's historical sense as displayed in this book is conventional in the mildly preposterous way of the time. Subjects have to be traced back to a remote beginning, and so *The History of St. Paul's* begins in Paradise, where Adam must have had a special place for his devotions. A succession of significant devotional places is lightly sketched in, passing via the Temple at Jerusalem to early Christian places of worship, until we arrive in England, where Christianity was first formally encouraged by King Lucius in the second century. St Paul's receives its foundation under Ethelbert in the early seventh century, on a site where a Roman temple to Diana had stood. From this point onward, Dugdale has the support of Bede and other Anglo-Saxon historians, and he can make use of the cathedral charters available to him. In addition, manuscripts from the Cotton Library help him piece together an early Saxon history for St Paul's. From Norman times, the picture is fuller as documentation becomes more abundant, and Dugdale can diversify his account with details of the more notable bishops, of customs associated with the cathedral, of its liberties and endowments. He shows no interest in the building history of the church.

It soon becomes clear that his principal aim is to record the tombs and inscriptions. This is an understandable preoccupation for a herald. As far as Dugdale is concerned, St Paul's is a genealogical treasure-house, filled with invaluable data about the kinship lines of innumerable families. The most important elements of tombs of the gentry were the details of descent, marriage, and offspring, and the display of heraldry that conveyed information about earlier alliances. The effigies and epitaphs that impressed the eye and pleased the mind were secondary to the record of the bloodstock lines of the deceased. The heraldic duty of tracing these lines animated Dugdale and his colleagues to compile their great collections. It is debatable whether the profligate creation of knights and peers by James I had really devalued their task or had rendered it more valuable by setting a premium on families whose ancient lineage could be authenticated. In his survey of the tombs, Dugdale is tempted to embark on a brief history of the rites of burial and of funeral monuments, beginning with Abraham and Sarah, but he desists. Instead, he quotes Weever on the unvarying need of all societies to commemorate their dead by lasting monuments.[32]

This sentiment gives edge to Dugdale's expostulation against those who deface and despoil monuments, whether they are the reformers of Edward VI's time or the zealots of the revolutionary years. He invokes Spelman's *De Non Temerandis Ecclesiis* as expressing his own powerful feelings, finds examples to show the retribution that falls on those who sack sacred places, and gives warning that temporal judgements do befall offenders. Then he sets to work to catalogue the tombs as they stood in 1641. His account is greatly enhanced by Hollar's etchings of the celebrated monuments that filled the choir, which preserve much that would otherwise have been lost to posterity. John of Gaunt's slender-pinnacled tomb, John Colet's memorial, the festive monuments of the great Elizabethans such as William, Earl of Pembroke, Sir Christopher Hatton, Sir Nicholas Bacon, and Sir William Cockayne, all stuck about with pillars and obelisks, are carefully and understandingly delineated.[33] After the Fire, the only monument to survive of all those illustrated was the marble conceit of John Donne rising from his urn.

The indifference of Dugdale to architectural and monumental detail is remarkable to a modern reader. Although he spent a great deal of time inspecting churches and their contents, he is always silent about the architecture, and there is no evidence in his letters that he derived any pleasure from it. His lack of reaction was common amongst antiquaries, who were generally so preoccupied with the inscriptions that they forgot the church. Only Aubrey seems to have taken a conscious delight in the buildings he visited,

---

[32] Dugdale, *St. Paul's*, 44.

[33] As with the *Monasticon*, the plates for *St. Paul's* were paid for by well-wishers, at £5 a time. For example, John King, Bishop of London, wrote to offer his contribution: 'I have a sequestered person's mite to offer Mr. Dugdale, when he decyphers my father's gravestone' (*Sir William Dugdale*, ed. Hamper, 318).

and of published antiquaries, only William Somner, in his *Antiquities of Canterbury* (1640), showed any interest in the style of a medieval building.[34]

The Antiquities of Warwickshire has always had a large following. Anthony Wood's rapture at his first sight of it is well known, and it immediately kindled in him an ambition to make a similar collection of the antiquities of Oxfordshire. (Wood never completed this collection, but some of the material was diverted to his book on the history of antiquities of Oxford University, published in 1674.) The intensity of his response may have been exceptional, but it was a fair indication of the book's reception. *Warwickshire* is the finest of the seventeenth-century county descriptions, the fullest, the most methodical and detailed, reproducing great numbers of accurate and reliable documents relating to county families. It was also the most attractively presented. It was the culmination of a tradition which had begun with Lambarde's *Perambulation of Kent* in 1576, and which had included Norden's Middlesex, Carew's Cornwall, and Burton's Leicestershire.[35] Dugdale's book was dedicated to Sir Christopher Hatton, who had been so helpful to him at the beginning of his career, and who had arranged his access to so many repositories of public records. Dugdale acknowledged too his indebtedness to Sir Simon Archer, who had originally proposed to write a survey of Warwickshire, and whose collections had been so useful to him. There is an 'Epistle to the Gentrie of Warwickshire', his principal audience, in which he makes the predictable comment that he

---

[34] For example, see Somner, *Canterbury*, 164. Somner 'confirmed the date of the architecture of parts of the cathedral that he had established from historical sources by comparing it with other pieces of that age' (Michael Hunter, *John Aubrey and the Realm of Learning* (London, 1975), 166n.).

[35] It is a measure of Dugdale's powers of perseverance that he carried the voluminous *Warwickshire* through to publication when one considers how many county histories were begun but failed to reach print in the seventeenth century because their authors were overwhelmed by the scale of their collections. Robert Cotton was gathering material for Huntingdonshire, Henry Spelman for Norfolk, Christopher Hatton as well as Augustine Vincent for Northamptonshire; Samson Erdeswick, was preparing Staffordshire, as was Walter Chetwynd; Roger Dodsworth hoped to give an account of Yorkshire, Thomas Risdon of Devonshire, and Matthew Hale of Gloucestershire; Edward Bysshe undertook Surrey, both Thomas Blount and Silas Taylor attempted Herefordshire, John Philpot Kent, and Simonds D'Ewes Suffolk. John Aubrey made considerable collections for Wiltshire, but they were published only in the nineteenth century.

wishes to memorialize the ancestors of the local gentry, and to show 'in what Honor they lived in those flourishing Ages past'. His aim, he declares, is 'to incite the present and future Ages to virtuous imitation' of those same worthy ancestors.

As in his other books of the 1650s, a sense of impending ruin fills the pages. He remarks in his Preface that because there was so much war and destruction in Saxon times, it is virtually impossible to construct a picture of Saxon Warwickshire. The Civil War and its effects have given a modern urgency to his work, and he writes that he has caused the engravings of so many tombs to be made 'for preserving those Monuments from that Fate which Time, if not contingent Mischief, might expose them to'.[36] Time and again he reverts to the catastrophe of the Dissolution, which swept away so large a part of the medieval record. This event 'gave the greatest blow to Antiquities that ever England had, by the destruction and spoil of so many rare Manuscripts, and no small number of famous Monuments'.[37]

In the background of the work is Camden's *Britannia*, which laid down the antiquarian groundplot for the English counties. Dugdale imitates Camden's topographical method of following the rivers to progress from site to site. The history of towns is briefly given, with speculations on the origin of the place-names. Regional commodities are noted. The important business is to record the families associated with each place, to speak of their more famous deeds, and to list their intermarryings and burials. Camden himself had deliberately omitted this aspect of county history because it would have been too voluminous a task and would almost certainly have provoked outcries from families who felt they had been inadequately treated. A glance at the hundreds of escutcheons that fill the pages of *Warwickshire* tells one immediately that genealogy is the prime concern of the book.[38] *Warwickshire* did not break new ground but

---

[36] Epistle to the Gentrie in Dugdale, *Warwickshire* (1656).

[37] Preface, ibid.

[38] The favourable response to this genealogical information is exemplified by the letter to Dugdale from Thomas Pecke of Norfolk, dated 22 June 1659: 'If posteritie would converse with their consumed Ancestours, they are forc'd to entreat such worthyes as you to descend into the Dormitories . . . they should thankfully reward the labour of those who brush ye dust from the tombes of their Great-grandfathers.' Pecke went on to urge Dugdale to write an 'Antiquities of Norfolk'. (*Sir William Dugdale*, ed. Hamper, 353.)

consolidated the old preoccupations. As a recent survey of the topographical tradition points out, Dugdale had virtually no sense of pre-history, made little reference to archaeological finds, and did not attend to the natural history of the county.[39] These were rising interests which would be seriously addressed after the Restoration, as the wider curiosity aroused by Royal Society investigations began to spread.

Dugdale deviated from his usual paths after the appearance of *St. Paul's* to publish a *History of Imbanking and Drayning of Diverse Fennes* (1662). This account of recent drainage schemes in the Fens offers a somewhat deceptive impression of Dugdale's reasons for producing the work. It is dedicated to Charles II, and presents the land improvements as evidence of the benefits of Stuart rule, for much is made of James I's and Charles I's encouragement of such schemes, and Charles II is urged to continue the good work. The achievements of the Dutch engineer Vermuyden in the reign of Charles I are deservedly admired. However, Dugdale disguises his own involvement in the big Commonwealth project for fen drainage that was carried out in the 1650s. From 1649 onwards, a group of entrepreneurs, mainly London merchants and landowners from East Anglia, had combined to carry out large-scale reclamation schemes in the Fens. John Thurloe, Secretary to the Council of State, was heavily involved, as was the Puritan Lord Gorges. Dugdale's friend John Marsham was also a participant. The chief surveyor and organizer of the project was the mathematician Jonas Moore. It appears that Dugdale was prevailed upon to 'advertise' the scheme by writing a learned discourse which would emphasize the historical importance and utility of the undertaking. Dugdale's diaries show that he was travelling round the East Anglian counties in 1657–8 and he must have begun writing his book after 1658, when *St. Paul's* was out of the way. With the restoration of the monarchy in 1660, however, it may have been imprudent to declare one's involvement with an important Commonwealth project, so Dugdale disguised his closeness to the managers of the scheme.

---

[39] Mendyk, *Speculum Britanniae*. Dugdale's *Warwickshire* is discussed on pp. 105–10. It is however worth noting that when Dugdale made his heraldic visitation of Cumberland, he made drawings of henge monuments and also of the hogback tombs in Appleby churchyard. These drawings are preserved at the College of Heralds, MS C39.

Instead of a work praising one of the great economic successes of the Commonwealth years (for the Fens were indeed made much more productive and habitable), Dugdale eventually produced a scholarly treatise on the history of 'imbanking and drayning', which sits rather oddly amongst the rest of his writings. In fact, it was a book that had to ignore its own *raison d'être*, for political considerations made Dugdale emphasize the antiquarian aspects of the subject and overlook the achievements of a Cromwellian project.[40]

Almost instinctively, Dugdale took his subject back to Genesis, when God ordered the waters to be gathered together, and saw that it was good. The problems of reclaiming the earth after the Flood exercise Dugdale for a while, and then he turns to the historical record of ancient drainage schemes in Egypt, Greece, and Italy under the Romans. The subject is pursued down the centuries: he conducts a survey of the marshlands of England, and he accumulates surprising amounts of information about medieval attempts to dry out these lands. Naturally, he looks admiringly to Holland, where so much land had been recovered from the sea, and where the Dutch led the modern world in the knowledge of 'imbanking and drayning'. But Dugdale's thoughts keep reverting to the Romans. Vermuyden's successful activities had uncovered Roman roads and many evidences of the remote past, which had given support to the idea that the Romans had indeed tried to drain some part of the Fens, so for more information Dugdale enlisted the help of Thomas Browne of Norwich, who knew more than most about East Anglia and ancient practices.

An animated correspondence went on between them from 1658 to 1660, in which Browne gave his opinions on Roman drainage skills, indicated the track of Roman roads and communicated news of urns and coins that had come to light. He companionably suggested that they get together to excavate a barrow so that Dugdale could see how these mounds were constructed. Characteristically, Browne launched into a sublime discourse on the great drainage schemes of antiquity, from Babylon to Rome. The familiar

[40] I am indebted to Frances Willmoth of Emmanuel College, Cambridge, for information concerning Dugdale's involvement in the fen drainage scheme. For an overall account of the fenlands project, see her book *Sir Jonas Moore: Practical Mathematics and Restoration Science* (Woodbridge, Suffolk, 1993), 88–121.

voice expounds: 'And beside what you finde in Natalis Comes, concerning Acharnania, the exiccation of meeres and fennes seemes to have been no unknowne thing in Greece. . . .'[41] Discussion of submerged lands brings up the question of great fishes' bones found far inland, unlike any known today. Browne suggests they may belong to some creature from the time of the Flood, and stumbles on to a truth when he declares, 'The greatest antiquities of mortall bodies may remaine in petrified bones, whereof some may be older than the Pyramides.'[42] When Dugdale questions him about burnt trees found deep underground, Browne imagines an earlier race of men, 'our uncivilized predecessors', who might have cleared the ground by burning, as he has observed in Ireland, and has heard is the practice in Virginia and the West Indies.

The research for the book on the Fens exposed Dugdale to a broad range of stimulating ideas relating to geological and climatic change, fossils, natural history, and the history of technology, ideas which would become the common currency of intellectuals after the Restoration in the new ethos generated by the Royal Society. Even familiar subjects such as Roman roads appeared in a new light. Browne pointed out that these roads were originally broad and raised above the level of the surrounding terrain, 'probably occasioning the first name of high wayes'. Had these roads in the post-Roman era been the passageways for the devastating raids of the Mercians upon the East Saxons? Elias Ashmole put a more radical query: why had the great Roman roads become so neglected? Perhaps, he suggested, it was because Christianity had caused people to go to new and different places, so the old roads were no longer used.[43] In fact, *A History of Imbanking and Drayning* shows little sign of the intellectual activity that accompanied its composition. Dugdale's habitual conservatism descended on the subject, and appropriately, it is a dry book. Its date of publication, 1662, was also the date of incorporation of the Royal Society, and its technological subject matter was in keeping with the Society's Baconian programme, but the book quite failed to engage with the spirit of the new Society.

Dugdale's relations with other antiquaries helped to clarify his

---

[41] Browne to Dugdale, 11 Dec. 1658, in *The Letters of Sir Thomas Browne*, ed. Geoffrey Keynes (London, 1946), 342. [42] Ibid. 344.
[43] Letter from Ashmole to Dugdale, 20 Apr. 1657, in *Sir William Dugdale*, ed. Hamper, 325.

place in the historical scheme. Spelman had the greatest influence over him, and introduced him to the methods of making searches into manuscript collections, seeking out the oldest documents, extracting evidence, interpreting it, and making comparisons for authenticity. The study of charters and the knowledge of ancient laws were essential to this kind of activity. From Spelman, Dugdale understood the necessity of Anglo-Saxon for antiquarian research of a legal and institutional nature. From Spelman too, Dugdale picked up his horror of the sacrilegious treatment of the Church at the Dissolution, an emotion intensified by the new wave of violence brought by the Civil Wars and the Commonwealth. Dugdale was trained up in Anglo-Saxon by Spelman, but he received the greatest assistance in this area from William Somner, who became a close friend and who helped him particularly with the Anglo-Saxon documents relating to the *Monasticon*.[44] Somner was able to give much assistance with the Canterbury records for the *Monasticon*, and it was to Somner that Dugdale turned for final approval of *Warwickshire* before it went to press. In return, Dugdale was one of the chief promoters of Somner's Dictionary in 1659. Dugdale was also friendly with an older master of Anglo-Saxon, the German-born Francis Junius, who was a member of the Arundel circle. He too was compiling an Anglo-Saxon dictionary, although it did not see the light of day until 1743, and their correspondence is full of references to Anglo-Saxon manuscripts. Dugdale's closeness to the major figures of Anglo-Saxon scholarship was further strengthened by his friendship with Gerard Langbaine, the Provost of Queen's College, Oxford. It was Dr Langbaine who suggested to Dugdale the fine idea for promoting the sale of *Warwickshire* by leaving a bound copy for four months in the great east window of the Bodleian Library, where strangers would notice it and wish to buy it.[45]

Of the younger antiquaries, Dugdale was very helpful to Anthony Wood, whom he first met in 1667, introduced by Thomas Barlow of the Bodleian; Barlow arranged for Wood to have access to the Cotton Library. In that same summer, when Wood gained entrance to the records in the Tower through the goodwill of the

---

[44] See Marsham's acknowledgement of this service in the Preface to *Monasticon*, p. v.

[45] It is not known whether this suggestion was adopted. See *Sir William Dugdale*, ed. Hamper, 312.

Keeper, the old Puritan lawyer William Prynne, he was conducted into the White Tower, 'where he was strangely surprised to see such a vast number of charters and rolls,' and found Dugdale working there on his *Baronage of England*.[46] The two dined together every day 'at a cook's house near the Tower', and thereafter, relations between them were mainly cordial. Because Wood's work too was mostly with manuscript collections, they had much to communicate to each other. Dugdale's entrusting of his biographical memoir to Wood at the end of his life is a measure of his esteem for the Oxford antiquary.

With John Aubrey, relations were less close. Aubrey greatly admired *Warwickshire*, and became involved in a collaborative scheme to compile an account of Wiltshire on the same principles. He ardently supported the preservationist ethic of the *Monasticon*, and contributed an illustration to volume II by having Hollar engrave a sketch he had commissioned before the Civil War of Osney Abbey, which by 1661 had almost totally disappeared. Dugdale encouraged Aubrey to make a collection of coats of arms based on historical principles, and urged him to print his 'Templa Druidum' on Stonehenge and stone circles, but Dugdale was not interested in the fieldwork that so attracted Aubrey, and Aubrey's fondness for speculation and hearsay were not at all to Dugdale's liking.[47] Aubrey for his part all too readily admitted his dislike of archival research: 'this searching after Antiquities is a wearisome Taske; ... of all studies I take least delight in this.'[48] Aubrey embraced the multi-disciplinary antiquarianism that became fashionable after the Restoration, and this was a different genera-tion's taste. Dugdale was willing to encourage the new generation: for example, he drew up 'Directions for the Search of Records, and making use of them' for the benefit of Robert Plot as he began his

---

[46] *The Baronage of England* was published in 1675. A vast compilation of family histories from the time of the Conquest, it brought together and printed a wealth of material from medieval records and so became the indispensable repository of genealogical information that formed the basis for most subsequent research in this field. Like the *Monasticon*, the *Baronage* developed out of collections gathered by Dodsworth in the 1640s. The book is valuable for its integrity of documentation in a subject notorious for exaggerated and misleading claims of lineage. Dugdale was scholarly enough, and by this time wealthy enough, to trace family histories fairly and impartially, uninfluenced by the ambitious claims of powerful families who affected some illustrious descent or distinguished connections.

[47] See Hunter, *John Aubrey*, 149.   [48] Ibid. 151.

Natural History of Staffordshire, a county survey of a much more modern kind than *Warwickshire* had been. Dugdale's own outlook remained basically a documentary one until his death.

Dugdale's most sympathetic companion amongst the younger antiquarians was his own son-in-law, Elias Ashmole (1617–92). As a junior heraldic officer, Ashmole had accompanied Dugdale on his visitations of the north-west midland counties in 1662 and 1663; he married Dugdale's daughter (as his third wife) in 1668. Their heraldic interests drew them together, and Ashmole's major antiquarian work, *The History of the Institution, Laws, and Ceremonies of the most Noble Order of the Garter* (1672), was in the traditional Dugdalian form of a documentary study of an institution.

Although William Dugdale died as late as 1685, he was essentially an exponent of a late-Renaissance type of historiography, which concentrated on reconstructing the society and institutions of medieval or pre-Norman times from a methodical and critical study of manuscript records. It was almost entirely a text-based study, appealing to virtually no other forms of evidence beyond the written page. When he declared on the title-page of his *Antiquities of Warwickshire* that it was 'illustrated from Records, Leiger-Books, Manuscripts, Charters, Evidences, Tombes and Arms', he was stating his working principles in a form that would have been entirely familiar to Selden or Spelman. Once the new spirit of the Restoration got abroad, however, these principles would begin to look limited, and too restricted in their scope.

9

A Mid-century Miscellany:
Thomas Browne, William Burton, and
Thomas Fuller

In the 1650s, many royalist gentlemen up and down the country were inclined to take their minds off contemporary discomfiture by thinking about the remote past. Perhaps exclusion from public life gave them more time for their researches, for this was a period that saw the publication of a good deal of antiquarian writing. William Dugdale dominated the decade, and his books advanced knowledge of the past on many fronts: monastic history, architectural history, and regional history were transformed by his voluminous and methodical endeavours. Dugdale's interest in ecclesiastical history was matched at a more popular level by Thomas Fuller's *Church History of Britain*, which came out in 1655, the same year as the *Monasticon*. The posthumous publication of Inigo Jones's speculations about Stonehenge in 1655 brought Ancient Britain and the Romans back into prominence after two decades of relative neglect. The configuration of Roman Britain was the subject of William Burton's *Commentary* on the Antonine Itinerary (1658), in which he attempted to locate the towns and camps of the third century. Thomas Browne composed his meditations on what he took to be Roman urns, and published them in 1658. Across the decade James Ussher's chronologies appeared in various formats in 1650, 1654, and 1658, carrying his many readers through the eventful epochs of ancient history, and reminding them how time pressed on to its likely end. By looking here at the work of the lesser figures in this group, Browne, Burton, and Fuller, we can enlarge our sense of the diversity of antiquarian thought in the Commonwealth years.

Thomas Browne, the polymath of Norwich, had taken all knowledge as his domain in *Pseudodoxia Epidemica* (1646), his erudite exposé of a multitude of common misconceptions about the natural world that were current in his time. But he did not turn his full attention to antiquarian matters until the 1650s, when he was inspired by the discovery of some sepulchral urns in Norfolk to write *Hydriotaphia* or *Urn-Burial*. The success of this work encouraged him to extend his interest to barrows and earthworks, and his new reputation as an antiquary brought him into rewarding correspondence with Dugdale, Evelyn, and Aubrey.

Urn-Burial is a unique production: part excavation report, part meditation on the mystery of time and the vanity of human wishes. Contemplating these clay vessels and their ashy contents, Browne articulated emotions ignored by most antiquaries, acknowledging in these scanty remains the forlorn hope of men to preserve themselves from oblivion. He spoke of the vast futility of human ambition in the face of time, and recounted the extraordinary designs of men to ensure their posthumous passage through age after age. The accidents of fortune that have frustrated so many splendid schemes to perpetuate bodies, names, and memories add an exquisitely poignant savour to Browne's reflections: 'Who can but pity the founder of the Pyramids? Herostratus lives that burnt the Temple of Diana, he is almost lost that built it; Time hath spared the epitaph of Adrian's horse, confounded that of himself. In vain we compute our felicities by the advantage of our good names, since bad have equal durations, and Thersites is like to live as long as Agamemnon.'[1] This is the archaeology of sighs and tears, as Browne recognized when he described the urns as 'sad and sepulchral Pitchers, which have no joyful voices; silently expressing old mortality, the ruines of forgotten times'.[2]

Browne initially assumed that his Norfolk urns were Roman, though the illustration he provides (with a suitable melancholy quotation from Propertius) makes clear to modern eyes that they were Saxon. He was on the wrong track from the start because of this false assumption, but to be fair to him, it must be said that there was no sense at all of the artefacts of the pagan Saxons in his time, or indeed until the end of the eighteenth century. As Browne himself remarked in his dedicatory epistle, 'The supinity of elder dayes hath left so much in silence, or time hath so martyred the

---

[1] *Hydriotaphia: Urn-Burial* in *The Works of the learned Sir Thomas Browne* (1686) ch. 5. ('Hydriotaphia' literally means 'burial in an urn'.) The chapters of *Urn-Burial* are very brief, and succeeding quotations can be readily identified without notes.　　　　　　　　　　　　　　　[2] The Epistle Dedicatory, ibid.

Records, that the most industrious heads do finde no easie work to erect a new *Britannia*.'

The discovery of urns was a commonplace event; many antiquarian books noted similar finds on ancient sites: Camden, Stow, Weever, Dugdale all remark on them briefly, and they are always assumed to be Roman, in part because the word 'urn' itself derived from the Latin 'urna', and also because cremation was known to be a Roman practice.[3] It is important to Browne that the urns should be Roman, for that puts him in touch with the high civilization of antiquity, and allows him to invoke the illustrious classical names that give such splendour to his discourse. These dull earthen pots command a profound respect because of their Roman origin; indeed, the incinerated fragments they contain offer physical contact with the Romans of the ancient empire, and 'remembring the early civility they brought upon these Countreys, and forgetting long passed mischiefs, we mercifully preserve their bones, and pisse not upon their ashes.'[4]

A review of the burial customs of the Romans arises naturally from contemplation of the urns, and from this rich subject Browne proceeds to the funerary practices of other nations of the ancient world. Greeks, Egyptians, Hebrews, Persians, Babylonians—all had their peculiar forms of burial, and distinctive beliefs concerning the fate of the soul. From all nations he gathers examples of extravagant or flamboyant disposal of the noble dead: in gold or silver urns, in enclosures of glass, beneath pyramids, obelisks, tumuli; raised high on pillars, or laid in the beds of rivers; burnt with perfumed woods, or buried amid precious stones. 'The

---

[3] Browne remarked in another context, and at a later time, on the inexhaustible supply of urns, and on their probable date: 'Now though Urnes have often been discovered in former Ages, many think it strange there should be many still found, yet assuredly there may be great numbers still concealed. For though we should not reckon upon any who were thus buried before the time of the Romans ... nor should we account this practice of burning among the Britains higher than Vespasian, when it is said by Tacitus, that they conformed unto the Manners and Customs of the Romans, and so both Nations might have one way of Burial. [The terminus would be the formal establishment of Christianity in the fourth century.] The Account of the buried persons would amount to about Four Millions, and consequently so great a Number of Urnes dispersed through the Land, as may still satisfy the curiosity of succeeding Times, and arise to all Ages.' ('Concerning some Urnes found in Brampton-Field, 1667' in *The Works of Sir Thomas Browne*, ed. Charles Sayle (Edinburgh, 1904–7), iii. 434).

[4] The Epistle Dedicatory in Browne, *Works* (1686).

Scythians . . . made their grave in the air; and the Ichthyophagi or fish-eating nations about Egypt, affected the sea for their grave.'

After the macabre cortège of burial customs that opens *Urn-Burial*, Browne devotes his second chapter to the discovery, contents, and condition of the objects that provoked his discourse. Clearly an ancient cemetery had been accidentally located:

> In a Field of old Walsingham, not many moneths past, were digged up between fourty and fifty Urnes, deposited in a dry and sandy soile, not a yard deep, nor farre from one another: Not all strictly of one figure, but most answering these described: Some containing two pounds of bones, distinguishable in skulls, ribs, jawes, thigh-bones and teeth, with fresh impressions of their combustion. Besides the extraneous substances like peeces of small boxes, or combes handsomely wrought, handles of small brasse instruments, brazen nippers, and in one some kind of Opale.

The opal was found in the urn that had been given to Thomas Browne by the landowner, and this jewel amid the ashes was the spark that set his imagination on fire, and caused him to see the beauty of buried things. It also suggested to him that the ashes might be those of a woman, and the opal a part of her decoration. He tries by minute and accurate description to assign a rough date to the finds, and to relate them to the romanized culture of East Anglia in the second and third centuries. His assumption is fortified by the presence of a Roman station five miles away from the cemetery, although he notes that the town adjacent to the urn-field has a Saxon name, Burnham. Browne is disappointed that no Roman coins were found with the urns, nor were they 'attended with lacrymatories, lamps, bottles of liquor, and other appurtenances of affectionate superstition' that would prove them to be Roman. But so numerous were Roman finds in Norfolk, and the discovery of coins so common, that he feels justified in believing his urns to be a relict of the Roman occupation, which he proves by many details to have been extensive and populous. He believes, reasonably in the circumstances, that they cannot be older than Boadicea's rising in 61 AD, nor later than the establishment of Christianity in the early fourth century, which gave 'the final extinction to these bone-fires'.

Browne's medical skills come into play when he minutely investigates the contents of the urns. From the character of the fragments of bone, he deduces that many of the remains are those of women and children. Burnt pieces of comb, small containers 'handsomely overwrought, like the necks or bridges of musicall instruments', 'brazen nippers to pull away hair' confirm his belief that these are female remains. The opal, 'yet maintaining a blewish colour', leads him into speculations about why precious objects are placed in graves, and, in one of those moments of imaginative speculation that frequently illuminate Browne's discourse with a strange unearthly light, reminds him of the ring of Cynthia's ghost, who returns from her cremation to upbraid her lover Propertius.[5]

As Browne continues to contemplate the unfamiliar objects amid the ashes, the thought occurs to him that the urns might not be Roman after all; there is nothing classical about them, and he suddenly wonders if they might not belong 'unto our British, Saxon or Danish Forefathers?' He remembers that Tacitus had written that 'the Romans early wrought so much civility upon the British stock, that they brought them to build Temples, to wear the Gown, and study the Romane Laws and Language'. It may be 'no improbable conjecture' 'that they conformed also to their Religion, rites and customs in burials'. According to Tacitus, the Germans also burnt their dead; the 'Saxons, Jutes and Angles' who settled in England were descended from the Germans, and most probably retained their customs. Moreover, the historians Saxo Grammaticus and Olaf Worm have provided evidence of Gothic cremation and urns in Denmark and Sweden. Browne's intuition here is right on target, and his archaeological reasoning is meticulous; he is prevented from recognizing the true nature of his find only by the absence of relevant data. Without examples of urns from an indisputable British, Saxon, or Danish source, and without illustrations of comparable material, he is at a loss. The ancient written record is helpful, but provides 'no assured conclusion'. Browne understands that the answers to his question lie in the character of the objects themselves, and in their location, and in the material remains surrounding them in the earth. But the practice of archaeology had not yet developed, nor indeed did the word seem known to Browne. He has grasped the principle of it, however, and it will not be long before we find him writing to William Dugdale to tell him to dig methodically and record whatever he finds when it comes to deciphering the enigmatic remains of the past.

After this valuable experience of honest doubt, Browne swings

[5] Propertius, bk. iv, vii.

back to the Roman hypothesis as the most likely explanation, for he needs some firm basis for his enquiries. He soars off again into ingenious speculations, beginning in facts, ending in fantasy. He taps his smooth black urn, and notes what a 'dully sounding' noise it makes, but this sad sound becomes the preface to a panegyric upon 'the artifice of clay': 'Hereof the House of Mausolus was built, thus old Jupiter stood in the Capitoll, and the Statua of Hercules made in the reign of Tarquinius Priscus, [that] was extant in Plinies dayes.' Then he spirals back down to his urn, to investigate more closely its contents, and to remark that it appears to have been stuffed, at the time of burial, with 'long roots of Quitch, or Dogs-grass wreathed about the bones'. How different, he muses, from the 'purple peece of silk' which closed 'the Homerical Urne of Patrocles'. It is this constant shuffling between the rude and provincial burial before him and the glories of the great funerals of antiquity that provides the pleasure of *Hydriotaphia*. He sensationalizes the past in every way, making it live again in imagination, and he brings it before the reader with a rousing immediacy. For example, as he observes that there are no vials of tears, 'vessels of oyles and aromaticall liquors' included in his urn, even though these in Roman times were often placed in 'noble ossuaries', he simultaneously speculates about the taste of such draughts, which 'far exceed the Palats of Antiquity. Liquors not to be computed by years of annual magistrates, but by great conjunctions and the fatal periods of kingdoms'.

In small specific ways Browne conveys, amid the frequent excursions of his learned fancy, a detailed and dependable account of the objects that have been recovered. Then he subjects some of the unidentifiable fragments to physical tests. What at first sight appeared to be pieces of wood, added to the cremated ashes, being dropped in water and exposed to flame prove to be bone or ivory. 'Our little Iron pins which fastened the Ivory works, held well together, and lost not their magneticall quality.' Other metal pieces that had remained unrusted were bronze, and began to develop verdigris after exposure to the air.

Having exhausted his urn's capacity for factual information, Browne is free to marvel at the metaphysics of death: the immortality of the soul and the hope of resurrection fill the fourth chapter of his discourse. His review of ancient beliefs and the way these beliefs were emblematized in the ceremonies of the grave is unforgettable. If ever there were a 'Thesaurus Sepulchralis' it is here, in *Urn-Burial*, where every conceivable funeral curiosity is engagingly displayed, and many that are inconceivable too. We are told why 'the souls of Penelope's Paramours conducted by Mercury chirped like bats, and those that followed Hercules made a noise like a flock of birds'. The question is put 'Why the Funerall Suppers [of the Greeks] consisted of Egges, Beans, Smallage and Lettuce, since the dead are made to eat Asphodels about the Elizian meadows?' We are reliably informed that a woman is 'unctuously constituted for the better pyrall combustion than a man' and regaled with the 'irregularities' and 'wild enormities' of antique funerals: of emperors half-burnt in the arena, of Mausolus his ashes swallowed in wine by his widow in a draught of 'passionate prodigality', of kings' bones burnt for lime. This is the romance of antiquarianism, the pleasure of rare knowledge exquisitely displayed.

The fifth and final chapter of *Urn-Burial* must be the most sublime and richly orchestrated passage of English ever composed. Sustained with astonishing virtuosity through paragraph after paragraph, it combines the mood of a requiem with the language of epic to evoke a vision of mankind everlastingly at war with time to preserve his identity beyond the grave. It is a meditation that begins in earth, with the Norfolk urns that 'in a yard under ground, and thin walls of clay' have 'quietly rested under the drums and tramplings of three conquests', and it ends in heaven, where the soul experiences 'the Gustation of God, and ingression into the divine shadow'. Browne soars far beyond the matters of antiquarianism, and the last chapter of *Urn-Burial* belongs more to religion and philosophy than to the study of the past.

The language and the imaginative flight of ideas of *Urn-Burial* are unique and unmatched, but in its subject matter it has antecedents and models. In particular there was a work of Continental scholarship that had a special relevance to Browne's purpose. On two occasions he refers to the recent discovery of the tomb of the fifth-century Frankish King Childeric near Tournai in the Low Countries in 1653. This was a notable occasion in archaeological history, for the grave was carefully excavated and the findings published at Antwerp in 1655 under the splendid title *Anastasis Childerici I, Francorum Regis, sive Thesaurus Sepulchralis*—'The Resurrection of Childeric'. The author was Jean

Jacques Chiflet, who was physician to the Archduke Leopold, Regent of the Austrian Netherlands, and the work was effectively the first methodical excavation report to be printed. Browne possessed this book, as is evident from his marginalia, and Stuart Piggott has suggested that he might have known Chiflet through their common association with the Leiden medical school.[6] At any rate, Browne seems to have been much influenced by this work, which detailed the royal treasures found with the body, and illustrated many of them accurately. Chiflet also attempted to reconstruct the funeral practices of the pagan Franks, and to recreate in small measure the cultural ethos of the Merovingian world over which Childeric had reigned. Although Browne had a humble subject with his ignoble urns, he also had before him this model of an archaeological report that went far beyond the immediate description of a grave, and he may well have set himself to show that an unremarkable find can give rise to reflections as sublime as any inspired by a royal tomb.

While Chiflet's book may have contributed to Browne's idea of a funerary treatise, other works seem to have shed their influence on *Urn-Burial* as well. John Selden's *De Diis Syriis* (1619), that remarkable disquisition on the gods of Syria and their rites, stood as an example of how a learned curiosity could suffuse a profoundly obscure topic with intellectual delight. More relevantly, the 'Discourse of Funeral Monuments' that prefaces John Weever's *Ancient Funerall Monuments* of 1631 parades a similar train of memorable and ingenious deaths, burials, and funeral customs before the reader. The solemn and elevated style of Weever's work also anticipates Browne's magniloquent prose. *Urn-Burial* has much in common too with the *De Funeribus Romanorum* (1625) of Johannes Kirchmann, the German scholar from Lübeck, whose compilation was the most thorough account in existence of Roman funeral rites.[7]

To return to 'the land of Moles and Pismires' where antiquaries dwell: with the publication of *Urn-Burial*, Browne acquired an immediate reputation as an opinionist on the remains of the ancient world. Dugdale, as we have seen, applied to him for information

---

[6] See Stuart Piggott, 'Sir Thomas Browne', *Oxford Journal of Archaeology* (1988), 257–69, especially 267.

[7] Extracts from all these authors are found in Browne's commonplace books. See Jeremiah Finch, *Sir Thomas Browne* (New York, 1961), 144 and 236 n. 3.

and ideas about fenland antiquities when writing his *History of Imbanking and Drayning*, and it would appear that Browne's tract 'Of Artificial Hills, Mounts or Burrows' was a response to a query from Dugdale about the origins of these mounds he so often met with.[8] Browne's reply is not very satisfactory. They might be Roman, Saxon, or Danish, and are either landmarks and boundary marks, or tombs of great men or fallen soldiers. His evidence is entirely from written sources: Virgil provides details to prove that the Romans raised funerary mounds, Wormius attests to the same custom among the ancient Danes. For the Saxons, however, Browne can only cite Leland's opinion, but with no solid detail. Although he advises his correspondent to look for objects in or near the mounds, the same difficulty handicaps him here as in *Urn-Burial*: Browne does not know what Saxon or Danish artefacts look like. He never entertains the thought that some mounds may be pre-Roman, and he has no concept that the ancient British made anything at all. Browne does stress the value of excavation, however, as the best means of advancing knowledge about fieldworks.

The correspondence with Dugdale allowed Browne to express his opinion about the fen country of East Anglia in antiquity, based on long familiarity with the region. He is persuaded that originally the fenland was forested, as the remains of large trees in the marshes prove; he imagines the first inhabitants clearing the forests by burning, a practice that is still carried on by the natives of America and Ireland, he notes. Between them, Browne and Dugdale discuss the probable geography of land and sea in eastern England in remote times, and the causes of change. No cataclysms, such as the Universal Deluge, are required to alter the landscape, but Browne secks for an explanation in geological and climatic change, and he posits the theory of a 'great winter', taken from Aristotle, that might have transformed the whole character of the land. He uses the presence of the skeletons of fish as proof that the sea once covered the inland areas; he is, however, puzzled by giant bones that seem like the bones of elephants, that are continually found in the fenland drainages. They cannot all be the remains of the elephants that Claudius brought over, and there is no record of

---

[8] Dugdale's letter to Browne dated 17 Nov. 1658 refers to this tract on tumuli. See *Letters*, 337–9.

'succeeding emperors' introducing large numbers of the beasts. He has to admit that 'many things prove obscure in subterraneous discoverie.'[9]

In considering the Roman occupation of the fenlands, Browne is able to prove that they must have engaged in very extensive drainage schemes for the improvement of the region, and suggests that these schemes must have involved the forced labour of the British population on a large scale. He imagines a major programme of public works in progress, and the building of causeways across the reclaimed land. His detailed knowledge of the Roman drainage projects undertaken by Claudius, Trajan, and Hadrian enables him to imagine the nature of the works in Britain. He is knowledgeable too about the construction of Roman roads, and although no 'noble consularie wayes' were built in East Anglia, he can identify the surviving roads and admire their composition and durability: 'raysed with small stones and gravell, of ample height and latitude, probably occasioning the first name of high wayes, now common unto all roades'. He assumes that these Roman high-ways remained well enough preserved to be used in Saxon times by the Mercians 'when they so often invaded and spoiled the East-Angles'.[10] These letters to Dugdale are full of suggestive comments that show what a valuable collaborator Browne could be, for all his ideas are brought out by enquiry. He had a most lively sense of Roman Britain; his interest in the British inhabitants is, however, minimal, and he believes that they cannot even have possessed the arts of agriculture at the time of the Roman conquest, but were wholly devoted to war.[11]

A fruitful correspondence also developed with John Evelyn, beginning at the time of the publication of *Urn-Burial*, devoted principally to what Evelyn would have called 'hortulan antiquities', that is to say ancient gardens and horticulture. Evelyn was clearly drawn to Browne's discourse on *The Garden of Cyrus*, which was printed together with *Urn-Burial*. Again, Browne's broad knowledge of Roman life and customs is shown to advantage as he is able to describe so many of the refinements of garden art among the ancient societies. He wrote too for Evelyn a learned tract on customs involving the wearing of garlands among the ancients,

[9] Browne to Dugdale, Oct. 1660, in *Letters*, 353–6.
[10] Browne to Dugdale, 11 Dec. 1658, in *Letters*, 344.
[11] Ibid.

with an account of the symbolic flowers used on such occasions, information which Evelyn requested for inclusion in his great study (never yet published in full) of the garden in all its aspects, 'Elysium Britannicum'.

One final antiquarian exercise of Browne's deserves mention: his account of the tombs and monuments in Norwich Cathedral, which was published posthumously in 1712 under the title 'Repertorium'. Although the title-page gives 1680 as the date when the work was compiled, it is clear from a letter to John Aubrey that Browne began collecting material for his survey in 1660, when he made the acquaintance of a 91-year-old 'understanding-singing man' who was himself a living memorial of ecclesiastical history.[12] Browne had already been taking an interest in church antiquities in 1658, when he was volunteering information about Norwich foundations for the *Monasticon*.[13] 'Repertorium' (an index or a catalogue) is in the tradition of Weever's *Ancient Funerall Monuments*, and is in fact a more detailed traversing of the same ground that Weever had covered for that book, for Norwich was one of the dioceses he combed. Browne was motivated to make his record after learning that over 100 brass inscriptions had been stripped away during the Civil Wars, with the result that many monuments were in danger of sinking into the anonymity he had so eloquently lamented in *Urn-Burial*. His catalogue is a piece of local piety, noting the graves of bishops, clerics, and Norfolk worthies, and giving a brief history of their achievements and lineage. He records coats of arms wherever they occur, but he cannot quote many inscriptions, for most have gone. Weever's collection already proves invaluable, for so much of what he recorded in the later 1620s had been destroyed by 1660. Like so many of his contemporaries, Browne had no interest in architectural or monumental detail, being concerned only with families, names, and deeds. 'Repertorium' is a utilitarian compilation, devoid of the stylistic splendour one might expect of a survey of monuments by Browne. It is enlivened, however, by recollections of the Cathedral before the Civil Wars, when all was brightly maintained, including a valuable description of the Combination Sermon formerly 'preached in the Summer Time at the Cross in the Green-Yard' to crowded

---

[12] Browne to Aubrey, 24 Aug. 1672, in *Letters*, 395.
[13] Browne to Dugdale, 16 Dec. 1658, in *Letters*, 339.

audiences as in an outdoor theatre, with the gentry in galleries and 'the rest either stood, or sat in the Green, upon long forms provided for them, paying a Penny or Halfpenny apiece, as they did at S. Paul's Cross in London.'[14] He remembers too the iconoclasm of the war times, when the richly-embroidered copes belonging to the Cathedral were carried to the market place, along with pieces of the Cathedral organ, and all were cast into a fire 'with shouting and rejoicing'. He recalls climbing to the very top of the steeple when scaffolding was put up at the Restoration, and how strange the country looked from on high. He adds a regretful remark that according to his estimation, only four monarchs have ever visited Norwich since the Conquest, and on this rather forlorn, provincial note, he ends.

Browne's involvement with local historical studies continued as an undercurrent to the end of his life. His prodigious learning made him an involuntary antiquarian, in fact, for he knew so much about the ancient world from his reading that he was qualified to offer an opinion on virtually any subject relating to antiquity. He developed a genuine if minor interest in field archaeology, and in *Urn-Burial* he raised an insignificant incident into an encounter with the past which reverberated through the intellectual community of the nation. This publication gave Browne a perhaps exaggerated reputation for antiquarian expertise, but it certainly commanded the respect of Dugdale, which was no small achievement, and it elevated his pursuits above those of the many educated country gentlemen in the last third of the seventeenth century for whom antiquarian interests held a firm but minor place.

In 1658, the same year as *Urn-Burial* was published, another account of a discovery of urns appeared. Whereas Browne conjured the genius of antiquity out of his urn, this new author was quite diffident about the importance of the objects in his possession: 'I would not note it, I must confess ... for I think there can be nothing more common', he writes modestly. But he goes on to tell of an urn-field near Sittingbourne in Kent, at the village of Newington to be precise, where 'in a very little compass of ground, have been taken out by digging within these few years, Roman pots

---

[14] 'Repertorium', in *Posthumous Works* (1712), repr. in Browne, *Works*, iii. 422.

and urns, almost of all sizes and fashions, and in number very many'; hundreds, if not thousands, in fact. The writer, like Browne, has been given an urn full of ashes, and he reproduces it in an engraving. It is undeniably Roman, with a Latin name scratched on it, and we learn that it is made of red clay. There follows a lengthy and serious disquisition on the use of urns by the Romans, closely linked to the discoveries in the field by Newington. To establish a rough date, he remarks that the practice of cremation probably faded out in the third century; he describes some of the funeral customs that would have resulted in small bowls and containers accompanying the urns, and he goes on to consider the sociology of urns, speculating that some great urns he has seen were possibly familial receptacles. He reasonably concludes that 'a common burying place' of the middle Roman period has been located, and plainly muses, 'so many ages of men have these poor earthen vessels (of so much better clay for durance than human bodies are) outlasted both the makers of them, and the persons to whose memories they were consecrated.'[15] The sentiments are identical with Browne's, though the language lacks the stylistic splendour and conceptual richness of Browne's presentation, exemplified by the 'drums and tramplings of three conquests'. The grasp of Roman antiquity that surrounds this other account of urn burial was, however, greatly superior to Browne's.

The author was William Burton, and the book *A Commentary on Antoninus his Itinerary*, the only substantial work on the Roman occupation of Britain to be published in the seventeenth century, besides Camden's, and Speed's *History of Great Britain*. William Burton (not to be confused with his namesake the chorographer in Leicestershire[16]) had a somewhat erratic career, achieving renown as an antiquary only posthumously. He was born in 1609, of a Shropshire gentry family, and was educated at St Paul's School, where he would have been an exact contemporary of John Milton. At Oxford, he became a protégé of Thomas Allen, the long-lived wizard of Gloucester Hall, who had developed

---

[15] William Burton, *A Commentary on Antoninus his Itinerary* (1658), 184.
[16] Both Burtons extended their antiquarian interests to the naming of their children: Leicestershire Burton called his son Cassibelan, and Antonine Burton named his daughter Appollonia.

antiquarian interests in his later years.[17] Burton qualified as a
lawyer (possibly at Clement's Inn) but through 'indigence', as
Anthony Wood informs us, was not able to make a career in law,
and fell into school-teaching, as assistant to the classical scholar
Thomas Farnaby at Sevenoaks in Kent, and ultimately became the
master of the Grammar School at Kingston upon Thames. It is clear
from his book on the Antonine Itinerary that he was friendly with,
and revered, John Selden, whom he may have met through Allen or
through his law studies, and James Ussher, whom he probably met
through Selden. Wood also names Gerard Langbaine, the Oxford
antiquary, as a close friend. Wood judged Burton to be 'an excellent
Latinist and noted philologist', and White Kennett, writing at the
end of the century, considered him to be 'the best topographer since
Camden'.[18] In his *Commentary*, he tried hard to present himself as
a lawyer, emphasizing his legal qualifications, using a portrait of
himself in his law gown, misleadingly noting that his book was
useful for 'the student of the laws', and dedicating it to the Lord
Chief Justice of the Upper Bench. But there is no evidence that he
practised law; on Wood's evidence he remained a schoolmaster
until ill health caused him to retire in 1656. He died 'of a dead
palsy', or paralysis, in December 1657, just before the publication
of his book.

The Antonine Itinerary, the fullest surviving list of Roman
stations and their relative disposition, had provided the original
substructure to Camden's *Britannia*, for it was an important part of
his design to settle the topography of Roman Britain and identify
the places named in the Itinerary. He had also been fascinated by
the challenge of Roman place-names that the Itinerary preserves,
recognizing that these names often contained British names that
had been Latinized, and to elucidate these was part of his intention.
In Camden, the concern with the Itinerary was almost lost to view

---

[17] Thomas Allen (1542–1632) had a precocious reputation as a mathematician
and philosopher, first patronized by the Earl of Leicester; he then became part of the
Northumberland circle at the end of Elizabeth's reign, along with John Dee and
Thomas Hariot. In the early seventeenth century, Allen was drawn into the newly
fashionable study of antiquities, and became the friend and associate of Camden,
Cotton, Savile, Spelman, and Selden. He accumulated a considerable library of
books that eventually passed into the Bodleian Library. When he died, Burton
delivered his funeral oration at the College.

[18] Wood in *Athenae Oxonienses* ii. col. 137; Kennett in 'Life of Somner' in
Somner, *Treatise*.

in the accumulating material about the British tribal zones, county topography, and the history of Saxon and post-Conquest events that filled up successive editions of *Britannia*. Burton went back to the Itinerary, subjected it to comparative analysis by looking at the variant editions that had been printed, related it to the other geographical texts about Britain that had survived from antiquity, and devoted a whole volume to identifying the towns and stations of Roman Britain, and providing as full an account as possible of the Roman occupation, its extent, and its cultural impact on Britain. His qualifications were that he was immensely well read in the Greek and Roman writers, possessed a modest understanding of the British language as it survived in Welsh,[19] and had examined in person many of the sites of Roman settlement.

The Itinerary, detailing the military routes of the Empire, had been compiled in the early third century, and had been preserved in one form or another in numerous manuscripts dating from the eighth century onwards.[20] Burton used the scholarly edition published by the Spanish humanist Hieronimo Surita at Cologne in 1609 as his principal text, supported by the sixteenth-century editions of Aldus and Josias Simler, and by the versions printed by William Harrison in his 'Description of Britain' affixed to Holinshed's *Chronicles* of 1577 and 1587. Burton naturally makes much of Camden's speculations about the names and sites of the British part of the Itinerary, but he also makes great use of the commentary on the Itinerary by the Tudor cleric Robert Talbot which had been printed by Ortelius, and another such commentary by the Cambridge divine William Fulke, to which he was directed by James Ussher. Burton acknowledges that it was Ussher who suggested that he undertake this work of annotating the Antonine Itinerary, and not surprisingly, Burton refers often in its pages to Ussher's own works on the state of Britain in the early centuries. Among the ancient writers, Burton is very well informed about Ptolemy's *Geography*, written in the late second century in Alexandria and containing in Book II detailed lists of towns and

---

[19] Burton was indebted to the work of the Welshman Humphrey Lluyd, physician, historian, and philologist, whose Latin Description of Britain (1572) was translated by Thomas Twyne as *The Breviary of Britaine* (1573). This work abounds in etymological speculations about British names.
[20] The fullest modern account of the Antonine Itinerary appears in A. L. F. Rivet and Colin Smith, *The Place Names of Roman Britain* (London, 1979), 148–84.

landmarks in Britain with their latitudes and relevant astronomical observations, which were intended to be used as the basis for a map projection.[21] In addition, he had access to the engravings of the map of the ancient world known as the Peutinger Table, annotated and published by Mark Velser in 1590.[22] This map, a thirteenth-century copy of a fifth-century draught (which may in turn be a revision of a third-century original), was a long roll of parchment sheets depicting the known world from Britain and Germany in the north to India and Ceylon in the east, which had been acquired by the German humanist Konrad Peutinger in 1508.[23] The sheet containing most of Britain and Spain had been lost, leaving only a portion of eastern Britain on the first surviving sheet, showing a handful of towns and roads, but offering a precious glimpse of how ancient eyes had imagined Britain. Finally, there was the *Notitia Dignitatum*, the register of ranks and offices in the Roman Empire, from *circa* 400, preserved in several late medieval manuscripts and printed in 1552 and 1593.[24] In its British section, the *Notitia* listed the major administrative posts and the stations where they were based.

With all this material to hand, William Burton set about annotating the fifteen routes across Britain detailed in the Antonine Itinerary, ascertaining the likely situation of each place mentioned, and elaborating on Roman subjects raised by his investigations. He accepts at the outset Surita's proposal (shared by modern scholars) that the Itinerary was compiled in the reign of Caracalla in the early third century, rather than the older view that assigned it to Antoninus Pius or Marcus Aurelius.[25] Burton's method, if such it may be called, is highly discursive. Each stage of his task provides an opportunity for a brief disquisition on some aspect of Roman life. He begins with an explanation of the purpose of itinerary tables in antiquity, with illustrations from Roman military historians and even St Ambrose; there are discourses on Roman units of measure and the tradition of mapping the Empire. The spread of the Roman conquest is discussed, as is the extent of Roman penetration beyond the Wall. The disposition of the legions is

---

[21] Ptolemy's *Geography* was first edited by Erasmus and published in 1533.
[22] Mark Velser, *Fragmenta Tabulae Antiquae* (Venice, 1590).
[23] See Rivet and Smith, *Place Names*, 149–50.
[24] Ibid. 216–25.   [25] Ibid. 152.

another question that he resolves, and he discourses on the different status of Roman towns, on the civitas, colonia, municipium, and their rights and privileges. He builds up a varied picture of romanized Britain, with its religious cults, its civic ceremonies, and the ubiquitous military presence. To illustrate all these matters, Burton brings his vast acquaintance with classical literature. There cannot be a reference to Britain in the Greek and Roman authors, in poetry and prose, that is not extracted and applied to the business of commentary, and all antique praise of things British, whether of dogs, oysters, or sea-monsters, is eagerly seized on.

Where a Roman site is known by remains, Burton will often describe the scene, tracing for example the vestiges of Rutupia by Sandwich, 'the draught of its streets crossing one another, which appear in the Feilds, and are known to have been so by the thinness of the Corn in them after it is come up'.[26] At Cataractonium, now Catterick, 'what a world of Rubbish is to be seen every where.' Urioconium, or Wroxeter, yields urns and coins and a convincing display of 'rubbish and decay': 'the place where sometime the city stood ... hath the ground blacker than elsewhere, where most excellent Barley comes up plentifully.' 'Rubbish', as he tends to call it, is a reassuring sight to Burton, sure evidence that he has located one of the Antonine stations. The very term, however, shows a general lack of archaeological intelligence. 'Rubbish' comprehends the remains of walls, arches, vaults, pavements, and potsherds, anything that is not recognizable as a valuable curiosity, such as inscriptions, coins, or artefacts of any kind. Burton has no desire to identify buildings or to plot the layout of a town: to establish its position is sufficient. Then it can be praised by literary means, by applying suitable passages of Roman literature, or, as in the case of Verulamium, close to St Albans, it can be coloured by modern writing, such as Spenser's elegiac verses on the ruins, and even some lines of Sannazaro. To make the stones speak for themselves, as Aubrey tried to do, is no part of Burton's design.

Where the location of an Antonine site remains a mystery, Burton's critical faculties are called into play. Although he had visited many known Roman sites, Burton was not a prospector in the field for missing places. He checks his three editions of the text to see if variant mileages from a known town are given, he looks

---

[26] Burton, *Itinerary*, 27.

into Ptolemy for further assistance, he looks at place-names in the area where the station is likely to be found. Finally, he will consult Camden. Cambodunum provides a good example of his technique. It is twenty or so miles from the next station on the second itinerary, Calcaria (or Tadcaster), going west. The next station beyond is Mamucium (possibly Manchester). Ptolemy confuses the issue by recording a town called Camulodunum among the Brigantes, who occupied the Yorkshire region. Bede provides a helpful clue by mentioning a place called Campo Dono extant in the seventh century, where Paulinus built a church. Burton is lost, and turns to Camden for a solution. Camden has noted that Paulinus's church was dedicated to St Alban, and plumps for the village of Almondbury by Leeds as the likely site of the Roman town, for he suspects that the name is a corruption of Albanbury. So Burton settles for Almondbury too.

Wherever he can, Burton will scratch through the Roman name of a place to find a British word beneath it. In this respect he is usually indebted to Humphrey Lluyd's etymological guesses. He will then trace the name through its various Saxon evolutions, generally with the help of Gildas, Bede, and Nennius. Nennius's 'History of the Britons', written in the ninth century, contained a list of twenty-eight 'cities' of Saxon England, and the relevant passages of his work were most accessible to him through Ussher's citation of them in Chapter 5 of his book on the antiquities of the British Church. (This detail allows Burton to introduce numerous admiring references to Ussher in his Commentary.) Selden is also invoked from time to time, especially to clarify the religious cults of Roman Britain. For example, at Vinnovia (Binchester), Burton explicates an altar stone dedicated to the 'Deae Matres' or 'Mother Goddesses' by a long digression on the cult of the divinities of the earth derived from the 'incomparable Mr. Selden's *De Diis Syriis*', to show how variations of worship of the same deities prevailed all across the Empire from Syria to the north of Britain.

While William Burton's book on the Antonine Itinerary did not notably advance scholarly understanding of Roman Britain, because it was essentially a knitting together of material from other men's looms, it did convey with much detail how totally Britain had been absorbed into the Roman Empire. Burton was able to bring to bear such a wealth of Latin and Greek references to Roman Britain that he made even a minor military station appear to have occupied an honourable position in the classical world. The sheer accumulation of information about Roman Britain was impressive in itself, even though Burton could not devise any satisfactory method for its presentation. Lack of method is a major problem with Burton's book: any slight occasion will send him off into a fascinating digression about some aspect of Roman culture as it applied to Britain. Every now and then he will engage in personal reminiscence, as when he recounts how his grandfather died for joy upon hearing of the death of Queen Mary, which appears under his account of Urioconium; he obtrudes into his long survey of Roman London a lament for the decline of Latin among English gentlemen in his time, an interesting piece of social observation, but not exactly relevant to his subject. In an unguarded moment he admits that 'Neither was Bede any more than I any diligent eye-witness of his own chorographical descriptions' (p. 90), but in spite of that admission there is a good deal of evidence to show that he did visit many of the sites he writes about to assure himself that there are Roman remains extant there, even though he is not very curious about their nature. Above all, he did achieve his professed purpose, to identify the places mentioned in the Antonine Itinerary according to the best information available. The map of Roman Britain showing the routes and the towns, beautifully executed by Wenceslaus Hollar, gives a clear sense that the topography of the country in classical times had now been firmly established. Burton's book was evidently popular, for it survives in considerable numbers. It satisfied the curiosity of many gentlemen about the Roman inheritance of Britain, a feeling which, because of the classical basis of education in the seventeenth century, was much more intense than any curiosity about the Saxon or medieval background of the nation.

A good deal of information about Saxon and medieval England was laid out in another antiquarian work of the 1650s, Thomas Fuller's *Church History of Britain* (1655). Fuller (1608–1661) was a Churchman of mild Calvinist doctrine and strong royalist sympathies who kept his head down during the Commonwealth years as the parson of Waltham Abbey in Essex.[27] A man of verbose piety

---

[27] The most accessible biography of Fuller is the excessively indulgent book by William Addison, *Worthy Dr. Fuller* (1951).

who had written much by way of Christian consolation, he had conceived the idea of writing an ecclesiastical history in 1642, when the Church of England was first running into trouble.[28] It was published when the Church had been dismembered and its hierarchy abolished, and the tone of the book becomes, understandably, increasingly elegiac as it reaches the end of its long narrative with the death of Charles I. Fuller tells the reader that he wrote the first three books of the *History* in the last years of Charles's reign, and the remaining nine under the Republic: the bulky folio was very much the product of the author's retreat from the prominent position in Church life that he had previously enjoyed. He had already outlined his future role in his description of 'The True Church Antiquary', which appeared in *The Holy State* (1642), a collection of characters and biographies of men and women whose virtues contribute to the maintenance of an honourable Christian society. There the antiquary was charged to describe the devotional purity of the primitive Church, and to emphasize the decline of piety from those early years, laying much of the blame upon the corruptions that Rome had introduced into worship. The antiquary should beware of developing any sympathy with the Catholic Church of the Middle Ages, and should not be deluded into lamenting the ruin of the monasteries when he should be censoring the decay of the religious life of the monks. Fuller is conscious that the study of antiquity leads to a fondness for ancient ceremonies, but this too should be guarded against, for the true primitive Church did not use ceremonies. He should also be mindful that the present age in England can show Christians as admirable as any who have lived, and it should not be undervalued by contrast with antiquity.

There had not been a full ecclesiastical history of the English Church since John Foxe's *Acts and Monuments* in the 1560s, and Foxe's book had concentrated on the post-Conquest Church, with only a patchy account of Saxon times. Fuller had limited access to manuscripts and records, though he did from time to time visit the libraries of the Cambridge colleges and the Cotton Library: his book is constructed out of the material made available by the

---

[28] Fuller announced his intention of writing an ecclesiastical history in the Preface to *The Holy State* (1642).

antiquaries of the seventeenth century, and his marginal notes show what a wealth of material was now available to those who desired a scholarly clarification of British antiquities. Camden, Lambarde, Verstegan, Selden, and Weever recur with some frequency, Spelman's *Concilia* is used as an indispensable source of information about Church councils and canons, and Ussher's book on primitive Christianity in Britain serves as a guide across the mistier regions of the early centuries. Bede is sensibly used as the principal interpreter of the Saxon Church, often with the help of the commentaries of his Cambridge friend Abraham Wheelock. Another friend whose help is much acknowledged is William Somner, who provided so much detail about the see of Canterbury. In addition to these modern works, Fuller was able to refer to editions of almost all the significant medieval chroniclers, and the result is that he effectively offers a popular digest of these scholarly volumes. Given the vast spread of his subject, Fuller's method is to intersperse history with anecdote to help his reader along. As with most of Fuller's works, the zeal for anecdote sometimes overwhelms the narrative structure, but generally speaking, *The Church History of Britain* is a coherent account of the long Christian traditions of the country, viewed by a patriotic Protestant. It is over-credulous about origins, well informed about the Saxon Church, deeply prejudiced against Rome in the Middle Ages, and dense with detail about the Reformation. The most valuable parts are the presentation of the complexities of Elizabethan Church politics, and the fairly balanced account of the tumults in religion at the end of the 1630s and in the first year of the Long Parliament, an account rendered from the standpoint of moderate Episcopalianism.

Fuller's version of the early centuries of Christianity is shaped by his need to keep a healthy distance between Britain and Rome, and nationalism is often at odds with the evidence. He wants the gospel to have been brought by Joseph of Arimathea, but acknowledges that there is only tradition to support this belief, and no documentation for Joseph's presence in Britain survives from before the Conquest. However, Fuller is concerned to have the first touch of the new religion occur in apostolic times, free from any association with Rome, and the balance of probability is tipped by Spelman's inclination to accept the legend. He warily accepts the story of King Lucius's conversion to Christianity and his request to the Bishop of Rome for instruction in the faith, in the late second century. To make the story more acceptable, he emphasizes the primitive purity of Rome at that time, when the see was uncontaminated by any papal pretensions. For the most part, Fuller is content to follow Ussher ('that unparalleled critic in antiquity') in his description of a flourishing Church among the British that survived the Romans' departure, and was long resistant to the Rome-inspired mission of St Augustine to the Angles and Saxons. Like Ussher, he is severely critical of the Pelagian heresies of the fourth and fifth centuries, seeing them as a foreshadowing of the disruptive Arminian doctrines of the seventeenth century. When he moves on to describe the pagan religion of the Saxons, he is indebted to Verstegan for most of his material. In dealing with the conversion of the Saxons to Christianity, he criticizes their too-ready acceptance of the ceremonies and superstitions of Rome. In keeping with his intention of identifying a vigorous native Church, he stresses the simplicity of the Church of the British and its separateness from the new strain of religion introduced into the south of England, and maintains that the character of the British Church was essentially 'asiatick', that is to say derived from the practices of Syria and Egypt, whose influences were most evident in the earliest form of eremitic life in Britain.[29] The section devoted to the antiquity of the British Church concludes with a panegyric on the British language (now Welsh), which has remained unchanged, Fuller believes, since its inception at Babel, unadulterated by other tongues, and likely to persist in its 'full stately and masculine character' until 'the Dissolution of the World'.

Gradually Fuller's hostility toward the Saxon Church diminishes as he begins to appreciate its success in converting the remaining pagans to Christianity in the course of the seventh and eighth centuries. Of St Augustine he wrote, 'We commend his pains, condemn his pride, allow his life, approve his learning, admire his miracles, admit the foundation of his doctrine, Jesus Christ.' Although 'that doctrine which Augustine planted here [was] impure, and his successors made worse with watering, [it] is since, by the happy Reformation, cleared and refined to the purity of the Scriptures.'[30] Although there was much piety among the Saxons, their ready credulity often depresses Fuller. He anticipates Milton's view in *The History of Britain* (1670) that the Saxons' virility was

---

[29] See *Church History*, ii. 61.   [30] Ibid. 68.

sapped by an over-indulgence in religion and by an excessive fondness for the monastic life. Both men felt strongly that the Saxon commonwealth was undermined by so many men and women, and even princes, removing themselves from public life into religious seclusion.

Fuller's handling of Saxon Church history is both full and competent, thanks to the many scholarly aids available to him in the 1640s, and he keeps an eye open for ecclesiastical details that can be related to his own time. He gives prominence, for example, to the Laws of King Ina in the late seventh century (printed by Lambarde and Spelman) that indicated that the king had supreme jurisdiction over Church matters at that time.[31] What does jar, however, is his obsessive interest in the early history of Cambridge University, which he intrudes time and again into his narrative. He cannot let die the old Elizabethan controversy about the primacy of Oxford or Cambridge, associated particularly with the writings of John Caius, and insists at every opportunity on the foundation of Cambridge by King Sigbert in 631, after judiciously rejecting the claims made by Caius for a foundation in the fourth century BC by the Iberian Prince Cantaber, claims that were in turn derived from the speculations of the late medieval antiquary John Rous. The remarkable prominence of Cambridge University in Saxon affairs casts a disreputable shadow over Fuller's narrative, and it is a pity he could not have removed the whole issue into the *History of the University of Cambridge*, which he published in the same volume as his *Church History*.

The medieval centuries are copiously supplied by material from the chroniclers, and Fuller pushes his narrative along vigorously, propelled by a rancorous anti-papal prejudice. The fog of superstition and false doctrine that he imagines to have involved the Church is dispersed by Wycliffe, who receives a long admiring presentation as the harbinger of reform. After an extended treatment of the Reformation and Henry VIII's assertion of royal authority over the Church, Fuller devotes the sixth book of his *Church History* to a history of abbeys in England. He dedicates this section to William Compton, the heir to the Earl of Northampton, with a Spelmanesque epistle that compliments his family for being free from any taint of sacrilege incurred by the possession of former

[31] Ibid. 90.

Church lands.[32] There follows a competent account of the different religious orders worked up from his extensive reading. He is best informed about the Benedictines, as a result of the work of the English Benedictine monk Clement Rayner, whose *Apostolatus Benedictinorum in Anglia* (1626) Fuller greatly respects. From this book Fuller prints a letter to Rayner signed by Camden, Cotton, Selden, and Spelman, refuting the proposition that the Benedictines were the only order in England before the Conquest. Marvelling at this starry group of signatories, he modestly associates himself with them, and exclaims, 'England may see 400 years, yet not behold four such antiquaries her natives at once, the four wheels of the triumphant chariot of Truth for our British History. This Quaternion of subscribers have sticken the point dead with me that all ancient English monks were Benedictines.'[33]

His views about the monastic movement are deeply ambivalent. He admires the principle, but feels it lends itself too readily to abuse. He acknowledges that post-Reformation England lacks provision for the contemplative life, and suggests, vaguely, that some new format to express piety and 'works of thankfulness' should be devised that would meet the needs of devotionalists. The scholarship of the monks he reads with mixed feelings, sad that so much credulousness is exhibited, grateful that so much history and theology have been preserved. He writes a long lament for the lost books of medieval England that were casually destroyed at the Reformation. Monastic hospitality has a strong appeal for him: it was part of a communal tradition that has sadly declined in his own time. Yet Fuller cannot overlook the decay of monastic discipline, and recounts many examples of the wealth, self-indulgence, and licentiousness of monks over the centuries. He yields all too easily to jesting sallies at the horrors of 'monkery', and declares himself

---

[32] *Church History* outstrips most books published in the seventeenth century in its number of dedications. Every subsection has a new dedication, sometimes to men whom Fuller did not know, but who might prove friendly to the work. This system of multiple dedications is a clue to the financing of this extremely large volume, for most of those named would have contributed something to its cost. Almost all the dedicatees are royalist and male, many of them London merchants and city councillors, the majority of the remainder being Essex gentlemen. The volume as a whole is dedicated provocatively to a Stuart, Esmé, Duke of Richmond—but he was only 5 years old, and the son of Fuller's recently deceased patron.

[33] *Church History*, iv. 268.

happy 'to shovel up these vermin, now dead in England'.[34] Although Fuller's self-contained History of Abbeys seems diminutive when set beside Dodsworth's and Dugdale's massive accumulation of original documents gathered together for the *Monasticon*, he deserves the credit of having put together the first large, coherent picture of the monastic movement that illustrates its social dimension as well as its role in the ecclesiastical life of the kingdom.

Fuller was aware that the *Monasticon* was about to appear, and forbore to enter into rivalry with what he knew to be a much more scholarly work. But it is interesting to note that he regarded the *Monasticon* as entirely the work of Roger Dodsworth, and makes no mention of Dugdale. Both works were long in the press: *The Church History* was registered with the Stationers Company in September 1652; the first volume of the *Monasticon* was ready for the press in 1654. Both books are dated 1655. Dodsworth died in 1654, so Dugdale must have advanced himself to the dignity of co-author at the last stage of production. Fuller and Dugdale were almost contemporaries, and certainly knew each other, for Fuller calls Dugdale 'my worthy friend' in *The Worthies of England*, and praises his *Warwickshire* at length. Fuller was also a good friend of Sir Simon Archer, the gentleman with whom Dugdale was originally going to collaborate on that same *Antiquities of Warwickshire*, and who had first introduced Dugdale to Spelman, the meeting that eventually led to Dugdale's involvement with Dodsworth and the *Monasticon*.[35] Yet nowhere, to my knowledge, does Fuller associate Dugdale with this last work, and his silence about Dugdale's involvement might indicate how little Dugdale had to do with the first volume. It was Dugdale, however, who received all the public acclaim for this immense achievement, and it is his name that is inseparably attached to the book.

Elias Ashmole, who became Dugdale's son-in-law, was also a friend, and contributed the one notable illustration in *The Church History*, a view of Lichfield Cathedral etched by Wenceslaus Hollar, who was preparing many of the plates for the *Monasticon*. (There were only three illustrations in the entire volume, and Fuller himself, it might be noted, was indifferent to the visual attractions

---

[34] For references to the contemplative life, see *ibid* ii. 134–5; for libraries, see iv. 334–6; for hospitality, see iv. 280–91; for vermin, see iv. 266.
[35] Fuller dedicated the account of the Battle Abbey Roll to Archer (ibid. ii. 151).

of ecclesiastical buildings, for he was suspicious of 'ornament' and believed that usefulness was more important than beauty.) Ashmole was a native of Lichfield, and the inclusion of this particular view had an emotive force in 1655, because this was the cathedral most badly damaged in the Civil Wars, and the plate has a mournful function at the end of the book, to remind the reader of the glories of the Church that have now passed away.

Viewed against the ponderous scholars who were his contemporaries, Fuller's place can be better understood. He was a popularizer of antiquarian research, a digester of the solid works of scholarship that the first half of the century had produced. By his friendly narrative style and his frequent anecdotes, he made the long perspectives of Church history accessible to readers of the middling sort, and he gave the past a human face—not an inconsiderable achievement. His book *The Worthies of England* (1662) continued this tendency, being an attempt to populate Camden's *Britannia* and Speed's *History* with eminent or memorable figures, lest ancient virtue be forgotten. The model was *Britannia* with its division by counties, and the method was to fill the shires with human interest instead of historical and topographical matter. Weever had been inclined to do something similar as he toured the dioceses, but Fuller went much further and produced a novel kind of dictionary of national biography on geographical principles. The *Worthies*, another fat work of the 1650s, has its place on the margins of antiquarianism, but it is a book of praise rather than of enquiry, and altogether too diffuse to merit more than a passing mention here. It does, however, pay spacious attention to county families, and its resulting appeal to the gentry of the nation has ensured that Fuller's reputation has been sustained more by the *Worthies* than by his more admirable and impressive compilation, *The Church History of Britain*.

10

John Aubrey

The contrast between Sir William Dugdale and John Aubrey as antiquarians is extreme. Dugdale was methodical, persevering, and immensely productive of published work. Over the years he brought a succession of large folios to the press; his searching of records and extraction of evidence was a work of prodigious industry and regular procedure. No man in England made more copious use of the manuscript heritage of charters, deeds, and statutes, of parliamentary, judicial, and parish records. Aubrey's research was intermittent, on subject matter that was often unconventional; it was notoriously unmethodical, and resulted in one small published volume of miscellaneous observations. Dugdale worked from the secure base of his home in Warwickshire, where he was a respected gentleman of the county, and from the Office of Heralds in London. Aubrey conducted his operations amidst a tangle of lawsuits that led to the loss of his estates and fortune, flight from his creditors, and decades of living in temporary lodgings on the goodwill of friends. Much of his library was sold off, at intervals, to lighten his passage through life. The confusion in which Aubrey worked is easily imaginable, yet in these unpromising conditions, Aubrey carried through in a haphazard way a number of projects that were remarkably innovative in the way they opened up understanding of past societies. For all the difference in character, however, between these two scholars, it was Dugdale who effectively set Aubrey going as a purposeful antiquary.

John Aubrey was born in 1626, in Wiltshire. He acknowledged that 'I was inclined by my Genius from my childhood to the love of Antiquities; and my Fate dropt me in a countrey most suitable for such Enquiries.'[1] An early indication of his passion for preserving

[1] John Aubrey, *Monumenta Britannica*, ed. John Fowles and Rodney Legg (Boston and Sherborne, 1980), 'To the Reader', i. 17.

the remnants of the past came in 1643, when, as a student at Oxford, he paid an artist to make drawings of the ruins of Osney Abbey, which he feared would not long survive. The abbey was indeed demolished in the following year, but Aubrey was eventually able to contribute a plate of the ruins to Dugdale's *Monasticon* in 1661 and so perpetuate the memory of the place.[2] As he grew up during the Civil Wars, when so much of the religious fabric of the country was being mistreated, he developed an acute sense of the impermanence even of substantial buildings, and resolved to devote himself to recording whatever he could of the vanishing scene. (A phrase that especially appealed to him was that of Ausonius, 'Mors etiam saxis, nominibusque venit'—'death comes even to stones and names'.) Not only were churches and their contents in danger, but castles and country houses were also under attack in the 1640s. Immaterial features such as customs and beliefs were also dying as the ascendant Puritans put down immemorial practices on the grounds that they were pagan or papistical. The accelerated pace of change caused by the Civil Wars meant that older ways of living now seemed to belong to a vanished age, so Aubrey was eager to note details of behaviour and belief that he observed amongst the elderly or found surviving in the countryside. People themselves were living history, and Aubrey grew steadily more interested in recording the character and memories of his more remarkable acquaintances before they disappeared into oblivion. The result of so many varied preoccupations was a vast miscellaneous accumulation of notes that Aubrey tried vainly to shape into books, but the scale and diversity of his collections overcame his powers of organization. The confusion that marks Aubrey's works stemmed in part from his own personality and circumstances, but also in some measure from the fact that he was moving away from the traditional kind of antiquarian enquiry towards a more innovative approach, and was not able to articulate his principles or evolve a methodology adequate for his purposes. In retrospect, he can be seen as a pioneer of sorts, but to his contemporaries he appeared 'ingenious' but muddle-headed. Aubrey himself was well aware of his deficiencies, and often sighed for an 'Aristarchus' to order his papers. (Aristarchus first arranged

---

[2] Aubrey also contributed a plate to Dugdale's *St. Paul's* dedicated to the memory of his grandfather, the eminent lawyer William Aubrey.

the *Iliad* and the *Odyssey* into the books we know.) Later in his life he tried to get several friends to methodize his manuscripts, but to no avail.[3] Although his friendships did not rescue his work, the very fact of his having such a wide range of acquaintances meant that he was unusually well informed about current antiquarian activities in many areas.

The development of Aubrey's career as an antiquary has been so admirably described by Michael Hunter in his book *John Aubrey and the Realm of Learning* that all else must be extensions of or footnotes to his study. Aubrey's achievements need to be registered here because his approaches to historical subjects and his assumptions about what could be known about the past differed considerably from those of his contemporaries, and his enquiries show a movement away from documentary evidences to an emphasis on fieldwork, the study of sites and monuments *in situ*, and the development of an idea of 'comparative antiquity'. Above all, Aubrey had a capacity to envisage the societies of the past as coherent systems inhabited by imaginable people, and his powers of empathy with the remote past were quite extraordinary for his time.

The formative influence on Aubrey's early career was Dugdale's *Antiquities of Warwickshire* (1656), which raised so much admiration among its readers that a natural desire to emulate it followed. Aubrey in Oxford was immediately inspired to begin a survey of Wiltshire, and he was encouraged by his friends from that proto-scientific circle associated with Wadham College who included Christoper Wren, William Petty and Seth Ward. His aim was to provide a description of the county noting those matters that were gaining in importance as a result of the prevalence of Baconian values in his Oxford circle: the agricultural economy, soil types and crops, and mineral resources, all viewed with the prospect of their improvement in mind. The effect of weather on the land and even on character might be reflected upon, as Robert Hooke advised him. In addition, the traditional preoccupation with county

---

[3] He gave the manuscript of 'The Natural History of Wiltshire' to Robert Plot, 'Wiltshire Antiquities' to Thomas Tanner, his study of place-names 'Villare Anglicum' to Edward Lhwyd, the 'Remains of Gentilisme' to White Kennett, and 'Monumenta Britannica' to Tanner and Lhwyd for editorial shaping, but his papers were too disordered.

families, their genealogies and monuments, and the history of the shire, would be included in Aubrey's design, which he styled 'The Natural History of Wiltshire'. Furthermore, in 1659, several Wiltshire gentlemen met in Devizes to consider how they might honour their county, so rich in antiquities, and they projected another scheme on lines similar to Dugdale's *Warwickshire*; parts were assigned, and Aubrey undertook to write a description of the north division of the county. The other contributors soon dropped out, but Aubrey would persevere with what became known variously as his 'Wiltshire Collections' or his 'Wiltshire Antiquities'. So with two Wiltshire enterprises moving forward, Aubrey was heavily committed to regional studies. Not surprisingly, he soon became a correspondent and friend of Dugdale, receiving advice from him and looking up references in return.[4]

As he worked his way round Wiltshire, Aubrey soon found himself bored with the conventional recording of monumental inscriptions and parish registers: 'I am tyred with transcribing, this hott weather.' More congenial was the business of describing the natural phenomena of the county according to the Baconian principles approved of by his Oxford friends. The book by Bacon most significant in this context was *Sylva Sylvarum*, his natural history, in which he urged his readers to take a more observant and analytical view of the physical world, in order to understand its properties and consider how it might be more serviceably exploited for the good of society. Bacon had also left guidelines for the compilation of regional natural histories in his 'Parasceve ad Historiam Naturalem et Experimentalem' which was printed at the end of the *Novum Organum*. So, Aubrey compiled chapters for his Wiltshire book that were devoted to 'Air, Springs Medicinall, Soils, Minerals and Fossils', as well as to the flora and fauna and to the endemic diseases of the region. (In his final ordering of subjects, which he made in the latter part of his career, he was much influenced by Robert Plot's book on Oxfordshire, for his acquaintance with that work caused him to arrange his data according to Plot's scheme.) Vague criteria of usefulness are fitfully applied

---

[4] For Aubrey's friendship with Dugdale, see Hunter, *John Aubrey*, 149. Dugdale became particularly concerned that Aubrey should write up and publish his work on the development of heraldry in England, a project that Aubrey called his 'Chronologia Aspidologia'.

to his collections. For example, he is concerned to identify the healthiest areas of the county for residence, and illustrates his findings with odd instances taken from personal experience: 'The leather cover of bookes in my closet at Chalke would be all covered over with a hoare mouldiness, that I knew not of what colour the leather was; when my bookes in my closet at Easton-Piers (in the Vale) were not toucht at all with any mouldiness.'[5] In his account of the soils of Wiltshire, he makes an attempt to relate soil types to character and attainments in an early attempt at environmental determinism.

Perhaps the earth affects accent and voice: anyone may observe that generally in the rich vales they sing clearer than on the hills, where they labour hard and breathe a sharpe ayre. This difference is manifest between the vale of North Wilts and the South. So in Somersettshire they generally sing well in the churches, their pipes are smoother. In North Wilts the milkmaydes sing as shrill and cleare as any swallow sitting on a barne. . . . According to the severall sorts of earth in England (and so all the world over) the Indigenae are respectively witty or dull, good or bad. . . . In North Wiltshire, and like the vale of Gloucestershire (a dirty clayey country) the Indigenae, or Aborigines, speak drawling; they are phlegmatique, skins pale and livid, slow and dull, heavy of spirit.[6]

Consideration of the different kinds of soil in the county had a practical relevance to the crops that could best be grown there, or cattle raised. Aubrey mused about the possibility of producing 'a mappe of England coloured according to the colours of the earth; with marks of the fossils and minerals.'[7] Characteristically, his idea for a geological map lay unknown in manuscript, while the public suggestion of such a project was put to the Royal Society by Martin Lister in 1683. This concern with soil types, their properties, and ultimately their improvement, was a distinctively Baconian matter, and one that exercised the attention of the circle around Samuel Hartlib in the 1650s. The Royal Society inherited this preoccupation, for husbandry and the advance of agriculture was a practical matter of immediate value to many of its members. The most notable presentation of the subject to the Society was John Evelyn's *Terra, or a Philosophical Discourse of Earth*, made in 1675. The prominence of chapters on soil, minerals, and stone

---

[5] Aubrey, *The Natural History of Wiltshire*, ed. John Britton (Newton Abbot, 1969), 15.   [6] Ibid. 11.   [7] Ibid. 10.

in *The Natural History of Wiltshire* show how Aubrey was modifying the topographical genre of the county history away from antiquarian concerns towards the Baconian agenda that was current in Oxford in the 1650s and that would be taken up by the Royal Society in the 1660s. Aubrey became a member of the Society in 1663, and eventually joined its Georgical committee, concerned with agriculture.

In his perambulation of Wiltshire, Aubrey was always on the look-out for medicinal springs, a phenomenon that excited him considerably. The identification of such springs was an approved Baconian practice, for Bacon had emphasized their contribution to health and longevity. For Aubrey there was an ulterior motive in the discovery of these 'chalybeate waters', for he seems to have had dreams of exploiting them commercially for his own benefit. Behind the Baconian desire to deliver information for the general good lay the personal concern with repairing his private fortune. He actually kept a little book of potentially profitable schemes that could be developed out of the discoveries he made in compiling his natural history. He entitled it 'Faber Fortunae', and in it he noted such projects as the creation of spas around mineral springs, details of where iron and tin and copper could be mined in Wiltshire, coal in Surrey, and lead in North Wales.[8] He also speculated about linking the Thames to the Avon by a canal, so opening a route from London to Bristol. All came to nothing.

Aubrey's proto-scientific tendencies emerged in his discussion of fossils, or 'formed stones' as he termed them, in Wiltshire. He tried to categorize these, and recognized that most of them were marine in origin; he realized that these objects bore on the early history of the world, but was not content with the received notion that they were deposited by Noah's Flood, nor did he believe that they grew in the earth, as some thought. Aubrey was moved to speculate on the processes that formed the earth's surface in a digression that he entitled 'An Hypothesis on the Terraqueous Globe'. It is unclear when he added this section to his manuscript of *The Natural History of Wiltshire*, but it reflects the theories that his friend Robert Hooke was proposing in the mid-1660s.[9] He agreed that

[8] See Hunter, *John Aubrey*, 109–10.
[9] Hooke had expressed his views on fossil remains in *Micrographia* (1665), where in Observation 17 he had stated that they were 'the Shells of certain shell-fishes, which, either by some Deluge, Inundation, Earthquake or some such other means,

the common discovery of 'petrified fishes' shells gives clear evidence that the earth hath been all covered over with water', but their presence on elevated ground indicated to him that the surface of the earth had been violently disrupted in the past. Aubrey could imagine that catastrophic geological events had taken place: 'As the world was torne by earthquakes, as also the vaulture by time foundered and fell in, so the water subsided and the dry land appeared.'[10] This was a quite unbiblical account of geological deformation, but Aubrey was not inhibited by the conventional wisdom that allowed only the Flood of Genesis to have shaped the earth; he was moving towards a more complex understanding that the earth had a history of change by catastrophe, and speculated that maybe there was fire at the centre that both warmed the earth and was the cause of cataclysms. Nor was Aubrey persuaded that the earth was only some six thousand years old as biblical chronologers maintained, for he noted that 'the world is much older than is commonly supposed.'[11] There are strong indications of a secular mentality in Aubrey.

This spacious sense of time, coupled with an appreciation of the process of change in time, had valuable consequences for Aubrey's approach to antiquities. In making his 'Wiltshire Collections', he had to describe the ancient monuments that were numerous in the country, most notably Stonehenge and Avebury, and for the first time in the annals of antiquarian enquiry he was able firmly to entertain the idea that these were prehistoric structures, built by the native British at an indeterminate date before the Romans came. His imagination had first been stirred by reading Inigo Jones's propositions about Stonehenge which Jones's disciple and relative John Webb had worked up into a book entitled *Stone-Heng Restored*, published in 1655, three years after the architect's death. Jones's book 'gave me an edge to make more researches', Aubrey noted in his introduction to 'Monumenta Britannica'.[12] Since Stonehenge was so notable and enigmatic a structure that much

---

came to be thrown to that place.' In 1665 he was also preparing his lectures on earthquakes, which he was convinced had done much to disfigure the earth's surface.

[10] *Natural History*, 46.

[11] Manuscript note in Aubrey, *Natural History*, quoted in Hunter, *John Aubrey*, 59.   [12] *Monumenta Britannica*, i. 20.

speculation was aroused about its origins, it is worthwhile recapitulating some of the more striking ideas in circulation so that one can appreciate the advanced nature of Aubrey's thinking, which depended more on fieldwork and comparison than on literary sources or ingenious theory.

The main medieval tradition regarding the stones derived from Geoffrey of Monmouth, who had described how Merlin had magically transported them from Ireland to serve as a burial place for the British nobles slain by the Saxons after Hengist had treacherously lured them unarmed to a parley. Originally the stones had been in remotest Africa, whence they had been removed by the giants who first inhabited Ireland. Giraldus Cambrensis repeated the story in his *Topographia Hibernia* (*circa* 1185). (The Latin phrase used to denominate Stonehenge in these works is 'Chorea Gigantum', 'the Giants' Dance', a phrase which persisted in use until well into the seventeenth century.) Another long-surviving story, also derived from Geoffrey of Monmouth, had Stonehenge a burial place for the British King Aurelius Ambrosianus, who had led the British resistance to the Saxon invaders in the post-Roman era. Polydore Vergil was willing to accept this last explanation in the early sixteenth century. Leland had passed by the monument without mention, referring only to 'sepultures of men of warre' in the region. Camden may not have visited Stonehenge on his perambulation of Wiltshire. He gives only a general description, and admits his ignorance about its origin: 'Our Countrimen . . . marvel from whence such huge stones were brought, . . . as also by what means they were set up. For mine own part about these points I am not curiously to argue and dispute, but rather to lament . . . that the authors of so notable a monument are thus buried in oblivion.'[13] In the early seventeenth century, Robert Bolton had proposed that Stonehenge was the burial place of Boadicea.[14]

Legend, then, enveloped Stonehenge. Serious enquiry began, it appears, as a result of King James's curiosity when he visited the monument in 1620, and asked Inigo Jones, as his Surveyor, for an

[13] Camden, *Britannia* (1610), 251.
[14] Edmund Bolton, *Nero Caesar* (1624). Dio Cassius had stated that Boadicea was buried with solemn and magnificent pomp: where better than at Stonehenge, asked Bolton. Bolton was a lawyer with literary and historical interests, who proposed the formation of an 'Academy Royall' to James I in 1617; antiquarian enquiries were amongst the subjects that the Academy was intended to advance.

opinion on its origins. Jones undertook a little digging on the site, made a plan of the stones and read widely among the ancient historians and the medieval chroniclers. His conclusions were surprising, for he determined that Stonehenge was a Roman temple, in a weatherbeaten Tuscan order, dedicated to Coelus, god of the heavens. His reasons were circumstantial, theoretical and deductive. He unearthed Roman coins and sacrificial oxheads in the vicinity, but a more compelling argument for a Roman origin arose from the geometry of the monument. After surveying the site, Jones drew up a neatly schematized plan that showed a regular and harmonious design: an outer circle, with an inner hexagon formed by the central stones. The two components were linked by an abstract geometry of four equilateral triangles inscribed within the circle. Jones related this sophisticated geometry to the plans of Roman circular temples, and found the form and proportions of Stonehenge consonant with the prescriptions of Vitruvius in his *De Architectura*. From his wide reading among the authors of antiquity, he discovered that circular, open temples were built in various parts of the Roman world. As for the god honoured by such a temple, he considered first Diana, then Pan, but finally settled for Coelus, one of the primal gods of the Romans, whose identity he unconvincingly extracts from Diodorus Siculus and Apollodorus.

At the beginning of his treatise, Inigo Jones raised the possibility that Stonehenge was an ancient British structure, built for the Druids, but he dismissed the notion because he believed, from Roman evidence, that the British were a barbaric nation, with no knowledge of architecture, while the Druids were creatures of the woods and groves who had no need of stone temples. To any reader of *Stone-Heng Restored*, the question must arise, how could Jones, who had seen Roman architecture at first hand, possibly imagine Stonehenge to be a Roman work? The answer must be that he found the geometrical scheme of the monument proof that it was designed by a higher civilisation; its rough state is the consequence of its construction in a barbarous land and of the effects of time. *Stone-Heng Restored* is a fine example of the triumph of theory over observation, and the tendentious use of literary material to elucidate an archaeological object; an example of the old humanist approach, in fact. But Jones had schematized the geometry of Stonehenge to suit his theories, and must have known he had imposed an unjustifiable perfection on the design. One might guess that Jones was deeply suspicious of his own findings, which may be why he never published them in his own lifetime. John Webb was not doing his master any great credit by presenting them to the world.

Jones's book provoked a rejoinder in 1663 from Walter Charleton, a doctor with broad scientific and antiquarian interests, and an early member of the Royal Society. Charleton proposed a Danish origin for Stonehenge, but his views also depended more on reading than on observation. Charleton had been profoundly impressed by the work of the Danish scholar Olaf Worm, *Danicorum Monumentorum Libri Sex* (1643), which was the first systematic survey of the field monuments of Denmark. Worm's book circulated widely in England, for Worm used English antiquarian sources quite extensively in his recreation of early Danish society. He accepted that the Danes were closely related to the Saxons, and he greatly respected Verstegan's account of Saxon beliefs and customs, which he quoted at length, paying particular attention to the information Verstegan provided about Saxon religious practices. He also drew on the writings of William of Malmesbury, Camden, Selden, Speed, and Spelman. In the late 1620s, he was exchanging letters with Spelman on the subject of runes found on the Bewcastle cross. Worm corrected Spelman's runes, and translated them into Latin; Spelman marvelled at this display of erudition, and confided to a friend his admiration for 'vester Mystagogus Wormius! Erit mihi magnus Apollo.'[15]

Danicorum Monumentorum gave a well-documented account of barrows, tumuli, standing stones, and henge monuments, all of which Worm attributed to the ancient Danes, though he was willing to assume that many of them were raised in centuries that coincided with the Roman empire. In the chapter 'De Sepelendi Ritibus' he described the burial customs of the Danes as he had reconstructed them from medieval writers, and by inference from Roman historians, particularly Tacitus, whose ethnographic description of the Germanic peoples was an indispensable source of information. He explained how monoliths were probably grave-markers of noble warriors, and described the rites of burial. He

---

[15] Spelman to Palaemon Rosencrantz, 14 May 1629, *Olai Wormii et ad eum Doctorum Virorum Epistolae* (Copenhagen, 1751), 425. The phrase may be translated as 'your interpreter of the mysteries, Worm! He will be as great Apollo to me.'

offered ideas about how great stones were moved and raised; he listed the grave goods that had been found in barrows. His account of stone circles concluded that they were meeting-places for councils of the ancient Danes, and the greater ones were probably places where their kings were elected and crowned. Worm's book was extensively and credibly illustrated. In particular, there is a notable engraving of what looks like a neolithic complex at a site called Leire (ancient Lethra), showing an oval enclosure of great stones, with mounds and standing stones nearby, and a neighbouring village, all set in a pleasant landscape. Here, Worm maintained, 'coronationi Regum deputata area [erat], saxis undique cincta. Vicinum habet collem, cui coronatus iam insistebat, jura populo daturus, et omnibus conspiciendum se praebiturus.' ('Here was the place where the kings were crowned, surrounded by stones; on a nearby hill, the king was shown to the people, and took the oath.')[16] It was probably this illustration and explanatory text that caught the attention of Walter Charleton, and caused him to interpret Stonehenge in the context of ideas provided by Olaf Worm. The Danes had, after all, occupied much of England in the eighth century, and had overrun Wessex; why should they not have introduced their characteristic monuments, such as Worm had described? Stirred by this possibility, Charleton entered into correspondence with Worm, and was strengthened in his conviction that Stonehenge was 'designed to be a Court Royal or place for the Election and Inauguration of ... Kings'.[17] He took over Worm's opinion that ancient stone monuments were of several kinds: 'Sepulchra, tombs; Fora, places of judicature; Duellorum strata, places of combat or duels, and Comitalia loca, places wherein Kings and supreme commanders were elected by the general suffrage of the people.'[18] To these he added the notion that some were Danish victory monuments. He instanced the stones called the Hurlers in Cornwall, and the Roll-Right Stones in Oxfordshire which, following Camden, he believed still preserved the name of the Danish war-lord Rollo. Stonehenge by its size was evidently the chief ceremonial centre of the Danes, who were both numerous enough to move the stones, and had the basic technology

[16] Worm, *Danicorum Monumentorum Libri Sex* (1643), 22.
[17] Walter Charleton, Dedicatory Epistle, *Chorea Gigantum, or Stone-Heng Restored to the Danes* (1663).   [18] Ibid. 40.

to raise them. The stones themselves had been deposited there by the Universal Deluge. Pleased with his conclusions, Charleton indulged his fancy to imagine the occasion of the work. The Danes, having conquered the Saxons, 'in a confidence to perpetuate their newly acquired power, employed themselves, during that time of leisure and jollity, in erecting Stone-Heng as a place where to inaugurate their supreme commander King of England.'[19] He even envisaged the noblemen standing on the lintels to shout their acclamations for the new leader. As they lay exhausted by 'luxury and revelling' and stone-lifting, into their camp came Alfred disguised as a minstrel to spy on them. Nowhere in his *Chorea Gigantum* did Charleton scrutinize Stonehenge itself. He approached it entirely through the books of Inigo Jones and Olaf Worm, believing that only written sources could cast light on 'the Founders of this prodigious Fabrick'. He admitted that much was speculation, and remarked disarmingly, 'It is no Dishonour to even the best Marks-man, not to hit the white, when he is forced to shoot in the Dark.'[20] John Webb returned to vindicate Jones's Roman thesis in a volume of tedious repetitions in 1665, and the subject would have continued to attract vain speculations if Aubrey had not cut through the foolishness with a bold new pragmatic assessment in the 1660s.

Aubrey was a friend of Walter Charleton who, indeed, proposed Aubrey for membership of the Royal Society in 1663.[21] One day that year Charleton was discussing the question of Stonehenge with the King, Charles II, to whom he had dedicated *Chorea Gigantum*,[22] and with the President of the Royal Society, Lord

---

[19] Walter Charleton, Dedicatory Epistle, 47.   [20] Ibid. 47.

[21] Hunter, *John Aubrey*, 45n.

[22] Stonehenge had acquired a new dimension of legend as a result of King Charles's pausing there in his flight after the Battle of Worcester in 1651. The restoration of Stonehenge to its true founders and the restoration of the King to his throne is a theme played on by both the commendatory poems by Robert Howard and John Dryden. These poems, and Charleton's dedicatory epistle, form part of the mythologizing euphoria of the early Restoration years. Charleton's identification of Stonehenge as a royal court was a particularly apt notion, and Charles had in some way validated the proposition by his presence there. The truth was now known about the monument, and it was also an affirmation about the importance of monarchy: so ran the refrain of these panegyrics.

Brounker. Aubrey's name was mentioned as a man knowledgeable about antiquities, who had made the discovery of an even greater stone monument at Avebury, which 'did as much excell Stonheng, as a Cathedrall does a Parish Church'.[23] The King asked Aubrey to wait upon him the next day. Aubrey brought a drawing of Avebury done from memory, and as a result of their conversation, Aubrey had the privilege of showing the King around the site shortly afterwards. 'His Majestie then commanded me to write a description of it, and present it to him: and the Duke of Yorke commanded me to give an account of the old Campes and Barrows on the Plains.' Aubrey happily complied, to the King's satisfaction; but characteristically, he was not able to fulfil the royal command to publish his views. He saw the opportunity to compile a comprehensive discourse on field monuments, and set about enlarging his enquiries. He had already made a good beginning with his work on Wiltshire antiquities, which he was able to draw on for his report to the King. He now felt that he should remove his chapter on antiquities from 'The Natural History of Wiltshire' volume, add to it the relevant material from his 'Wiltshire Collections', and develop his observations into a separate treatise which would be a survey of the remains of ancient Britain. The new project would eventually be called 'Monumenta Britannica'. The title reflects that of Olaf Worm's book *Danicorum Monumentorum*, and the scope of the two projects is not dissimilar, covering the ancient fieldworks of the country, with an attempt at classification and an interpretation of their function. Beyond those aims, there was an attempt to imagine the societies that raised these structures. One of the limitations of Worm's survey was his reluctance to date his monuments earlier than the second or third centuries AD; he also assumed that the people who built them were the forebears of the modern Danes. Aubrey was willing to imagine a genuinely prehistoric origin for British stone circles and barrows, and had a sense that the British tribes responsible for them were remotely different from the later inhabitants of the island.

The nucleus of Aubrey's design was the section 'Templa Druidum' or 'The Temples of the Druids', into which he incorporated his research into Stonehenge and Avebury. Concerning Stonehenge, he had reacted against Inigo Jones's neat reconstruction

[23] *Monumenta Britannica*, i. 21.

of the site, recognizing that Jones's measurements were as false as his reasoning. Aubrey made his own survey, without any pre-conceived ideas. He also believed that a great deal could be learned about monuments and their function by cross-referencing and comparison with similar examples. In this respect, his secret weapon was Avebury, which he considered almost as a personal possession, a sentiment fortified by the resemblance of his own name to that of the monument. He was the first to recognize that the great stones dispersed over a wide area at Avebury constituted a formal monumental complex; the presence of the village had hitherto obscured the ancient scheme. He had found himself among the stones while on a hunting party at the beginning of 1649, and realized the importance of the place. He returned many times to map the site and reflect on its significance. He taught himself the use of surveying instruments, and employed a plane-table to take accurate measurements. He traced the bank and fosse, and proved to his satisfaction that these were not part of a defence system, and therefore the site was not an ancient camp.[24] He identified the great avenue, and suspected that it had a ceremonial function. He noted depressions in the earth, and tried to imagine what had caused them. He guessed where missing stones must have been. He was able to reconstruct a secondary circle of stones within the greater circle. He also tried to locate the complex within the landscape by remarking the approach roads and the relationship of Avebury to Silbury Hill and neighbouring barrows. What he saw at Avebury helped to clarify the pattern at Stonehenge: he detected the circle of post-holes inside the bank where the smaller stones had been, by analogy with Avebury, and these are now called Aubrey-holes after him. As he wrote in his introduction to *Monumenta Britannica*, his aim was to restore the form of these ancient monuments 'after a kind of algebraical method, by comparing those that I have seen one with another, and reducing them to a kind of Aequation, so . . . to make the stones give evidence for themselves.'[25] He rephrased this idea in a cancelled passage of the manuscript: 'As the Divines do interpret Scripture by Scripture, so I shall explaine these obsolete

---

[24] There is a passing reference to Avebury in the 1610 edition of Camden's *Britannia*, where it is described as 'an old Campe with a faire trench' with 'four gappes as gates, in which stand huge stones as jambes'.

[25] *Monumenta Britannica*, i. 32.

Antiquities one by another, displaying together those that I have seen (or have been very well enformed of), for there is no Historie reaches so high as to decide this trifling Controversie.'[26] Or again: 'these Antiquities are so exceeding old, that no Bookes do reach them: so that there is no way to retrieve them but by comparative antiquitie, which I have writt upon the spott from the Monuments themselves.'[27]

Once Aubrey had hit on the comparative method, he knew he had to extend his enquiries beyond Wiltshire. Indeed, he knew that these stone monuments were to be found all over Wales and Scotland as well as England, a reason in itself for believing them to antedate the Romans. He deduced that they were places of ceremony and ritual, and imagined that they must be associated with the ancient religion of Britain. The only known religion in ancient Britain was that presided over by the Druids, and so Aubrey became persuaded that these stone monuments were connected with druidical activities, a suggestion that Inigo Jones had made at the beginning of *Stone-Heng Restored*, only to dismiss. Aubrey was strengthened in this belief by finding in Camden details of a monument in Denbighshire called Kerrig y Drudion that seemed to preserve in its name some remote memory of its association with Druids. This discovery he termed 'the Hinge of this Discourse', for it provided the vital clue to the context of megalithic remains. He needed to know more about Welsh and Scottish monuments, and so entered into protracted correspondence with the Scottish antiquarians Sir Robert Moray and Dr James Garden of Aberdeen (who furnished invaluable details of Scottish monuments and customs) and later he received help from Edward Lhwyd, the Pausanias of Wales. So the manuscript of *Monumenta Britannica* grew, incorporating reports from correspondents, excerpts from the ancient historians, and drawings and plans of all kinds of standing stones and earthworks.

Aubrey took pains to quash the theory that the Danes had erected stone monuments in Britain. 'These vast perennial memorials, seem rather to be a work of a people settled in their country, than of such roving pirates, who for their security must be continually upon their guard, and consequently have but small leisure or reason for erecting such lasting monuments. And that we

---

[26] Ibid. 43.   [27] Quoted in Hunter, *John Aubrey*, 181.

find also these monuments in the mountains of Caernarvonshire, where no history does inform us ... that ever the Danes had been.'[28] They were clearly British constructions. Eager to put together a full picture of the Druids, who he thought were the real cause of so much building, he drew in material from numerous classical sources to describe their practices and beliefs and to ascertain the extent of their authority. He then added a section on the Bards, who were associated with the Druids. It was part of Aubrey's secular, modernistic outlook that he tried to depict the Druids as a serious priesthood; he was not drawn into discussing them as ancient Magi in possession of a secret primeval wisdom, as Jacobean antiquaries would have been disposed to do. Druids and Bards needed to be placed in the context of a functioning society, and so Aubrey set himself to reconstruct the character of primitive society in Britain, again using the comparative method, and exploiting observations of the wild Irish or the Virginian Indians to help him evoke the condition of Britain in pre-Roman times. Some of this material ended up in his Wiltshire collections, as he always found it easier to imagine the Ancient Britons on Salisbury Plain than anywhere else. The way in which Aubrey's antiquarian researches were backed by an imaginative idea of primitive society is best evinced in the memorable introductory section to that Wiltshire manuscript:

Let us imagine then what kind of countrie this was in the time of the ancient Britons, by the nature of the soile, which is a soure, woodsere land, very natural for the production of oaks especially. One may conclude that this North-division was a shady dismall wood; and the inhabitants almost as salvage as the Beasts, whose Skins were their only rayment. . . . They were 2 or 3 degrees I suppose less salvage than the Americans.[29]

Behind ancient remains lies the life of men and women (mainly men, it has to be said) engaged in the common pursuits of agriculture and war, the features of which can still be traced by intelligent observation of the landscape, aided by objects found in the earth, and by the survival of customs and usages, to Aubrey's own time. It is quite remarkable how Aubrey was able to reconstitute the British past by combining archaeological data, ethnological detail, and the reports of the ancient historians.

[28] *Monumenta Britannica*, i. 125.
[29] Introduction to *Natural History*, 4.

The first book of *Monumenta Britannica* was finished by 1665, and the manuscript up to that point looks like a fair copy ready for the press. With its numerous drawings of stone circles and standing stones from all over the British Isles, it provided clear evidence for the existence of an extensive category of ancient stone monuments that were British in origin and pre-historic in time. The Druids are introduced for contextual purposes, but the manuscript is basically a Royal-Society-style exercise in the classification of ancient stone monuments, where straightforward measured descriptions prevail over theory or speculation.[30] It is recognizably an archaeological treatise, effectively the first of its kind to be written in England.

Aubrey then decided to continue the manuscript to cover the many kinds of ancient earthworks visible in the English landscape: camps, hill-forts, defensive ditches, tumuli, and barrows. This section became an accumulation of short descriptive pieces, identifying the sites and noting their condition. Aubrey is hesitant about assigning any of these earthworks to pre-historic times: he describes a few of the hill-forts and camps as British, without venturing a date. Great ditches were usually the work of the Saxons, and most burial mounds are assigned to the Danes. For the most part, he believes the British fortifications were thrown up as defences against the Romans. The great majority of the camps are either Roman or Danish, the former being distinguished by their squarish shape, the latter by their round formation. He includes in his manuscript much historical documentation to illustrate the layout of Roman camps and the military tactics of the Romans, mostly taken from Polybius, Caesar, and Sir Henry Savile's commentaries on Tacitus.

So familiar did Aubrey become with the geography of Roman Britain that he was able to compose a map of the south-west showing the Roman and British settlements, camps, and hill-forts, and the roads and tracks connecting them. The map brings out the overlay of Roman authority on the British tribes, and illustrates the coexistence of two sturdy peoples. It is not a thinly sketched

---

[30] Aubrey's concern to make accurate measurements in his field work may be contrasted favourably with Dugdale's practice, as exemplified in his 'Visitation of Cumberland' manuscript, which Aubrey used for accounts of stone circles in the north-west of England. Of the 'Long Meg' monument Dugdale wrote 'The diameter of this circle is about the diameter of the Thames from the Heralds' office.' See *Monumenta Britannica*, i. 115.

map. The dense concentration of settlements and earthworks in the region of Malmesbury, Salisbury, and the Welsh Marches in particular indicates how populous the land had been, and also how extensive was Aubrey's understanding of the archaeology of ancient Britain.[31] Modern towns are marked on the map to emphasize the continuing pattern of habitation from antiquity.

With the exception of this map, one cannot judge the second section of *Monumenta Britannica* to be of lasting value, but by bringing together notes on so many different kinds of earthwork, Aubrey conveyed the impression of intense and enduring activity over the whole of the country in the early ages of its history. Clearly a great deal was going on in those times, even if it was only fitfully illuminated by the Roman and Saxon writers. Aubrey left no doubt that early Britain had experienced a very eventful history. There were no longer any glamorous Trojans or Greeks, no legendary kings or Arthurian heroes stirring up matter for a British chronicle, but nameless people had undoubtedly warred across the country, and the hills and plains and river valleys were everywhere marked with their records. Aubrey could not penetrate through to any knowledge of the shadowy men who lived on the darkened slopes of oblivion, but his work aroused an anticipation that more might eventually be known with the progress of learning. As he remarked in his introduction to *Monumenta Britannica*, 'this Inquiry I must confess is a groping in the Dark: but although I have not brought it into a cleer light, yet I can affirm, that I have brought it from an utter darkness to a thin Mist.'[32]

Physical remains were not the only survivals of antiquity that fascinated Aubrey. He became convinced that popular customs and ceremonies might be a tenuous link between the present and the vanished societies of the ancient world. He had always been interested in taking down notes of odd customs and old wives' tales, and eventually he gathered enough information to make a manuscript collection that he called 'Remains of Gentilisme and Judaisme'. It was his contention that 'the Britons imbibed their Gentilisme from the Romans, and as the British language is crept into corners, sc. Wales and Cornwall, so the remains of Gentilisme are still kept there, which customes (no doubt) were anciently all over Britaine and Gaule: but the Inundation of the Goths drove it

[31] The map is dated 1668, and is reproduced in *Monumenta Britannica*, i. 594–5.
[32] Ibid. 25.

out together with the language.'[33] He was not entirely convinced by this thesis, asking in parenthesis why it was, 'the British Language being utterly lost in England, that so many Roman Customes should yet remain?' Nevertheless, he liked to think that many surviving customs had in fact been introduced by the Romans, because there were so many similarities between them and the practices described in Roman authors, especially by Ovid in his *Fasti*, or Calendar of Festivals, and by Pliny in his *Natural History*. Judaism is seen as another source of pre-Christian customs that spread into England, though Aubrey does not explain how they came. His assumption is that 'in the infancy of the Christian Religion it was expedient to plough (as they say) with the heifer of the Gentiles: that is, to insinuate with them, and let them continue and use their old Ethnick Festivalls, which they new-named with Christian names.'[34] His method generally is to note a custom and then to seek a Roman source in order to establish continuity with the remote past, as for example with his reflections on harvest ceremonies:

Home Harvests are observed (more or less) in most Counties of England. . . . When they bring home the last load of Corne: it is done with great joy and merriment: and a Fidler rides on the loaded Cart, or Wayne, playing: a Barrell of good Beer is provided for the Harvestmen, and some good Rustique Cheer. This Custom (no doubt) is handed down to us from the Romans: who after this manner celebrated their Cerealia [Sacra Cereris] instituted by Triptolemus.

In Herefordshire, and also in Somersetshire, on Midsommer-eve, they make fires in the Fields in the waies: *sc.* to Blesse, the Apples. I have seen the same custome in Somersetshire, 1685; but there they doe it only for the custome-sake: but I doe guesse, that this custome is derived from the Gentiles, who did it in remembrance of Ceres her running up and down with Flambeaux in search of her daughter Proserpina, ravisht away by Pluto: and the people might thinke, that by this honour donne to the Goddesse of Husbandry, that their Corne, &c. might prosper the better.

Memorandum: the sitting-up on Midsommer-eve in the Church-porch, to see the Apparitions of those that should dye, or be buried there, that Yeare: mostly used by women: I have heard 'em tell strange stories of it. Now, was not Ceres Mother-in-law to Pluto, king of the infernal Ghosts? and Virgil makes Aeneas to sacrifice a barren cowe to Proserpina for his Trumpeter Misenus.[35]

[33] 'Remains of Gentilisme and Judaisme' in *Three Prose Works*, ed. J. Buchanan-Brown (Fontwell, 1972), 132.   [34] Ibid. 133.   [35] Ibid. 143.

Aubrey gathers together an extraordinarily rich range of rural customs and superstitions, some familiar, such as church-ales, which he traces back to the love feasts of the early Church, to Roman convivia, and to Greek and Hebrew feasts after sacrifice, and many unfamiliar, such as sin-eating, where a poor man symbolically eats the sins of the deceased, a practice Aubrey relates to the scapegoat of the Old Testament. Although Aubrey tried to organize his material into categories—festivals, marriages, funerals, omens, divination, oaths, etc.—it is so miscellaneous that it virtually defies classification, and personal anecdotes mingle promiscuously with objective reporting. He was conscious that these survivals were relics of ancient belief, flotsam from the lost religions of the ancient world. He did not realize that he was imposing too restrictive an origin by assuming that they descended from Roman customs introduced into Britain by conquest. The view today would be that they were remnants of beliefs and customs that prevailed all over Europe in immemorial times, part of a universal common culture which lay behind all religions, concerned with preservation against misfortune, the courting of good luck, and the ensuring of fertility.[36]

Aubrey's ideas were uncommon, but not unique. Robert Herrick, for example, had developed similar opinions after becoming familiar with the folklore of Devonshire in the 1630s. Herrick assumed these rustic practices were of Roman origin because they corresponded with ceremonies in Latin writers, particularly Ovid. He was much inclined to use his poetry as a means of participating imaginatively in these innocent rituals, acting out the part of an honorary Roman in a Britain that still retained in its folk memory a continuity with classical times. Rituals of propitiation and sacrifice were especially dear to him, and his poetry is imbued with a vital pantheism which Aubrey, never a committed Church-man, would have found congenial.[37] In Herrick's verse too, one feels a spirit of preservation at work, as if the poet felt that by rehearsing the rituals

---

[36] Aubrey might have deduced that the customs he recorded were older than the Romans and wider in distribution, from the notes that his friend Balthazar Cramer, the German amanuensis of the Royal Society, added to his manuscript, informing him of similar customs that survived in Germany in parts beyond the control of the Romans.

[37] Working with folkloric material that reached back into unknown antiquity might have encouraged a disposition to Deism in Aubrey. Buchanan-Brown thinks it significant that Aubrey lent his manuscript to the notorious Deist John Toland for security (Introduction to Aubrey, *Three Prose Works*, p. xxxiv).

of rural life he would help to perpetuate them. Aubrey felt that the old Catholic Church had been tolerant of the pagan customs that had so long cohabited with Christianity, such as May-poles and May-games, which he guessed were derived from the pagan festival of Florialia. It was the zealous Protestantism of the Reformation that had begun to purge these heathen vestiges, and the process was much intensified as the Puritans gained a national ascendancy in the 1640s. The Laudian Church, itself so partial to ceremony, was no enemy to ancient customs. (Robert Herrick, not surprisingly, had Laudian inclinations.) Part of the ideology of Puritanism involved the suppression of any practices that seemed like pagan or Catholic survivals infringing on a reformed Christian society. In the 1640s and 1650s a combination of religious zeal and social upheaval was sweeping away long-lingering customs all over England, for war and Puritanism left no part of the country undisturbed. As late as Jacobean times, old men might invoke saints to protect their oxen or sheep or households. 'They did pray to God and St. Oswald to bring the sheep safe to the fold. . . . The country people call St. Oswald St. Twosole. . . . In those days when they went to bed, they did rake up their fire and make a cross in the ashes, and pray to God and St. Sythe to deliver them from fire and from water and from all misadventure.'[38] These gestures of propitiation were on the verge of extinction. Even the immemorial bonfires were beginning to flicker out:

Still in many places on St. John's night they make Fires, that is Bonfires, on the Hills, but the Civil Warres coming on have putt all these rites or customes quite out of fashion. Warres not only extinguish Religion and lawes, but superstition, and no suffimen [i.e. fumigation] is a greater fugator of Phantosmes, than Gun-powder.[39]

Elsewhere he considers print a great destroyer of traditional habits in that it supersedes oral transmission and intrudes modern notions into backward places.

Before Printing, Old-wives Tales were ingeniose: and since Printing came in fashion, till a little before the Civil-warres, the ordinary sort of People were not taught to read: now-a-dayes Bookes are common, and most of the poor people understand letters: and the many good Bookes, and variety of Turnes of Affaires, have put all the old Fables out of dores: and the divine art of Printing and Gunpowder have frighted away Robin-good-fellow and the Fayries.[40]

[38] Ibid. 163.   [39] Ibid. 207.   [40] Ibid. 290.

Almost alone amongst his contemporaries, Aubrey was anxious to record odd superstitious stories and old wives' tales, not knowing what blurred memory of ancient beliefs or events lay concealed in them, but conscious that they retained something of value. 'I know that some will nauseate these old fables, but I do profess to regard them as the most considerable pieces of Antiquity that I collect: and that they are to be registered for posterity, to let them understand the encroachment of Ignorance on Mankind.'[41] His instinct to collect the old fables and customs was well founded, though he hardly knew what to do with them. Many he first gathered as curiosa for his *Natural History of Wiltshire*; much later, when he gathered them into the 'Remains of Gentilisme', he tried to give them significance by relating them to the ceremonies of classical times. He was unwittingly the pioneer of folklore studies, and it is typical of him that in showing this curiosity for non-written, a-historical material, he was centuries in advance of scholarship and fashion, and thus unappreciated in his own time.[42]

Aubrey's sense of history seems to have been of settled ages punctuated by catastrophe. He entertained an affection for the sturdy primitive Britons, but welcomed the Roman invasion as the imposition of a higher culture. The Saxon invasions were generally referred to as a 'deluge' of barbarism, and the Danes were worse. He had no respect for anything done by the Saxons, 'who lived sluttishly in poor houses where they ate a great deal of beefe and mutton, and drank good ale in a brown mazard; and their very Kings were but a sort of Farmers.'[43] He scarcely credited that the Saxons could build with stone, and did not share at all the favourable seventeenth-century estimate of their Christian culture. He writes little about the Normans, but has a characteristic antiquarian fondness for the Middle Ages, which he tends to imagine as a time of splendid building when learning was cultivated in hospitable monasteries across the length and the breadth of the land. Outside, the endless broils of the barons were fought out, though Aubrey sees these conflicts as high-spirited exercises which

---

[41] Quoted in Hunter, *John Aubrey*, 167.

[42] The manuscript of the 'Remains' seems to have inspired an interest on the part of White Kennett, who had it in his possession in the 1690s, and who began to compose his own 'History of Custom' (never completed). John Evelyn annotated the manuscript copiously, and showed in his notes an interest in rustic ceremonies which is not evident elsewhere in his work.   [43] *Natural History*, 4.

kept the nation fit. Then came the orgy of destruction that was the Reformation. Aubrey nowhere records any satisfaction at the emergence of Protestantism: the cost in ruined buildings, dispersed libraries, and vandalized art was not compensated by the benefits of the reformed religion. In his own lifetime the Civil War, which he was inclined to see as another upsurge of radical protestation against a cultivated conservative establishment, had had a devastating effect on the whole inheritance from the past— buildings, works of art religious and secular, customs, beliefs, ownership of land, and family lineage. Even the landscape had been changed, with woods and trees cut down and fortifications raised. Aubrey's observations begin, 'When I was a boy, before the Civil Warres', as if he were the survivor of a lost civilization. Images of shipwreck recur in his writings: there is scattered wreckage everywhere, and it is far beyond the means of a single man to reclaim so much. This did not deter him.

Not only was Aubrey conscious of times of dramatic alteration in society, but he was also aware of the process of continuous change that went on over long periods of relatively settled government. Michael Hunter has drawn attention to Aubrey's observant notes on various aspects of medieval art and society which chart the gradual evolution of form and style.[44] Aubrey was the first to trace the development of Norman and Gothic architecture by the changing shape of the arch and fenestration. He included his 'Chronologia Architectonica' in the fourth part of 'Monumenta Britannica': it contains over fifty drawings and refers to over eighty buildings in ten counties as it tries to characterize the styles prevalent in different reigns, and so devise a chronology for post-Conquest architecture.[45] Oxford and London provided the majority of the examples, for Aubrey found details of the building record easier to come by in those places; he was careful to provide examples for which a clear date could be established, and the comparative method helped to confirm his sense of the succession of styles and ornamental detail. Here, long before Thomas Rickman formulated his account of the phases of Gothic in 1817,

---

[44] Hunter, *John Aubrey*, 162–71.
[45] See Howard Colvin, 'Aubrey's *Chronologia Architectonica*', in John Summerson ed., *Concerning Architecture* (London, 1968), 6–8. The date on Aubrey's manuscript is 1671, but he would have been collecting his examples over the decades.

was a sound basis for a guide to medieval architecture and beyond (for he also recorded the progress of the fashion for Italianate design from the time of Edward VI); but it was never published.

Along similar lines he put together a history of costume that he called 'Chronologia Vestiaria', based on examples culled from tombs, stained glass, and illuminated manuscripts, and left many notes about the introduction of new fashions in the generations before his own. He began to compile a record of the way the shape of shields on tombs changed over the centuries, his 'Chronologia Aspidologica', a matter of some interest to his heraldically-minded age. Of greater value was his study of handwriting styles from Saxon times to the seventeenth century, one of the first systematic accounts made in England on the subject of palaeography.[46]

In field after field, Aubrey was innovative but ineffectual. Gifted with such powers of observation, an indefatigable gatherer, Aubrey knew he suffered from the antiquarian's Achilles' heel, lack of organization, which led to failure to publish. He tried, sometimes successfully, to ally himself to people who could bring method to his papers. For example, he made over a mass of accumulated biographical data to Anthony Wood, who made extensive use of it for his *Athenae Oxonienses*, the great dictionary of Oxford authors. He had high hopes that the Scottish entrepreneur, John Ogilby, would see him into print. In the early 1670s Aubrey agreed to write a 'Perambulation of Surrey' for Ogilby, who was planning to issue a great atlas to be called *Britannia*, which would contain detailed road maps and city plans with a modern description of the English counties, emphasizing the economic vigour of the nation and showing a scientific interest in the land. Charles II extended his patronage to the work, which was intended to be a valuable new survey of the kingdom as well as an invigorating piece of national propaganda. Aubrey was commissioned to do Surrey, and he went about the county from July to October 1672. To assist his surveyors, Ogilby had devised a questionnaire in conjunction with Wren, Hooke, Gregory King the statistician, and Aubrey himself.

---

[46] See Hunter, *John Aubrey*, 165. Hunter notes the existence of Spelman's unpublished treatise of 1606, 'Archaismus Graphicus' (the manuscript of which is in the British Library), and reminds the reader that Jean Mabillon's important work *De Re Diplomatica* was published in 1681, not long after Aubrey had drawn up his lists of examples.

This was designed to elicit a great variety of useful information relating to natural history, mineral resources, and land quality, as well as historical and antiquarian matters.[47] Financial problems caused the scheme to be much reduced, and when it was published in 1675, *Britannia* did not contain Aubrey's survey of Surrey, and many other counties were deficient. In any case, Aubrey's collections were not altogether suitable to Ogilby's plan. They were too much dominated by monumental inscriptions from churches, and genealogical material, more in the tradition of Weever and Dugdale than in the Baconian spirit of investigation intended by Ogilby. Aubrey's work was eventually published in 1718 as *The Natural History of Surrey*.

It was to his friends in the Royal Society that Aubrey looked most hopefully for support and discipline. He knew many of the leading members, and the Society itself offered just the facilities that Aubrey needed: collaborative help, advice about methodology, a forum for discussion, and the possibility of publication in the *Transactions* to help preserve discoveries. He started well, for in July 1663, soon after his induction to the Society earlier that year, he was presenting a paper on Avebury. This was the first occasion on which an antiquarian subject was discussed at the Society, and Aubrey's paper was effectively the first presentation of a true archaeological paper in England, none having been offered to the Society of Antiquaries in the earlier part of the century.[48] He provided a measured plan, offered a discussion of the monument in relation to other artefacts, made deductions from the structure, and did not force preconceptions on his material. Informed observation was paramount. In this he differed from Walter Charleton's presentation of Avebury at the same meeting, for although Charleton also submitted a measured plan, his discourse was influenced by his conviction, derived from books, that all stone circles were Danish in origin. After the presentations and discussion, the members asked Aubrey and his Wiltshire friend James Long to investigate further and to excavate around and below a great triangular stone. The dig did not take place, but the pattern that is

---

[47] See Katherine van Eerde, *John Ogilby and the Taste of his Times* (Folkestone, 1976), 129–39, and Hunter, *John Aubrey*, 71.

[48] See *Avebury Reconsidered*, ed. P. Ucko, M. Hunter, A. Clark, and A. David (London, 1991), 19–20.

forming here of observation and comparison, leading to a hypothesis to be strengthened by systematic excavation, marks the beginning of recognizably modern methods of field archaeology.

In most respects, however, the Royal Society did not solve Aubrey's problems, even though it provided plenty of stimulus and friendship. He was not, at bottom, in sympathy with the principles of mensuration, quantification, and verification advocated by the Society, preferring anecdotal evidence, ingenious insight, and the pleasures of exotic information: 'I think . . . that you are a little too inclinable to credit strange relations', the naturalist John Ray reprimanded him in 1691. His wandering life after his bankruptcy in 1671 and the gradual dispersion of his private library thereafter affected his ability to work consistently; the perennial disorder of his manuscript collections grew worse. All he ever brought to publication were his *Miscellanies* in 1695, an assortment of papers, gathered over many years, on paranormal phenomena, coincidence, portents, and dreams, 'The Oeconomia of the Invisible World', as he described it in his Preface.[49] In the last phase of his life he became quite closely associated with the younger generation of antiquaries who were emerging in Oxford, men such as Arthur Charlett, White Kennett, Thomas Tanner, and Edmund Gibson, and the benefits of Aubrey's work began to appear in public as his papers were consulted by those scholars whom Gibson recruited to revise and enlarge Camden's *Britannia* in the 1690s. Later, William Stukeley used Aubrey's work on Avebury as the starting-point for his own researches, but because Aubrey's papers were stowed in the Bodleian Library, and not available in print, his long-term influence was much smaller than it should have been. In his lifetime, however, one of his most valuable functions was to give an edge to the curiosity and intelligence of his fellows, 'like a whetstone which can make iron sharp, though itself unable to cut'.[50]

An attempt to produce a new-style county history written in

---

[49] Aubrey recognized his own magpie tendencies. The running title for some of his papers was Στρωματα, the Greek word for a miscellany. Under this heading he grouped his various 'chronologias', and eventually his 'Monumenta Britannica'. It could be said that most of Aubrey's manuscript volumes were miscellanies of one kind or another.

[50] Aubrey quoted this phrase from Horace's *Ars Poetica* in a letter to Wood in 1673. (Hunter, *John Aubrey*, 63.)

conformity with the Baconian values of the Royal Society was eventually made by Robert Plot (1640–96), who published his *Natural History of Oxfordshire* in 1677.[51] The author was an Oxford chemist, who became Secretary to the Royal Society in 1682, and next year was appointed as the first Keeper of the Ashmolean Museum. In his dedication to Charles II, he called for a comprehensive series of county surveys that would serve as a repository of information about the resources and trades of England. Enough was known about the topography, history, and gentry of the nation; what was needed was a detailed description of the natural characteristics of all parts of the island so that understanding might be increased and trade promoted. There is an unspoken dismissal here of Ogilby's *Britannia* project, which had had a similar aim but had ended up more as a road atlas and gazetteer. Plot's programme was entirely Baconian at the start, and the plan of his book is best understood in the light of Bacon's 'Parasceve ad Historiam Naturalem' or 'Preparative towards a Natural History' in which he laid out the desiderata for the genre, listing dozens of topics that might be explored so that natural phenomena might be better understood and their usefulness exploited. Bacon's suggestions were renewed by Robert Boyle in a submission to the Royal Society in 1666 of 'General Heads for the Natural History of a Countrey'. According to Bacon, a natural history should be eminently factual and utilitarian, interested in 'Things', even if those things were mean or dirty or not convention- ally suitable for gentlemen's attention, such as the operation of the mechanical trades. He warns against three topics that swell the bulk of regional histories in an unprofitable way. The first of these is the description of antiquities, which should be disregarded along with quotations from ancient authors and old controversies and opinions relating to antiquity. (Likewise, philological speculations are discouraged, and at this point Bacon cautions authors against the vice of oratorical convolutions and eloquent flourishes, as hostile to clear sense.) Secondly, picturesque descriptions and illustrations of plants and animals should be avoided; only details that enlarge scientific understanding need to be given. Finally, 'superstitious

---

[51] Plot also published *The Natural History of Staffordshire* in 1686, constructed on lines similar to *Oxfordshire*.

narrations' of the inhabitants should be excluded as unworthy of a mature history.[52]

Plot's 'Epistle to the Reader' strikes many Baconian notes, proposing to discuss natural phenomena first, followed by unnatural events such as prodigies and monstrosities, which by their defects may throw the true workings of natural processes into relief. He intends also to illustrate how nature may be 'restrained, forced, fashioned or determined by Artificial Operations' for the benefit of society. All this will be carried out in 'a plain, easy, unartificial style, studiously avoiding all ornaments of language, it being my purpose to treat of Things'. So *Oxfordshire* begins with an account of the local meteorology, the healthiness of the air, and consideration of ways in which weather can be related to the onset of 'dearths, famines and disease'. Plot then devotes an unusually long section to the echoes of Oxfordshire, responding to Bacon's pronounced interest in acoustics. We learn where in Woodstock Park we can find an echo that will return a full Latin hexameter, and the location of a similar polysyllabic echo in Magdalen College. Much geometry is applied to diagrams of these scenes, but an explanation of the mystery of echoes remains elusive. The waters of Oxfordshire are also the subject of extensive enquiry, their effect on health noted, and their chemical content assessed. Then soils and their qualities are analysed, with details of the distribution of building stone in the county.

Antiquity, however, soon gains entrance to Plot's discourse through the question of the history of the earth. He is deeply interested in fossils or 'formed stones', and several plates of accurate illustrations accompany his text. He is inclined to think that certain kinds of stones simulate animal or vegetable forms in the earth—they are a 'lusus naturae' or sport of nature. When he discusses fossil shells, he takes issue with Hooke's views in *Micrographia* that their presence in high places is evidence that the sea once covered the whole of England, preferring Martin Lister's compromise views, expressed in the *Philosophical Transactions*,

[52] Francis Bacon, 'Parasceve ad Historiam Naturalem: Aphorismi de Conficienda Historia III', in *Novum Organum*, in *Works*, ed. J. Spedding (1864), ii. 48–50. See also Mendyk, *Speculum Britanniae* 114–35, for a useful discussion of Bacon's influence on seventeenth-century natural histories. Mendyk deals with Robert Plot in ch. 11 of his book.

that low-lying areas may well once have been under water, and the shells turned to stone by the action of 'petrifying juices', similar to those springs that covered objects with limestone deposit, to the gratification of virtuosi everywhere. Shells found on high ground must have been thrown away by the inhabitants in ancient times, Plot believes. He is reluctant to allow fossils to open up deep vistas of time, however, for he is nervous about venturing far into pre-history. The problem was raised more acutely by the massive bones that were regularly dug up in the country. The favoured explana-tion of these bones was that they were the remains of the elephants that the Emperor Claudius had brought with him in his conquest of Britain, but Plot was sceptical. The Roman History of Dio Cassius (Book 60) records that Claudius gathered elephants for his expedition, but it doesn't say they actually came, and Suetonius nowhere mentions them. In any event, Plot doubted that Claudius would have taken elephants to Cornwall, where more great bones had recently been found, and discovery of such bones was not uncommon all over England. To settle this question firmly, he made a practical move: there was, even at the time of writing, a live elephant in Oxford, and Plot compared the ancient bones and teeth with the living creature, and he found no resemblance. So what were these great bones? He dismissed as an old fable the notion that giants inhabited the island of Britain in the dawn of time, but at this point uncritical assumptions begin to take over: 'It remains that (notwithstanding their extravagant magnitude) they must have been the bones of men or women.'[53] His reasoning is as follows. The Bible preserves the memory of Goliath, who was nine feet, nine inches tall. Reports from travellers in primitive places speak of men and women who were nine or ten feet tall. Luxury has diminished human size, and civilization has had a reductive effect on stature. In the barbaric world, where men continue to live according to simple nature, giants will still be found. This display of sophistry is instructive, for it shows that Plot has no effective method for conducting a 'scientific' enquiry, but relies for the most part on that trusted seventeenth-century habit, conjecture. There is an unwilling-ness to look at the bones attentively, or to attempt a classification, and in any case, he had no sense of comparative anatomy. Ideas that could have helped him, such as climatic change and the

---

[53] Robert Plot, *The Natural History of Oxfordshire* (Oxford, 1677), 136.

extinction of species, were not yet available, and Plot himself was incapable of imagining them. The only sure guides were the Bible and the classics. The short span of world history assumed in the biblical scheme inhibited speculation about processes of long, slow change. In the earth sciences, intellect was boxed in by the limitations of inherited beliefs, and although Bacon's counsels about experimental philosophy could and would eventually open the box, the leaders of the Royal Society found, just as Bacon had warned in the *Advancement of Learning*, that the prison walls of ancient authority were too strong to be broken. Space was infinite, as Newton proved, but time was still tightly sealed.

Plot proceeds erratically to carry out his Baconian mission. His account of trees in Oxfordshire leads to a barely informed disquisition on how they grow and why they die. The discussion of plants, animals, and birds is kept short, as being familiar; only phenomena such as albinoism are lingered over in the hope (unfulfilled) of penetrating into the secrets of nature. Plot includes a section on the customs of Oxfordshire, without tracing them back to Roman times as Aubrey had done; he uses them rather to define the community of Oxfordshire folk. Supernatural phenomena also find a place in his natural history, poltergeists, knockings, apparitions, etc. being introduced under the Baconian justification that exceptions to the laws of nature need looking into, in order to enlarge our sense of how nature works. A novel departure, but still Baconian in spirit, is Plot's survey of the inventions that have come out of Oxfordshire. Most of these belong to the seventeenth century, and many are the products of Royal Society men in Oxford: telescopes, mathematical instruments, new kinds of clocks, and advances in hydraulics. Some appear more charming than useful, such as Dr Wilkins' waterworks, which 'could raise a Mist in his Garden, wherein one might see an exquisite Rainbow in all its proper colours'.[54] But Plot also admires Dr Wilkins' invention of 'The Real Character' for a universal language, his system of ideograms that would enable learned men of any nation to communicate with a high degree of specificity about 'Things and Notions'. More Baconian information is gathered under the heading of trades practised within the county, where Plot respect-fully appreciates common 'mechanick' skills, such as brick-making

---

[54] Robert Plot, *The Natural History of Oxfordshire*, 235.

and glass-making, and reveals the mysteries of less well-known businesses, as in his account of starch. The effect of this survey is to project Oxfordshire as a rich, varied county, full of natural resources and human enterprise, an honourable part of the King's dominions, and a region full of promise to projectors of new business.

Plot finishes with a long section on antiquities. Knowing of Bacon's desire to exclude this topic from regional histories, one can interpret their inclusion here either as an act of resistance to Baconian authority, or as a submission to conventional English antiquarian habits. One can well imagine that the audience for this kind of book—gentlemen and above—expected a discourse on antiquities, and were as intrigued by their past as they were satisfied by their present. Plot goes to some lengths to make the study of antiquities profitable to the mind, and he does try to advance the understanding of ancient society by his observations. He attempts to explain the function of the remains that his readers encounter and sometimes uses them as clues to the state of knowledge in the society that produced them. So, ancient British coins may be used to distinguish tribal regions or to identify units of value, but Plot also uses them to demonstrate the state of metallurgy amongst the British by analysing their composition. Tumuli call forth explanations of Roman military burial practices, also of Danish practices, for Plot believes that both cultures raised these mounds. The uses of urns and lachrymatories are explained; mosaic pavements are represented as functional objects, being the floors of Roman generals' tents, marking the status of the commander.[55] Archaeological finds are no longer just curiosities, but provide instructive information about the societies that produced them.

He does not always maintain such an improving educational tone, and he allows speculation to thrive when he deals with the main stone monuments of the county. The Roll-Right Stones were to Oxfordshire what Stonehenge was to Wiltshire and in assessing them, Plot forgets his Baconian restraint and enthusiastically

---

[55] This belief was based on a detail in Suetonius' 'Life of Julius Caesar' where the historian remarked that Caesar 'carried tessellated and mosaic pavements with him on his campaigns'. (Suetonius, *The Twelve Caesars*, trans. Robert Graves (Harmondsworth, 1957), 29.) This statement confused archaeological thinking about such pavements for generations. John Aubrey and Christopher Wren, however, believed they were the floors of Roman villas. See *Monumenta Britannica*, i. 24, 243 and 247.

engages in controversy with Charleton's theories about the ceremonial purposes of Danish monuments. That it is a Danish work,
he has no doubt, because of the etymological link with Rollo the
Dane—a striking demonstration of the good sense of Bacon's
warning against following the ignis fatuus of etymology. The
ancient Britons are scarcely mentioned in Plot's survey. All that he
can associate with them are isolated standing stones, the significance
of which remains unclear: either they are the grave-markers of
fallen warriors, or maybe they were the actual gods of the Britons (a
notion which Edward Lhwyd afterwards entertained).[56] By rapid
movement across the stepping stones of Strabo and Pausanias, he
links ancient Britain with the Mediterranean world, and speculates
that the earliest recorded practices of the Greeks may not have been
dissimilar to those of the primitive British. So Plot's Baconian
intentions are beginning to unravel at the end of his *Natural
History*, for he is on the verge of fruitless, unprovable controversy.
He checks himself just in time, hastily terminating his argument and
telling the reader that he must make up his own mind, and then
closes his book with a brief, uncontentious, unremarkable account
of Saxon history.

The Natural History of Oxfordshire is altogether an informative
and profitable book, which adds to the stock of knowledge of
national assets. It has a low level of dependence on literary or
historical texts, and its achievements are gained by steady observation of objects and things. The generous space allocated to
antiquities, in spite of Bacon's reservations about their worth,
shows how necessary they had become to the intelligent reader's
total understanding of a region. The uncertainty that clouds the
past is guaranteed to provoke controversy about the builders of
monuments and their purpose, and Plot cannot avoid becoming
engaged in arguments that produce more heat than light, but he is
careful not to be drawn in too deeply. He does not have a unified
vision of antiquity in any case, and one feels he is learning about
antiquities as he encounters them. The depth of time in which he
sets antiquities is too short to satisfy later expectations, but it is
normal for his own age. He is however not dogmatic about the

---

[56] Plot's views were strengthened by Edward Stillingfleet's recommendation of
this idea, that the stones themselves were objects of worship, expressed in his
Origines Sacrae (1662).

remains of the past; he does see them as functional and tries to contextualize them, and his opinions are presented in the form of hypotheses, open to further correction. In these respects, he is a worthy exponent of Royal Society values and, along with Aubrey, leads forward to the fuller understanding of antiquity attained in the next two generations, when hypothesis will be informed by excavation, measurement and comparison.

11

Phoenicia Britannica

While the Royal Society was beginning to encourage a critical, comparative approach to antiquities, and Aubrey was drawing, measuring, and speculating about remains in the field, the old stories of exotic origins for the British still found their adherents. The most remarkable of these recidivists was Aylett Sammes (1636?–79?), an Essex gentleman who had attended Christ's College, Cambridge, between 1655 and 1657, and then moved to study law at the Inner Temple. His life remains undocumented and obscure, but we know that he spent several years 'wholly employed' in reading the works of ancient history that contributed to form his highly opinionated volume *Britannia Antiqua Illustrata*. This handsome folio was printed for the author in 1676 (a fact which suggests a reluctance on the part of the booksellers to underwrite it) and dedicated to the Lord Chancellor, Heneage Finch, whose family had connections with Christ's, and whom Sammes may have come to know as a young lawyer. His Preface expresses his conviction that the antiquity of Britain has not been sufficiently looked into: Camden had taken too short a view when he concluded that Britain had been settled by Gallic and Belgic migrants from the Continent, for the first movement of civilized people had occurred long before, when the Phoenicians came. Sammes declares that

not only the name of Britain itself, but of most places therein of ancient denomination are purely derived from the Phoenician tongue, and that the language itself for the most part, as well as the Customs, Religions, Idols, Offices, Dignities of the Ancient Britains are all clearly Phoenician, as likewise their instruments of war, as slings and other weapons, their scithed chariots . . . As to that concordance which was between the Ancient Britains and Gauls in point of language and some other customs, I have shown it proceeded not from hence, that they were the same people, but from their joint commerce with the Phoenicians.[1]

[1] Aylett Sammes, *Britannia Antiqua Illustrata* (1676), A3v.

The evidence for this remarkable claim is of the kind that Camden would have approved: philological. Indeed, Camden himself had left the door open to such an interpretation when he was reflecting on the origin of the British word 'caer' ('a city') and noted that

Carthage in the Punic tongue was called, as Solinus witnesseth, Cartheia, that is the new City. I have heard likewise that Caer in the Syriack tongue signified a City. Now seeing that the Syrians, as all men confess, peopled the whole world with their colonies, it may seem probable that they left their tongue also to their posterity, as the mother of all future languages.[2]

Since the Phoenicians were a Syrian people, Sammes had no doubt that Camden's speculation was well founded, and that the British tongue was coloured by its Syrian origin. Leland had believed that the main body of the British or Welsh language 'consisteth of Greek and Hebrew words' but was at a loss to explain why. Sammes readily supplied the answer. The Phoenician language was one with Hebrew, and according to legend, and to Herodotus, the Greek language originally derived from the Phoenician: hence the apparent affinity between British and these other ancient tongues. William Burton, in his Commentary on the Antonine Itinerary, had been struck to find that a town in Britain, Rutupis (Richborough), had the same name as a town on the coast of Barbary. The mystery is solved, Sammes announced, if we imagine that the Phoenicians gave names to their colonies in Britain in the way that Britain gave names to its colonies in America, *scilicet* by a perceived resemblance of the new plantation to a place in the home country.

The case for the Phoenicians as the earliest settlers of Britain had been first argued by John Twyne (1501?–81), the Tudor churchman and historian, in his *De Rebus Albionicis*. This work, published posthumously in 1590, takes the form of two books of British antiquities addressed to his son, and is based on recollections of an antiquarian discussion that took place, or is imagined to have taken place, in Canterbury, shortly before the dissolution of the monasteries. The conversation is led by the Abbot of St Augustine's, and the interlocutors are Nicholas Wotton, afterwards an important Tudor diplomat and the first Dean of Canterbury, Dygon, a monk of St Augustine's, and Twyne. They talk about the original settlement of Britain, which the Abbot believes was by

---

[2] Ibid. A4, quoting Camden, *Britannia* (1610).

Albion, son of Neptune, and the race of giants he brought with him. There is a sceptical dismissal of the Trojan history. Instead, Twyne suggests that after the coming of the giant race and long before the imagined entry of the Trojans there had been another phase of settlement, by the Phoenicians. They were likely to have been the first discoverers of Britain after the legendary times. Twyne takes advantage of the clue that Strabo provided to predicate a Phoenician settlement in the north, and he gives his argument a contemporary relevance by quoting the opinions of the Spanish humanist Vives about the energetic and enterprising nature of the Phoenicians expressed in his commentary on Augustine's *City of God* (bk. VIII, ch. ix). (Augustine himself was associated with the great Phoenician city of Carthage.) Wotton and Dygon, speakers in this antiquarian symposium, had just come from escorting Vives to Oxford, so he is at the centre of their thoughts. Their discussion focuses on the Phoenician colonies on the Atlantic coast of Spain, and Twyne argues that there must have been a northwards extension of Phoenician influence from those colonies. He instances various examples of this influence in language and culture. The word 'caer' is picked out as the Punic term for a castle or encampment; coracles were introduced by the Phoenicians; the primitive Welsh huts preserve an ancient form of dwelling; even the dress of Welsh countrywomen is instanced as a Phoenician habit.[3] Twyne's proposals were vigorously presented, and most unexpected for the time.

A new impetus to consider the possibility of a pervasive Phoenician influence in early Britain came from the French scholar Samuel Bochart, who had devoted a whole book to the voyages of the Phoenicians throughout the world, and had extensively demonstrated their presence in Gaul. Sammes was effectively proposing to extend Bochart's evidence to Britain. Bochart was a Protestant pastor and controversialist based in Caen who was also a highly proficient orientalist, strong in Hebrew.[4] In 1646 he

---

[3] For an account of John Twyne, see Kendrick, *British Antiquity* (1970), 105–8.

[4] Bochart was born in Rheims in 1591, and received his education at Saumur, Oxford, and Leyden. He gained a certain fame from his success in two set-piece disputations with a Jesuit priest in 1618 and 1628. His *Geographia Sacra* (Paris, 1646) was 'un ouvrage qui fit sensation' in 1646, and one of its consequences was that Queen Christina of Sweden invited him to Stockholm to work on the Arabic manuscripts in the Royal Library there. He returned to Caen after a year. In 1663 he

published his *Geographia Sacra*, an imposing folio in two parts, enigmatically entitled 'Phaleg' and 'Chanaan'. Here is an imaginatively elaborated history of the Phoenicians, in which every passing reference to this people in biblical or classical writings is amplified and exploited. Bochart confidently identifies the Phoenicians with the Canaanites whose land was occupied by the Jews. He assumes that the Phoenicians were being described in Chapter xxvii of the Book of Ezekiel, which is a long elegy for the city of Tyre and its overthrow; this chapter is an important point of reference for associating the Phoenicians with the Israelites. After lengthy wars, they were driven from their country, regrouping in new colonies along the coast of North Africa and becoming an enterprising nation of seafarers and traffickers who penetrated to the ends of the known world and beyond. Forty-six chapters are required to describe their voyages and plantations around the coasts of the Mediterranean and the Black Sea, their outreach into the Red Sea, to Persia, Ophir, and India. No seas were too wide, no gulfs too deep for these glorious navigators. On the basis of a remark in Diodorus Siculus, that Punic sailors had sailed to an island 'amoenissimam et beatissimam in mare Atlantico, a Libya plurimum dierum navigationum' ('a most agreeable and beautiful island in the Atlantic Ocean, many days' sailing from Libya'), Bochart has them reaching the New World, conjuring up a vision of Phoenician barques skimming by Cuba or Jamaica, and making landfall in Brazil.[5] Almost certainly they had the use of the magnetic compass.

For English readers of Bochart, the most absorbing chapter was 'Phoenicia in Britannia et Hibernia et Cassiteridibus', dealing with the Phoenician presence in Britain, Ireland, and the Tin Islands. The basis for Bochart's speculations is Book III of Strabo's *Geography*, which contains a long description of the extended voyages and trading expeditions of the Phoenicians, and gives an account of their contact with the islands called Cassiterides, rich in tin

---

published *Hierozoicon*, a work on the animals in the Bible, and later brought out a series of sermons on Genesis. He died in 1667, of an apoplexy. (*Dictionnaire de Biographie Française.*) Bochart was friendly with the Irish antiquary James Ware, whom he met when Ware was living in exile in France during the Interregnum. Ware, however, did not subscribe to Bochart's thesis of Phoenician ubiquity.

[5] Bochart, *Geographia Sacra*, ch. 38. Thomas Browne was also disposed to believe that the 'Tyrians and Carthaginians' had a share in the peopling of America. See 'Notes from Commonplacebooks' in Browne, *Works* (1904–7), iii. 286.

and lead, where they exchanged pottery, copper utensils, and salt for these metals. The Cassiterides, ten in number according to Strabo, were commonly identified with the Scilly Islands, and Strabo observes that their location was known only to the Phoenicians.[6] It was an easy step to imagine that if the Phoenicians had reached the Scillies, they must have visited the mainland as well, especially Cornwall, where tin and lead were also mined. Since Strabo emphasized the tendency of the Phoenicians to plant settlements along the coasts where they traded, it was quite possible that colonies were established in Britain. Pliny (bk. VII, ch. xxxvi) is brought in to reinforce the argument. Tacitus too, in his *Agricola*, had remarked that the Iberians had established colonies in Britain, and the coastal inhabitants of Celtiberia or Spain were, according to Strabo, of Phoenician origin. Bochart notes that Strabo often called Britain 'Bretannica' in his *Geography*, and this may be an indication of the Phoenician origin of the country's name, from 'Barat-anac', that is 'terra stanni', the land of tin. Considering the tribal names of Britain, Bochart is of the opinion that the Silures preserved a Phoenician denomination, relating to their costume: men who wore breeches. He also confects a Phoenician etymology for Ireland, meaning the uttermost place of habitation. Bochart is confident in refuting Camden's view that the British Isles were not known to the ancient world before Caesar, finding allusions to them in Homer (whose informants about the remoter parts of the world were Phoenician, according to Strabo[7]) and in Polybius. He proceeds to devote a whole chapter to the Phoenician words that had survived in the British, that is to say the Welsh, language.[8]

Bochart's book concludes with a long disquisition on the Phoenician language, which he assumes to be cognate with Hebrew, since the Phoenicians came from the land of Canaan. His Phoenician etymologies are in effect all Hebrew. He does address

---

[6] Strabo, *Geography* (Loeb edition), III. v. 11. Strabo had enjoyed a new prominence in the seventeenth century as a result of the fine edition with annotations prepared by Isaac Casaubon, published in 1587.

[7] Ibid. III. ii. 14.

[8] e.g. among geographical words, 'dun' and 'crag' are deemed to be Punic, as is 'caer', 'a city'. Bochart declares the 'Caled' of Caledonia to be a Punic word for 'hard' or 'rocky'. The British town Camelodunum, associated with Camelot in folk legend, contains the Punic root 'kimal', 'head-place of a people'. (Bochart, *Geographia Sacra*, 726.)

the locus classicus of Phoenician, the incomprehensible speech at the beginning of Act v of Plautus's play *Poenulus*, which is believed to be the only authentic surviving example of Punic, and he makes some sense of it by approximating the words to Hebrew.[9] Finally, he recommends as an invaluable insight into Phoenician beliefs and practices the one preserved literary work of the nation, the Phoenician History by Sanchoniathon, a mythic account of the Creation and the times before the Flood, with the genealogy of the Phoenician people, translated into Greek by Philo Byblius and preserved in part by Eusebius. The effect of this concluding strategy is to remind the reader that the Phoenicians in turn had their own documented antiquity that reached back to the beginnings of time, and that they were an ancient and honourable nation worthy to plant the world.

Given Bochart's panoramic presentation of the ubiquity of the Phoenician presence in ancient times, it is understandable that Aylett Sammes could compose a folio volume devoted to their affairs in Britain. The arguments and opinions that fill *Britannia Antiqua* are based entirely on Sammes' uncritical reading, and on his complete assimilation of Bochart's ideas. Nowhere does Sammes look for evidence in the field, nor does he produce a single object of Phoenician origin to give substance to his claims; he does, however, make liberal use of fanciful etymologies. His ingenious imagination manœuvres freely in seas of possibility. From the great library of the ancient authors Sammes takes whatever suits his purposes without any consideration for chronology or for geographical impediments. Remote nations go smoothly about the business of settling Britain, that most desirable of habitations. Sammes shows commendable restraint in restricting Phoenician settlement to the coasts of Britain, for he is mindful of Caesar's remarks that the inland people claimed to be longer established than the coastal tribes, and of different origin, and he remembers too Tacitus's reports that the Germans had planted the most northern parts of the island. So Sammes fills Britain with a Germanic race while the more civilized Phoenicians bring their

---

[9] Plautus's play, *Poenulus* ('The Little Carthaginian'), is dated to *c.*190 BC. Modern scholarship continues to believe the speech to be an example of Punic rather than an utterance of nonsense. See Maurice Sznycer, *Les Passages Puniques et Transcription Latine dans le 'Poenulus' de Plaute* (Paris, 1967).

cultural influences to bear on the littoral regions. He very reasonably dismisses the traditional notion that Britain had been settled by the sons of Noah after the Flood, arguing that mankind could not have multiplied sufficiently to fill the world, and lacked adequate means of transport to disseminate themselves. He pertinently cites Sir Walter Raleigh in *The History of the World* that 'The Spaniards, in some parts of America, scarcely proceeded into the continent ten miles in ten years.' In the primitive world of Europe, progress would have been just as slow.

It is easier to imagine Britain settled a long time after the Flood by those skilled shipmakers and navigators, the Phoenicians, along with the Cimmerians, or Celts. By a series of etymological shifts (from Cymri, as the Welsh call themselves, to Cimbri, to Cimmerii), and by means of promiscuous and unspecific exploitation of sources such as Pliny, Plutarch, Diodorus Siculus, Suidas, Livy, Caesar, and Strabo, Sammes traces a line of migration back to the Black Sea. The Cimmerians were known as Celts to the Greeks, and Sammes assumes that they become Germans in their northern European phase. Passing swiftly down the Rhine, they strike out for Britain as for the promised land. So, by a pincer movement, the land is filled: 'but whether the Cimbri entered the Northern and Eastern parts of this Island before the Phoenicians arrived in the West, is a thing altogether unsearchable, but I have showed, in all likelyhood, that it was seven or eight hundred years after the Flood before any part of it was inhabited.'[10] Sammes included in *Britannia Antiqua* an engraved map showing the Cimmerians or Cimbri processing across the top of Europe on their way from the Black Sea to Britain. Dressed in pointed hats, and carrying staves, with horses and wagons, they look like purposeful settlers who know where they are heading. The map itself bears the names of all regions in Latin and Phoenician to demonstrate the universal spread of 'the grave Tyrian traders'.

Sammes's main evidence for the Phoenician presence lies in the large number of British words that, he contends, contain Punic roots. Pages are filled with imaginative etymologies, and words that have an approximate sound to what he deems to be 'Phoenician' are eagerly enlisted for his argument. For example, the prefix 'tre-' so common in Cornish place-names, is declared to be descended

---

[10] Sammes, *Britannia Antiqua*, 15.

from the Phoenician 'Tira', by contraction 'Tra', signifying 'a castle', so that such places 'were Forts built by them to secure their Trade'.[11] The British word 'pen', 'a hill', is clearly derived from the Phoenician 'Pinnah', we are assured. Sammes professes a magisterial command of Phoenician, 'which was but only a Dialect of the Hebrew' (and being a dialect allows it to be manipulated rather loosely for etymological advantage), so that the unlettered, un-qualified reader can only gaze in amazement (or disbelief) at the version of history that Sammes reveals. And not only the Phoenicians and the Cimmerians were involved in the settlement of Britain: before long the Greeks were in on the act, following the Phoenicians to their trading places, and placing colonies here too. Anglesey was the place of their landfall, for that is where the order of Druids had their headquarters, and the Druids, as we know from Caesar's testimony in Book v of *De Bello Gallico*, used Greek. They preserved it as the language of religion and learning in a way similar to the Roman clergy 'who stick fast to the ancient Latin tongue'. The strange omission of their British colonies from the Greek histories is explained by their remoteness and by the excessive preoccupation of the Greeks with their Mediterranean affairs. However, memories of Britain lingered on in the legends of the Fortunate Isles, the Isles of the Hesperides, and other half-glimpsed western paradises. As a further concession to Caesar's historical reporting, Sammes also allows that there must have been a late influx of Belgic settlers into the south-eastern parts of the island, for Caesar's testimony to their presence has to be trusted.

Lest one might think the author too liberal in leasing out the British Isles to so many ancient nations, Sammes shows his critical mettle by taking a stand against the Trojans. He glows with scepticism. Brutus, he notes, makes a suspiciously late entry into the historical record via Geoffrey of Monmouth's twelfth-century Chronicle; there is no mention of Brutus amongst the classical writers; he seems a convenient fiction to justify a false etymology for Britain. So Brutus is discarded. Yet, reflects Sammes, the Trojan tradition is so strong, and has had so many supporters down through the centuries, that it has become part of the fabulous past of Britain, just as the Greek gods and heroes were part of the fabulous age before the First Olympiad when historical time began.

---

[11] Ibid. 60.

So Sammes will narrate the story of Brutus and his Trojans, who belong to a different kind of national history from the well-documented Phoenicians, Cimmerians, and Greeks. Tradition, when it has a broad enough base of belief, is an alternative form of history, and given the mistiness of remote times, may preserve distorted memories of distant events. Having made that concession, he softens, and persuades himself that there was a Trojan presence in Britain, but Brutus was not part of it: Aeneas was the key figure. Sammes constructs a king-list for his Celtic Cimmerians which eventually incorporates a tributary line from Troy. Starting with Noah, he acknowledges Japhet his son 'the first British Monarch', but only in title, as a biblical King of the Islands, for 'he never journeyed hither'. Then Sammes cuts into the fictitious but ever-convenient genealogies of the pseudo-Berosus via Samothes, the supposed son of Japhet and leader of the Celts. The pseudo-Berosan lines of descent lead down to Aeneas, and several generations after Aeneas, Sammes lights on Silvius Britannicus as a King of Trojan stock who also figures in Geoffrey of Monmouth's British History: he serves as the first Trojan King of Britain. Thereafter, the familiar British kings make their appearance, Lud, Locrine, Lear, and the like, and so through to the Roman conquest.

In the matter of religious worship and belief, these Celtic Cimmerians appear to have lost their gods *en route*, for Sammes would have them all drawn into the ways of worship of the Phoenicians, whose gods seduced the British as easily as they did the Israelites in Canaan. The priests of the British were the Druids, who accompanied the Celtic settlers. Sammes imagined that the Druids exercised a function similar to that of Bishops in the Anglican Church, maintaining the discipline of religion and ensuring a uniformity of worship. But the gods of power whom the Druids served were, in Sammes's view, those brought by the Phoenicians, many of them familiar from the Bible and the classical writers, though often disguised by their Punic names. Here are Moloch or Taran or Jupiter, Tutates or Mercury, Hizzus or Mars, Belessus or Apollo, and variants of Venus, Diana, Minerva, and Ceres. Curiously, and inconsistently, Sammes makes no use of Selden's treatise *De Diis Syriis* to elaborate his account of the Phoenician gods and their ceremonies in Britain, even though the Phoenicians were acknowledged by Sammes to be a Syrian people, and Selden's work was the most thorough enquiry into their beliefs. Although Sammes quotes from other works by Selden, *Marmora Arundelliana* and *Jani Anglorum* (which he uses to show Selden's tolerance for the Brutus story—a complete misreading of Selden's opinion), he inexplicably ignores *De Diis Syriis*, and delivers an account of British religious rites out of Caesar and Tacitus. There is much about the Bards and the Druids, the former reciting the memorable histories of the race and 'singing the praises of Heros at their Apotheosis, which in Ancient Times was not only esteemed glorious for the dead, and useful to the living, but also a religious and acceptable act to the Gods'. The Bards, like the Greek poets of the fabulous age, had 'the whole body of their Divinity in verse'.[12] Mercifully, Sammes does not expatiate on this body of divinity, but the Druids are extensively discussed, as one might expect. They were a less ancient order than the Bards, and gradually superseded them as the Bards, 'who formerly sang of the essence and immortality of the Soul, the works of Nature and the celestial bodies', became 'the divulgers of idle and empty genealogies', and eventually 'degenerated by degrees into the nature of common ballad-makers'.[13] The Druids, who were Celtic, learned much from the Bards, who had been Phoenician in origin, but their great advances in knowledge were made in the days when the Greeks planted colonies here, for then they learned the Pythagorean mysteries, such as the transmigration of the soul, and also learned the use of the Greek language, which they thereafter continued to employ for their public communications, as Caesar reported. They became 'the sole interpreters of religion', presiding over ceremonies and sacrifices; their authority extended over the whole Island, and into Gaul, and their power was independent of the civil government. The supreme Druid was chosen by election amongst the order. Sammes is able to favour the reader with an illustration of a Druid, based on the description given by Selden in his *Jani Anglorum* of some statues found in Germany that were believed to represent Druids. A much more memorable illustration is that showing the wicker man filled with sacrificial victims about to be burnt, derived from the account in Tacitus. 'The most esteemed sacrifice to their Gods, they deemed Murtherers, Thieves and Robbers and also other criminals, but for want of these, Innocents often suffered.'[14] Folk recollections of

[12] Sammes, *Britannia Antiqua*, 99.   [13] Ibid. 100.
[14] Ibid. 141.

12. An Ancient Briton, from Aylett Sammes' *Britannia Antiqua Illustrata* (1676). The image is derived from a description in Strabo. The landscape suggests a fairly advanced economy in early Britain.

these great wicker figures may have given rise to stories of giants in Britain in ancient times, but upon further consideration Sammes inclines to the belief that the Phoenicians themselves may have been of gigantic stature, being products of nature in her prime, and the age of their navigation to Britain coinciding, in his computation, with the age of the giants mentioned in the Bible. He calculates the settlement of Britain to have occurred some 2,560 years after the Creation of the world, and some 800 to 900 years after the Flood.

The paramount cult in the exotic Bretannica of Aylett Sammes was that of the Phoenician Hercules. The documentation of this deity shows Sammes's eclectic imagination at the height of felicitous invention as he threads together a number of ancient authorities, draws inspiration from Bochart, and adds a few speculative touches of his own. Sammes was able to retrieve evidence for the Phoenician Hercules from the surviving Phoenician History of Sanchoniathon, where Hercules was a primitive hero, a King of Tyre. The Greeks called him Palaemon and made him a god of the sea. He was supposed 'by many' to be 'contemporary with Moses, and to have flourished in the days of Joshua, when the Israelites expelled the Canaanites from their land'.[15] He led the Phoenicians in their colonization of the Mediterranean coast, and at the limits of the known world he raised the Pillars of Hercules by the Straits of Gibraltar. (Sammes is even able to quote the Phoenician inscription on these pillars, as recorded and translated into Greek by Procopius, and goes on to provide an account of the Herculean temple that had stood beside the Pillars, including a description of its ceremonies, from Strabo, Appian, Diodorus, and Arrian.) Book v of the pseudo-Berosus is also a source of information about the eminence of this hero, whom he styles the 'Lybian' Hercules, and the late Roman historian Ammianus Marcellinus has the 'Tyrian' Hercules leading men 'to inhabit the sea-coasts of Gaul, lying upon the Ocean', a detail Bochart had amplified in his account of the Phoenician settlement of Gaul. Sammes would have him go a little further: 'Seeing that Hercules arrived into those seas, why may he not be supposed to be in Britain also?'[16] Could he not have been the first discoverer of the

---

[15] Sammes, *Britannia Antiqua*, 141.

[16] Ibid. 142. The Tyrian Hercules enjoyed some prominence in seventeenth-century accounts of British antiquity. John Speed mentioned him as overcoming the

tin mines that made Britain so attractive to the ancients? Sammes finds support for his theory in Ptolemy's *Geography*, where a landmark on the western coast of Britain is listed as 'Herculis Promontorum', a place that Camden, following tradition, associates with Hartland Point in north Devon. Camden regards Hercules as a metaphor, not an historical person; indeed he denies that Hercules was ever in Britain, but Sammes eagerly seizes on the name from Ptolemy to give substance to his belief. At the same time he assures the reader that this Hercules was worshipped in Britain under the name of Ogmius, and from Lucian he is able to provide a description of his cult. When Sammes attempts to locate the centre of this cult in Britain, it comes as no surprise to find Stonehenge named as the chief temple dedicated to Hercules, who was a god associated with great pillars and the tutelar deity of the island. The old legends of Stonehenge built by giants were a recollection of the mighty Phoenicians. Even Inigo Jones's judgement that the temple was of the Tuscan order is exploited by Sammes with the remark that 'the Tuscans were, (as Grotius and others prove) of Tyrian original, and in all probability brought with them (from Phoenicia into Italy) that order of building; so that what one colony of the Phoenicians carried into Italy, another, with the same reason, might bring it into Britain.'[17]

The customs and the manners of the Britons Sammes is content to recite from familiar sources, notably Caesar and Tacitus, whilst endeavouring to find a Phoenician origin for these practices. These may be as various as the use of fermented barley as a drink or the habit of computing the day from the setting of the sun, not the rising. Of liquor, Sammes remarks, 'We read in Herodotus that the Egyptians did make a sort of drink with Barly, the particulars whereof he describeth. Now why may not this custom be thought to come from them by means of the Phoenicians, who found Britain very fruitful in that grain?'[18] Why not indeed? The method of measuring the day is related to the Jewish custom, and of course the Phoenicians had originally resided with the Jews in Canaan.

---

giant Albion and then settling the island. (*History of Great Britaine* (1614), 162; Speed quotes Bale and Pomponius Mela as his sources.) Verstegan had referred to him in *Restitution*, and Selden had described his cult in *De Diis Syriis* and in *Historie of Tithes*.

[17] Sammes, *Britannia Antiqua*, 398.   [18] Ibid. 108.

The only aspect of ancient British life on which Sammes has anything insightful to report is the matter of their chariot warfare. He writes intelligently about the use of chariots in battle and the tactics and manœuvres that they were capable of, and makes an effort to distinguish various types of chariot, from the evidence of Roman writers. He also writes credibly about the displays of vaunting and taunting that the charioteers employed in the face of the enemy, and the fearsome means they had to strike terror as they attacked. Inevitably, however, chariots are identified as Asiatic vehicles, associated with the Egyptians and Assyrians and Greeks, and therefore another Phoenician import. Caesar reported that chariots were unique to the British, for he had not encountered them in battles with other tribes or nations in Europe, a detail Sammes uses as proof of the special relationship between Britain and Phoenicia. In fact, modern archaeology has shown Caesar's view to have been mistaken, for the Gauls and the Belgae did have chariots, as we know from the many chariot burials that have been unearthed. Present evidence suggests that all the Celtic peoples had chariots, but by Caesar's time they were evidently reserved for ceremonial purposes, and not used in battle, because they were not effective against Roman infantry, and the Continental tribes had come to rely on infantry and cavalry when fighting the Romans.

The wayward fancies that characterize Sammes's book are accompanied by a strong visual imagination. *Britannia Antiqua Illustrata* lives up to its title with a number of startling engravings which bring the world of ancient Britain to the reader in a series of disconcerting images of strange rituals and monstrous gods. The finest invention is that of an ancient Briton, who towers over a landscape showing a well-developed civilization with castles, a viaduct and a port. This swarthy figure is worked up out of the description given by Strabo in Book III of his *Geography*, where he depicts the inhabitants of the Tin Islands as 'men wearing black garments, clad in side-coats descending to their ankles, going with staves like the Furies in Tragedies'.[19]

Once Sammes reaches the Roman conquest, his book loses a good deal of its fascination. He combines the Roman history of Britain under the emperors with the British history from Geoffrey of Monmouth, thus giving the British and their kings a separate

[19] Quoted by Sammes, ibid. 117.

13. The Wicker Man, as imagined by Aylett Sammes. A sacrifice of malefactors offered to the gods, derived from Caesar's account in Book vi of *De Bello Gallico*.

14. Aylett Sammes' image of a druid, based on John Selden's account of statues found in Germany. Druids evidently possessed their own sacred books.

identity beneath the overlordship of the Romans. Christianity makes its appearance in Gospel times with Joseph of Arimathea in the reign of Arviragus, under the Emperor Claudius, and Sammes reprints the engraving of the first church in Britain at Glastonbury from Spelman's *Concilia*.

He is not however particularly concerned to chart the progress of Christianity in the Island. Racial origins and philology are what engage him most. His treatment of the Roman centuries is perfunctory, and numerous inconsequential digressions mark his fading concentration. The arrival of the Saxons challenges him to track them to their source, which he identifies variously as Scythia or Cimmeria. The Saxons are proved to be another branch of the Cimmerian Celts who first settled the greater part of Britain; they had occupied Germany and their language had greatly diverged from the old British tongue over the centuries. He readily confuses Saxon with Gothic, and embarks on a disquisition on the Gothic language which inspires no more confidence than his presentation of Phoenician. He pours scorn on Verstegan for his suggestion that the father of the German nation had been Tuisco, and engages in a protracted scholarly denunciation of Annius of Viterbo for perpetrating his fraudulent edition of Berosus and introducing so much specious history into circulation, including that notorious will-o'-the-wisp Tuisco. (He seems to forget he has made use of the pseudo-Berosan genealogies earlier in his book.) It is evident to Sammes that Woden was the true leader of the Saxons, who brought them into Germany, just as Hengist and Horsa brought them into England. Sammes's discussion of Woden draws heavily on Snorri Sturrelson, and is an unusually early use of the Icelandic Edda, which he cites both in the original and in the translation by Rossenius. Sammes makes no effort to speculate on the consequences of the Saxon influx into the post-Roman British world, and his book peters out in a bald narrative of the petty Saxon kings, and ends by reprinting the laws of King Ina, which he has translated from the Anglo-Saxon. He offers no commentary on these laws, which provide so much scope for social exploration. There was the prospect of a second volume of *Britannia Antiqua*, but Sammes died in 1679 and nothing more appeared.

Aylett Sammes may seem to be an antiquarian who explored the uttermost peninsula of absurdity, but in his time he was not so exceptional as he now seems. It is worth noting that Sammes's opinions were seriously considered by Edmund Gibson in the 1695 edition of Camden's *Britannia*, and though not accepted, they were given an honourable place in the footnotes of the introductory section on Britain. The Phoenician thesis was a tempting one to develop, and Sammes was not alone in exploiting this line of thought. It could be worked up out of Strabo, who was a reliable author, and part of its appeal was that it offered a possible pre-history for Britain that could be authenticated from an ancient source. The Trojan thesis had long been suspect because of the total lack of support for it from any writer in antiquity, but the Phoenicians were a well documented race, noted for their numerous colonies and ranging voyages, and they could plausibly be associated with the Israelites in their Syrian homeland. They were attractive too because they were a named people, and met that universal desire among all the nations of Europe in medieval and Renaissance times that their founders should be notable and distinguished. The idea of settlement by anonymous primitive tribesmen was too unpalatable to be entertained.[20]

Thanks to Samuel Bochart, the Phoenicians had been vastly magnified in the seventeenth century, so that their role in antiquity seemed almost as important as that of the Greeks and Romans. Bochart's opinions had been echoed by Robert Sheringham in his *De Anglorum Gentis Origine Disceptatio* of 1670. Sheringham (1602–79) was a fellow of Caius College, Cambridge, a royalist who was dispossessed of his fellowship and spent the Commonwealth years in Rotterdam, where he taught Hebrew and Arabic, returning to Cambridge at the Restoration. Sammes appears to have known him personally, and quotes his book extensively. Sheringham followed Verstegan (whilst often differing from him) in emphasizing the Germanic character of the English, believing that the Saxons, Jutes, and Angles virtually obliterated any previous racial cultures in Britain. He was concerned to explore the origins of the Germanic peoples, and in particular was fascinated by the Goths, whose language and customs he examined in detail. He was

---

[20] A similar preference for a less prosaic past is apparent in Sammes's insistence that Britain must always have been an island. He dismisses Verstegan's opinion that Britain was probably once joined to the mainland, not on the basis of geological evidence, but because 'it seems more glorious for this excellent part of the Earth to have been always a distinct Nation by itself, than to be a dependent Member of that Territory to which it hath often given Laws' (*Britannia Antiqua*, 16).

an open-minded man to say the least, and not governed by obsessions. ('Disceptatio' means 'discussion', or 'reflection': a non-assertive word.) As one might expect, he was most respectful of Tacitus, but in seeking to go further back, tracing the Cimbri who feature so prominently in Tacitus, he tried to relate them to the Trojans who were so disseminated throughout Europe according to the various legends of national foundation. He identified many similarities between British/Welsh words and Greek (giving several pages of examples), and he assumed Greek to have been the language of the Trojans. But he also entertained the possibility of a link between the German tribes and the Phoenicians, whom, following Bochart, he assumed to have been ubiquitous in Europe long before the Trojan War.[21] In the absence of any more convincing theories of population movements and settlement in pre-historic times, the continuing attraction of the Trojans and the Phoenicians, and behind them, the biblical migrations after the Flood, can be well understood.

If Sammes can be said to have any disciple, that doubtful honour must fall to Charles Leigh (1662–1701), the Lancashire physician and naturalist, educated at both Oxford and Cambridge, who in 1700 published *The Natural History of Lancashire, Cheshire and the Peak in Derbyshire, with an Account of the British, Phoenician, Armenian, Greek and Roman Antiquities in those Parts*. Confidently dedicated to the Chancellor of Oxford, the Duke of Ormond, and to the University of Oxford, this volume took seventeen years to write, and is 'critically curious in each observation and experiment'. The format owes much to Robert Plot's *Natural History of Oxfordshire*, with much attention paid to the Baconian concerns of the properties of earth, air, and water in the region, information about the flora and fauna, and a lengthy contribution to the debate about the nature of fossils. But in Book III, on antiquities, we are led into an antiquarian *Wunderkammer* to be shown 'Heathen Altars, Sacrificing Vessels, Coins, Fibulae, Lamps, Urns, Tyles, Fortifications, Signets, Pagods etc.' We are given a discourse on 'the Armenian, British and Phoenician Languages ... their Deities, the Asiatic Manner of Fighting, the Eastern and British Way of Computing Time and divers other things', and informed that 'the whole Island was chiefly and primarily inhabited by Colonies from

---

[21] Robert Sheringham, *De Anglorum Gentis Origine Disceptatio* (1670), ch. 4.

Asia long before either the Greeks or Romans came hither.' Leigh offers a highly localized version of Sammes's thesis, with equally slender evidence. Britain was a Phoenician colony (he is persuaded from his reading of Strabo). 'Since therefore we may reasonably suppose the Phoenicians were in those northern parts, to me there appears no difficulty how they might transplant themselves into Lancashire.'[22]

The ancient inhabitants in the north-western region were the Brigantes and the high point of Leigh's historical romanticism comes when, by means of singular etymological evidence, he describes their entrance into their chosen land and the foundation of New Canaan on the Ribble.

As to the Brigantes, it is reasonable to conclude a greater part of them Phoenicians, a People of Syria, very industrious Improvers of Navigation, since we have a remarkable River in Lancashire called Ribble, by Ptolemy stiled Bellisama, which word undoubtedly he derived from the Phoenician words Belus and Sama, signifying in that language, the Moon or Goddess of Heaven, she being supposed to have a particular influence over Waters, and at that time the Deity they adored. Hence it is evident, that before the Greeks traded into Brittany, the Phoenicians had been there, and no doubt discovered the greatest part of the Island. Since therefore a River in this Country, in those early days, retained a Phoenician name, as the Greek geographer Ptolemy makes it manifest it did, to me it seems an undeniable conjecture to suppose that the name must be attributed to it from the People of that Country, viz. Phoenicia, that resided near it; probably in the pleasant and beautiful town now stiled Preston.[23]

Leigh provides a florid account of the Phoenicians setting sail for Lancashire, in their ships from Tyre, 'ships made of the fir-trees of Senir, and their masts the cedars of Lebanon . . . oars from the oaks of Bashan. Benches of ivory from the Ashurites, brought out of the Isles of Chittin; embroidered linen from Egypt for their sails, blue and purple from the Isles of Elisha.'[24] What sounds like a Miltonic evocation of ancient splendour is in fact a quotation from Ezekiel xxvii, the biblical description of Tyre and its riches made by 'their prodigious merchandizing', with the elegy for its destruction by the Israelites, the event that caused the flight of its people and the dissemination of Phoenician colonies abroad. Leigh reverts to this

---

[22] Charles Leigh, *Natural History of Lancashire* (1700), iii. 4.
[23] Ibid. 3.   [24] Ibid. 62.

history of the Phoenician diaspora on several occasions, for it provides for him the explanation of the presence of this energetic people in the remotest places.

Nor did the Phoenicians come alone: according to Leigh, Lancashire was quite an Asiatic melting pot in antiquity, for their next neighbours were the Persians, 'who spake the Armenian Language'. Leigh believes it probable, on the slenderest philological evidence, that the Phoenicians brought some Persians along with them in their continued trafficking with the Bretannick Isles. He picks up the detail from Caesar about the use of chariots as a distinctive feature of warfare in Britain, and like Sammes, cites these chariots as proof of contact with the Middle East, imagining that they were first bartered by the Phoenicians for the products of the flourishing cloth industry that Leigh assumes to have existed in Lancashire in pre-historic times. Before the Phoenicians came, the north had been inhabited by giants. (The skull of a giant not long since dug up in Pepper Street in Chester was adequate evidence for Leigh of their presence.) Before the giants, the land had belonged to the descendants of Samothes the son of Japhet, for Leigh is happy to find space for the posterity of Noah in the wonderland that was ancient Lancashire.

Much of Leigh's account of Lancashire antiquities is a sustained fantasy, helped along by a perverse use of etymological skills that yoke together any similar-sounding words in unrelated languages. Ancient history is a gigantic bran-tub from which Leigh continues to pull out astonishing objects, which he identifies with casual ease. A large gold torc recently found in Staffordshire most probably belonged to Boadicea, because Dio Cassius, in his Life of Nero, had reported that she wore such an ornament; and because there is no gold in Britain, it is equally probable that the torc was traded here by the Phoenicians. So much for evidence. When it comes to Roman artefacts discovered in Lancashire and Cheshire, Leigh lists them, gives their inscriptions, and often illustrates them, but makes no attempt to deduce any historical information from them. Patterns of settlement, times of occupation, religious cults, networks of communication—these are of no interest to the author, who regards all things that have come out of the soil essentially as curiosities. Archaeology had no place in his scheme of antiquities.

Interest in the Phoenicians persisted, encouraging the publication in 1720 of a full translation of the Phoenician History by

Sanchoniathon, which had been preserved in Greek in the works of Eusebius. This translation, with extensive commentary, was by Richard Cumberland, who had been Bishop of Peterborough.[25] He had undertaken it, according to the Preface, in the late 1680s, about a decade after the publication of Aylett Sammes's book. Cumberland's work made available for the first time in English an authentic piece of Phoenician writing about the early history of the world, and the challenge to a Christian commentator in the seventeenth century was to harmonize this account with the biblical record. In Cumberland's opinion, Sanchoniathon's narrative preserved the history of the idolatrous line of Cain, whereas the Bible preserved the history of the worshippers of the true God in the line of Seth. He attempts to align the unfamiliar characters of this History with the known record transmitted by Hebrew and classical writings; so, for example, he interprets the mythological figure of Ouranon as the Phoenician name for Noah, and his son Cronus as Ham, who restored idolatry after the Flood and whose progeny founded the empires of Assyria and Egypt. Working within the constraints of the Bible as a true and literal record of primal antiquity, Cumberland manages to deliver a fairly intelligent contextualization of the Phoenician History. Central to his manner of proceeding is the assumption that all the gods of the gentile world had been mortal men, and could be placed in a scheme of history that was already partially known from other sources. The god Thoth therefore, who had collected the most ancient stories of the Phoenicians, and who seemed to be a heathen counterpart to Moses, he identified with the magus Hermes Trismegisthus; the service that Sanchoniathon had rendered posterity was to have preserved these records of Hermes. So Cumberland in his commentary gave Englishmen a sense of Phoenicia's place in the primitive Mediterranean world. He illustrated the observations made by his contemporary Edward Stillingfleet in *Origines Sacrae* (1662), a survey of the earliest accounts of the beginnings of human history (which naturally gave priority to the Books of Moses), in which he placed the Phoenicians among 'the nations with the greatest name in the world for learning and antiquity', and made

[25] Richard Cumberland (1632–1718) had attended Magdalene College, Cambridge, and was a friend of Pepys. He was made Bishop of Peterborough in 1691.

them responsible for transmitting to the Greeks the art of writing.[26] Stillingfleet had quoted Herodotus and Diodorus Siculus to the effect that the earliest known inscriptions in the world were in Phoenician, and his book helped to reinforce the impression that the Phoenicians were an important race of the highest antiquity and culture. His own view of Sanchoniathon's History was that it was 'misty and unreliable', but Richard Cumberland demystified it to some extent and strengthened its credibility by its commentary; the treatment by these two writers of the Phoenicians' role in history was reasonable and sensible by the standards of the time, and they had no inclination to acclaim them as the discoverers or settlers of Britain. They did, however, celebrate the fame of Phoenicia.

William Stukeley gave the Phoenicians a further lease of life when he accepted them as the first planters of Britain in his books on Stonehenge and Avebury (1740 and 1743). Driven by his obsession with Druidic lore, he deduces the Druids from Tyre, whence they had come as part of 'an oriental colony' of Phoenicians soon after the Flood, bringing with them to Britain an authentic recollection of the religion of Abraham. The leader of these colonists, Stukeley declares, was the Tyrian Hercules, a figure he takes over from Sammes's book. In the extravagance of Stukeley's imaginings, the Tyrian Hercules was 'a worthy scholar of Abraham', and the transmitter of a form of patriarchalism to the new-found-land of Britain.[27] Another early-eighteenth-century enquirer into the Druids, Henry Rowlands, author of *Mona Antiqua Restaurata* (1723), was similarly respectful of Bochart and Sammes's theories concerning the peopling of the British Isles, even to the extent of believing that Welsh, the surviving form of the ancient British language, was a descendant of the Hebrew tongue.

A century after Sammes, the hypothesis was applied to Ireland. In 1772, Charles Vallencey published *An Essay on the Antiquity of the Irish Language*, 'being a collation of the Irish with the Punic Languages'. In this work, he denied the conventional view, aired by Bochart and Sammes, that Phoenician was closely associated with Hebrew, maintaining instead that it had many similarities with

---

[26] Edward Stillingfleet, *Origines Sacrae* (1662), 25. The other nations who in Stillingfleet's scheme were the equals of the Phoenicians were the Chaldeans and the Egyptians.
[27] Stuart Piggott, *William Stukeley* (London, 1985), 99–100.

Irish. But Vallencey was also convinced that Irish was spoken in the Garden of Eden, so he did not find a very large audience in the Age of Enlightenment. In his opinion, the round towers of Ireland were of Phoenician design and had been used for purposes of astronomy. This art too had come to Ireland from Phoenicia, which nation had in turn learned it from the Chaldeans, so early Irish culture was considerably indebted to Mesopotamia.[28] Such views harmonized easily with the old foundation legends of Ireland which derived the original Scoti from Scota, the daughter of the Egyptian pharaoh in the time of Moses.

The Phoenicians-in-Britain thesis has never entirely lost its appeal, sustained by the plausibility of the idea that they must have visited the island in search of tin, and by the inferences that can be drawn from Strabo's description of the Phoenicians as the greatest voyagers, merchants, and settlers of pre-Roman times. If Sammes had restricted himself to exploring the possibility of contacts between Britain and Phoenicia, his book might have been esteemed as a work of intelligent historical conjecture, but his total addiction to the theory led him to procrustean distortions as he tried to make every known feature of Ancient Britain fit a Phoenician scheme. Yet undeniably he articulated a view that many imaginative readers accepted, and the thesis has continued to attract believers well into the twentieth century, despite the complete absence of convincing archaeological evidence for any such connection.[29]

[28] See Norman Vance, 'Celts, Carthaginians and Constitutions: Anglo-Irish Literary Relations 1780–1820' in *Irish Historical Studies*, 22 (1981), 216–39. Vance notes that James Joyce, in his lectures on Ireland at Trieste in 1907, was assuring his audience that Irish culture and language owed much to the Phoenicians.
[29] See, e.g. L. A. Waddell, *The Phoenician Origin of Britons, Scots and Anglo-Saxons* (London, 1924). This book went into a third edition in 1931.

12

Britannia Revised

So diverse and industrious had the enquiry been into the antiquities of the nation in the course of the seventeenth century, that in the last decade a project was floated to bring out a new edition of Camden's *Britannia* that would reflect the remarkable advances in antiquarian understanding in the hundred years since its first publication. The prime mover of this project was Edmund Gibson, a young Fellow of Queen's College, Oxford. He himself was a precocious antiquary, whose enthusiasm and discipline qualified him to be an admirable editor of the *Britannia*. Born in 1669 in Westmorland, Gibson had become fascinated by antiquarian studies as a student, and in particular he was drawn into Anglo-Saxon scholarship by the influence of George Hickes who had brought that subject to a new eminence in Oxford in the 1680s.[1] His talents were rapidly revealed by the edition of the *Anglo-Saxon Chronicle* that he published in 1692, with a Latin translation and notes. Abraham Wheelock had already printed a version of the *Chronicle*, based on a manuscript in Cotton's library and on the manuscript at Corpus Christi College, Cambridge, but Gibson was able to draw on further versions to produce a much more substantial edition of this collection of documents, which forms such an important continuous record of events in England from the late sixth century until the Conquest.[2] In the same year, Gibson published an account of the manuscripts in the collection of Thomas Tenison, then Bishop of Lincoln, and those given to the Ashmolean by Sir William Dugdale. In 1693, he brought out an edition of Quintilian, and provided notes to an edition of William

---

[1] Hickes published the first full Anglo-Saxon Grammar in 1689 under the title *Institutiones Grammaticae Anglo-Saxonicae et Meso-Gothicae*.

[2] See Douglas, *English Scholars* (1943), 83–4, for an account of this edition, and his strictures upon it for its tendency to make the Chronicle appear 'a single homogeneous authority derived from a single mind'.

Somner's *Roman Ports and Forts in Kent*. His promotion of Somner continued in 1694 with a translation of his *Julii Caesaris Portus Iccius*, on the identification of a Kentish port in Caesar. Behind Gibson's versatile scholarship, one can detect an eagerness to conserve, order, and inform that is the mark of the true antiquary. Some time in 1692, he conceived the plan of bringing the *Britannia* up to date, and incorporating into a new edition the most valuable additions to antiquarian knowledge that had accumulated in print or in manuscript since the last printing of the work in 1637.[3]

Gibson was able to recruit a team of scholars and exert pressure on them to deliver their manuscripts with such effect that the 700-page folio was printed in 1695, within three years of its inception. Gibson was 26 at the time. His editorial method was both deeply respectful of Camden and intelligently innovative. He gave the 1607 edition the status of a classical text, causing it to be translated anew from the Latin, and insisting on its integrity as an important historical document that must not be altered. He relegated Philemon Holland's additions of 1610 to the bottom of the page as footnotes. Then, at the end of each county, the various contributors were entitled to make their own additions, which were a summary of the recent improvements of knowledge relating to their region, and notes on places and monuments that Camden had overlooked. In many cases, the new additions virtually matched the size of Camden's original entries. 'An exact translation of Mr Camden's text has been made, in a uniform style though by many hands,' the Preface notes. Several of the contributors produced their own translations of their county; for the rest, Gibson recruited a number who were able Latinists, including the historian Laurence Eachard, and James Wright the chorographer of Rutland. Translation of the medieval Latin poetry often quoted by Camden for historical illustration (as well as for the literary edification of his reader, who he hoped would develop a taste for the verse of the Middle Ages) was entrusted to White Kennett, who produced smooth easy couplets that were faithful to the sense.[4] All the translators are

---

[3] Gibson's project had the backing of Dr Arthur Charlett, the influential Master of University College, who is described in the Preface to the *Britannia* as 'the Great Promoter of this Work'.

[4] Gibson pauses to praise in particular Kennett's rendering of the poem on the marriage of the Thames and the Isis in Oxfordshire, a poem he was convinced was of

acknowledged in the Preface. 'The version is plain and easy,' remarked Gibson, sustaining the trend towards firm, clear English that the Royal Society encouraged in the interests of efficient communication.

Mindful that the original framework of the *Britannia* had been the Antonine Itinerary, Gibson helpfully printed the Itinerary at the beginning of his new edition so that the underlying structure could be understood. Maps were newly commissioned from Robert Morden reflecting the great advances in surveying that had been made since the days of Saxton and Speed. (Accuracy comes in at the expense of atmosphere, however: the sea monsters have fled the coasts, and the sailing ships that used to decorate the seas with their argonautical magic have become more prosaic vessels; the imaginative sense of the power of the land, which had been complemented by the mythological frontispiece to the book, has given way to a utilitarian spirit.) A further improvement was the inclusion at the end of each county of a section on rare plants of the region, furnished by the naturalist John Ray. These contributions were fortuitous, arising out of Gibson's friendship with Ray, but they show how the vogue for county natural histories was closely allied to an interest in antiquarian learning.

Gibson made it clear in his Preface that he had resisted strong pressure from the gentry, from whose ranks most of his subscribers came, for much more information about county families and their seats. The eternal vanity of English gentlemen was a threat to serious antiquarian studies, forever trying to make the past illustrate their own lineage. Let them look into Dugdale, he advised, and quench their self-conceit in his pages. The other notable subject that Gibson excluded was that of monasteries and their history. Camden himself had avoided this subject as too sensitive to be handled; in any case, little information concerning the monasteries was available at the beginning of the century. By the 1690s, thanks to Dugdale and his associates, the topic had become so voluminous that it would have overwhelmed the new *Britannia*. Besides, recent scholarship in this field was already being summed up by Thomas Tanner in his *Notitia Monastica*, which was also published in 1695.

Camden's own composition. It certainly is a fine imaginative sequence in Renaissance Latin, in the Ovidian mythological mode, in which British names mingle mellifluously with classical deities; Kennett turned it into assured Augustan verse which has its own distinction.

The scale of antiquarian research in the seventeenth century is made evident to the reader by the 'catalogue of some Books and Treatises relating to the Antiquities of England' which is printed, together with a list of Scottish and Welsh material, before the main body of the text, occupying five large folio pages. What a world of curious learning has been explored! Commentaries on British, Roman, Saxon, and medieval antiquities, county histories and perambulations, legal and ecclesiastical histories, books of monumental inscriptions, surveys of the nobility and of the worthies of the nation, descriptive catalogues of museums and private collections, regional phenomena, investigations of mineral springs and spas, treatises on fossils and thunderbolts, topographical poems: a very considerable library could now be assembled by an aspiring antiquary. Gibson notes too the location of important collections of material in manuscript, such as John Aubrey's, and informs his readers of the existence of unpublished county histories. Among the English counties, the ones that remained seriously under-investigated by 1695 were Bedfordshire, Huntingdonshire, Lancashire (soon to be remedied by Leigh's History), Lincolnshire, Suffolk, and, rather surprisingly, Yorkshire. The overall impression conveyed by the catalogue, however, is that the nation has been exceptionally attentive to its past, and that Camden's *Britannia* has produced a remarkable progeny of books.

The group of antiquaries that Gibson persuaded to contribute to the new *Britannia* was remarkable for its intellectual brilliance and for the prevalence of young scholars. There was a good deal of talent among his own contemporaries at Oxford which could be brought to bear on his edition, and a survey of the major contributors provides an opportunity to sketch the flourishing scene of antiquarian scholarship towards the end of the century. It is not surprising that Gibson's team was mainly based at Oxford, for that university had now become the natural home, as some might say, of antiquarianism. We may begin with Thomas Smith, one of the senior members of the group, who was author of the 'Life of Camden' that prefaced the 1695 volume and introduced Camden to English readers for the first time. Smith was an antiquarian of wide and unusual interests. Born in London in 1638, he had gone up to Queen's College in 1657, taken holy orders, and had been elected a fellow of Magdalen in 1666. As early as 1664 he had published a book on Druidic lore and authority, *Syntagma de*

Druidum Moribus ac Institutis, in which he had brought together
all the information furnished by classical authors about the Druids,
and argued for their familiarity with the secret wisdom concerning
the mysteries of the natural world and the progress of the soul
which had descended from Adam to the Patriarchs of Israel, to the
poets of Greece in the earliest times, and to the various philosophic
sects of antiquity. He turned from this demonstration of Britain's
participation in the mainstream of ancient wisdom to observations
of the state of the Eastern Church in his own time as a result of his
service as chaplain to the English ambassador in Constantinople in
the late 1660s. He became a proficient commentator on the affairs
of the Greek Church, and on its historical evolution from the
apostolic age. This interest led him on to an attempt to understand
Jewish theological traditions and the customs of the Jews, resulting
in books on the Talmud which earned him the soubriquet of
'Rabbi' Smith. His career at Oxford was derailed by the controversy
over the oath of allegiance to the new monarchs William and Mary.
He refused to swear, on the grounds that theirs was not a legitimate
succession, and lost his fellowship as a non-juror. He moved to
London and lived in the household of Sir John Cotton, grandson of
the great antiquarian, and seems to have become the librarian of the
Cotton Library. At any rate, he compiled a catalogue of the Cotton
collection, published in 1696, which became invaluable for its
description of manuscripts that were destroyed in the fire of 1731.
Working among the Cotton papers brought him in touch with
Camden's manuscripts, with the consequence that he published
Camden's surviving letters in 1691, and was able to piece together
his biography from material in the library, perhaps aided by the
family reminiscences of John Cotton. This 'Life of Camden',
originally composed in Latin to introduce his edition of the
Epistolae, was now translated into English for the benefit of a new
audience.[5]

Of the younger contributors to the revised *Britannia*, Thomas
Tanner (1674–1735), who compiled the additions to Wiltshire, was

[5] Camden's life had been briefly sketched by Thomas Fuller in his *Holy State*
(1642), where he was represented as 'the antiquary as English worthy', a true
Protestant and an honourable preserver of the dignity of Britain. There was,
however, too much sententious approval of Camden's merits for this to be anything
other than an appreciative retrospect.

outstanding. His career shows how addictive the pursuit of antiquities could be. He was the son of a vicar from Wiltshire, who had been an undergraduate at Gibson's college, Queen's, and by 1695 was chaplain and fellow of All Souls. By this time he had already made considerable collections towards a natural history of Wiltshire, having consulted with John Aubrey and benefited from his notes and fieldwork. A mark of Tanner's precociousness was the proposal he made in 1693 to edit the whole works of John Leland, a formidable undertaking, given the volume and complexity of Leland's papers in the Bodleian, but one that needed to be done if England's first true antiquarian and topographer were to be properly placed on record. It is surprising how long it took to get Leland into print. Though he was universally acknowledged as the father of antiquarian studies in England, that acclaim had not translated itself into a scholarly publication of his collections. Here was this wonderful detailed description of England and its antiquities in the years of the Reformation, when the splendours of the medieval Church could be seen for the last time, yet it still lay in manuscript. Various transcriptions of the 'Itinerary' had been made, by John Stow in the late sixteenth century, and then by William Burton the Leicestershire historian, by William Dugdale in 1657, by Thomas Gale, and by Robert Plot; several anonymous transcriptions were in existence too.[6] Tanner failed to carry his project of publication through, but it was eventually taken up and realized by his friend Thomas Hearne in 1710–12. Tanner did, however, manage to prepare for the press Leland's account of the early English writers, 'Commentarii de Scriptoribus', which he vastly enlarged to make a comprehensive annotated register of British authors from earliest times until the Reformation; it was eventually published as *Bibliotheca Britannica* in 1746, though the work for it dates back to the 1690s.

Tanner's finest achievement was the publication in 1695, when he was only 21, of *Notitia Monastica*, in which he gathered together details of all documents relating to the monasteries of Britain. Effectively a supplement to Dugdale's *Monasticon*, it offers a survey of the growth of monasticism in the British Isles, followed by a summary of every monastery's foundation, its landholdings

---

[6] For an account of the state of Leland's manuscripts, see Lucy Toulmin Smith, *Leland's Itinerary in England and Wales* (Fonthill, 1964), vol. i, pp. xx–xxxii.

and income, with a catalogue of all surviving charters, legal records, and historical notices concerning the abbey. It is clear that Tanner's gifts lay in the direction of ordering, classifying, and making serviceable complicated documentary evidences. This talent was further exercised in his contributions to Edward Bernard's invaluable catalogue of the manuscripts in the Bodleian Library which came out in 1697, for which Tanner described the collections left to the Library by the Stuart antiquarians Francis Junius and Richard James. His methodical habits and purposeful plans gained him the trust of older antiquarians. It was to Tanner, along with James Bisse of Wadham, that the cantankerous and ever-suspicious Anthony Wood entrusted his books and manuscript collections as he died in November 1695. Tanner and Bisse were also given custody of his private papers, and Tanner alone received, with great ceremony, the continuation of *Athenae Oxonienses* that Wood had compiled, containing much prickly commentary on living writers, which was eventually incorporated into the enlarged edition of 1721. More importantly, for the purposes of *Britannia*, Tanner managed to persuade John Aubrey to loan him the manuscript of 'Monumenta Britannica' so that its observations on British field monuments could finally be given to a larger audience in the 'Additions' to Wiltshire.

So, for the first time, Stonehenge is roundly declared in print to be a monument raised by the ancient British, 'for it does not appear that any other Nation had so much footing in this Kingdom, as to be the Authors of such a rude and yet magnificent Pile.' Aubrey's views are presented as the most intelligent thinking on megalithic structures; his suggestion that these might have been Druidic temples is noted, but not debated. His recognition of Avebury as an important pre-historic site is also now put on record. The description of Stonehenge is for the first time given with accurate measurements, and with great specificity of detail. It is accompanied by a new illustration by Johannes Kip which offers a more credible image of the monument, although the ruggedness of the stones is exaggerated, and the wild landscape owes more to fantasy than to observation. The affinities with other rude stone monuments is pointed out, and the existence of such structures in regions where neither Romans nor Danes had penetrated is cited as evidence that the Britons were the most likely builders; a higher estimate of their technical abilities must now be accepted, and they must now be

15. A lively representation of Stonehenge from the 1695 *Britannia*, engraved by Jan Kip.

credited with considerable powers of design. Tanner's interest in the Britons was largely fostered by his relationship with Aubrey. His own inclinations were toward the recovery of Saxon history, and he greatly expanded the account of Saxon activity in the region around Stonehenge, taking advantage of the advances in knowledge about the Saxons that derived from the publication of chronicles and from the generally clearer picture of Saxon settlement that had been built up in the course of the seventeenth century.

It may be observed generally that the majority of the additions in the 1695 *Britannia* are characterized by a greatly improved understanding of the Anglo-Saxon language and of Saxon history, areas of scholarship that were particularly prominent at Oxford in the last decades of the century. The 'Additions' to the county of Oxfordshire, in the care of Edmund Gibson and White Kennett, show the full benefits of these researches. Saxon place-names are given in a more accurate form than Camden was able to provide; details of Saxon Church history are introduced from Spelman's *Concilia* and from later archival research: so, for example, we learn of the councils held at Burford and Eynsham. From the *Anglo-Saxon Chronicle* comes much more information about historical events, mainly battles, although these conflicts still seem to be summed up by Milton's phrase about 'the wars of kites or crows, flocking or fighting in the air',[7] for there is still no overall sense of Saxon society or policy.

Saxon or Danish origins are suggested for most earthworks, barrows and tumuli in Oxfordshire (round barrows are thought to be Danish, square or 'quinquangular' ones Saxon). The Roll-Right Stones remain a mystery: they are associated with Stonehenge, but also considered in relation to the Danes. Excavations have been undertaken, but no bones found within the circle. Some ceremonial function may provide an explanation for this monument, and such was the persisting influence of Wormius's book on Danish Monuments that Gibson and Kennett fall back on the notion that the enclosure may have been for the election of leaders in the time of the Danes. Aubrey's opinions about the likelihood of their being ancient British in origin had not circulated sufficiently to make an impact, and the inhabitants of these parts before the Romans remained largely unimaginable.

---

[7] John Milton, *The History of Britain* (second edn., 1677), 216.

White Kennett (1660–1728), who was responsible for Oxfordshire, was another example of an antiquarian who was early in the field. As an undergraduate at Oxford, he had come to the notice of Anthony Wood, who had employed him to collect epitaphs and details of eminent Oxonians for his great dictionary of literary biography *Athenae Oxonienses*. He became friendly with George Hickes, who taught him Anglo-Saxon, by now thought to be an indispensable adjunct to antiquarian studies. He took orders and became a vicar in Oxfordshire; he developed an intense interest in the deeply-layered history of individual parishes, and opened this area of research with the publication in 1695 of *Parochial Antiquities Attempted in the History of Ambroseden and Burcester*. Perhaps through an association with John Aubrey, he grew fascinated by folklore, and began to make collections towards a 'History of Custom' which never saw the light of day. Like many Oxford antiquaries in the late seventeenth century, Kennett felt the obligation to keep alive the memory of earlier workers in the vineyard of the past, and see their manuscript works put into print. So, he composed a biography of William Somner which prefaced the edition of Somner's *Roman Ports and Forts in Kent* that he brought out in 1693, and he was instrumental in publishing Sir Henry Spelman's *History of Sacrilege* (1698), which Edmund Gibson had omitted from his edition of Spelman's posthumous works, *Reliquiae Spelmanniae*, on grounds of prudence, since many men could be offended by the printing of details of property appropriated from the Church. Kennett was not so reluctant to offend; indeed, he became increasingly a clerical controversialist, and although he rose to be Bishop of Peterborough in 1718 (replacing Richard Cumberland who had translated the Phoenician History), he was lost to antiquarianism.

Robert Plot (1640–96), whom one might have expected to furnish the 'Additions' to Oxfordshire and Staffordshire, was entrusted with Kent and Middlesex. Kent was the most per-ambulated county, and Plot derived much material from Lambarde and from John Philpot's *Villare Cantium* (1659) and Richard Kilburne's *Survey of Kent* (also 1659). Plot is much concerned with the identification of Roman sites, and the lines of Roman roads, pulling into the *Britannia* William Burton's judgements from his Commentary on the Antonine Itinerary. He notes, too, recent archaeological finds of Roman materials, and draws attention in particular to the remarkable quantities of 'Roman brick or tile, Opus Musivum, coins, fibulae, gold-wire, ear-rings and bracelets' that have been turning up at Reculver as the cliffs crumble, certain evidence of a once important settlement there. Saxon data is plentifully added to Camden's reports, and much about the growth of Canterbury and its Cathedral from Somner. Plot is careful to record more recent developments in the county: he praises the new observatory at Greenwich as an adventurous scientific enterprise of which the nation should be proud, and he admires the naval facilities at Chatham (though there is no mention of the humiliation of the English fleet by the Dutch there in 1667). He takes note of novel economical activity at Canterbury, where a large group of Huguenot exiles has established an important silk manufacture. Finally, Plot injects a note of sensationalism with the report of a woman of Kent who 'had at her decease, lawfully descended from her, 367 children; 16 of her own body, 114 grandchildren, 228 in the third generation and 9 in the fourth.' Plot would regard this as an example of natural phenomena, but it is also a sign of how multifarious a book the 1695 *Britannia* had become.

Middlesex is rather briefly annotated by Plot, considering that the City of London falls into this county. He decided to recount the history of disasters that had befallen the City, culminating in the Great Fire, and one senses a lingering fondness for marvels, wonderful accidents, and curious information. Yet he also pays attention to the excavations that have been carried out beneath St Paul's in the course of laying the foundation for the new Cathedral, and he is able to report that no traces were found of a temple to Diana that legend asserted had stood on the site, but that a Roman cemetery was uncovered, containing a mass of bones and urns and lamps. Although Plot wonders at 'the stupendous pile, now erecting', he nowhere mentions the name of the architect, nor is Wren's name given in relation to Chelsea Hospital or Hampton Court, both of which are singled out for their excellent architecture. It is probably true to say that architects were still not recognized as important figures who left their mark on the landscape as powerfully as any king or commander.

A figure who would have been astounded by Plot's failure to acknowledge Wren was John Evelyn (1620–1706), one of the foremost judges of contemporary architecture, just as he was an arbiter in so many of the areas of national life. Evelyn was brought in by Gibson to improve the commentary on Surrey, where his own family had been long established. With his boundless curiosity, his excellent knowledge of classical authors, and his prominent position in the Royal Society, he should have been an outstanding contributor, but he proved to be over-inclined to comment on gentlemen's seats and on the amenities of modern garden design. He adds little to our knowledge of antiquities, although a good deal of incidental information is imparted, such as the recollection that the Earl of Arundel was trying to trace the line of Stone Street, the Roman way, through the county, until the Civil Wars put an end to his probings. He also recounts a folk custom that his friend John Aubrey would have seized on as evidence for the survival of classical traditions in Britain, when he describes how rose-trees are planted on the graves of young lovers in the churchyard at Okeley, and cites Greek and Roman examples of the same custom.

Evelyn's friend Samuel Pepys (1633–1703) was an unexpected participant in the *Britannia*, writing in his professional role as a maritime administrator about the royal arsenals in Kent, with notes on Plymouth and Harwich. He respectfully chides Camden for overlooking the naval bases that assured the seaworthiness of Elizabethan ships, going on to impress the reader statistically with the five-fold growth of the Royal Navy from Camden's time to the present. Pepys writes in a brisk workmanlike way, emphasizing the efficient functioning of the docks and yards, for which he could take some credit, and he is much concerned to strike a modern note amidst all the talk of antiquity.

Among antiquarians making their first appearance in 1695, Ralph Thoresby is notable. A Yorkshireman, born in 1658 and based in Leeds, he had already gathered together an impressive private 'Musaeum' which probably constituted the most extensive collection of Roman artefacts in the north of England. He undertook the 'Additions' to the West Riding of Yorkshire, a region he describes with intimate and detailed familiarity. He expertly traced the network of Roman roads and military stations, making many improvements on Camden's account, but he had relatively little interest in Saxon or medieval antiquities, and his post-Roman entries are generally disappointing. Like Evelyn, he displays an interest in detailing the seats of the gentry that was not called for in the *Britannia*, and there is a corresponding indifference to the commerce of the region that contributed so much to its distinctive character. One would scarcely know that the wool trade was prospering, and enlarging towns steadily, or that Thoresby himself was the son of a wool merchant. At Halifax he lingers over the town guillotine as a unique instrument of punishment, and even places an illustration in the text, but he has nothing to say about the economic growth of the place. Camden had included the wealth and commodities of a region in his original description of the land, but his successors were more disposed to fill out the historical record than to attend to manufactures. The study of antiquities was a pursuit that befitted a gentleman, such as Thoresby had become.

As one reads Thoresby's 'Additions', one is repeatedly made aware of the shadow of Roger Dodsworth, the Yorkshire antiquary of early Stuart times, who had assembled immense collections of topographical and ecclesiastical materials, but had brought nothing to the press. Dugdale had effectively usurped his title to the monastic collections, but no 'Antiquities of Yorkshire' had ever been raised on the foundations Dodsworth had laid. Dodsworth had been encouraged by Thomas, Lord Fairfax, who had pensioned him, and who did what he could to preserve his materials, trying to find a scholar to extract a book of Yorkshire antiquities from them, but to no avail. When Fairfax died, he bequeathed Dodsworth's collections to the Bodleian Library. They filled 120 volumes in manuscript.[8] Thoresby greatly honoured Fairfax for 'the peculiar respect he had for Antiquities', and he recalled with gratitude Fairfax's order to prevent the sacking of York Minster after the battle of Marston Moor. So many antiquarians were royalist by temperament that Fairfax stands out as a relatively rare example of a major parliamentarian who cherished the past. Fairfax's own cabinet of coins and medals was purchased by Thoresby's father John, and became a prized part of Thoresby's Musaeum. The best examples of Saxon coins in this collection were sent to Gibson to be engraved for the 1695 *Britannia*. Thoresby himself secured a

---

[8] Fairfax hoped one Nathaniel Johnston, a Yorkshire physician, would undertake the task, but he 'grew weary of the work'. Dodsworth had transcribed a vast quantity of documents relating to Yorkshire monasteries kept in St. Mary's Tower, York, just before it was blown up in the siege of 1644. When Dodsworth's papers were taken to the Bodleian, in 1673, they were soaked by rain in transit and would have quite perished if not for the initiative of Anthony Wood, who dried them on the leads of the library, 'which cost him a month's time to do'. See Wood, *Fasti*, ii. 699–700.

permanent reputation as an antiquary with the publication in 1715 of *Ducatus Leodiensis*, a topographical description of Leeds and its region, one of the first books to be devoted to the local history of a town that was not of outstanding national importance. This work was accompanied by an elaborate catalogue of his Musaeum and his manuscript collections, which excited the interest of antiquaries all over the country.

The remaining parts of Yorkshire and Northumberland were given to the care of William Nicolson (1655–1727), another of the talented antiquaries nurtured by Queen's College, Oxford. He came from a clerical family in Cumberland, and while he was at Oxford he fell under the spell of Anglo-Saxon. He was also attracted to the modern Germanic and Nordic languages, and spent some years abroad to acquaint himself with them at first hand. His earliest reflections on antiquity were made in letters published in *Philosophical Transactions* in 1685, concerning runic inscriptions in the north of England. He returned to his native county as a chaplain to the Bishop of Carlisle, and his considerable familiarity with the Border regions made him an excellent choice to write the 'Additions' to Northumberland. Camden had already been particularly attentive to this county, where so many visible traces of the Roman occupation survived. He had made an expedition along the Wall with Cotton in 1600, had inspected the military stations and the defensive forts, and collected gravestones and altars which became the trophies of their engagement with the past. Here at the utmost limits of the Roman Empire, the romance of Empire was at its height and Camden had been able to identify many of the cohorts, composed of Dalmatians, Batavians, Sabines, or Gauls, who manned the Wall against the barbarians beyond. In the wilderness of Northumberland, where the resources of Rome were exerted in one final act of territorial definition, Camden found place names and inscriptions which spoke of the presence of Hadrian or the orders of Marcus Aurelius. The initial stages of the Antonine Itinerary, which began on the northern frontier of Britain, could be located here: Bremenium, Corstopitum, Vindolanda— their still-remaining walls brought one very close to the days when Latin was the lingua franca of the Borders.

There was little that Nicolson could add to Camden's Roman knowledge, but his Saxon scholarship was put to use in clarifying the complexity of Northumbrian history in Saxon times, and relating events to places. In the land of perpetual skirmish between Romans and Picts, English and Scots, Nicolson is a competent guide. He shows much more interest than Camden in the progress of Christianity in the north-east, an interest fuelled by Bede and by the lives of the Saxon saints, and he portrays with vigorous strokes the flourishing of Northumbria in the time of the Saxon kings. Nicolson wrote for the honour of the north. Camden had quoted disparaging remarks from the memoirs of Aeneas Sylvius Piccolomini, later Pope Pius II, who once as a papal legate found himself travelling hazardously in the Borders, an experience which he remembered as a journey among the barbarians; Nicolson counters with a warm description of the amenities of modern life in Northumberland, where good order is maintained, where the gentry are 'preservers of the true old English hospitality', and where red wine is available in quantities to satisfy any visitor from the Mediterranean. Turning somewhat reluctantly away from the colourful confusion of the past, Nicolson is also prepared to promote the reputation of the north-east in his own time, drawing his reader's attention in particular to the prosperous condition of Newcastle and its region, based on sea-coal.

When Camden came to deal with Wales and Scotland, he was somewhat diffident about his expertise, for these were unfamiliar countries to him, and he had to rely on correspondents for information, particularly in the case of Scotland. Gibson in 1695 put these regions into the hands of the two leading masters of Celtic antiquities, Edward Lhwyd and Sir Robert Sibbald. Lhwyd, who was born in 1660, had attended Jesus College, the Oxford resort of Welshmen, from 1682 to 1687.[9] He then became the assistant to Robert Plot, the Keeper of the Ashmolean Museum, and began to develop the characteristics of a late-Restoration virtuoso, albeit with a Welsh bias. As an undergraduate he had shown the Oxford Philosophical Society a fireproof asbestos paper he had invented. Once at the Ashmolean, he rapidly became an expert on British

---

[9] Lhwyd is well served by two volumes of biographical material: *The Life and Letters of Edward Lhwyd*, edited by R. T. Gunther in *Early Science in Oxford* (Oxford, 1945), and Frank Emery, *Edward Lhwyd 1660–1709 FRS* (Cardiff, 1971). See also Frank Emery, 'Edward Lhwyd and the 1695 *Britannia*', in *Antiquity* (1958), and Gwyn Walters and Frank Emery, 'Edward Lhwyd, Edmund Gibson and the Printing of Camden's *Britannia*, 1695', in *The Library*, 5th series, 32 (1977), 109–37.

shells and plants, and then moved on to make a study of fossils, or 'formed stones', as his contemporaries called them. These interests were pursued at the same time as he was refining his skills as a philologist of the Celtic languages and acquainting himself with the various kinds of field monuments that were associated with the Ancient Britons. Native patriotism prompted him to exhibit to the Philosophical Society examples of Roman coins from Denbigh, pearls from Cardigan and crystals from Caernarvon; in 1688 he was sending back to the Physic Garden at Oxford specimens of plants that he had collected on and around Snowdon. So many new varieties did he find that his friend John Ray the botanist was able to devote a section to Welsh Alpine flora in his book of British plants, *Synopsis Methodica Stirpium Britannicorum*, published in 1689–90. Plot had introduced Lhwyd to Ray and to the natural scientist Martin Lister and from them Lhwyd seems to have learnt the Royal Society methodology of descriptive and analytical classification, which would serve him well in his many collections. He also came to know John Aubrey, with whom he became a close friend and correspondent.[10] Aubrey, together with his friend Edmund Wild, excited in Lhwyd a passion for British monuments, and Lhwyd in return was able to further Aubrey's speculations by his reports on stone structures in Wales.

When Gibson approached him in 1693 to contribute to the new *Britannia*, Lhwyd agreed to undertake Denbighshire, Merioneth- shire and Montgomeryshire, but as the other Welsh contributors dropped out, Lhwyd took it on himself to update the whole of the principality. He immediately proposed to make an antiquarian tour to cover the ground in person and gather material, and to this end made a modest request to the publishers Churchill and Swalle for £10 in expenses, but such was their indifference to Wales that they were initially willing to offer him only £5, imagining that the work could well be carried out in Oxford. Finally they gave in, and

---

[10] One of Lhwyd's letters found Aubrey at an appropriately imaginative lodging in London ('For Mr. Aubrey at the Tobacco Roll and Sugar Loaf, Maydenhead Lane'), and contained a complaint about public ignorance of the new 'scientific' institutions that were beginning to appear: 'The people at Oxford do not yet know what ye Musaeum is, for they call ye whole buylding ye Labradary or Knaccatory and distinguish no further' (*Life and Letters of Edward Lhwyd*, 134).

Lhwyd spent two intensive months in Wales in the summer of 1693 and wrote up his contributions within the year.[11]

Without a doubt Lhwyd's 'Additions' to the Welsh counties are outstanding; indeed they transform this part of *Britannia* from a fairly inadequate sketch of unfamiliar terrain to the most rewarding part of the whole volume. Camden did not know Wales, and he was primarily interested in trying to associate existing place-names with stations on the Antonine Itinerary (often by means of etymological similarities) and locating the tribal areas mentioned in Ptolemy's *Geography*. He made extensive use of Giraldus Cambrensis's *Description of Wales*, written in the late twelfth century (which he had printed in his 1602 edition of early chronicles) but he was rather short of modern information about the province. Lhwyd's long familiarity with the central counties of Wales, improved by his antiquarian tour and supplemented by a purposeful correspondence with gentlemen, clergy, and schoolmasters in those parts he could not reach, meant that he could offer a much more comprehensive commentary than Camden. He also made good use of the unpublished 'Description of Pembrokeshire' by the Elizabethan chorographer George Owen, a work notable for its early attention to the geology of a region; this had been available to Camden, but Lhwyd was able to take better advantage of it because he knew the land in greater detail.

Lhwyd's 'Additions' to the Welsh counties are commonly longer than the original entries, and he often develops an observation into a brief disquisition upon a topic, so one can well understand why Thomas Hearne thought that Lhwyd's contributions were quite the best feature of the work.[12] Understandably Lhwyd is inclined to work his way back into the past by means of etymology. Welsh is the surviving form of the ancient British language, so Lhwyd had a greater title than most antiquaries to riddle out the traces of primitive meaning in place-names and topographical terms. For example, he remarks of the river Wye:

[11] Lhwyd asked for £10 for travel plus twenty copies of the *Britannia* upon publication, and the publishers did eventually agree to this, after trying to beat down his request by half. The 1695 *Britannia* was sold at £1.12.00 a copy, with 6/- asked for the binding.

[12] *Remarks and Collections of Thomas Hearne*, ed. C. E. Doble *et al.* (Oxford Historical Society, 1885–1915) i. 217.

The British name of this river is Wysk, which word seems a derivative from Gwy or Wy. . . . At present it is not significative in the British; but is still preserv'd in the Irish tongue, and is their common word for water. There were formerly in Britain many rivers of this name, which may now be distinguished in England by these shadows of it, *Ex, Ox, Ux, Ouse, Esk,* etc. Because such as are unacquainted with etymological observations, may take this for a groundless conjecture; that it is not such will appear, because in Antonine's Itinerary we find Exeter called *Isca Danmoniorum* from its situation on the River Ex, and also a city upon this river Usk (for the same reason) called Isca Leg. II.[13]

Confronting the mysterious pyramidal heaps of stones found on many Welsh mountains, some of considerable size, Lhwyd explicates the meaning of the word 'kairn', narrates how cairns are still built up over the graves of malefactors and suicides in his own time, suggests that this custom was formerly widely observed and not restricted to outcasts, shows from Virgil that cairns marked honourable places of burial in Roman times, insists that the practice of accumulating stones over a grave was far older and more widespread than the Roman Empire (for cairns occur in Ireland and Scotland), and speculates that the huge cairns on Plinlimmon—'a hundred cart-load of stones'—were the pre-Christian funeral monuments of the chieftains of a tribe. Here is a spacious, imaginative mind at work, using language, literature, customs, and fieldwork to interpret a practice which has persisted over thousands of years.

Edward Lhwyd makes an important methodological advance in his Welsh Additions, a simple but significant way of presenting information about material remains: he gives extremely specific details of structures or objects, indicating their dimensions and condition, describing what was found with or near them and at what depth, and noting who has possession of removable items. So, for example, he gives a minute account of a tessellated pavement found in 1689 in the garden of Mr Francis Ridley, near Monmouth:

[13] 'Additions' to Brecknockshire in Camden, *Britannia* (1695), col. 592. Likewise Lhwyd notes that the word 'Taw' appears variously in many Welsh river names and speculates that it may have been a defunct British word for water or river; perhaps 'the Britains might call that river Tav, Tavwy or Tavwys, before the Roman Conquest; which they afterwards called Tamesis' (Caer-Mardhin-Shire, ibid. col. 625). He supplies several examples of the phonetic process by which the Romans Latinized British words.

he notes the size of the tesserae, the materials and colours, and records the pattern and the images in the decoration. He is particular in his description of finds of coins, giving details of the emperors' heads. He describes Roman bricks found at Caerleon bearing a legionary hallmark, 'not inscribed but stamped with some instrument', which suggest the presence of an army brickworks there. He gives a specific account of Roman copper ingots, and describes a number of Roman brooches and shows how they fastened. This kind of information is of enduring value, and allows later generations of antiquarians and archaeologists to make use of his material. When he does not understand what he is looking at, such as a peculiar layout of stones, or an inscription of meaningless letters or symbols, he will none the less describe it accurately in the hope that a later scholar will make use of it, and in many cases he actually provides illustrations of the stones he has encountered.

Indeed, he makes more intelligent use of illustration than any of the other contributors, to record a wide variety of odd objects that have been unearthed. Here is the enigmatic statue found near Caerleon, made of alabaster, of 'a person in a coat of mail, holding in the right hand a short sword, and in the left a pair of scales,' on which are balanced a maiden's head and breasts, and a globe: 'we must leave the explication to some more experienced and judicious Antiquary;' but a good illustration is placed on record. Painted or embossed vases and plates are also recorded, whose 'elegant figures . . . might be made use of for the illustration of Roman authors'; Roman beads and jewellery are also accurately sketched in his plates, providing models by which future finds might be identified.

Accomplished Roman scholar as he was, Lhwyd's most important advances were made in the field of British antiquities, and he made it clear in his contribution to the *Britannia* that the scale of British remains was far greater than had yet been imagined. Monoliths, triliths, stone circles, stone enclosures of various forms, horizontal stones, cairns, barrows, tumuli, and earthworks are presented as the remains of a complex and technically proficient society which flourished in the British Isles before the Romans, and which may have formed part of a wider pre-historic culture that extended across Europe: 'I think it probable, should we make diligent enquiry, that there may be Monuments of this kind still extant in the less frequented places of Germany, France and Spain; if not also

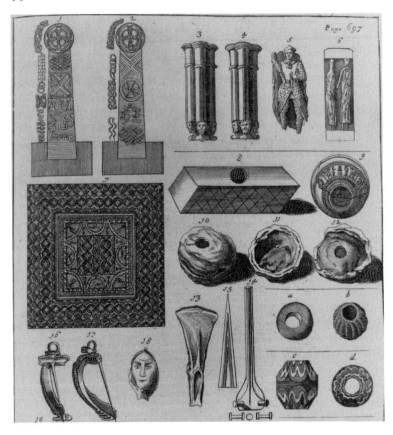

16. An illustration from the 1695 *Britannia* showing miscellaneous antiquities, including Celtic crosses, a mosaic pavement, a bronze axehead, brooches for fastening cloaks, and adder-beads or druid amulets.

in Italy.'[14] His own diligent enquiry had located many such sites, hitherto unnoticed, many of which were in the last stages of disintegration. In Gower, for instance, at the Kevn Bryn circle, the great stone in the centre

is much diminished . . . as having five tuns or more broke off it to make mill-stones. I guess the stone originally to have been between 25 and 30 tuns in weight. The carriage, rearing and placing of this massy rock is plainly an effect of human industry and art; but the pulleys and levers, the force and skill by which 'twas done, are not so easily imagined.[15]

He is fully persuaded that these stone monuments are the work of the ancient British, and erected long before the Roman occupation. Their rudeness conveys an evident antiquity, from a time before men had the use of iron. He has no reason to believe that the Saxons or Danes built these piles, for their number and magnitude indicate they were the work of long-settled communities: 'such vast perennial memorials seem rather to be the work of a people settled in their own country, than of such roving pirates.'[16]

These conclusions were his own, formed by observation and reflection. He had read Aubrey's 'Templa Druidum' from the manuscript of 'Monumenta Britannica', as his notes several times acknowledge, and agreed with Aubrey's attribution of these stone complexes to the ancient British. He agreed too that many of them were sacred sites. But Lhwyd was his own man, and formed his views independently. Nor did he readily associate the Druids with these sanctuaries, as Aubrey had done, but kept an open mind about the possibility. Roman sources, after all, made Druids priests of woods and groves. Perhaps a clue to the function of these stone circles might be supplied from a Celtic source rather than a classical one, and Lhwyd cites an early Life of St Patrick to telling effect. He is discussing the great circle called Y Gromlech in Pembrokeshire (which had an eighteen-foot monolith at its centre, and 'a piece broken off, about ten foot long and five in breadth, which seems more than twenty oxen can draw'); he notes that

Irish historians call one of their chiefest idols *Cromcruach*, which remained till St. Patrick's time in the plain of Moy-sleuct in Brefin. This Idol is described to have been *auro et argento caelatum*, and said to be attended

[14] Pembrokeshire, ibid. col. 637.
[16] Pembrokeshire, ibid. col. 637.
[15] Glamorganshire, ibid. col. 620.

with twelve other Idols much less, all of brass, placed about him. *Cromcruach*, at the approach of St. Patrick, fell to the ground, and the lesser Idols sunk into the earth up to their necks.[17]

Lhwyd wonders if their story is not a memory of stone circles still in active use in historical times as 'a place of idolatrous worship'. Perhaps the standing stones *were* the idols, worshipped as gods. This would certainly be a fresh interpretation of the function of standing stones. He reinforces his belief with information supplied by the Scottish antiquary Dr James Garden of Aberdeen to John Aubrey, included in *Monumenta Britannica*, which tends to the same conclusion.

Lhwyd had much in common with Aubrey: a fascination with the ancient Britons, a fondness for natural history, a highly observant eye, and an uncommon talent for the cross-fertilization of ideas. Though both had speculative imaginations, Lhwyd was more methodical and disciplined, and kept fuller records. Concerning the relation of Druids to stone monuments, as proposed by Aubrey, Lhwyd, as mentioned, kept an open mind. He was willing, on etymological grounds, to follow Aubrey in believing that the stones at Kerrig y Drudion in Denbighshire were associated with Druidic ceremonies. He conceived of the Druids as a working priesthood spread across the Celtic world, but certainly not possessed of any mysterious powers. However, he believed that superstitions associated with Druidic practices might still linger on in Wales, and in a remarkable flight of imagination which Aubrey would have applauded, he suggests how a surviving curiosity of Welsh folklore may preserve 'a relic of the Druids' doctrine'. He records the widespread belief that around Midsummer's Eve, snakes gather in companies, and by communal hissing create a kind of bubble that then passes around one of the snakes, hardening into a ring as it comes off the tail. These rings, glass or earthen amulets, are held to be fortunate and to prosper the owner. They are known in Welsh as snake-rings, and 'I have seen at several places about twenty or thirty.' Lhwyd remembers Pliny's account of the magical snake-egg, created by 'the spittle and secretion of angry snakes' that the Druids used to ensure good fortune, and proposes that the snake-rings prized by the Welsh (which he thinks are Roman beads) are a

[17] Pembrokeshire, ibid. col. 637.

similar phenomenon and a vestige of Druidic religion.[18] Who is to say he is wrong?

In his extensive contributions, Lhwyd did more than any of his predecessors to enlarge understanding of the societies that inhabited the land before the Romans. He moved away from a dependence on classical sources, with their fairly repetitive information based on limited contact, and formed a picture from their material remains supplemented by folklore and the classical reports. He drew attention to the high degree of social organization and technical skill needed to erect the great stone complexes. He made it clear, too, that the British had considerable metal-working skills. In particular, he notes the discovery of several caches of weapons, axe-heads, bolts, daggers, and swords, made of brass (though they were obviously bronze) and is sure that they are British, not Roman. He links them to similar finds described in Robert Plot's *Staffordshire*, and gives an illustration of an axe-head, dagger, and hasp that we can recognize as Bronze-Age implements. Lhwyd's comments here show the mental effort involved in getting round the idea that the Romans were the sole exponents of civilization in the lands of northern Europe:

For my own part, I must confess, that for a long time I suspected these instruments Roman, supposing them too artifical to have been made by the Britains before the Romans civilized them; and that they were not swords, etc. but intended for some other uses. But seeing they had gold and silver coins before that time (as all Antiquaries allow) and that 'tis scarce questionable but that the golden Torquis described in the last County was theirs; and also that Pliny tells us the Druids cut down their Misseltoe with golden sickles: I know but they might have more arts than we commonly allow them, and therefore must suspend my judgement.[19]

Lhwyd illustrates some of these gold and silver coins of the British that bore no signs of any Roman influence, and could thereby deduce the existence of a moderately developed economic system. The long disquisition on torcs in Merionethshire pays tribute to the elaborate goldwork of the Britons, and as he investigates the etymology of the word 'torc', and finds analogies in languages, such as Irish, that were not in contact with Rome, he is emboldened to

---

[18] See Denbighshire, ibid. cols. 683–4. Pliny's account is in the *Natural History*, XXIX. iii. See also Stuart Piggott, *Druids*, 117–19.

[19] Caernarvonshire in Camden, *Britannia* (1695) col. 672.

think that perhaps the Latin language absorbed words from older languages, such as the Celtic group, and was not always in a position of linguistic hegemony over its subject nations.

Nor ought any one to think it absurd, that I thus endeavour to derive Latin words from the Welsh, seeing there are hundreds of words in that language, that agree in sound and signification with the Latin, which yet could not be borrowed from the Roman, for that the Irish retain the same, who must have been a colony of the Britains, long before the Roman conquest.[20]

Not the least of Lhwyd's achievements in the *Britannia* was creating a cultural space in which the society and productions of the ancient Britons could be admired as something different from and independent of classical civilization, which had hitherto over-shadowed all contiguous cultures.

All things Celtic attracted Lhwyd. He was possibly the first to recognize the characteristic patterns of braided interlace and knotwork as features of a culture that he could trace throughout Wales, northern England, Scotland and Ireland. He was unclear about the identity of this culture, as of the significance of the decoration, but he was struck by the frequency with which these designs occurred on early Christian monuments and sculpture, and he left an account of the style for the benefit of aftercomers who might make something of it. He described the 'certain endless knots' of a cross in Pembrokeshire, and the 'chequered carving' on a monument in Flintshire, and provided an accurate illustration of the latter. He linked his discoveries with similar examples depicted by Robert Plot in his *Staffordshire* (where Plot believed they were of Danish origin, a view that Lhwyd did not share) and with the Bewcastle Cross in Cumberland.

Lhwyd's researches for the *Britannia* emboldened him to undertake a work that would bring together his knowledge of Celtic languages and ancient British antiquities and his interest in natural history. In 1695, encouraged by a group of Welsh gentry, he issued a proposal for his 'Natural History and Antiquities of Wales' together with an 'Archaeologia Britannica' which would be a comprehensive account of Wales, historical, geographical, and philological. He would establish the affinities between the Welsh/British language and the Irish, Scottish, Cornish, and Breton

---

[20] Merionethshire, ibid. cols. 658–9.

tongues, and this would be the foundation of a study that would enquire into the existence of a common culture which prevailed in these regions in pre-Roman times. He issued a questionnaire, 'Parochial Queries', to gather information about his proposed topics from knowledgeable people all over Wales, and then set about his travels, for he believed above all in the importance of personal inspection of sites of interest. For several years he travelled intensively, going as far afield as the Scottish islands, Ireland, Cornwall, and Brittany, making his collections, and in 1707 he published his *Glossography*, the first part of his project. This book confirmed Lhwyd's pre-eminence as a Celtic philologist, but the other parts of his scheme, which would have formed a composite cultural survey of Welsh antiquity, failed to appear. The account of the antiquities, customs, traditions, and folklore of the Welsh, which could have complemented the linguistic material and thrown light on the mentality of the Celtic peoples of which the British were part, proved too difficult to compile. Nor could Lhwyd order his notes on all the monuments in Wales presumed to be British and raised no later than the Roman conquest. His details of Roman monuments in Wales, and those of the time of the British princes, remained in manuscript, as did his lists of inscriptions, his observations on ancient British coins and camps and burial places, and his extensive collections relating to the natural history of the region. Lhwyd endured the frustrating experience of so many antiquaries, of being overwhelmed by the volume of his collections. When he died in 1709, Thomas Hearne examined his papers and declared them to be 'undigested'. They were dispersed, and so in the end it was Lhwyd's contributions to the 1695 *Britannia* which best showed his remarkable gifts as an antiquarian.

While Wales, thanks to Lhwyd's 'Additions', came to be the most rewardingly described region of the updated Camden, Scotland was only modestly improved, by the attentions of Sir Robert Sibbald. In a nation where antiquaries were few, Sibbald was pre-eminent.[21] (The only comparable figure was Dr James Garden, the Professor of Divinity at Aberdeen, who was John Aubrey's prolific correspondent on highland customs and folklore, and an important commentator on pre-historic monuments in Scotland.[22]) Sibbald

[21] Sibbald's 'Life' may be found prefixed to his *History Ancient and Modern of Fife and Kinross* (1710).
[22] For an account of antiquarian activity in Scotland in the seventeenth century,

(1641–1722) was an Edinburgh physician who had devoted himself to the study of the Scottish past. Following the fashion of the last quarter of the seventeenth century for combining antiquities with natural history, he had compiled *Scotia Illustrata* (1684). This work was modelled on the Baconian design of Plot's *Oxfordshire* of 1676, with sections devoted to the virtue of the air and soil, to the geology of the land and its mineral wealth, descriptions of the products of Scotland, its flora and fauna and fossils, and an estimate of its people. The antiquarian content is modest. Sibbald's contributions to the *Britannia* were likewise biased towards natural history and geography. Camden in his treatment of Scotland had been primarily concerned to trace the remains of the Romans there, mainly in the lowlands where they had established camps and settlements beyond the Wall as a result of the campaigns of Julius Agricola in the first century. He had also been eager to discourse upon the Picts and to draw together the many references to that obscure nation by the writers of antiquity. Sibbald generally adds a 'descriptio' to Camden's county entries, seeking to emphasize the flourishing condition of modern Scotland, and he cannot be said to have advanced knowledge of Scottish antiquities in a way that was permanently valuable. Sibbald's interests as an antiquarian focused on representations of Scotland by the ancient geographers, and he mounts his hobby-horse in the discourse concerning 'The Thule of the Ancients', where he is able to review the extensive literature relating to this utmost limit of the world. He readily accepts Samuel Bochart's assertion that the Phoenicians had first discovered and named Thule, which, after copious citation and comparison, he concludes to be not Iceland nor Orkney nor Shetland, but the north-east part of Scotland. His views on Thule had already appeared in a separate publication of 1693, but their inclusion at the end of the *Britannia* gave that work a pleasing termination, for it indicated that this once unimaginably remote land was now a place of letters and learning.

The opinions offered by Sibbald were almost entirely the result of a scrutiny of ancient texts. He had little inclination for fieldwork,

see Mendyk, *Speculum Britanniae*, 213–22, where he traces the thin line of antiquarians from the late-Elizabethan chorographer Timothy Pont through the two Gardens, Robert and James, to Sibbald and his contemporaries, James Wallace the historian of Orkney and Martin Martin the Pliny of St Kilda (whose account Sibbald drew on extensively for the *Britannia* 'Additions').

preferring to remain in his library evaluating the writings of ancient historians and geographers. His cabinet of curiosities was an agreeable setting for the discussion of antiquarian matters. Like Camden in late-Elizabethan England, Sibbald in late-Stuart Scotland found it gratifying to demonstrate the involvement of his native country with the Roman Empire and, by extension, with classical culture, but he tended to do this by reporting information he had received, rather than by examining artefacts on site. He was however aware that the spirit of the age was in favour of fieldwork, even though it was not his forte. In the Preface to *Historical Enquiries Concerning the Roman Monuments and Antiquities in ... Scotland* (1707) he wrote,

Amongst the Sciences and Arts much improved in our time, the Archaeologie, that is the explication and discovery of Ancient Monuments, is one of the greatest use: for the ancients, by Triumphal Arches, Temples, Altars, Pyramids, Obelisks and Inscriptions upon them, and Medals, handed down to posterity the history, religion and policy of their times, and an account of the Sciences and Arts that flourished certainly in these times, of which records are not found. The only sure way to write history, is from the proofs that may be collected from such monuments.

The conception of ancient civilization projected by 'Triumphal Arches, Temples, Altars, Pyramids, [and] Obelisks' is exalted and romanticized, far removed from the spoil-heaps and rusted fragments of a dig.

Sibbald in Edinburgh was no isolated antiquary. He was in correspondence with Edward Lhwyd, and entertained him when the latter came to Scotland in 1697 to gather materials for his 'Archaeologia Britannica'. Sibbald was also in touch with William Nicolson, who was working on the northern counties of England for the *Britannia*. The contributors to that project now formed a network across England and Scotland. Oxford and London were still the vital centres of antiquarian study, but now there were reputable antiquaries in every shire, communicating with one another, and bringing their notes, discourses and observations to the press, certain now that a sufficient audience existed for their works. This numerous tribe provided Edmund Gibson with the recruiting ground for his revised *Britannia*, which was truly the product of nationwide enquiry into the past, a fitting summary of the state of learning at the end of the great century of antiquarianism.

Conclusion

So, by the end of the seventeenth century, the various kinds of antiquarian activity—topographic, literary, legal, ecclesiastical, and archaeological—had made considerable progress in piecing together the many pasts of Britain. The legendary British History had largely been discredited as implausible and unsubstantiated, and the figure of Brutus would scarcely survive even among the fictions of the poets in the eighteenth century. Belief in the original settlement of Britain by biblically-derived groups, most notably the offspring of Japhet, would, however, persist as long as the Bible enjoyed its unquestioned status as the principal record of the early world. The primitive character of pre-Roman Britain was universally accepted by the time Gibson's edition of *Britannia* was published, and the insightful observations of Aubrey and Lhwyd would be rewardingly developed by William Stukeley in his *Stonehenge* (1740) and *Abury* (1743), books which preserved the details of his exceptional fieldwork at those sites, and presented his speculations about Ancient British society and religion.[1] Ever since William Dugdale had first drawn attention to a polished flint axe in his *Warwickshire* and suggested it might belong to a class of 'weapons used by the Britons before the art of making arms of brass or iron was known',[2] there was a growing willingness to recognize a gradual evolution of skills among the ancient British inhabitants of the island, although no very lengthy time-scale was envisaged for this development.

Clarification of the state of the Ancient Britons was only the first of those problems that were considered to belong to the domain of the antiquary in the seventeenth century. In practice, any aspect of society up to the Reformation was assumed to be of antiquarian interest, such was the looseness of definition associated with the subject. Indeed, when Humfrey Wanley was drawing up a scheme

---

[1] See Piggott, *William Stukeley*, (1985). Stukeley's contribution to our understanding of the British remains in Wiltshire still manages to impress, in spite of his extravagant opinions about the nature and content of Druidic belief.

[2] Dugdale, *Warwickshire*, 788.

for a revived Society of Antiquaries in 1707, he considered that all 'such things as shall precede the Raigne of James the first, King of England', were fair game for the antiquary.[3] One can say with some confidence that antiquarian enquiry was the most productive area of historical research in the seventeenth century, for the writing of history, as a form of narrative discourse, lagged far behind the compilation of antiquarian treatises in this period. These treatises, whether Camden on the ancient British coinage, Selden on tithes, Somner on Roman ports and forts, or Browne on urn-burial, were in fact the main avenues for the advancement of knowledge about the past in the seventeenth century, and they reached out in an impressive variety of directions, indicative of the intellectual enterprise of English scholars in the Stuart age.

Few phases of the history of Britain remained unvisited by the antiquaries. The Ancient British world, as we have remarked, was becoming both clearer and more complex as the seventeenth century progressed. The Roman occupation of Britain had been the initial focus of Camden's seminal book, and attention to Roman Britain never lapsed thereafter, though the focus slowly moved from the military to the cultural consequences of the occupation. Camden had begun the process by gathering together an anthology of remarks concerning Britain from a broad range of Latin writers, including poets, and had been able to infer much about the trade of the island, its special products, and the reputation of its inhabitants, as viewed from the Mediterranean. His introductory essay, 'The Romans in Britain', which formed part of the prefatory material of the *Britannia*, offered a balanced account of the military history of the occupation as it could be deduced from the Roman writers together with a description of a settled society exhibiting the benefits and amenities introduced by a superior culture.

Numerous later works reminded English readers of the presence across four centuries of a classical civilization in Britain. The several editions of John Stow's *Survay of London* drew attention to the remains of a great Roman town lying beneath the visible Elizabethan city. Edmund Bolton attempted to illustrate events from Romano-British history by means of Roman coins and medals in his *Nero Caesar* (1624 and 1627). Every volume of county history produced during the seventeenth century added to the

---

[3] Quoted in Evans, *Society of Antiquaries*, 36.

knowledge of the material evidences of Roman Britain. In the mid-century, William Burton renewed interest in the military layout of the province, and Thomas Browne reconstructed many of the civil ceremonies of Britain in his *Urn-Burial* and in miscellaneous tracts. In the masques at court in the reigns of James I and Charles I, Roman settings were applied to contemporary subjects to dramatize the felicitous idea that Stuart Englishmen were the rightful inheritors of a full classical culture. From the marriage masque *Hymenaei* of 1606 to *Britannia Triumphans* of 1638, images of Roman splendour on British soil were projected to the members of the court. The intellectual community in the reign of Charles II and his successors took the analogies between Roman Britain and their own society for granted in the Augustan ethos of the Restoration. The enlarged documentation of the 1695 *Britannia* consolidated the advances made in Roman studies, and paved the way for the compendious and magisterial work of John Horsley, *Britannia Romana*, in 1732.

Perhaps the most impressive achievements of the antiquarian movement in the seventeenth century lay in the clarification of the Saxon past. Here more than anywhere the blank spaces of history were filled in, because sustained interest in the Anglo-Saxon world resulted in the publication of numerous texts that previously had been inaccessible, or unknown. At the end of Elizabeth's reign, Saxon England was only faintly imaginable, and the language barely understood, but by 1700 the Saxon centuries had become filled with personalities and events, and the language had become familiar to a large body of scholars at Oxford and Cambridge. The curiosity about the Saxons aroused at the beginning of the century by Camden and Verstegan had been immensely productive. Impelled by the desire to know more about the conditions of the early Church and about a crucially formative phase of national identity, scholarship had progressed steadily. Selden, Spelman, and Ussher all appreciated the need for much fuller information about pre-Conquest institutions, and it was the concern particularly of Spelman and Ussher to give Saxon studies a secure base that led to the foundation of the Lectureship at Cambridge in 1640. Up to the Restoration, Anglo-Saxon was maintained by a thin line of notable scholars who could trace their intellectual lineage back to the circle around Archbishop Parker in the 1560s and 1570s. When the first holder of Spelman's

Lectureship, Abraham Wheelock, died in 1653, the funds were used to support the research of William Somner, and the eventual fruit of Spelman's initiative was the publication of Somner's Dictionary in 1659. Only then could Anglo-Saxon scholarship develop along a broader front as the language was finally made openly accessible to industrious students. The flourishing of Saxon studies in the Restoration period, so well described by David Douglas in his book *English Scholars*, was in large measure due to the stimulus provided by Somner's work.[4] By the end of the century the main corpus of Anglo-Saxon writing was in print, and the secular and religious history of a complicated age had been pieced together. The Anglo-Saxon Chronicle had been well edited, along with the Saxon version of Bede's Ecclesiastical History, by Wheelock. Francis Junius published an edition of the works of Caedmon in Amsterdam in 1655. The Saxon Heptateuch, the major hagiographies and several collections of Saxon laws were available. The Latin works of Gildas, Nennius, Bede, and Asser had all been ably edited. A new domain of scholarship had been established.

The other major area of scholarship to be opened up was monastic history, which received the attention of some of the most accomplished antiquaries of the century. It is ironic that one of the great triumphs of Protestant scholarship in the seventeenth century should have been the detailed reconstruction of the monastic movement that had been the principal casualty of the Reformation. Yet such was the case, and the work of Dodsworth, Dugdale, Tanner, and Wharton still to this day remains fundamental to the study of monasticism in Britain.

Scholarly reconstruction of the world of the monasteries gave rise to a pleasing development: illustration. Volume I of the *Monasticon* in 1655 was the first extensively illustrated antiquarian work. Verstegan's *Restitution* had a number of small engravings which had been drawn by the author, and which, in Anthony Wood's opinion, 'advantaged the sale of it much'. Those plates, though beautifully executed, are few and fanciful (except for the depiction of fossils). Weever's *Ancient Funerall Monuments* had a few pictures, mostly of brasses. The works of Selden, Spelman, and Ussher were almost devoid of illustration. Dugdale, however, recognized that illustration could greatly enhance understanding.

---

[4] Douglas, *English Scholars* (1943); see in particular ch. 3, 'The Saxon Past'.

The profusion of plates by Wenceslaus Hollar and Daniel King in the *Monasticon* reinforced the text by showing the magnificence of the buildings, and in some cases their poignant decay. Ground plans of monasteries, architectural details, even the costumes of the different orders brought home to the reader a fuller sense of the monastic movement than the reprinting of documents alone could have done.

The 1650s saw a sudden vogue for illustrated antiquities: Inigo Jones's *Stone-Heng* in 1655 (where most of the plates were imaginary reconstructions or geometric schemes), Dugdale's *Warwickshire* (1656) and *St. Paul's* (1658), Daniel King's book on Cheshire, *Vale-Royall of England* (1656), and his *Cathedrall and Conventuall Churches of England and Wales* (1656). Thereafter it became customary for books dealing with antiquities to contain engravings of a miscellaneous character, with the 1695 *Britannia* having an unusually diverse range, as well as a new sequence of county maps by Robert Morden.[5]

The increasing diversity of illustrated material went along with the steadily growing appreciation of the significance of objects and sites that marked the emergence of an archaeological mentality. This process was a lengthy one. The 1598 edition of Stow's *Survay of London* had contained an account of the excavation of a Roman cemetery in Spitalfields in 1576. Camden and Cotton had explored Hadrian's Wall for Roman remains in 1600, but they did not keep a record of the precise location of their finds. Inigo Jones had excavated at Stonehenge in 1620, again without keeping a serviceable record. Thomas Browne's description of his buried urns has an archaeological dimension, but it is obscured by rhetoric and moralizing. Aubrey practised a fairly consistent methodology when he surveyed Ancient British sites, but his findings were not published, and so did not have the influence they merited. Significantly, Aubrey was an early member of the Royal Society, and made a detailed presentation of his research at Avebury to the Society in 1663. The importance that the Royal Society gave to accurate measurement, specific data, and circumstantial evidence clearly had consequences in the antiquarian field, and when the new methodology was linked to an altered attitude to ancient

---

[5] For a useful brief account of antiquarian illustration, see Stuart Piggott, *Antiquity Depicted* (London, 1978).

remains, then the development of an archaeological approach to the past was possible. There had to be a recognition that all material remains could contribute to the understanding of the past. Even though they might appear insignificant, they carried a message. Potsherds were as important as gold cups, post-holes as pillars, but one needed to know exactly where they were found, and in what relation they lay to other objects. Robert Plot was prepared to cast an appraising eye over a wide range of remains, as he declared in the chapter 'Of Antiquities' in his *Natural History of Staffordshire*. He wrote of his design

to omit, as much as may be, both persons and actions, and chiefly apply my self to things; and amongst these too, only such as are very remote from the present Age, whether found under ground, or whereof there yet remain any footsteps above it, such as ancient Medalls, Ways, Lows, Pavements, Urns, Monuments of Stone, Fortifications, etc. whether of the ancient Britans, Romans, Saxons, Danes, or Normans. Which being all made and fashioned out of Natural things, may as well be brought under a Natural History as any thing of Art.[6]

Plot, however, did not document his works with the specificity one would have expected from a man who associated himself with Royal-Society values, nor did he have any profitable methodology for his research. The systematic description and assessment of sites and artefacts would not come until the eighteenth century, with William Stukeley as an early exponent of the new science.

The archaeological tendency was only incipient in the seventeenth century. Most antiquaries were concerned primarily with the written records of the past, and operated from bases where the written word was paramount: the Church, the Law, the Heralds' Office, and towards the end of the century, the universities. All these institutions had a conservative bias, so it can be no surprise that the majority of antiquaries were themselves of a conservative as well as of a conservationist character, and they were slow to adopt new methods of enquiry.

Looking back over the century, one can recognize that there were several phases in the process of conserving and reconstructing the past. In the early days of Camden, Cotton, and the Society of Antiquaries, the mission was to piece together the fragments of England's past in order to make a coherent, critically sustainable

[6] Plot, *The Natural History of Staffordshire*, 392.

history of the nation, and elucidate the means by which its distinctive institutions came into being. Associated with this research was the need to document the long record of Christianity in Britain as part of the post-Reformation defence of the credentials of the Church of England. Ecclesiastical antiquarianism soon established itself as an exceptionally rewarding field because of the wealth of documents available and the continuous history of the subject. The immense vistas back into both biblical and classical antiquity opened up by Selden and Ussher were achievements of a high order that enabled well-educated Englishmen to understand their own national position in the long process of development of European society.

Concerned as they were with clarifying the early history of the Church and the growth of its institutions, many Stuart antiquaries were also conscious that the Church in their own day was physically deteriorating through neglect, and that there was a serious need to preserve a record of buildings, monuments, and inscriptions that were being casually or wilfully effaced. This motive fortified the activities of William Somner at Canterbury, of John Weever, William Dugdale, and all the transcribers of epitaphs and inscriptions. It also drove John Aubrey to begin his collections.

Worse than neglect was war. The hostilities that broke out in 1642 threatened ruin to cathedrals, castles, and country houses, and on occasion destroyed libraries and archives with a wantonness not seen since the dissolution of the monasteries. The Civil War gave an urgency to the recording of endangered objects. Dugdale's frenzied journeys around the country on the eve of the war were the most notable example of this activity, and Roger Dodsworth in Yorkshire redoubled his efforts to transcribe monastic papers, and to compile a documentary record of his county. Aubrey began his antiquarian career by attempting to keep notes on the devastations caused by war or Puritan zeal in the regions he knew best, Wiltshire and Oxfordshire. At Slaughterford in Wiltshire, for example,

Here is a prettie small Church, the most miserably handled that I ever saw, the very barres are taken out of the windowes by the fanatique rage of the late times; here have been two good South windowes, and the doores are gone and the paving, and it serves for any use, viz. Weavers. The font has gone to make a trough.[7]

---

[7] Quoted in O. L. Dick, *Aubrey's Brief Lives* (London, 1950), p. xxxvii.

In adverse times, the antiquarian spirit flourished. Thomas Lord Brudenell, a royalist imprisoned in the Tower during the Civil War, 'made extensive . . . collections by abstracting several of the records there deposited', and he may stand as a representative of lives circumscribed by war that found relief in antiquities.[8]

If publication of antiquarian material was untimely in the 1640s, in the 1650s it became a notable feature of the intellectual life of the Protectorate. Long-accumulated collections were finally released to the press. These works seem to have found a large audience, and one suspects they had a certain consolatory appeal for readers of a conservative cast of mind, with their evocation of lost worlds, often formal and ceremonious. Perhaps too the consciousness of recent radical changes in Britain sharpened curiosity about earlier societies that had grown and faded in this island.

With the Restoration, the revived Church of England again enjoyed scholarly support from antiquarians. Dugdale's completion of Spelman's *Concilia* in the 1660s strengthened the Church's sense of its own ancestry and canonical inheritance, while the second and third volumes of the *Monasticon* (1661 and 1673) added to the well-established tradition of ecclesiastical scholarship in England. Dugdale's researches were encouraged by Archbishop Sheldon, whose own antiquarian proclivities were further evidenced by the reconstructed Roman theatre he commissioned Wren to design as his leaving present to Oxford. A new generation of historically-minded clerics emerged in the Restoration, who applied their learning 'to discover in the past a church similarly independent of Rome and equally subjected to bishops'.[9] None of them had the intellectual stature or polymathic erudition of their formidable predecessors, but their works still command respect. Their most notable representatives were Edward Stillingfleet and Henry Wharton. Both were close to another Archbishop who was sympathetic to antiquarian studies, William Sancroft. Stillingfleet's *Origines Britanniae* was the last of the great scholarly defences of the Church of England's position as an authentically ancient and continuous institution, and he devoted his scholarship to elucidating the earliest era from the first plantation of Christianity to the

---

[8] *Sir William Dugdale*, ed. Hamper, 296. Antiquarian research had a known power to mitigate adversity: Raleigh had written *The History of the World* in the Tower, and Selden had prepared his edition of Eadmer during a term of imprisonment. [9] Douglas, *English Scholars* (1943), 252.

conversion of the Saxons. It is a fluently written folio full of judiciously deployed material provided by earlier antiquaries, and tinged with a critical spirit directed against 'Fabulous Antiquities' in Church history.[10] Wharton's great achievement was the publication in 1691 of *Anglia Sacra*, a two-volume compendium of documents bearing on the history of the Anglican sees which printed, often for the first time, a broad range of material from medieval chronicles relating to the cathedral churches that had formerly been monastic institutions, as well as early lives of bishops in the Saxon and Norman Church. By bringing together so much valuable source material and providing it with a context, he enabled scholars to undertake a comparative study of English medieval chronicles dealing with the affairs of the Church. In conjunction with the ecclesiastical works of Spelman, Ussher, and Dugdale, *Anglia Sacra* made possible a broad and detailed understanding of the English Church across Saxon and medieval times: its history, laws, economic basis, administrative structure, and its politics could all be reconstructed.

The grand comprehensive titles of the antiquarian works of the seventeenth century speak of the assurance of generations of scholars as they confronted the complexity of the past, confident they could bring definition to subjects that were profoundly obscure or misunderstood, by the application of their tireless scholarship, and by their passion for antiquity. The ambitious projects of the men whose work has been surveyed in this book can intimidate a modern reader by their scope and grandeur; yet the achievements of the antiquaries matched their ambitions. By the end of the century the nation's past, so recently a *terra incognita*, had become an atlas full of detailed maps. Though there was still much speculation, yet there had been a remarkable increase of knowledge and understanding. A restitution of decayed intelligence in antiquities, to recall Verstegan's phrase, had indeed taken place.

---

[10] For example, Stillingfleet doubted the story of Joseph of Arimathea, was sceptical about the historicity of King Arthur, and would not accept the tradition that King Alfred had been the founder of Oxford University.

Select Bibliography

PRIMARY SOURCES

ASHMOLE, ELIAS, *The Institution, Laws and Ceremonies of the Most Noble Order of the Garter* (1672).

AUBREY, JOHN, *The Natural History of Wiltshire*, ed. John Britton (London, 1847; repr. Newton Abbot, 1969).

—— *Brief Lives*, ed. A. Clark (2 vols.; Oxford, 1898).

—— *Three Prose Works*, ed. John Buchanan-Brown (Fontwell, 1972).

—— *Monumenta Britannica* ed. John Fowles and Rodney Legg (parts 1–3; Sherborne, 1980–2).

BERNARD, NICHOLAS, *The Life and Death of . . . Dr. James Ussher* (1656).

'BEROSUS BABILONICUS', *Antiquitates* (Paris, 1510).

BOCHART, SAMUEL, *Geographia Sacra* (Paris, 1646).

BOLTON, EDMUND, *Hypercritica, or a Rule of Judgment for Writing or Reading our Histories*, in *Critical Essays of the Seventeenth Century*, ed. J. E. Spingarn (3 vols.; Oxford, 1907), i.

BROWNE, THOMAS, *The Works of the learned Sir Thomas Browne* (1686).

—— *The Works of Sir Thomas Browne*, ed. Charles Sayle (3 vols.; Edinburgh, 1904–7).

—— *The Letters of Sir Thomas Browne*, ed. Geoffrey Keynes (London, 1946).

BURTON, WILLIAM (1575–1645), *The Description of Leicestershire* (1622).

BURTON, WILLIAM (1609–1657), *A Commentary on Antoninus his Itinerary* (1658).

CAMDEN, WILLIAM, *Reges, Reginae, Nobiles et alii in Ecclesia Collegiata B. Petri Westmonasterii Sepulti* (1600).

—— *Anglica, Normannica, Hibernica, Cantabrica a Veteribus Scripta* (Frankfurt, 1602).

—— *Britannia*, trans. Philemon Holland (1610).

—— *Britannia*, ed. E. Gibson (1695).

—— *Remains Concerning Britain*, ed. R. D. Dunn (Toronto, 1984).

—— *Epistolae*, ed. T. Smith (1691).

CAREW, RICHARD, *The Survey of Cornwall* (1602).

CHARLETON, WALTER, *Chorea Gigantum, or Stone-Heng Restored to the Danes* (1663).

COMMELIN, H., *Rerum Britannicarum Scriptores Vetustiores* (Heidelberg, 1587).

COTTON, ROBERT, *Cottoni Posthuma*, ed. J. Howell (1651).

D'EWES, SIMONDS, *The Autobiography and Correspondence of Sir Simonds D'Ewes*, ed. J. O. Halliwell (2 vols.; 1845).

DRAYTON, MICHAEL, *Poly-Olbion*, in *The Works of Michael Drayton*, ed. J. W. Hebel (5 vols.; Oxford, 1933).

DUGDALE, WILLIAM, *Monasticon Anglicanum* (1655, 1661, 1673, Eng. trans. 1718).

—— *The Antiquities of Warwickshire* (1656).

—— *The History of St. Paul's Cathedral* (1658).

—— *The History of Imbanking and Drayning of Divers Fens and Marshes* (1662).

—— *Origines Juridiciales* (1666).

—— *The Baronage of England* (1675–6).

—— *The Life, Diary and Correspondence of Sir William Dugdale*, ed. W. Hamper (1827).

EARLE, JOHN, *Micro-Cosmographie* (1628).

EVELYN, JOHN, *The Diary of John Evelyn*, ed. E. S. de Beer (6 vols.; Oxford, 1955).

FORTESCUE, JOHN, *De Laudibus Legum Angliae*, ed. J. Selden (1616).

FOXE, JOHN, *Actes and Monuments of these latter and perillous dayes, touching matters of the church* (2 vols.; 1610).

FULLER, THOMAS, *The Holy State* (1642).

—— *The Church History of Britain* (1655).

—— *The Worthies of England* (1662).

GASSENDI, P., *The Mirror of True Nobility*, trans. W. Rand (1657).

GUNTON, SYMON, *The History of the Church of Peterburgh* (1686).

HACKET, JOHN, *Scrinia Reserata* (1693).

HARRISON, WILLIAM, *The Description of England*, ed. George Edelen (Ithaca, NY, 1968).

HEARNE, THOMAS, *A Collection of Curious Discourses*, (Oxford, 1720); ed. J. Ayloffe (2 vols.; 1773).

—— *Remarks and Collections of Thomas Hearne*, ed. C. E. Doble *et al.* (10 vols.; Oxford, 1884–1915).

HOLLAND, HENRY, *Monumenta Sepulchralia Sancti Pauli* (1614 and 1633).

JONES, INIGO, *The Most Notable Antiquity of Great Britain Vulgarly Called Stone-Heng Restored* (1655).

KING, DANIEL, *The Cathedrall and Conventuall Churches of England and Wales Orthographically Delineated* (1656).

LAMBARDE, WILLIAM, *Archaionomia* (1568).

—— *A Perambulation of Kent* (1576).

LEIGH, CHARLES, *The Natural History of Lancashire, Cheshire and the Peak in Derbyshire* (1700).

LELAND, JOHN, *The Itinerary*, ed. Lucy Toulmin Smith (5 vols.; Fontwell, 1964).

LHWYD, EDWARD, *Archaeologia Britannica: Glossography* (1707).
—— *The Life and Letters of Edward Lhwyd*, ed. R. T. Gunther, *Early Science in Oxford* (Oxford, 1945).
LLUYD, HUMPHREY, *The Breviary of Britayne*, trans. T. Twyne (1573).
MILTON, JOHN, *The History of Britain* (1670; 2nd edn. 1677).
NICHOLAS, N. H., *A Memoir of Augustine Vincent* (1827).
NORDEN, JOHN, *Speculum Britanniae* (1593).
OGILBY, JOHN, *Britannia* (1675).
PARR, RICHARD, *The Life . . . of James Ussher* (1686).
PEACHAM, HENRY, *The Compleat Gentleman* (1634).
PEIRESC, NICHOLAS F. DE, *Lettres de Peiresc*, ed P. Tamizey de Larroque (7 vols.; Paris, 1888–98).
PLOT, ROBERT, *The Natural History of Oxfordshire* (1677).
—— *The Natural History of Staffordshire* (1686).
POWELL, THOMAS, *Directions for Search of Records* (1622).
RALEIGH, WALTER, *The History of the World* (1611).
ROWLANDS, HENRY, *Mona Antiqua Restaurata* (Dublin, 1723).
SAMMES, AYLETT, *Britannia Antiqua Illustrata* (1676).
SAVILE, HENRY (ed.), *Rerum Anglicarum Scriptores post Bedam* (1596).
SELDEN, JOHN, *Jani Anglorum Facies Altera* (1610).
—— *Titles of Honor* (1614).
—— *De Diis Syriis* (1617).
—— *The Historie of Tithes* (1618).
—— *Marmora Arundelliana* (1628).
—— *Mare Clausum* (1635).
—— *Opera Omnia*, ed. David Wilkins (3 vols.; 1726).
SHERINGHAM, ROBERT, *De Anglorum Gentis Origine Disceptatio* (1670).
SMITH, THOMAS, *Catalogus Librorum Manuscriptorum Bibliotecae Cottonianae* (1696).
—— *Catalogue of the Manuscripts in the Cottonian Library, 1696*, ed. C. G. C. Tite (Woodbridge, Suffolk, 1984).
SOMNER, WILLIAM, *The Antiquities of Canterbury* (1640).
—— *Dictionarium Saxonico-Latino-Anglicum* (1659).
—— *A Treatise of the Roman Ports and Forts in Kent*, ed. White Kennett (Oxford, 1693).
SPEED, JOHN, *The Theatre of the Empire of Great Britaine* (1611).
—— *The History of Great Britaine* (1611 and 1614).
SPELMAN, HENRY, *De Non Temerandis Ecclesiis* (1613 and 1646).
—— *Archaeologus. In Modum Glossarii ad Rem Antiquam Posteriorem* (1626).
—— *Concilia, Decreta, Leges, Constitutiones, in Re Ecclesiarum Orbis Britannici* (1639).
—— *De Sepultura* (1641).
—— *English Works*, ed. E. Gibson (1727).
—— *The History and Fate of Sacrilege* (1698).

Spelman, Henry, *Reliquiae Spelmanniae*, ed. E. Gibson (1727).

Sprat, Thomas, *The History of the Royal Society* (1667).

Stillingfleet, Edward, *Origines Sacrae* (1662).

—— *Origines Britannicae* (1685).

Stow, John, *The Survay of London* (1618).

Tanner, Thomas, *Notitia Monastica* (1695).

Torinus, G., *Itinerarium Provinciarum Omnium Antonini Augusti* (Paris, 1512).

Twyne, John, *De Rebus Albionicis* (1590).

Twysden, Roger, *Historiae Anglicanae Scriptores Decem* (1652).

Ussher, James, *A Discourse of the Religion Anciently Professed by the Irish and the British* (1631).

—— *Britannicarum Ecclesiarum Antiquitates* (1639).

—— *The Annals of the Old and New Testament* (1658).

—— *The Whole Works of the Most Rev. James Ussher*, ed. C. R. Elrington (17 vols.; Dublin, 1847–64).

Vergil, Polydore, *Anglica Historia* (1534).

Verstegan, Richard, *A Restitution of Decayed Intelligence in Antiquities* (Antwerp, 1605).

Ware, James, *The Historie of Ireland* (1633).

—— *De Hibernia et Antiquitatibus* (1654).

—— *Works Concerning Ireland* (2 vols.; 1739 and 1746).

Webb, John, *A Vindication of Stonehenge Restored* (1665).

Weever, John, *Ancient Funerall Monuments* (1631).

White, Richard, *Historiarum Britanniae* (11 vols.; Arras and Douai, 1597–1607).

Wood, Anthony, *Athenae Oxonienses* (2 vols.; 1691 and 1692).

Worm, Olaf, *Danicorum Monumentorum Libri Sex* (Copenhagen, 1643).

—— *Olai Wormis et ad eum Doctorum Virorum Epistolae* (Copenhagen, 1751).

Wortley, Francis, *Characters and Elegies* (1646).

Wright, Joseph, *Monasticon Anglicanum Epitomized in English* (1693).

SECONDARY SOURCES

Adams, E. W., *Old English Scholarship in England from 1566 to 1800* (New Haven, 1917).

Allen, D. C., *The Legend of Noah* (Urbana, 1949).

Atkinson, R. J. C., *Stonehenge* (London, 1956).

Berkowitz, David S., *John Selden's Formative Years* (Washington, 1988).

BINNS, J. W., *Intellectual Culture in Elizabethan and Jacobean England: the Latin Writing of the Age* (Leeds, 1990).

BOUGAERTS, THEO, *The Correspondence of Thomas Blount 1618–1679: A Recusant Antiquary* (Amsterdam, 1978).

BRINKLEY, R. F., *Arthurian Legend in the Seventeenth Century* (Baltimore, 1932).

BURKE, PETER, *The Renaissance Sense of the Past* (London, 1969).

BURTON, EDWARD, *The Life of John Leland* (London, 1896).

BUTT, J., 'The Facilities for Antiquarian Studies in the 17th Century', *Essays and Studies*, 24 (1938), 64–80.

CHIPPINDALE, C., *Stonehenge Complete* (London, 1983).

CHRISTIANSON, PAUL, 'Young John Selden and the Ancient Constitution, 1610–18', *Proceedings of the American Philosophical Society*, 128/4 (1984), 271–315.

COLLINGWOOD, R. G., and MYRES, J. N. L., *Roman Britain and the English Settlements* (Oxford, 1936).

CORBETT, MARGERY, 'The Title-Page and Illustrations to the *Monasticon Anglicanum 1655–1673*', *The Antiquaries' Journal* (1986), 102–9.

CORY, I. P., *The Ancient Fragments: The Phoenician Theology of Sanchoniathon; Berossus; Manetho* (1828).

CURTIUS, E. R., *European Literature and the Latin Middle Ages*, trans. W. R. Trask (New York, 1953).

DANIEL, GLYN, *The Origins and Growth of Archaeology* (Harmondsworth, 1967).

—— and RENFREW, COLIN, *The Idea of Prehistory* (Edinburgh, 1988).

DENHAM-YOUNG, N., and CRASTER, H., 'Roger Dodsworth and his Circle', *Yorkshire Archaeological Journal*, 32 (1934), 5–32.

DOUGLAS, DAVID, *English Scholars* (London, 1939; 2nd edn. 1943).

EMERY, FRANK, *Edward Lhuyd 1660–1709 FRS* (Cardiff, 1971).

—— 'Edward Lhuyd and the 1695 *Britannia*', in *Antiquity* (1958).

EVANS, JOAN, *A History of the Society of Antiquaries* (Oxford, 1956).

FERGUSON, ARTHUR B., *Clio Unbound* (Durham, NC, 1979).

FOX, LEVI (ed.), *English Historical Scholarship in the Sixteenth and Seventeenth Centuries* (London, 1956).

FUSSNER, F. SMITH, *The Historical Revolution: English Historical Writing and Thought, 1580–1640* (London, 1962).

GOTTFRIED, RUDOLPH, 'Antiquarians at Work', *Renaissance News*, 11 (1958), 114–20.

GRAFTON, ANTHONY, *Joseph Scaliger* (Oxford, 1983).

—— *Defenders of the Text* (Cambridge, Mass., 1991).

HALES, WILLIAM, *A New Analysis of Chronology* (4 vols.; 1830).

HALL, D. H., 'History of the Earth Sciences', *History of Science*, 14 (1976), 149–95.

HAMILTON, ALASTAIR, *William Bedwell the Arabist, 1563–1632* (Leiden, 1985).

HAVERFIELD, F. J., 'Julius F VI: Notes on Reginald Bainbrigg of Appleby, on William Camden and on some Roman Inscriptions', *Proceedings of the Cumberland and Westmorland Archaeological Society*, 11 (1911), 343–78.

HAY, DENYS, *Polydore Vergil* (Oxford, 1952).

—— *Annalists and Historians* (London, 1977).

HAYNES, D. E. L., *The Arundel Marbles* (Oxford, 1975).

HELGERSON, RICHARD, *Forms of Nationhood: the Elizabethan Writing of England* (Chicago, 1992).

HILL, CHRISTOPHER, *The Economic Problems of the Church* (Oxford, 1956).

—— *The Intellectual Origins of the English Revolution* (Oxford, 1965).

HOGDEN, M. T., *Early Anthropology in the Sixteenth and Seventeenth Centuries* (Philadelphia, 1964).

HONIGMANN, ERNST A. J., *John Weever* (Manchester, 1987).

HOUGHTON, WALTER E., 'The English Virtuoso in the 17th Century', *Journal of the History of Ideas*, 3 (1942), 51–73, 190–219.

HOWARTH, DAVID, *Lord Arundel and his Circle* (New Haven, 1985).

—— 'Sir Robert Cotton and the Commemoration of Famous Men' in the *British Library Journal*, 18/1 (1992).

HUDDESFORD, WILLIAM, *The Lives of those Eminent Antiquaries John Leland, Thomas Hearne and Anthony Wood* (2 vols.; Oxford, 1772).

HUNTER, MICHAEL, 'The Royal Society and the Origins of British Archaeology', *Antiquity*, 65 (1971), 113–21, 178–91.

—— *Science and Society in Restoration England* (Cambridge, 1981).

—— *John Aubrey and the Realm of Learning* (London, 1975).

JAYNE, SEARS, *Library Catalogues of the English Renaissance* (London, 1956).

JESSUP, FRANK W., *Sir Roger Twysden 1597–1672* (London, 1965).

JOHNSON, G. W., *Memoirs of John Selden* (1835).

JOSTEN, C. H. (ed.), *Elias Ashmole (1617–1692): His Autobiographical and Historical Notes, his Correspondence and Other Contemporary Sources Relating to his Life and Work* (Oxford, 1966).

KENDRICK, THOMAS D., *British Antiquity* (London, 1950; repr. 1970).

KLIGER, SAMUEL, *The Goths in England* (Cambridge, Mass., 1952).

KNOX, R. BUICK, *James Ussher, Archbishop of Armagh* (Cardiff, 1967).

LEVINE, JOSEPH M., *Dr. Woodward's Shield* (Berkeley, Calif., 1977).

—— *Humanism and History* (Ithaca, 1987).

LEVY, F. J., *Tudor Historical Thought* (San Marino, Calif., 1967).

—— 'The Making of Camden's *Britannia*', *Bibliothèque d'Humanité et de la Renaissance*, 26 (1964), 70–97.

MacDougall, Hugh A., *Racial Myth in English History: Trojans, Teutons and Anglo-Saxons* (Hanover, NH, 1982).

MacGregor, Arthur, *Tradescant's Rarities: Essays on the Foundation of the Ashmolean Museum 1683* (Oxford, 1983).

McKisack, May, *Medieval History in the Tudor Age* (Oxford, 1971).

Marsh, Henry, *Dark Age Britain* (London, 1970).

Mendyk, Stan E., *Speculum Britanniae: Regional Study, Antiquarianism and Science in Britain to 1700* (Toronto, 1989).

Momigliano, A., *Studies in Historiography* (London, 1966).

Mosshammer, Alden A., *The Chronicle of Eusebius and Greek Chronographic Tradition* (Lewisburg, 1979).

Newdigate, B. H., *Michael Drayton and his Circle* (Oxford, 1961).

Oates, J. C. T., *Cambridge University Library: A History*, i (Cambridge, 1986).

Parry, Graham, 'Wenceslaus Hollar, the Antiquarians' Illustrator', *Ariel*, (Apr. 1972).

—— *Hollar's England: A Mid-Seventeenth-century View* (Salisbury, 1980).

—— *The Seventeenth Century: The Intellectual and Cultural Context of English Literature 1603–1700* (Harlow, 1989).

Pattison, Mark, *Isaac Casaubon* (1875).

Pennington, Richard, *A Descriptive Catalogue of the Etched Work of Wenceslaus Hollar 1607–1677* (Cambridge, 1982).

Piggott, Stuart, *The Druids* (London, 1975).

—— *Ruins in a Landscape* (Edinburgh, 1976).

—— *Antiquity Depicted: Aspects of Archaeological Illustration* (London, 1978).

—— *William Stukeley* (London, 1950; rev. edn. 1985).

—— 'Sir Thomas Browne and Antiquity', *Oxford Journal of Archaeology* (1988), 257–69.

—— *Ancient Britons and the Antiquarian Imagination* (London, 1989).

Pocock, J. G. A., *The Ancient Constitution and the Feudal Law: English Historical Thought in the Seventeenth Century* (Cambridge, 1957).

Popkin, R. H., *Isaac Lapeyrère* (Leiden, 1987).

Powell, Anthony, *John Aubrey and his Friends* (London, 1948).

Powicke, F. M., 'Sir Henry Spelman and the *Concilia*', *Proceedings of the British Academy*, 16 (1931), 1–37; repr. in *Studies in History*, ed. Lucy Sutherland (London, 1966).

Rivet, A. L. F., and Smith, Colin, *The Place Names of Roman Britain* (London, 1979).

Rossi, P., *The Dark Abyss of Time* (Chicago, 1984).

Shapiro, Barbara J., *Probability and Certainty in Seventeenth-Century England* (Princeton, 1983).

Sharpe, Kevin, *Sir Robert Cotton 1586–1631* (Oxford, 1979).

SOMMERVILLE, J. P., 'John Selden, the Law of Nature and the Origins of Government', *Historical Journal*, 27 (1984), 437–47.

—— *Politics and Ideology in England 1603–40* (Harlow, 1986).

SYKES, N., *Edmund Gibson* (London, 1926).

THOMAS, KEITH, *Religion and the Decline of Magic* (London, 1971).

TOULMIN, S., and GOODFIELD, J., *The Discovery of Time* (London, 1965).

TREVOR-ROPER, HUGH, *Renaissance Essays* (London, 1985).

—— *Catholics, Anglicans and Puritans* (London, 1987).

—— *From Counter-Reformation to Glorious Revolution* (London, 1992).

TUCK, RICHARD, ' "The Ancient Law of Freedom": John Selden and the Civil War', *Reactions to the English Civil War*, ed. J. S. Morrill (1982), 137–61.

UCKO, PETER, HUNTER, M., CLARK, A., and DAVID, A. (eds.), *Avebury Reconsidered* (London, 1991).

VAN DORSTEN, J. A., *Poets, Patrons and Professors: Sir Philip Sidney, Daniel Rogers and the Leiden Humanists* (Leiden, 1962).

VAN EERDE, KATHERINE, *John Ogilby and the Taste of his Times* (Folkstone, 1976).

VAN NORDEN, L., 'The Elizabethan College of Antiquaries', Ph.D. thesis (University of California, Los Angeles, 1946).

—— 'Peiresc and the English Scholars', *Huntington Library Quarterly*, 12/4 (1948–9), 369–90.

—— 'Sir Henry Spelman on the Chronology of the Elizabethan College of Antiquaries', *Huntington Library Quarterly*, 13 (1949–50), 131–60.

WAGNER, ANTHONY, *Heralds of England: a History of the Office and College of Arms* (London, 1967).

WALTERS, GWYN and EMERY, FRANK, 'Edward Lhuyd, Edmund Gibson and the Printing of Camden's *Britannia*, 1695', *The Library*, 5th series, 32 (1977), 109–37.

WARNICKE, RETHA, *William Lambarde, Elizabethan Antiquary, 1536–1601* (Chichester, 1973).

WEBSTER, CHARLES (ed.), *The Intellectual Revolution of the Seventeenth Century* (London, 1974).

WEISS, ROBERTO, *The Renaissance Discovery of Classical Antiquity* (Oxford, 1969).

WILLIAMS, F. B., *Index of Dedications and Commendatory Verses in English Books before 1641* (London, 1962).

WOOLF, D. R., *The Idea of History in Early Stuart England* (Toronto, 1990).

WORMALD, F., and WRIGHT, C. E., *The English Library Before 1700* (London, 1958).

Index

Abbot, George, Archbishop of
  Canterbury 167, 223 n.
Abraham 126, 145, 240
Adamnanus 136
Aelfric 187
Africanus, Sextus Julius 143–4
Agarde, Arthur 44, 78, 159 n.
Ailred of Rievaulx 227 n.
Alfred, King 41, 210, 366 n.
Allen, Thomas 17, 261–2
Alured 172
Ambrose, St 121
Ammianus Marcellinus 319
Ancient Britons 20, 23 n., 28–32, 45,
  290, 296, 305, 349–55, 358; Aubrey
  on 290; Camden on 28–32; Selden
  on 99–103
Andrewes, Lancelot 115, 123, 168, 172
Anglo-Saxon 54–6, 49, 64–8, 81, 150,
  171–2, 223, 344; revival of 2, 4,
  150, 181, 184–7, 360–1
Anglo-Saxon Chronicle 42, 331, 339,
  361
Anne, Queen 4
Annius of Viterbo 55, 99, 323
Anstis, John 225 n.
Antonine Itinerary 23, 39, 55 n., 249,
  262–7, 333, 340, 344, 347, 348
Appian 319
archaeology 39, 243, 250–8, 282–3,
  287–92, 299, 348–55, 362–3
Archer, Sir Simon 187, 219, 226,
  241, 272
Arianism 35
Arminianism 140–1
Arrian 319
Arthur, King 47
Arundel, Earl of, *see* Howard, Thomas
Ashmole, Elias 6, 154, 187, 224,
  235 n., 245, 248, 273–4
Ashmolean Museum 301, 331, 345
Asser 42, 81, 361
Athelstan 172
Aubrey, John 7, 12, 13, 14, 15, 16–17,
  19, 33, 47, 74, 216, 228, 240, 247,
  259, 275–307, 334, 339, 355, 357,

362, 364; and architecture 297–8;
and Avebury 287–9, 299, 337; and
Dugdale 247, 274–8, 291 n.; and
Lhwyd 346, 351–2; and Wood 298;
and 1695 *Britannia* 334, 337, 339.
Miscellanies 300; 'Monumenta
Britannica' 281–92, 297, 337, 351;
'Natural History of Wiltshire'
278–81, 287, 296; 'Remains of
Gentilism' 292–7; 'Wiltshire
Antiquities' 278, 281, 290
Augustine of Canterbury, St.
  141 n., 170, 184, 196, 215, 232, 270
Augustine of Hippo, St. 121, 140, 310
Avebury 19, 287–9, 299, 329

Babel 32, 45, 53, 59, 65
Backhouse, William 238
Bacon, Sir Francis 30, 93, 152, 278,
  301–2, 304–6, 325
Bacon, Sir Nicholas 240
Bainbridge, Reginald 92
Baker, Father Augustine 52 n., 70
Bale, John 2, 27, 49, 56, 57 n., 78, 154,
  320 n.
Barclay, John 8 n.
Bards 31, 110–12, 155, 290, 317
Barlow, Thomas 187, 238, 246
'Battle of Maldon' 82
Beauchamp, Sir John 211
Bede 34, 42, 80–1, 170, 181 n., 266–7,
  269, 361
Bedwell, William 115–16, 150
Benedictines 70–1, 232, 272
Benlowes, Edward 237
Beowulf 81
Bernard, Nicholas 153
Berosus 9, 55–7, 316, 319, 323
Bini, Severinus 168 n., 170
Bisse, James 337
Blount, Thomas 241 n.
Boadicea 25, 29, 103, 252, 282, 327
Bochart, Samuel 154, 310–13,
  324–5, 329, 356
Bodenham, Wingfield 238
Bodin, Jean 114

Bodleian Library 153, 222, 262, 337, 343
Bodley, Sir Thomas 79, 132–3
Bolton, Edmund 41 n., 282, 359
Boyle, Robert 301
Boys, John 187
Brehon Law 153
Bridgeman, Orlando 187
Bromley, William 15 n.
Brooke, Ralph 200
Browne, Sir Thomas 14, 16, 64, 195, 216, 249–61; *Urn-Burial* 19, 249–58, 260, 360, 362; *Garden of Cyrus* 258; 'Repertorium' 259; and Dugdale 243–4, 256–8; and Evelyn 258–9; on Phoenicians 311 n.
Browne, William *Britannia's Pastorals* 20, 113 n., 199
Brudenell, Thomas, Lord 365
Brutus 10, 26, 53, 60, 62, 72, 99, 108, 215, 315, 316
Buchanan, George 76 n., 84
Burton, William 19, 249, 260–7, 340, 359; *Antonine Itinerary* 260–7; and Ussher 263–6
Burton, William 336; *Description of Leicestershire* 43 n., 202, 219, 241
Bysshe, Edward 241 n.

Caedmon 150, 361
Caesar, Julius 25, 28, 31, 90, 102–3, 109, 111, 215, 291, 313–15, 317
Caius, John 271
Camden, William 1, 3, 5, 6, 8, 9, 13, 16, 21, 22–48, 78, 127, 174, 200, 227, 261–3, 272, 282, 285, 289, 309, 320, 344; *Annals* 76; *Britannia* 1, 3, 5, 6, 8, 9, 12, 13, 20, 22–48, 100, 108, 133, 190, 198, 200, 242, 274, 288 n.; *1695 Britannia* 331–57; *Epistolae* 4 n., 26, 335; *Reges* 211; *Remains* 37–8, 54–7, 67–8, 75, 199, 203, 210, 214; and the Ancient Britons 28–32, 298; and the British History 26–8; and chronicles 75; and coins 30; as herald 42; as poet 332 n.; and Roman Occupation 33–6; and Saxons 37–8, 40, 41; and Stonehenge 41; relations with Cotton 39, 43, 45 n., 70, 72–5, 77; with Ortelius 22–3; with Peiresc 8; with Spelman 44; with Ussher 133
Campion, Edmund 134, 135 n., 154
canon law 122, 166–7

Canterbury 14, 181–9, 309, 341, 325
Canute, King 172
Capella, Martianus 120
Caracalla, Emperor 264
Carew, George 78, 241
Carew, Richard 43 n., 46, 66
Carey, George 71
Carleton, George 118
Carr, Robert, Earl of Somerset 86
Cartismunda 103
Cartwright, William 180
Casaubon, Isaac 8, 26, 119 n., 152, 185
Casaubon, Meric 8, 185–6
Cecil, Robert 102
Cecil, William 41, 79
Celestius 137
Celts 36, 314, 316, 351–5
Charles I, King 18, 19, 61, 124, 125, 140, 163, 169, 178, 243, 268
Charles II, King 19, 243, 286–7, 301
Charleton, Walter 81, 299; *Chorea Gigantum* 7, 19, 69, 284–6, 306
Charlett, Arthur 225 n., 300, 332 n.
chariots 321, 327
Chaucer, Geoffrey 82, 198
Chetwynd, Walter 241 n.
Chiflet, Jean Jacques 255–6
Childeric 255
Chippenham 40
Christianson, Paul 10, 105, 121
Christmas, Gerard 209
chronograms 213
chronology 15, 19, 127, 143–9, 249
Clapham, Margaret 238
Clarendon, Lord 223
Claudian 33
Claudius, Emperor 33, 34, 257–8, 303, 323
Clifford, Lady Anne 211
Cockayne, Sir William 240
Cole, William 236
Colet, John 240
Colt, Maximilian 209
Columbanus 136
Comnena, Anna, Empress 125
Compton, Henry 238
Compton, William 27
Constantine, Emperor 34, 35, 139
Constantius Chlorus, Emperor 35
Coryate, Thomas 71
Cotton, John 94 n., 187, 335

Cotton, Sir Robert 26, 30, 37, 70–94, 272, 363; *Henry III* 85–90; *Cottoni Posthuma* 91–2; and Church history 4; Conington 40, 74, 92, 93–4; library 5, 6, 8, 42, 76–84, 97, 170, 198, 203, 222, 239, 241 n., 268, 331, 335; closure of library 19, 90; manuscripts 81–3, 331; Genesis ms. 83–4, 93; memorials 94; political alignment 18; relations with Camden 70, 72–3, 92; with King James 72, 85–92; with Selden 94–7; with Ussher 133, 137; with Weever 203–4

Cotton, Thomas 187
Cramer, Balthazar 294 n.
Cromwell, Oliver 153, 188
Cujas, Jacques 114 n.
Cumberland, Richard 328–9, 340
Cure, Cornelius 209
customs 12, 13, 292–6, 340, 342, 355

Danes 62, 64, 253, 257, 284–6, 290–1, 296, 305–6, 337, 339
Daniel 144
Daniel, Samuel 71, 95, 200
Davies, John 78
Davison, Thomas 236
Dee, John 262 n.
Dering, Sir Edward 18, 78
D'Ewes, Sir Simonds 17, 18, 79, 187, 203, 225 n., 241 n.
De Montfort, Simon 86
De Thou, Jacques-Auguste 26, 73, 76
De Vere, Aubrey 238
Dethick, William 44
Dio Cassius 31, 33, 282 n., 303, 327
Diodorus Siculus 283, 319, 329
Dionysius of Halicarnassus 144, 145
Dodsworth, Roger 10, 15, 17, 71, 222, 225, 227, 231, 234, 241 n., 247 n., 273, 343, 361, 364; fate of manuscripts 343
Domesday Book 77 n.
Donne, John 13–14, 71, 95, 135–6, 209, 238, 240
Douglas, David 68, 361
Douglas, Gavin 198
Drayton, Michael 71, 200; *Poly-Olbion* 20, 109–13
Dryden, John 286 n.
Druids 30, 31, 34, 102, 155, 215, 289–92, 315, 316–17, 329; and Greek 102–3, 315, 317, 334–5, 337,

351, 352–3; Selden on 102–3, 110–12
Duchesne, André 80
Dugdale, Sir William 6, 10, 11, 13, 16, 18, 19, 47, 71, 93, 154, 186–8, 216, 217–48, 251, 260, 291 n., 331, 333, 361; *Antiquities of Warwickshire* 1, 43 n., 222–3, 225–6, 241–3, 247, 277, 358, 362; *Baronage* 15, 202, 224–5, 247; *History of St. Paul's* 7, 18, 223, 236–40, 243, 362; *Imbanking and Drayning* 93, 243–5, 257; *Monasticon* 7, 10, 15, 18, 194, 224–5, 227–36, 246, 259, 273, 276, 361, 365; title-page to 157 n., 231–2; *Origines* 224; relations with Aubrey 247, 274–81; with Browne 244–5, 253, 257–8; and Somner 246; and Spelman 172, 219–20, 223, 246, 248
Du Tillet, Jean 114 n.

Eachard, Laurence 332
Eadmer 80, 125, 365 n.
Earle, John 20
Edward the Confessor, King 87, 105, 172, 196
elephants 33, 303
Eliot, Sir John 90
Elizabeth, Queen 78, 84 n., 103–4, 113 n., 163, 192–3
Elphinstone, John 82
epitaphs 47, 190–216, 364
Erasmus, Desiderius 123
Eratosthenes 144, 145
Erdeswicke, Samson 241 n.
Ethelbert, King 184
etymology 9, 30, 32–3, 58, 155, 312, 314–15, 347
Eusebius 55, 143, 145–6, 313, 328
Evelyn, John 150, 235 n., 279, 341

Fairfax, Thomas, Lord 19, 222, 234, 343
Farnaby, Thomas 262
Favyn, André 114 n.
Finch, Heneage 308
Fletcher, John: *Bonduca* 20
Florio, John 66
Fortescue, Sir John 107
fossils 62, 93, 278, 280–1, 302–3, 346
Foxe, John 49, 130, 142 n., 268
Fulke, William 263

Fuller, Thomas 20, 249, 355 n.; *Church History* 18, 19, 235 n., 267–74; *History of Cambridge* 271; *Holy State* 157 n., 268; *Worthies* 216, 273–4; and Dugdale 273; and Ussher 269–70
Fulman, William 17

Gale, Thomas 81, 336
Garden, James 289, 352, 355, 356 n.
Gaunt, John of 240
Geoffrey of Monmouth 2, 9, 26, 27, 32, 52, 62, 99, 109, 196, 282, 315–16, 321
Gervase of Canterbury 227 n.
giants 27, 303, 319, 327
Gibson, Edmund 7, 164, 300, 324, 330–57; and 1695 *Britannia* 330–58; as editor of Somner 332; *Life of Spelman* 157, 176
Gildas 36, 42, 80, 133, 136–7, 169, 266, 361
Giraldus Cambrensis 138, 282, 347
Glastonbury 169, 323
Gomer 32, 54, 56, 99
Gorges, Lord 243
Gorlaeus, Abraham 93
Goropius Becanus 56, 65
Gostwyck, Roland 118
Gower, John 82, 200
Gregory, St 231–2
Greneway, Anthony 52 n.
Gresham, Sir Thomas 49
Greville, Sir Fulke 22, 73
Grotius, Hugo 124, 320
Gruter, Jan 5, 26, 73

Hadrian, Emperor 34, 258
Hadrian's Wall 39, 74, 92, 250, 362
Hakluyt, Richard 23
Hale, Matthew 241 n.
Hales, William 128 n., 143 n.
Hamilton, Alastair 115
Hanmer, Meredith 115
Hardyng, John 196, 200
Hariot, Thomas 262 n.
Hatton, Sir Christopher 221, 240–1
Hearne, Thomas 44, 72 n., 347, 355
Hebrew 65, 114–15, 132, 150, 309–10, 312–13, 324, 329, 335
Heinsius, Daniel 118 n.
Hengist 62
Henry III, King 85–90, 231

Henry VIII, King 162–3, 165, 231–2, 271
Henry, Prince of Wales 93, 104 n., 113 n.
Henry of Huntingdon 199
Henry of Marlborough 154
Hercules 55, 254, 319–20, 329
Herodotus 309, 320
Herrick, Robert 294–5
Heyward, Edward 113
Hickes, George 81, 185, 331, 340
Higden, Ralph 99
Higgins, William 7 n.
Hill, Chrisopher 165
Hobbes, Thomas 128
Hoccleve, Thomas 198
Holinshed, Raphael 27, 131, 184, 263
Holland, Henry 13, 47, 211–14
Holland, Hugh 71
Holland, Philemon 48, 211, 332
Hollar, Wenceslaus 11, 234–8, 267, 273, 362
Homer 238, 254, 277
Honigmann, Ernst 190, 202 n.
Hooke, Robert 277, 280, 298, 302
Horace 238
Horsa 62
Horsley, John 360
Hotman, François 26, 73, 98, 114 n.
Howard, Henry, Earl of Northampton 71, 91
Howard, Robert 286 n.
Howard, Thomas, Earl of Arundel 8, 83, 90–2, 125–8, 221, 342
Howard, Lord William of Naworth 92
Hugford, Henry 7 n.
Humphrey, Duke of Gloucester 211–12
Hunter, Michael 277

Ina, King 104, 271, 323
Inns of Court 71, 76, 97, 129, 224

Jacob, Wiliam 1, 187
James I, King 19, 44, 51, 53, 85, 107, 113 n., 203, 243, 282; *True Law* 101–2; relations with Cotton 72, 85–92; with Ussher 134
James, Richard 126, 337
Japhet 32, 54–5, 155, 316
Jerome, St 145, 146
Jewel, John 130, 142
Johnston, Nathaniel 343 n.

Jones, Inigo 11, 34, 71, 125, 236, 281, 362; *Stone-Heng Restored* 281–4, 287–9, 320, 362

Jonson, Ben 7, 34, 60, 71, 84, 95, 96, 108, 360; *The Alchemist* 65

Joscelin, John 68, 185

Joseph of Arimathea 10, 35, 139, 169–71, 196, 269, 323, 366 n.

Joyce, James 330n.

Junius, Francis 8, 73, 81, 128 n., 150, 181, 186–7, 246, 337, 361

Kennett, White 4, 13, 17, 184, 188–9, 262, 277 n., 300; contributions to 1695 *Britannia* 332–3, 339, 340; *Life of Somner* 4 n., 181–5, 189

Kilburne, Richard 43 n., 340

King, Daniel 234–5, 237, 362

King, Gregory 298

King, John 213, 240 n.

Kip, Johannes 337

Kirchmann, Johannes 256

Lambarde, William 37, 59, 68, 78, 105, 181, 184, 185–6, 241, 271

Langbaine, Gerard 130 n., 153, 246, 262

Langland, Robert 198

Lapthorne, Richard 84 n.

Laud, William, Archbishop of Canterbury 17, 18, 82, 136, 140, 169 n., 172, 205, 213, 227, 239

Laudianism 182, 184, 204–5, 295

Layamon 82

Lear, King 9, 316

Le Gros, Thomas 236

Leigh, Charles 325–7, 334

Leland, John 2, 16, 27, 44, 78, 206, 257, 282, 309, 336; transcription and publication of 'Itinerary' 336

Lhwyd, Edward 12, 13, 21, 33, 277 n., 289, 306, 345–55, 357, 358; and Ancient Britons 349–54; and 1695 *Britannia* 346–55; and Celtic Studies 354–5; and natural history 346; relations with Aubrey 346, 351–2

Lichfield 14, 221, 235, 273–4

Lightfoot, John 95 n.

Lilly, William 187, 219

Lipsius, Justus 26

Lisle, William 68, 78, 79

Lister, Martin 19, 279, 302, 346

Lluyd, Humphrey 23 n., 263 n., 266

Locrine 9, 316

Loggan, David 237

Long, James 299

Lucan 31, 33, 94, 104, 195

Lucian 320

Lucius, King 34, 139, 170, 196, 211, 215, 239, 269

Lucretius 109

Lud 9, 316

Lydgate, John 198, 200

Magna Carta 78, 112, 176, 231

Malmesbury 40, 42, 292

Manetho 55

Marmion, Shakerley 20

Marsham, Sir John 154, 187, 228–9, 243

Martin, Martin 356 n.

Mary, Queen of Scots 50, 76 n.

Mary Tudor, Queen 267

masques 360

Mausolus 254–5

Merlin 41

Middle Temple 71

Milton, John 261; *History of Britain* 69, 103, 270–1, 339 n.; *Paradise Lost* 116–17, 148; *Samson* 117

monasticism 10, 11, 194, 227–36, 271–3, 333

Montacute, Thomas 47

Moore, Jonas 243

Moray, Sir Robert 289

Morden, Robert 333, 362

Moses 111, 143

Munday, Anthony 214

Munster, Sebastian 54

Natalis Comes 245

Neckham, Alexander 41

Nedham, Marchamont 124

Nennius 27, 34, 81, 133, 138, 155 n., 215, 361

Nicolini, Domenico 168 n.

Nicolson, William 344, 357

Noah 9, 127, 280, 316, 328

Norden, John 8 n., 43 n., 241

Norman Conquest 105, 114, 174–6

Norwich 1, 259–60

Notitia Provinciarum or *Dignitatum* 23, 25, 264

Nowell, Laurence 37, 68, 78, 81, 185–6

Ogilby, John 298–9, 301

Orderic Vitalis 80

Origen 34, 93, 169
Ortelius, Abraham 7, 22, 23, 26, 65, 263
O'Sullevan, Philip 135 n.
Ovid 293, 294, 333 n.
Owen, George 347

Panzani, Gregorio 93
Paris, Matthew 231–2
Parker, Matthew 2, 49, 77, 130, 139, 185, 195, 360
Parliaments 90–2, 102–7, 177–9
Patrick, St 131, 133, 137, 138, 171, 351
Pausanias 306
Peacham, Henry 6
Pecke, Thomas 1, 242 n.
Peiresc, Nicholas Fabri de 8, 26, 73, 80, 83, 128, 174
Pelagianism 137–8, 270
Pelagius 35, 137, 140
Pepys, Samuel 328 n., 342
Petavius, Dionysius 146, 147
Peterborough 13
Petty, William 128 n.
Petty, Sir William 277
Peutinger, Conrad 264
Peutinger Table 264
Philipot, John 43 n., 241 n., 340
Philo Byblius 313
Phoenicians 308–30
Piccolomini, Aeneas 345
Picts 36
Piers Plowman 82
Plato 28
Plautus 313
Pliny the Elder 28, 31, 111, 293, 312, 352–3
Plot, Robert 20, 21, 216, 247, 277 n., 278, 300–7, 336; Oxfordshire 301–7, 325, 345, 356; Staffordshire 353, 363; and 1695 Britannia 340–1
Pococke, Edward 116, 182
Pocock, J. G. A. 177
Polybius 109, 291
Pomponius Mela 320 n.
Porphyry 53
Powell, Thomas 76 n.
Priscian 187
Procopius 29, 319
Propertius 33, 250, 253
Prynne, William 247
Ptolemy 23, 39, 146, 263, 320, 347

Ptolemy Philadelphus 149 n.
Purchas, Samuel 124
Puteanus 26
Pythagoras 103

Quintilian 331

Radcliffe, Ralph 52 n.
Raleigh, Sir Walter 13, 314, 365 n.
Ray, John 333, 346
Rayner, Clement 52 n., 70 n., 272
Risdon, Thomas 241 n.
Robert of Gloucester 196, 199–200, 215 n.
Robertes, Foulke 118
Robinson, John 239
Rogers, Daniel 23 n.
Rolle, Richard 200
Roll-Right Stones 285, 305, 339
Rous, John 271
Rowlands, Henry 329
Rowlands, Richard, see Verstegan, Richard
Royal Society 19, 243, 245, 280, 299–300, 304, 306, 308, 333, 362
Rubens, Peter Paul 187
Rudolph II, Emperor 52
Rushworth, John 236

Sackville, Thomas: Gorboduc 20
St Albans 196, 265
St Paul's Cathedral 206–7, 211–14, 341
Sammes, Aylett 6, 21, 69, 308–30; on Druids 112, 315–17
Samothes 55–7, 60, 99, 327
Sanchoniathon 313, 319, 328–9
Sanders, Francis 160
Sandys, George 195
Sannazaro, Jacopo 265
Savile, Sir Henry 8 n., 42, 134, 291
Saxo Grammaticus 253
Saxons 37–8, 51–69, 104–5, 139, 175–6, 196, 243, 257, 270–1, 284, 296, 323, 360–1
Saxton, Christopher 333
Scaliger, Joseph 45 n., 114 n., 146, 152
Scoti 36, 37, 155
Scotus, Sedulius 136
Scudamore, Lord 164 n.
Scythia 36, 58, 155, 210, 252
Sedgwick, William 221, 237
Selden, John 5, 6, 8, 10, 16, 26, 73, 78,

80, 95–129, 186, 192, 203, 248, 262, 272, 360, 364, 365 n.; *Analecton* 97; *De Diis Syriis* 116–18, 128, 256, 266, 316, 320 n.; *De Jure Naturali* 128–9; *Eadmer* 125; *England's Epinomis* 107; *History of Tithes* 13, 96, 118–24, 161, 163, 199, 320 n.; *Jani Anglorum* 97–102, 317; *Marmora Arundelliana* 125–8, 130 n., 143, 146, 317; *Titles of Honor* 7, 113–14, 199; and *Poly-Olbion* 20, 99 n., 108–13; and oriental languages 114–17; friends 95; relations with Arundel 125–8; with Camden 100, 113; with Cotton 90, 95, 119, 121; with Ussher 129, 130, 149; with Ware 154

Shadwell, Thomas 20
Shakespeare, William 46, 200; *Cymbeline* 20; *King Lear* 20; *Love's Labour's Lost* 66
Sharpe, Kevin 76 n., 77, 79, 84
Sheldon, Gilbert, Archbishop 172, 223, 365
Shelton, Thomas 52 n.
Sheringham, Robert 69, 324–5
Sibbald, Sir Robert 345, 355–7
Simeon of Durham 227 n.
Simler, Josias 263
Sleidanus, Johannes 131, 142
Smith, Thomas 70 n., 75, 77, 334–5
Society of Antiquaries 5, 19, 43, 44, 72–3, 79, 105, 114, 209, 210, 217, 363
Somner, William 6, 11, 21, 181–9, 246, 269, 332, 341, 364; *Antiquities of Canterbury* 182–5, 241, 341; *Dictionary* 1, 7, 19, 64, 223–4, 361; as poet 18; and Dugdale 246; and Ussher 171
Speed, John 5, 75, 184, 261, 274, 319 n., 333
Spelman, Clement 162–3
Spelman, Sir Henry 5, 8, 16, 17, 26, 44, 68, 73, 84, 157–81, 236, 248, 271–2, 360; *Concilia* 15, 157, 168–73, 180 n., 223, 224, 323, 339, 365, 366; *De Non Temerandis* 118, 150–2, 242; *De Sepultura* 165, 180 n., 203; *Glossarium* 15, 134, 173–77, 223; *History of Sacrilege* 161 n., 164–5, 340; relations with Camden 173, 174; with Dugdale 172, 219, 246; with Selden 174; with Somner 171;

with Ussher 168, 169, 172, 181; with Worm 284; and Anglo-Saxon 171–2, 181, 246
Spenser, Edmund 53, 66, 265; *View of Ireland* 154–5
Stanley, Thomas 187, 228 n.
Stanyhurst, Richard 52 n., 53, 131, 134
Stephens, Jeremy 163–4, 169 n.
Stillingfleet, Edward 10, 306 n., 328 n., 365, 366 n.
Stone, Nicholas 209
Stonehenge 11, 41, 247, 249, 281–7, 289, 320, 329, 337–9, 362
Stow, John 27, 43, 44, 184, 199, 214, 251, 359, 362
Strabo 28, 306, 311–12, 319, 321, 326, 330
Stukeley, William 300, 329, 358
Sturrelson, Snorri 323
Surita, Hieronimo 263–4
Surius, Laurentius 168 n.
Syncellus, Georgius 55, 146

Tacitus 23, 25, 28, 31, 32, 56–8, 100, 102, 105, 253, 284, 291, 312–13, 317
Talbot, Robert 263
Talbot, Thomas 44
Tanner, Thomas 277 n., 300, 335–7, 361; *Notitia Monastica* 11, 227 n., 333, 335–6
Tate, Francis 68
Tavistock Abbey 68
Taylor, Jeremy 216
Taylor, Silas 241 n.
Tenison, Thomas 331
Theodoret 169
Thor 59
Thoresby, Ralph 342–4
Thorkelin, Grimur 81
Thurloe, John 243
Thynne, Francis 44, 78
Toland, John 294 n.
Trajan, Emperor 258
Tregian, Francis 52 n.
Trojans 9, 27, 28, 51, 52, 99, 109, 292, 310, 315, 324
Tuisco 54, 56, 59
Twine, John 184, 309–10
Twyne, Brian 17
Twyne, Thomas 23 n., 263 n.
Twysden, Sir Roger 10, 186, 227–8, 230

Ussher, James, Archbishop 5, 8, 13, 16, 18, 26, 53, 75, 95, 116 n., 130–56; 186, 262–3, 270, 360, 364, 366; *Annals* 146–52; *Antiquitates* 83, 139–41, 269; *De Successione* 83, 142; *Discourse of Religion* 83, 134; *Sylloge* 138–9; and chronology 15, 19, 127, 143–9; concern with Apocalypse 131, 134; relations with Cotton 133, 137, 138; with King James 138, 139; with King Charles 139; with Selden 129, 134, 143, 149; with Somner 186; with Spelman 134; with Ware 153, 156
Uther Pendragon 41

Vallencey, Charles 329
Varro 7
Velser, Mark 264
Vergil, Polydor 2, 27, 28, 123 n., 177, 282
Vermuyden, Cornelius 243–4
Verstegan, Richard 3, 4, 8, 21, 49–69, 174, 186, 203, 269–70, 284, 323–4, 360, 361, 366; early writings 49–50; *Restitution* 51–69, 320 n.; illustrations 59–61, 63; friends 52; and Saxons 57–68
Villiers, George, Duke of Buckingham 85–90, 124, 136, 209
Vincent, Augustine 17, 202–3, 224, 241 n.
Virgil 33, 195, 238, 293, 348
Virginia 257, 290
Virginia Company 124–5
Vitruvius 283
Vives, Juan Luis 310
Vortigern 20
Vossius, Gerard 8, 152

Walker, Sir Edward 229
Wallace, James 356 n.
Walton, Brian 116, 150
Wanley, Humfrey 81, 358–9
Ward, Seth 277
Ware, James 19, 21, 78, 135 n., 153–6, 311 n.
Warner, John 183, 187
Webb, John 281, 286
Weever, John 6, 13, 17, 21, 47, 82, 182, 190–216, 227, 240, 251, 256, 269, 299, 361, 364; and medieval literature 197–200
Westminster Abbey 211
Wharton, Henry 10, 361, 365–6
White, Richard 52–3, 99
Wilkins, John 304
William of Jumièges 80
William of Malmesbury 125, 183, 199
Williams, John 125
Wiltshire 40, 278–81, 287, 290, 296, 335–9, 364
Woden 59
Wood, Anthony 1, 6, 17, 49, 114, 123, 129, 164, 219, 224 n., 241, 246–7, 262, 298, 337, 340, 343; on Dugdale 219; on Selden 114, 123, 129
Woolf, D. R. 114 n.
Worcester 13
Worm, Olaf 8, 253, 257, 284–7, 339
Wortley, Francis 172 n., 180
Wotton, Sir Henry 228 n.
Wotton, Nicholas 309–10
Wren, Sir Christopher 277, 298, 305 n., 341, 365
Wright, James 230, 332
Wycliffe, John 79, 84, 271

York 20, 25, 222
Young, Patrick 126